D1044989

Politics, Economy and Society
in Contemporary China

Politics, Economy and Society in Contemporary China

Bill Brugger

and

Stephen Reglar

Stanford University Press
Stanford, California
1994

NOV 1 6 1995

DS
779.2
.B78
1994

Stanford University Press
Stanford, California
© 1994 Bill Brugger and Stephen Reglar
Originating publisher: The Macmillan Press Ltd
First published in the U.S.A. by
   Stanford University Press, 1994
Printed in Hong Kong
Cloth ISBN 0-8047-2349-4
Paper ISBN 0-8047-2350-8
LC 93-86794
This book is printed on acid-free paper.

OCLC: # 30484893

NOV 1 6 1995

Contents

Acknowledgements

The authors have drawn on some parts of earlier works and have reproduced a few passages verbatim (Brugger 1981 a and b; Brugger 1971). In all cases we are grateful to the publishers (International Thompson Publishing Services and UNESCO) who have given their permission for direct quotation. Thanks also are due to Professor Ted Wolfers and the staff of the Department of History and Politics at the University of Wollongong for making time available for one of the authors. We are, of course, grateful for the contributions from students at the Flinders University of South Australia to whom a draft text was directed. For constructive comments, thanks are due also to Tony Saich, Yvonne Corcoran-Nantes and Noel Tracy. For editorial work, thanks go to David Jolley. For much wider support, particular thanks go to Suzanne Brugger and Rosemary Reglar.

Introduction

Since the eighteenth century Western accounts of China have oscillated between excessive admiration and excessive horror. That oscillation has continued up to the present in characterisation of the Communist Party and the régime it created. In the mid-1920s, Chinese Communists were regarded as extreme revolutionaries. Then during the Second World War, when that Party moderated its policies, Communists were seen as patriotic agrarian reformers. The Cold War thinking of the 1950s saw the new Chinese régime as 'totalitarian' in Soviet mode and when the Chinese Communist Party broke with the Soviet Party in the 1960s as even more sinister. The Cultural Revolution of the mid-1960s confirmed all the worst fears of cold-warriors whilst offering inspiration for a while to Western radicals. Then the opening-up of China in the early 1970s began to produce amongst some scholars a very favourable view of the 'Chinese road to socialism' and Mao Zedong's model of economic development. While many economists were sceptical, China was proclaimed a developmental success. Then after 1978, when the Chinese Communist Party changed tack and rejected many of Mao's policies in favour of market socialism, the World Bank revised downwards its estimate of China's gross domestic product and the favourable assessment of Mao's strategy began to evaporate. The mood changed later to one of extreme optimism for China's economic reform and gave rise to hopes for a future democratic agenda.

During the 1980s, the Party blocked most moves towards the latter for fear of renewed Cultural Revolution-type turmoil but most commentators were mesmerised by economic success. When the economic reforms were beset by major problems, they were often explained away as inevitable setbacks in a transition to what Francis Fukuyama (1992) was later to call 'the end of history' (the triumph of liberal capitalist democracy). To question aspects of the reform process (as one of the present authors did) was often to invite criticism as a 'Maoist'. Then the Tiananmen massacre of 1989

1

caused a massive shock and gave rise once again to negative assessments of China, both political and economic. Yet before long, while there was no political reform, the government embarked on a new round of market reforms which are beginning to engender a new mood. Now one hears talk of huge rates of growth and estimates that China will become the largest economy in the world by 2010.

General works on China have reflected those changes of mood. Such a text, written by one of the present authors at the end of Mao's life in the mid-1970s (Brugger 1981a and b), adopted an orientation very different to any such book produced today. All writing inevitably reflects the milieu in which it is written but general texts are usually required to exhibit a greater degree of balance than most theses which are constructed around a discrete argument. Such balance is often illusory. In part this is because of the paucity of data. For example, output data on collectivised Chinese agriculture in the 1970s testified to great success. When input data became available, the Chinese agricultural 'miracle' was seen as a costly failure. Sociological survey work, moreover, has only really been possible since 1978 and only covers a small part of a huge country. Balance is also difficult to achieve by scholars in abstract disciplines which take historical context insufficiently seriously. For example, by the standards of the 1990s, the model of economic management adopted in China in the 1950s and copied from the Soviet Union was inappropriate. But is the current assessment being made according to standards of 'intensive' development (where productivity is important) and applied inappropriately to a stage of 'extensive development' where labour and resources are cheap and the cost of energy is not seen as vital? Also consider once again the assessment of collective agriculture. To be sure, changes in agriculture did not significantly raise the per capita standard of living of peasants, but they may perhaps be seen as providing some of the infrastructure without which privatised agriculture of the 1980s would have been less spectacular.

Economics is notorious for being wise after the event. But the discipline of history is not much better. Because of ideological controls (both traditional and Communist), the old historical method of basing one's account on contemporary documents and testimony will be distorted by adherence to the official line or to radical repudiation of that line. Throughout the past forty years documents have surfaced dealing with the events of decades previously and these have been interpreted by people whose memories have been twisted by the traumas of civil war, mass campaigns and Cultural Revolution or who have been socialised into new discourses of power. One wonders sometimes about the veracity of contemporary accounts by people who always knew that the Cultural Revolution was wrong. The 'narrative unity' of a person's life is often achieved by unwitting distortion.

This book is not so presumptuous as to claim to be following the slogan, beloved of Deng Xiaoping, 'seeking truth through facts'. It seeks to marshal various conflicting arguments around controversial themes. It tries to be open-minded though sometimes a judgmental tone is adopted (for example, that members of the 'Gang of Four' were inept politicians). While conflicting arguments may be found concerning all aspects of Chinese society, the themes included in this book are chosen to highlight questions of general relevance. For example, is collective agriculture necessarily wasteful? What is the best way of extracting a rural surplus for industrial development and what should the degree of that extraction be? Is collective agriculture in centrally planned states best seen in terms of a centrally controlled system based upon coercive direction or should it be seen in terms of patron–client relations. If it is the latter, then can one expect a freer market fundamentally to alter social relationships? If, moreover, it can be established that in the past local leaders were not so much simple agents of the state as gatekeepers between state and society, why should we expect a decline in direct state control to lead to a freer society?

Why was it the case that the Chinese government, in the 1960s and 1970s, did almost everything proposed by Western social scientists to solve problems of urban inequality, urban concentration and sprawl and to prevent the growth of an under-class and yet failed to solve the problem of urban bias? Is it true that attempts to create urban communities will necessarily lead to greater coercion? Is urban anomie the price of urban freedom? Is it possible for a rapidly industrialising socialist state to provide housing and maintain it? When one cannot afford a universal social welfare system, is it advisable to create a stratified one based on privileged units of production? Is it harmful to fuse together units of production, administration and residence and, when such units exist, how does one separate them out again? Moreover, will a privileged state sector in industry create a labour aristocracy hostile to economic reform?

We have chosen to look at law in this work precisely because developments in China raise questions as to the general conditions for the 'rule of law'. Is a formalised legal system a necessary but not sufficient condition for that rule of law? How can a party, which claims to act in its superior knowledge of the way forward, be seen as subject to the law or, more generally, what is the connection between law and policy in a developmental state? What is the relationship between formal law and notions of proper behaviour which looks askance at formal rules (traditional and Communist) and between that formal law and informal mediation? Will law always take on the form of commodity exchange and what are the implications for a state which professes socialism? What are the proper functions of the police? Even more important, what are the necessary conditions and possibilities for adhering to human rights?

With regard to intellectuals, we ask what is their relationship to class, so important in a socialist state. How does a ruling party deal with intellectuals necessary to it but also despised as élitist? What is the role of censorship? How may academic and literary creations be bent to serve political causes? What is the proper relationship between the state and the academics, writers and artists it employs? More specifically, what happens when critical Marxism is used to criticise official 'Marxist' ideology? How does one separate theory from ideology? Is it possible, moreover, for a democratic orientation to be developed from a scientific discourse?

For many feminists, of course, the history of the Chinese revolution and economic development is the history of Chinese men. Has socialism relegated the liberation of women to second place or, more insidiously, has it replaced traditional patriarchy by 'patriarchal socialism'? Now socialism is being diluted, has the privatisation of agriculture reinforced the power of the family patriarch? Is a freer labour market producing a part-time disposable and predominantly female labour force? Does a 'one child' population policy discriminate in favour of males? Do state-run women's organisations relegate the interests of women to those of the ruling party? Has a new 'feminine mystique' and availability of domestic technology subordinated women even more effectively than the monochrome, technologically deprived, collective society of the past?

Finally we turn to the question of national unity versus ethnic identity. Does a socialist policy demand ethnic assimilation and how should it treat traditional holders of power whose position is often based on religion? What should a socialist policy towards religion look like? How may a central government promote the economic development of peoples it considers backward? And what should be the policy of a government toward ethnic minorities which straddle often hostile borders? Perhaps even more important, how much regional autonomy can the state tolerate? Can any intelligent speculation be made on the relationship between a state with great coercive power and regions with dynamic economies oriented to regions outside the country (for example, the Pearl River Delta)?

The above are questions of considerable general concern. They are also very topical. One only has to consider the current European debates about the small farm and economies of scale and, of course, the problem of reorganising East European agriculture. More generally there is currently considerable interest in peasant motivation and the relationship between market and what have been called 'moral economies'. Problems of third world cities, moreover, are as salient as ever and the relationship between the market and welfare provision has been a problem of all urban areas during the past decade of privatisation. Perhaps most important is the widespread discussion concerning the conditions for the development of a civil society – a term much used in the final days of European socialist states and thereafter. One notes also the general concern in recent years about human rights and the rule of law – a factor which extends beyond obvious bounds to matters of foreign policy and trade and even to internal United States politics. Feminist concerns, too, have become central to social science analysis, if insufficiently so to government policy. Finally, in this 'year of indigenous peoples', the preservation of cultural identity is seen as vitally important. The break-up of the Soviet Union has focused our attention on the role of the nation state in shaping ethnic identity (directly and as a reaction to government policy). It is probably no exaggeration to say that the Soviet Union has been falling apart along fault lines of its own making. Does China offer a useful point of comparison?

Our rationale for choosing the themes of this book, therefore, is first their general relevance and second their topicality. This thematic work is aimed at senior level undergraduate university courses and taught post-graduate courses. It presumes some familiarity with general developments in China during the past half century and the beginning student is advised to start with a general chronological account (for example, Meisner 1986) before attempting this text. To help such students two initial chapters are provided which give an outline of political and economic developments, though the economic arguments are more detailed than one usually finds in introductory texts. We ask questions about the successes and failure of the Soviet model as applied to China and about collectivised agriculture and economic reform. Rather than praising or condemning Mao, we question the coherence of his ideas and strategy. We look at the rationale behind that enormous production extravaganza of the late 1950s known as the Great Leap Forward. We examine the ideas behind the Cultural Revolution of the mid to late 1960s and the measures taken to repair the damage. We consider the tortuous process of developing a reform agenda and five cycles of reform and repression which characterised the 1980s and early 1990s. Those cycles have had both an economic and a political dimension. On the economic front, repeated periods of boom were followed by loss of control, inflation and application of the brakes. On the political front, relaxation of controls and encouragement of criticism have given rise to fears of turmoil and new repression.

The first two chapters form the basis of the thematic chapters which follow dealing with the rural sector, the urban sector and industry, law, intellectuals, women and minority nationalities. Each of those later chapters may be read by students interested in the various areas with a little prior knowledge. We hope, therefore, that our discussions will be of use to general courses which deal with rural development, urban problems, comparative law, feminism, ethnicity and the like. Whilst the book is aimed at students of political science and sociology it is intended also to be of interest to students of economics.

Part 1

Overview

1

China Under Mao

Early twentieth-century China was characterised by a dilapidated Confucian state at the mercy of foreign powers which disintegrated into revolution, warlordism, corruption and despair. Yet there was said to exist pockets of dynamism in a sluggish economy, experiments at modernisation within an ossified patriarchal bureaucracy and an 'Asiatic' economy within a growing network of market relations.

Typically the 'Asiatic' economy has been described in terms of thousands of isolated villages engaged in subsistence farming. In fact, in China, where some 30 per cent of agricultural produce was marketed in the early twentieth century, discussions focusing simply on a 'subsistence economy' are inappropriate. While large areas could be so characterised, other areas had developed trading networks. By the 1930s, an industrial sector had developed, contributing some 20 per cent to gross domestic product. Most heavy industry was concentrated in the North East (what was then the state of Manchukuo) whilst other modern industries were found largely in the coastal 'treaty ports'. Characteristically most light industry consisted of small firms. There was a significant degree of foreign ownership, though this tended to be located in a few areas (for example, banking, insurance, mining, energy, textiles, ship-building and some light industry).

Crisis, Revolution and Reconstruction

That economy was said to have experienced crisis. Western scholars have debated the dimensions of the crisis. One argument, disputed by many, focuses on the inability of traditional farming methods to produce enough food in a situation where there was little new land

9

to open up. Others blame the social and political structure for inhibiting necessary investment. Still others stress the role of imperialism. Accounts range from those which denounce the latter for blocking development to those which praise it for providing an economic stimulus. A third position sees foreign economic activity and the establishment of treaty ports in the East as having only a small impact on the overall economy. In accordance with the methodology outlined in our introduction, this chapter will not adjudicate that debate. Suffice it to note that the surrender of tariff autonomy, the cost of foreign wars and domestic ones, due in part to foreign powers destabilising the legitimacy of the régime, generated dislocation and resentment which was a vital factor in the Chinese revolution.

Clearly though, since 85 per cent of the population lived in the countryside, the major issue in the Chinese revolution was land ownership. Some scholars consider rural society to have been relatively egalitarian. Though a third of land was rented out in the early twentieth century, land-holdings were small, the largest farms (0.5 per cent) averaging only 10 hectares and the difference between landlord and poor peasant consisting only of a few acres. When one considers, however, that the average size of a farm was only one hectare, the difference was considerable. Rents, moreover, were high (about 50 per cent of crop) and landlords were the principal money-lenders. Rural China was by no means egalitarian. As for the dimensions of the crisis, it may well have been the case that food production kept pace with population increase, but there is no doubt that there was chronic indebtedness, considerable downward mobility, a sharp increase in the numbers of poor peasants and a drift of peasants into bandit gangs. All that was exacerbated by famine which on average killed 4.5 per cent of the population in each generation, perhaps reaching almost 9 per cent in North China; needless to say these were the poorest of the population (Riskin 1987: pp. 22–33).

The Early Years of the Communist Party

Such was the economic milieu in which the Communist Party of China (founded 1921) grew up. Its ideology derived initially from two sources – the Bolshevik Revolution of 1917 and the May

Fourth Movement of 1919. The first of these showed that radical transformation was possible in conditions of economic backwardness and that a radical Party, organised on military lines, could lead the way. The second exposed Chinese intellectuals to Enlightenment thinking and demonstrated the material constraints on that thinking. Not surprisingly, the founders of the Party reflected influences as diverse as Dewian pragmatism, anarchism and Hegelian and Chinese cosmology. But one enduring characteristic emerged, which Arif Dirlik (1989) traces to the influential Japanese Marxist Kawakami Hajime – an economically determinist view of history, located within a framework of broader ethical concerns. This was very different from that Western Marxist tradition which followed the determinism of Karl Kautsky. It contrasted also with the Leninism of the advisers sent to China by the Communist International (Comintern) who initially sought to achieve a tactical alliance among workers, peasants and those defined as the 'national bourgeoisie'.

Tactical considerations (Vladimir Ilyich Lenin's insistence that Communist Parties should ally with the 'national bourgeoisie') led to the Party being persuaded to enter into an alliance with Sun Zhongshan's (Sun Yat-sen's) Soviet-aided *Guomindang*. Faulty Comintern advice concerning that alliance, however, led to tragedy in 1927 when *Guomindang* forces and their supporters massacred large numbers of Communists. The crises of the late 1920s almost entirely concerned tactics and the relative roles of the rural and urban struggle though clearly there were ideological implications. Those who stressed the role of the urban proletariat were perhaps influenced by the views of Leon Trotsky (or were accused of that by his enemies). Trotsky rejected the 'two stage' theory of revolution which had become dominant in Soviet and Comintern thinking. This held that the 'bourgeois-democratic' revolution based on alliances of workers, peasants and domestic capitalists had to be completed before the socialist revolution was begun. Persisting with such a position, Trotsky believed, would lead to a collapse of socialist fervour and a 'deformed' state. Those who inclined towards Trotsky felt vindicated by the disastrous results of the multi-class 'united front' in 1927 and still believed that the urban workers' movement could thrive. Mao Zedong resisted that position as much as he could, though for a time the Workers and Peasants Red Army which formed the core of a Communist-led

'Soviet Republic' in Jiangxi was used to capture cities. After the collapse of the Jiangxi Soviet and the subsequent Long March (1934–5), however, Mao was able to develop a rural strategy – eventually enshrined in the 'Yan'an way' (named after the principal war-time base) which for a while was shored up by a new 'united front' with the Nationalist *Guomindang* to resist Japan (Selden 1971). The Yan'an way symbolised a number of gradualist policies (with rent reduction replacing land reform), though clearly it stressed firm Party leadership, tempered by what was known as the 'mass line' (integrating central policy with mass sentiments) which involved the rustication (*xiaxiang*) of urban personnel to ensure compliance. The theoretical exposition of Mao's position was known as 'new democracy' or later 'people's democratic dictatorship', supporting a 'four class bloc' of workers, peasants, petty bourgeoisie and national capitalists and prescribing 'dictatorship' over the remainder.

During the Yan'an period, rectification was geared to opposing the uncritical adoption of Soviet models of revolution ('dogmatism') and studying Marxism without any concrete aim ('subjectivism'). Indeed, Mao made the point that Marxism had to be judged solely by its utility (Mao, *Selected Works*, 3: p. 43). Whilst Marxism was seen as a universal guide, it was also, and more importantly, a practical tool, reinforced by the rustication programme. Though one might question the dichotomy drawn by Franz Schurmann (1966: pp. 17–104) between pure (universal) theory (*lilun*) and thought (*sixiang*), there is a lot of truth in his argument that 'thought', as used by the Chinese Communist Party, incorporated the relationship between revolutionary theory and practice, so important in the 'sinification of Marxism'. Without stretching the point, Mao's Marxism was more akin to what we now consider the 'new physics' linking the observer and the observed in a network of purposive action, in contrast to Stalinist dialectical materialism (diamat) which was more akin to Newtonian physics and 'iron laws'. But such a conclusion may be contested by those who see Mao's writings of the time as derivative and unoriginal, subject to the creative application of others such as Chen Boda (Wylie 1979).

There was, moreover, a darker side to rectification. It was aimed at inculcating a Party line among 'patriotic' but insufficiently Communist 'intellectuals'. As such it was often very intolerant of dissent and sometimes descended to demonology and persecution. This will be examined in Chapter 6. Denunciation of intellectuals, under the rubric of 'sinifying Marxism', moreover, weakened considerably the universalistic ideas inherited by the Party from the May Fourth Movement twenty years previously.[1]

The onset of renewed civil war between Communists and *Guomindang* in 1946 intensified struggle and brought to an end many gradualist policies (see Hinton 1966). In particular the Land Reform Law of 1947 demanded the confiscation of all land owned by the (*Guomindang*) state and the redistribution of all land above the general average (which included not only that of landlords but also that of rich peasants). Peasants, however, still retained the right to buy and sell land (Selden 1979: pp. 208–18). The new policy, which made Yan'an gradualism redundant, required considerable leadership skills to mobilise the peasants and to sustain a stable policy. It failed, resulting in the summary execution of many landlords, in 'commandism' (the arbitrary issue of orders regardless of mass sentiments) and in much chaos. It was followed by a harsh rectification campaign to restore order. A new approach to land reform eventuated as the Party, having captured a number of major cities, turned its attention to urban areas. By late 1949, another land reform law was formulated which was much less radical than that of 1947 (Selden 1979: pp. 240–3). Such was the genesis of what was later referred to as 'the rich peasant line' (Liu Shaoqi, *Collected Works*, 2: pp. 215–33). Restricted for a while, land reform acquired a new momentum and renewed harshness after China's entry into the Korean War and was completed in 1952, as we shall see in Chapter 3.

The Establishment of Government and Control Over the Economy

Despite the fact that land reform had been much more radical than anything which had occurred in Yan'an, the Communist Party régime which took power over most of the country in 1949 celebrated the Yan'an model of administration (often romantically) for its administrative flexibility and the 'mass line'. The basic

---

[1] We are grateful to Tony Saich for this point.

Yan'an principles of 'new democracy' were adopted and enshrined in official state documents in September 1949 by a body known as the Chinese People's Political Consultative Conference, composed of representatives of a number of political parties and groups sympathetic to the Communist Party, geographical areas, religious bodies, minority nationalities, overseas Chinese and mass organisations.

The conference adopted a 'Common Programme' and two organic laws which were to serve as an interim constitution (Selden 1979: pp. 186–93). According to the formula of 'new democracy' or 'people's democratic dictatorship', as it was now known, citizen rights were given only to those who formally qualified as the 'people'. 'Dictatorship' was prescribed for the former exploiting classes and groups which constituted the remainder. Pending the establishment of a National People's Congress to be elected by all citizens, the conference set up a Central People's Government Council and a National Committee, with a smaller Standing Committee, to handle routine work. That Council was simultaneously a legislative, executive and judicial organ. It supervised a number of bodies, the most important being the Government Administration Council, headed by the premier, Zhou Enlai. This latter body, which consisted of five deputy premiers, a secretary-general and sixteen members, controlled all government ministries. There was also a People's Committee of Supervision, charged with investigating the operation of all ministries. Alongside the Government Administration Council stood a Revolutionary Military Council, a Supreme People's Court and a Supreme People's Procuracy. The judicial institutions, based on Soviet models, will be discussed in Chapter 5.

Initially, however, most real government power rested with six large administrative regions created by the field armies which had achieved victory in the civil war. Victory in that war had been sudden and had left the new régime in charge of cities with which most of its leaders had little experience, as we shall see in Chapter 4. Cadres (leaders) from a rural background, moreover, had to come to terms with an urban communist underground whom they distrusted as 'collaborators'. As early as 1948, therefore, leaders in the North East (the former state of Manchukuo) looked for advice to a Soviet leadership which was somewhat suspicious of a potentially 'Titoist' Party. Despite suspicions, Soviet-style planning was introduced into that area immediately after taking power. The task was immensely difficult since large amounts of equipment had been transferred to the Soviet Union following the Soviet invasion of 1945, factories had been destroyed and many managers and technicians had fled. Yet, in other respects, takeover was easy. The commanding heights of the economy, already nationalised in North East China, could readily be appropriated and Soviet concerns in the Soviet-occupied cities of Lushun and Dalian could serve as models.

Taking over the rest of the country, which was the task of military control commissions, was more complex. The urban economy, inherited by the Communist Party, had been devastated by war and chronic hyperinflation. Industrial production in 1949 was just over half its pre-war level. The task of economic reconstruction needed much vigour. At a central level, this was provided in major efforts by the People's Bank to control the money supply (successful by March 1950) and to squeeze the private banks, by the government reducing expenditure, taking over wholesale trade and much else. Vigour was evident in reorganising and (during the Korean War) extending state-controlled industry from 35 per cent of modern industry to 57 per cent by 1953. Vigour could also be seen in restoring the transport network and, more slowly, in bringing commerce under control. At lower levels, however, vigour was at first lacking. After military control, a number of campaigns were launched to combat laxness on the part of local leaders, to suppress 'counter-revolutionaries' in the face of war in Korea, to halt infiltration by secret societies and to bring the private sector of the economy to heel. Eventually all these campaigns coalesced into what was called the 'three' and 'five anti' campaigns (1951–2) – the first to revitalise and purge local leaders and the second to control the 'private sector'.

The campaigns caused some economic disruption and were severe. Nevertheless, the most frequent sanctions imposed by the people's tribunals set up to carry out the campaigns were fines or confiscation rather than more serious penalties (Gardner 1969: p. 523). Only 1 per cent of the business community, moreover, was subject to imprisonment and labour reform. Yet the long-term effects of the 'five-anti' campaign in particular were profound. Though the private sector (accounting for some 30 per cent of total production) remained in existence and thrived, it had become dependent upon the Communist Party and the government. Dependency had been achieved by instilling fear into private businessmen, driving them into debt to the state and by new state financial controls. More specifically, Party control was maintained through labour-capital consultative conferences (Gardner 1969: pp. 477–539). The way seemed clear for importing a model of planning derived from the Soviet Union.

The Soviet Model

After the 'three' and 'five anti' campaigns, attempts were made to generalise the Soviet model of planning and administration experimented with in the North East since 1948. By 1952–3, the government deemed that the achievements of economic rehabilitation had been outstanding though China's level of economic development was much lower than that of the Soviet Union at the start of its first five-year plan in the late 1920s. If one compares the Chinese economy in 1952 with that of the Soviet Union in 1928, one finds that output per capita of grain, electricity, coal, steel and cement were less than half and per capita rail mileage less than 10 per cent. Those different initial conditions must be borne in mind when we consider later the different outcomes (Riskin 1987: p. 53).

In accordance with Soviet practice, China's First Five Year Plan aimed to lay the foundations 'of a comprehensive heavy industrial structure in as short a period as possible, in the belief that heavy industry would provide the basis for light industry, which required machine tools, steel, chemicals and means of transport (e.g. locomotive production) and agriculture which needed chemicals, fertilisers, tractors and implements (CCP 1956: pp. 263–70). The emphasis placed on heavy industrial development is reflected in the fact that during the First Five Year Plan, 36 per cent of investment in capital construction went into heavy industry, compared with 6 per cent into light industry and 7 into agriculture (Guojia tongjiju, 1988: p. 569). More than 85 per cent of capital investment in the period, moreover, was allocated for 694 large industrial projects (especially 156 Soviet-aid projects), leaving only 15 per cent for more than 10,000 small projects. Such a strategy involved considerable Soviet aid. This took the form of low-interest loans but, because the repayment period was shorter than most, such 'aid' imposed a heavy burden.

The first institutions set up specifically to implement China's First Five Year Plan were the State Statistical Bureau and State Planning Commission (1952). Initially the former was ranked equal to the Government Administration Council, which meant that its first head, Gao Gang, who was transferred from the North East, was rated, in the formal government apparatus, equal to the premier, Zhou Enlai (though his status in the Party remained lower). In 1954, however, the Commission was placed under the new State Council together with a State Construction Commission, joined in 1956 by a State Economic Commission (to handle short-term plans), a General Bureau for the Supply of Raw Materials and a State Technological Commission.

The changes of 1954 reflect the adoption of a new government structure. The large administrative regions were abolished. The leaders of two of those regions, Gao Gang (the North East, where ironically the Soviet model was most prevalent) and Rao Shushi (East China) were under suspicion for fostering 'independent kingdoms'. Both were purged. Replacing regional administration, a strengthened central government was established. The National People's Congress took over most (though not all) functions of the Chinese People's Political Consultative Conference. A 'soviet' principle of election was adopted, with the Party scrutinising candidates and each level electing the next highest and with the electorate restricted to the 'people' (said to be 95 per cent of the population over 18). The First National People's Congress, in September 1954, approved a draft constitution similar to the Soviet Constitution of 1936 (PFLP 1961). It discussed types of ownership, policy towards social classes, rights and duties of citizens etc., but only mentioned the Chinese Communist Party in its preamble and then only with reference to its leadership before 1949. Such was the mood of 1954 which was very soon to change.

China was now (unlike the Soviet Union) established as a unitary multinational state with a single legislature, the National People's Congress. The congress was elected for four years and was scheduled to meet once a year. It chose a chairman of the People's Republic (at first Mao Zedong, who held that post until 1959 and then Liu Shaoqi until he was purged in 1968), who was consti-tutionally commander of the armed forces and chairman of a

Council of National Defence. Whenever necessary, the chairman could convene a Supreme State Conference consisting of the vice-chairman (at first Zhu De), the chairman of the Standing Committee of the National People's Congress (at first Liu Shaoqi) and the premier of the State Council (Zhou Enlai, who remained in that post until his death in 1976). The Standing Committee of the National People's Congress was set up to conduct the routine business of the congress when it was not in session and the State Council was the main executive arm of the government, consisting initially of the premier, a secretary general and the heads of thirty ministries and five commissions including the State Planning Commission. The only bodies placed equal to the State Council in 1954 were the Supreme People's Court (under Dong Biwu) and the Supreme People's Procuracy. The constitutional provisions of 1954 also included the establishment of a State Council Personnel Bureau to manage China's huge and growing bureaucracy. By 1955–6 formal salary scales for cadres were worked out, comprising some 30 grades for cadres and 18 for technicians, with variations for differences in the cost of living. A ranking system was also introduced into an army which was being remodelled on professional lines rather than in accordance with the old doctrine of civilian–military integration fostered during the days of 'people's war'.

Accelerated Co-operativisation and Socialisation

As some leaders saw them, the targets of the five-year plan could only be attained by syphoning off a greater surplus from agriculture and faster agricultural growth. Indeed, after a remarkable recovery in 1950–2, growth in food grains fell, leading in places to real distress. To maintain legitimacy, the régime could not raise significantly the level of taxes. It imposed, however, a state monopoly on grain and some other agricultural products with compulsory procurement quotas at low prices. It tried directly to raise those quotas to appropriate more of the 'surplus' and met with resistance from peasants who saw that the notion of 'surplus' was an artifact of the state marketing system. Many leaders felt, therefore, that there was a need to move to a new form of rural organisation which could determine the surplus to be extracted at the point of production. That same organisation might also promote economies of scale. There was a need also to check the process of class polarisation in the countryside. The answer was seen as accelerating co-operativisation. We shall consider the rapid collectivisation of agriculture in Chapter 3. At this point let us simply note that some commentators consider it to have been successful, whilst others see it as the creation of a system which sapped initiative. The Communist Party in the 1980s echoed its position of the early 1950s that collectivisation should not have proceeded until there was adequate mechanisation or, in Marxist language, until the productive forces had developed to a point where new relations of production were called for. Radical collectivisation was not appropriate for what in the mid-1980s was called 'the primary stage of socialism'.

In comparative terms, one is initially tempted to look favourably on the collectivisation process of 1955–6. Farm output rose throughout, whereas it fell disastrously in the Soviet movement of the late 1920s (Nolan 1976; Bernstein 1967). Shue (1980: pp. 321–44), whilst noting the excesses, speaks of the movement as exhibiting care in policy-formulation, flexibility in policy-implementation, the value of swift and bold assaults on problems followed by rectification, the careful cultivation of local peasant cadres, the skilful management of class struggle rather than offering empty promises according to which no one would suffer, and a good relationship between central and local leadership. Attempts made in the 'high tide' of 1956, moreover, to replace agricultural price planning by direct production planning (directly specifying sown areas and compulsory delivery targets) were nipped in the bud. Such production planning had characterised agricultural policy in the Soviet Union where it had led to imbalances, fewer crops, great inefficiencies, terms of trade grossly unfavourable to agriculture and a lack of incentives for peasants to cultivate economic crops. Chinese economists and leaders such as Chen Yun were aware of similar dangers in China. At a time when both Soviet and Chinese leaders were beginning to question the Soviet economic model, it seemed inappropriate to initiate the one set of Soviet policies which had so far been avoided. From the vantage point of agriculture, the First Five Year Plan, so far, looked more like that country's New Economic Policy rather than the centralised Stalinist system which had been applied to heavy industry (Lardy

1983: pp. 18–41). Not everyone will concur with Shue's favourable assessment of initial collectivisation. They would surely agree, however, that, if favourable conditions did apply in 1956, that was the last time they did so.

Radicalisation also occurred in industry. Chapter 4 will discuss the whirlwind process whereby private concerns were turned into 'joint public and private firms' or collectives. Here even Mao, who had promoted the process, complained of excessive speed. But surely one would expect speed in a situation where owners of small businesses held back investment, pending what was certain socialisation. Again one confronts the question, was socialisation at that time beneficial? In retrospect, when one considers the decline in services and retail outlets over the next few decades, the answer must be negative.

De-radicalisation, 1956

At the very peak of this 'socialist high tide' in April 1956, a decision was taken to de-radicalise policy. One reason for this was the Communist Party's desire to work out what to do in the wake of Nikita Khrushchev's denunciation of Stalin and the 'cult of personality' in the Soviet Union. Another reason was the need to deal with disruptions which had arisen in the radical 'socialist high tide' (Walker 1965: pp. 59–67). Third, it was clear that major problems were evident in the Soviet model of administration.

One such problem derived from the Party's insistence that 'the state plan' was 'law' . The result was a recurrence of 'commandism'. One is not surprised that various leaders inveighed against it, together with 'bureaucratism' and 'departmentalism'. From the Party's view of politics, commandism subordinated political goals to economic dictates. Soviet techniques, moreover, whilst seeking to centralise economic decision-making, produced protective measures which acted against centralisation. According to the ideal planning procedure of 'two up and two down', relevant ministries sent control figures down through a long chain of command to the enterprise which in turn worked out a draft plan to be sent back up, amended by higher levels and then sent down again. In practice, the plan was formulated with much haggling and much deception by lower levels, eager to underestimate their potential (and hence over-fulfil their targets). In all this, Party organisations might promote worker participation, serve local interests or act as agents of superior planning bodies.

Soviet planning techniques, moreover, made one person responsible at each level for operations, with a staff of specialists reporting directly to the manager (staff line management actualised in the particular Soviet variant of 'one person management'). The result was a system of parallel bureaucratic 'hierarchies', exemplified by the People's Bank and the Ministry of Commerce (Schurmann 1966: p. 190), with minimal horizontal integration and serious supply bottlenecks. Yet such concentration of power at the centre actually produced a situation where regional levels, which could conceal information, acquired power. Extended 'one person management' and vertical rule did not restrict what Mao called setting up 'independent kingdoms'. To combat the power both of local 'independent kingdoms' and ministerial monopolies on information, an elaborate supervisory system was created, eventually under a Ministry of Supervision modelled on the Harbin railway network. From the point of view of many Communist Party members (with local roots), both the ministries and the supervisory network eroded sufficient consideration of explicitly political goals.

At enterprise level, the Eighth Party Congress of 1956 tackled the erosion of collective political goals by abolishing 'one-person management'. Celebrating its demise, Li Xuefeng, the director of the Industrial and Communications Work Department of the Party Central Committee, noted that it had been resisted despite current Party policy. Li drew attention to the neglect of the 'mass line' principle in Party work, particularly in enterprise management, where, he thought, too much emphasis was placed on centralised authority and decision-making, resulting in a neglect of democracy. Enterprise management was influenced too strongly by considerations of technological advance and scientific method as means of promoting increased production. The new formula for enterprise management was 'responsibility of the factory manager under the unified leadership of the enterprise Party committee'. But the erosion of collective goals at enterprise level was not simply a result of managerial authority. Another problem, some Party leaders felt, was the Soviet model's incentive policy which demanded sharp wage differentiation and piecework. There was little attempt to address that problem in 1956. On the contrary the

1956 wage reform, which increased urban wages overall, led to even sharper differentiation which was to be the subject of much criticism the following year. Part of the criticism derived from simple egalitarian sentiments but one has to acknowledge that in some industries, with out-of-date machinery, considerations of productivity in wage payment must inevitably lead to charges of unfairness (Riskin 1987: p. 64).

At levels above the enterprise, the erosion of collective political goals and the problem of centralised suffocation had to be tackled by some kind of decentralisation. But what kind of decentralisation was the Party to promote? Two alternatives were put forward which Franz Schurmann has called decentralisation I (to enterprises as practised in Yugoslavia) and decentralisation II (to local regions, especially provinces). The former, promoted in part by Chen Yun at the Eighth Party Congress, proposed to give market forces a much greater role in development. Such was an effective means of involving all enterprises and co-operative personnel in decision-making. But radicals (and eventually Mao), fearing the recrudescence of capitalism, came to oppose it in favour of decentralisation to local areas, adopted at that time in the Soviet Union. Herein lay the major problem in Mao's economic thought. He opposed bureaucratic centralisation but did not realise that, short of an anarchistic system of self-reliant units, it could only effectively be replaced by a greater degree of market integration. That was a major cause of the repeated cycles of decentralisation, anarchy, fear of market growth and re-centralisation which have occurred ever since.

It was not until 1957, however, that radical policies prevailed and a full-scale programme of regional decentralisation was launched. In the meantime, fears about direct production planning (as opposed to price planning), economic chaos and extravagant targets led to the reopening of markets and the shelving of an ambitious twelve-year plan for agriculture put forward by Mao. But the momentum of collectivisation was unstoppable. By the end of 1956, 83 per cent of all households were enrolled in co-operatives, rising to 97 per cent in the summer of 1957. All the advocates of stability could do was sort out the various rural administrative units. One result of co-operativisation was the despatch of cadres from *xiang* (township) level to the villages with a resultant shortage of cadres at that level. Thus *xiang* were amalgamated and, in

December 1955, the next highest level the *qu* was abolished. In the spring of 1955, there had been some 219,000 *xiang*. By the time regulations were worked out as to optimum size in the autumn of 1956, there were only 117,000, with different optimum sizes in hilly and mountainous regions (Schurmann 1966: pp. 452–3).

In addition to fixing the size of the *xiang*, attempts were made to specify the size of the new higher-stage collectives and guarantee their operational autonomy. In September 1956, the prescribed size was 300 households in the plains, 200 households in hilly regions and 100 households in the mountains. Collectives were subdivided into *brigades* (corresponding often to the older co-operatives and consisting of 20–40 households) and *teams* (often corresponding to the old mutual aid teams containing seven to eight households) (URI 1971: pp. 407–30). As time went on, the early very large collectives were reduced in size to correspond more nearly to the old natural villages. With the old village reconstituted as a collective, a final step was taken to include everyone in the collective. Now most of the remaining rich peasants joined, though some joined and then left.

1956, therefore, was a year of consolidation and policies revealed a degree of caution. The Party structure, as announced at the Eighth Congress, revealed no dramatic departures from the model inherited from pre-1949 days. The congress noted that Party membership had risen to some 10.7 million, of whom the majority were classified as peasants (Schurmann 1966: pp. 129–36). Though large in absolute terms, it only represented some 1.7 per cent of the total population. The formal rules specified that the congress was the source of authority which determined the Party's general line. The congress elected a Central Committee of 97 full members which was required to meet periodically in plenary session. Those plenary sessions rarely initiated policy but, in the 1950s, were extremely important in making authoritative decisions (Chang 1970). Policy tended to be initiated either by the Politburo (seventeen and six alternates), or sometimes at meetings of provincial Party secretaries. The Politburo, along with the chairman (Mao Zedong), vice-chairmen and general secretary, were elected by the Central Committee. In 1956, a new body was created, the Politburo Standing Committee, to manage the day-to-day business of that extremely important decision-making body.

A number of other bodies existed at the central level of which perhaps the most important was the Party Secretariat under Deng

Xiaoping. In 1954, Deng had been appointed Party secretary general (*mishuzhang*), but in 1956 was elevated to the new role of general secretary (*zongshuji*). The Secretariat, which handled the routine business of the Central Committee, served probably as an important link between the Politburo and local Party organisations. Another body was the Military Affairs Commission which was linked to a newly created General Political Department (*zongzhengzhibu*) of the People's Liberation Army, the immediate task of which seemed to be to ensure that all People's Liberation Army companies established Party branches. Other committees existed to deal with propaganda and various branches of the economy, the latter running parallel to the state structure. There was also a Party Supervisory Commission, headed by Dong Biwu.

The organisation of the Party at provincial level was the same as at the centre. Provincial Party congresses elected committees, headed by a first secretary who was usually a member of the Central Committee. They set up a number of specialist committees to supervise various aspects of political and economic work and to control the 'Party fractions' (*dangzu*) at various levels of administrative organisation. Considering the continuity of leadership in the provinces, close links were maintained with the local military. At *xian* (county) and city levels, efforts were directed to recreating much the same kind of structure by abolishing many of the *ad hoc* organisations which previously had been directly responsible to the Central Committee.

Basic-level Party organisations were formed according to both geographical and functional principles with particular emphasis on establishing Party committees in each *xiang*. By 1956, there were 538,000 of these basic-level organisations each headed by a secretary. The Party organisation at *xiang*, factory, school, military company, street, state organ and maybe collective level was referred to as 'basic', in that it was the lowest level at which the principle of committee organisation applied. Though basic organisations could be set up where there were as few as three Party members, some of them were quite large and were subdivided into cells. The only other local-level Party organisations which need concern us here were local supervisory organs (which functioned in much the same way as the Central Supervisory Commission in checking up on the operation of lower levels) and the Party fractions which existed at most levels of administration.

The above is a fairly standard Communist Party structure, reflecting, as we have noted, the cautious atmosphere of 1956. But beneath the superficial picture of stability and the desire for consolidation, contradictory pressures were at work. In the Chinese Communist Party there was both a desire to restore explicitly political goals to an increasingly economistic Soviet model and a willingness to echo the de-Stalinisation moves taken in the Soviet Union. The latter led to the Eighth Congress omitting reference to Mao Zedong Thought in its new constitution. Yet it was soon to become apparent that the source of the political goals many leaders wanted to restore was precisely Mao Zedong Thought and Mao Zedong himself seemed bent on using charismatic methods of leadership to ensure their realisation. Within a year that issue was to become explosive. Second, while the Eighth Congress was critical of and endorsed changes in the Soviet model of administration, it adopted a very Soviet approach in its definition of 'socialism'. Having collectivised much of agriculture and socialised industry and commerce, the Party felt it could proclaim the basic achievement of 'socialism'. Socialism here was taken as a model – a matrix of features against which progress could be measured – rather than a process (Brugger 1981c). Thus the Party stressed that the main programme in China should focus not on class struggle but on developing production. As the congress put it, the basic contradiction in Chinese society resided in the relationship between the 'advanced socialist system' and the 'backward productive forces' (CCP 1956: pp. 1–116). The implications were profound. Most leaders argued that the forces of production should be consolidated and some even felt that some socialist relations of production might be too advanced and should be retarded. This step-by-step approach had been advocated in the Soviet Union in the 1920s where it was referred to as 'geneticist' (taking reference from its origin). Its philosophical defenders refuted teleology (the proposition that goal-oriented thinking shaped being) in seemingly esoteric terms by claiming there was no identity between thinking and being, or in simple terms that politics had no force independent of the forces of production. But clearly, the restoration of what Mao considered to be explicitly political goals (in particular the elimination of the gaps between worker and peasant, town and country and mental and manual labour) demanded teleology. Mao was soon to repudiate the formulation of the Eighth Congress.

An Assessment of the Soviet Model

At a macro-economic level, three aspects of the Soviet model, as it applied in China, were discussed at length by the Eighth Party Congress: its reliance on a high rate of capital formation, with a corresponding emphasis on industrial development, its priority given to the expansion of the capital goods industry and its preference for large industrial plants and for capital-intensive techniques.

Because of the overwhelming concentration of investment in heavy industry and the internal orientation of China's economy, with only a small percentage of its gross domestic product devoted to foreign trade, the operation of the Soviet model depended on the agricultural sector for savings. Development required a continuous squeeze on the resources of the agricultural sector to provide for the growth of heavy industry, even though some attempts were made between 1949 and 1957 to reduce the disparity in prices between agriculture and industry and to close the notorious 'price scissors'. Clearly, agricultural output was not growing fast enough. Agricultural productivity had to be enhanced to meet subsistence requirements and to feed the rest of the population. But peasants displayed what economists term a high 'income elasticity for food' (Lippit 1975: p. 98). A political solution was required.

Whilst the production of consumer goods rose significantly faster than population and food production roughly kept pace with the total population increase of 13 per cent, China's leaders required more of the economy. There needed to be more investment in commodity industries to overcome regional scarcities. But at a time when investment in capital-goods industries ought to have been cut, there was actually a further sharp increase in capital investment in 1956 and inflationary pressures grew rapidly on the consumer market. A perceived scarcity of goods caused a decline in government popularity (Vogel 1969: p. 186). Peasants lacked incentives to increase agricultural production and, without a steady growth of agricultural production and a corresponding increase in marketable agricultural surplus, some leaders felt that the investment rate in the industrial sector would decline and the whole economy would stagnate. Consider also that 80–85 per cent of the raw materials for China's 'light' industry came from the agricultural sector (Lippit 1975: p. 98). Stagnation in the growth of agricultural production plus increasing industrial growth led to a serious problem of under-utilisation of industrial plant capacity. In 1957 the production capabilities of the vegetable oil industry was 75 per cent of full capacity, with leather at 69 per cent, flour at 68 per cent, sugar 66 per cent, canned foods 53 per cent and the cigarette industry at 52 per cent (Chen Nai-ruenn 1967: p. 253). Such was remarked on by Liu Shaoqi at the Eighth Party Congress.

As noted in our introduction, from the vantage point of the 1990s, the Soviet model wasted resources. To a degree, the Soviet practice of concentrating on 'extensive development', or development which expands production by adding more inputs to the production process instead of using each input more intensively, can offset labour displacement caused by technological change. But, according to the thinking of most Chinese economists in recent years (and some in the mid-1950s), the Soviet model wasted labour power, as well as capital and raw materials. Its policies also encouraged workers to look to the possibility of high-paying jobs in already developed areas including the large cities (Riskin 1987: pp. 61–2). This occurred in spite of the fact that the First Five Year Plan directed three-quarters of investment in new plant capacity to inland regions and the coastal provinces' share of total industrial production declined.

However much we may tend to rationalise after the event, there was a glaringly obvious need at the time to curtail the growth of urban population. Between 1952 and 1957, it increased from 71.6 million to 99 million, rising still further to 131 million by 1960 (Guojia tongjiju 1988: p. 569). From 1952 to 1957, it grew by some 40 per cent compared with rural population growth of 9 per cent. A familiar third world problem loomed. There was a pool of unemployed people (6 per cent) in urban areas (State Statistical Bureau 1990: p. 123), living in conditions characterised by serious overcrowding and over-utilisation of resources. Mao's preferred solution was to rely on labour-intensive techniques in light industry, located in rural areas. That strategy, he felt, could more than cope with population increases (Gray 1973: p. 133).

A new economic strategy was required and Mao was groping for one. Yet, bearing in mind the desire to be open-minded expressed in our introduction, we should not underestimate the success of economic development under the plan (see Ishikawa 1984). The Soviet-inspired First Five Year Plan had been spectacular. An annual industrial growth of 18 per cent (though probably overstated due to an underestimate of early years) was higher than virtually every other country in the world and surpassed the industrial growth rate of the Soviet Union during its first two five-year plans (1928–37). A system, moreover, where state revenue consisted more and more in enterprise profits was easier to administer than one based on sales taxes at fixed prices with subsidies directed at enterprises unable to compete; such might incur huge administrative costs (as during the reform period of the 1980s) (Riskin 1987: pp. 73–4). Perhaps most significant, despite peasant opposition to high procurement quotas and despite high investment rates and local shortages of commodities, the overall standard of living of the masses did not decline. One can understand perhaps the nostalgia for the 'extensive development' of the early 1950s exhibited by Party leaders in the late 1970s. But, of course, their views were affected by bitter memories of what came later.

Radicalisation and Retrenchment, 1957–62

Mao's initial criticism of the mechanistic Soviet model of socialism in 1957 still remained within the parameters of a positive model, a quasi-socialist 'mode of production' brought about by agricultural collectivisation and the socialisation of industry and commerce. The achievement of that model was felt to have brought to an end 'large and extensive' class struggle. He criticised, however, the Soviet model's inability correctly to 'handle contradictions' – to distinguish among those between the people and the enemy (antagonistic) and those among the people (internal). The former demanded coercion but the latter persuasion. The downgrading of class struggle, however, meant that 'people' and 'enemy' were defined as behavioural or ideological categories without clear objective referents. It was easy, therefore, to diagnose a social problem in terms of the methods used to deal with it which, as we shall note in the later discussion of law and policing, could lead to arbitrariness. We only have to consider how the definition of 'correct' in 'correct handling' changed from that used in the movement to 'let a hundred flowers bloom' which solicited criticism in 1957 to that of the Anti-rightist movement which turned on the critics of the earlier movement and led to ideological persecution.

The Anti-rightist movement, which struck down many people in the state structure, gave enormous power to Party organisations which often overrode formal state structures and procedures. We shall comment on this in most of the following chapters, in particular those dealing with law and intellectuals. Indeed, the formal legal structures, set in place after 1954, were severely hampered and civil and criminal codes remained on the table for over two decades. Increasing egalitarianism in 1957 saw also a reduction in the salaries of cadres (followed by further reductions in 1959 and 1960). Perhaps most important, however, was the massive decentralisation of decision-making in late 1957.

By late 1957, decentralisation II had triumphed (Selden 1979: pp. 432–6). All light industry and a large part of heavy industry was transferred to provincial control. Provinces were allowed to retain a greater percentage of profits from centrally controlled industries in their localities. Local governments could now float their own bonds. In short, much greater provincial or municipal financial autonomy was enjoyed. At the same time, the planning system was decentralised to provincial level. Even the railways, where centralisation would seem to be crucial, were transferred to local authorities (Schurmann 1966: p. 209). In retrospect, it has been claimed that, at one fell swoop, the system had been shifted from 'centralised suffocation' to 'decentralised anarchy'. To counter this, various plans were put forward for 'large economic co-operation regions', though in general the government lost control of the economy in that great extravaganza of production and social transformation known as the Great Leap Forward.

The Great Leap was informed by adherence to an extreme 'teleological' view. Indeed, the parameters of that teleology extended beyond those expressed hitherto and, at one point, envisaged the rapid transition to 'communism' (a society governed by distribution according to needs rather than work). In the spirit of moral teleology and rejecting 'mechanical materialism', Mao took a stand against the 'theory of the productive forces' and came to reaffirm class struggle. Long before, he had remarked that while material forces generally play the decisive role, in certain circumstances the relations of production and what Marxists call the 'ideological superstructure' or simply mass consciousness and human relationships are decisive (*Selected Works*, 1: p. 336). Now he reaffirmed that view with a vengeance. For Mao 'politics' had to be kept 'in command'. Failure to see that was one of the weaknesses of Josef Stalin's (1972) position (JPRS 1974: p. 191). Stalin, he felt, ignored 'the superstructure', politics, the communist movement and the people. Thus Mao rejected Lenin's view that socialism would be more difficult in 'backward countries'. It would be easier because 'the poorer they are, the more people want revolution' (JPRS 1974: p. 259). The most beautiful words can be written on a blank sheet of paper (Schram 1969: p. 352). All that sounds populist but we should be wary of such a designation since a consideration of Marxian productive categories remained prominent in Mao's thought.

Even more significant, in rejecting the productive forces as the major dynamic in socialist society and replacing them by the more activist stimulation and resolution of contradictions, Mao began to chart a new view of revolution referred to as 'uninterrupted' (*buduan*). This held that in all things, social and natural, there is a struggle of opposites. Such struggle might result in balance but balance was only temporary and relative. Progress, therefore, consisting in the constant interaction of contradictions, was 'wave-like' or spiral. That dialectical view rationalised the disequilibria of the Great Leap Forward which caused much economic damage.

The dominant slogan of 1958 was produce 'more, better, faster and more economically'. Such had been the basis of Mao's twelve-year plan for agriculture, unceremoniously shelved in 1956 and re-published in slightly revised form at the Third Plenum of the Eighth Central Committee in late 1957 as the National Programme for Agricultural Development (Chao 1963: pp. 57–79). That plenum, occurring less than one week after a Central Committee directive had declared that, once the current programme of scaling down the collectives had been completed, there should be no change for the next ten years, ushered in a frenetic pace of development. In late 1957, national plans had called for an increase of 4.7 per cent in agricultural production during the coming year. Those figures were soon substantially altered. After a series of meetings in January 1958, which resulted in 'Sixty Work Methods' being put forward as guidelines for the Leap (*Current Background*, 892, 21 Oct 1969: pp. 1–14), it became clear that the Second Five Year Plan (commencing

1958) would be drastically revised. At the same time, the mass mobilisation effected during a water conservancy campaign in the winter of 1957–8, led to a further reduction in the size of private plots, the amalgamation of collectives, the deployment of troops in the rural sector and an intensification of the old Yan'an programme to send youth to the countryside (rustication). Campaigns came thick and fast and everyone was instructed to help agriculture. By February, there was every indication that the harvests in that year would be much better than in 1957, and that prospect fuelled optimism and led to continual raising of planned targets beyond those which could possibly be attained. To doubt those targets was to invite criticism as a 'conservative', and since decentralisation of authority had rendered the planning and statistical system inoperative, planning organs could only accept the highest possible estimate of prospective output.

Decentralisation, moreover, resulted in attempts being made to establish some kind of industry in each *xiang* to manufacture agricultural tools, to produce fertiliser and to process food. There were even attempts to set up small furnaces at *xian* level and lower, to turn out steel which proved to an expensive failure, as Mao admitted. To help rural industrialisation, technical cadres were sent, in ever increasing numbers, to the countryside to participate in labour, to train other technicians and to implement plans to establish a secondary school in every *xiang*. Yet it soon became clear that decentralisation had resulted in the centre losing its grip on local developments. Local governments, finding it extremely difficult both to remit funds to the centre and to finance the burgeoning local investment, further decentralised authority to *xian* and minor municipalities. By March 1958, leaders were unclear as to where operational decision-making power rested and, in a manner similar to two years previously, called for caution. Complaints of excesses began to appear in the press. Materials were said to be in short supply. There was much talk of 'reckless advance' (which were precisely the words once used to describe the 'little leap forward' of 1955–6) and of 'overcoming the ill wind of empty talk and false reports'. In response, the centre called a further series of meetings culminating in a re-convened session of the Eighth Party Congress (necessitated in any case, since the Second Five Year Plan was defunct). At that session, many leaders stressed the need to take stock of the situation and immediately afterwards undertook tours of the country to make an assessment of what was happening.

The result of those tours and Mao's insistence that experiments in mobilisation undertaken in Henan should be extended resulted in a revival of the Great Leap in the summer. Collective amalgamation in Henan had produced a mobilised and potentially transferable rural workforce, had freed women for agricultural work and, in the face of tension over Taiwan, had led to experiments in merging productive units with militia organisations, according to the slogan 'everyone a soldier' (*quanmin jiebing*). The first of these amalgamated units had appeared in April and was officially endorsed in July. By the end of that month 5,376 agricultural collectives in the Henan region had become 208 large 'people's communes' with an average population of 8,000 households. Nation-wide endorsement of the commune model took place at an enlarged Politburo conference at Beidaihe in August 1958 (Selden 1979: pp. 401–5).

An Assessment of Mao's Changed Strategy

As we have noted, by the summer of 1958, Mao had endorsed a set of policies geared to 'simultaneous development on all fronts' which welcomed imbalance. This was a dramatic shift from his initial reaction to the Soviet model. In 1956, Mao appeared to believe in 'objective economic laws', of which one was the 'law of planned and proportionate development'. Over the next two years, however, imbalance was disastrously to destroy proportions, resulting in huge waste and bad planning decisions (the production of unusable steel in local plants and, more seriously, reducing the area sown in grain). As a result of all that, Mao's 1956 call to improve the livelihood of the peasants resulted in the very opposite.

Consider also investment. In 1956, mistakenly perhaps, Mao celebrated China's not investing in heavy industry practically to the exclusion of light industry and agriculture, as in other socialist countries. But he still insisted that, while heavy industry remained the 'leading factor', the proportion of investment needed to be adjusted somewhat in favour of light industry and agriculture which had a faster lead time (*Selected Works*, 5 (1977): pp. 285, 286). What, in fact, happened was that investment in heavy industrial capital construction in the so-called Second Five Year Plan period increased from 36 per cent of total investment (the First Five Year Plan figure) to 54 per cent, with light industry remaining at about 6 per cent and agriculture increasing to about 11 per cent. In crude terms, what Chinese planners call the 'accumulation rate' rose from 25 per cent in 1957 to 44 per cent in 1959. (This refers to the ratio of accumulation to national income. It is larger than the Western concept 'net investment rate', because national income is smaller, omitting most services: see Riskin 1987: p. 145.) Over-investment in heavy industry, which reached alarming proportions during the Great Leap, has remained a problem ever since.

In 1956, moreover, while supporting decentralisation of authority, Mao was eager to see that transfer of power to local areas did not swamp the initiatives of enterprises. As he put it, one should pay careful attention to the relationship between the state, the enterprise and the individual producers (*Selected Works*, 5 (1977): pp. 289–92). The Great Leap Forward, however, involved radical decentralisation to regions which often damaged enterprise independence. Mobilisational policies and exhaustion, moreover, were the antithesis of caring for the interests of the individual producers.

Clearly, over the years 1956–8, Mao changed his mind or lost control over the major policy initiatives he took. From 'objective economic laws', he moved to the intoxicating idea of 'politics taking command'. From the geneticist planners, Chen Yun and Bo Yibo, he moved to a teleological view. When economic difficulties appeared, he retreated to 'objective economic laws' (which he saw as a 'great school'). Then, in temporary eclipse, he made notes effectively denying those economic laws. Bearing that in mind, few commentators nowadays, in China or in the West, have much good to say about Mao's Great Leap policies, which are seen as throwbacks to the Yan'an vision of self-reliant local areas and unsuitable to a developing, integrated commodity economy. Yet critics have to consider the Great Leap in the light of possible alternatives.

We have noted that whilst official figures for the 1950s show that overall the growth of food grains was higher than the increase in population, one could not be sure for how long the ratio might be maintained. There had been a surge in agricultural growth once peace had allowed agricultural infrastructure to be repaired, but it fell after that and there was every reason to believe that the rate would fall further. More seriously, relaxation of quotas had caused grain procurement to fall below 1953 levels. To those of a radical bent, the fact that the state was selling more grain than it procured and was running down stocks (Riskin 1987: pp. 70–1) required an attempt once again to introduce direct production planning. But, they felt, Soviet-style planning was over-centralised, inflexible and bureaucratic and placed too great a premium on technological development as the key to productivity. The proposed answer was decentralised, regional production planning. Since modern technology was scarce, moreover, a strategy was adopted which relied on social mobilisation to increase productivity and thus generate funds for agricultural mechanisation which would make savings available for industrial investment. The old policy of postponing social transformation until there was adequate mechanisation, abandoned during the leap of 1955–6, was now considered far too 'conservative'.

Since reliance on modern technology exclusively was not an option, 'walking on two legs', as a general policy, made much sense. Whilst mobilisational policies often resulted in chaos, many economists, following Ragnar Nurske, would see merit in a radical assault on rural under-employment. Whilst many small enterprises were wasteful and were closed down, it may be argued that they served the function of introducing new technologies and imparting skills which later, in a more market-oriented environment, proved invaluable. One wonders whether the phenomenal success of local industries in the 1980s would have been as great without the initiatives of the collectives, set in motion during the Great Leap. Also, while there was much wasteful large-scale construction during the Leap, many of the larger enterprises set up at that time eventually proved profitable.

That being said, it was abundantly clear to many leaders quite early on in the Great Leap that things were going very wrong. For two decades Party leaders argued one with another about the causes of the economic disaster which followed the Great Leap (policy, climate, bad leadership or betrayal). Mao's action, moreover, in dismissing defence minister Peng Dehuai, who had criticised the 1958 leap as manifesting 'petty bourgeois fanaticism' (Selden 1979: p. 479), caused a decay in Party norms and loss of confidence in internal Party procedures. Until 1959 the Party had maintained a belief that its procedures were governed by 'inner-Party democracy'. Members at any level were permitted to criticise policy provided that, when an authoritative decision was taken, they followed the

Party line. As many Party leaders saw it, Peng was merely following that procedure and in 1959 was criticising the excesses of 1958 in the same spirit as Mao who took the same tack in December of that year. Peng's dismissal was seen by many as Mao's violation of a code he himself had defended. Mao's action could only be seen as pique. Mao had placed himself above the rules of Party procedure.

Economic Crisis and Recovery, 1959–66

In the wake of the Great Leap, Mao retired to the Politburo's 'second front' (mooted in 1956), leaving Liu Shaoqi and others to repair the damage. Meanwhile in 1959 China suffered from its worst natural calamities for several decades. In the years 1959–60 approximately half the land under cultivation was hit by floods and drought (State Statistical Bureau 1990: p. 375). Grain production (corrected figures)[2] fell from 193 million tonnes in 1958 to 165 in 1959 and 139 in 1960, rising slightly to 143 in 1961. After an annual rise of 3.7 per cent, cereal production fell from 1958 to 1960 by almost 30 per cent. Between 1959 and 1961 there was a net loss of population of between 14 and 28 million (Aubert 1988: p. 106; Riskin 1987: p. 136; Lardy 1983: pp. 146–52). Such was a symptom of famine. In that situation China turned from a net grain exporter to a net importer and remained so for some time since decentralisation had made inter-provincial grain transfers extremely difficult. Perhaps saddest of all was the fact that such imports did not begin until 1961. Before that time leaders believed they had 100 million tonnes more than they did.

The crisis of 1959–61 was directly attributable to the Great Leap Forward. The autumn harvest of 1958 was not gathered in its entirety. A reduction of the area sown in grain in the winter of 1958 led to a food shortage and the situation was further exacerbated by the poor harvests of 1959. Meanwhile grain procurement had been stepped up. Furthermore, a premature reduction of material incentives and the abolition of the private sector led to a loss of

---

[2] Grain statistics include tubers, which at different times were calculated at a quarter or a fifth of dry weight. The corrected figures convert the pre-1964 figures to one-fifth (Aubert 1988: p. 106).

peasant confidence. The boom of 1958 encouraged rather than reversed the drift of peasants to the cities, which harsh policies of household registration failed to halt, and there developed a rural labour shortage which hindered production. The planning system, moreover, was in tatters. Added to this, Soviet withdrawal of assistance in 1960, in reaction to the Leap and to ideological and strategic factors, may have halted development of a significant sector of industry and added to the general demoralisation.

In the years 1960–2, remedial policies were adopted. A sixty-article document on agriculture shifted management of agriculture back to production teams, (which with a reduction in the size of communes soon came to comprise some 24 households). The document ratified contracting of tasks to small groups or individuals and allowed for a significant private sector. The key slogan was 'agriculture as the base and industry as the leading factor'. That order of priority was to result in the designation of high and stable yield grain-producing areas and a shift to concentration on the rice lands of the Central South. Such specialisation according to principles of comparative advantage ran diametrically counter to Great Leap self-reliance. There was a greater shift also towards investment in agriculture, with the number of (largely Soviet made) tractors in 1961 quadrupling the figure of 1957. The sudden removal of Soviet assistance in 1960, however, halted tractor deployment and, before long, other forms of investment fell off sharply. Agriculture might have been designated the 'base' but it never achieved anything like priority in investment. At the same time, in industry, most small rural enterprises were closed down and workers were returned to agriculture.

The urban labour force which had doubled during the Great Leap was reduced by 20 million by the simple expedient of sending workers to the countryside. A seventy-article document on industry of late 1961, whilst paying lip-service to some Great Leap innovations such as the triple alliance among cadres, technicians and workers (enshrined in a constitution authorised by Mao for the Anshan Iron and Steel Works but not published at the time), called for halting unplanned capital construction projects, the closure of enterprises making a loss, a halt in industrial recruitment and restoring former co-operatives. This was done according to another slogan: 'consolidation, filling out and raising standards'. There was much talk of 'balance' rather than the old Great Leap affirmation of the positive role of disequilibrium. The investment rate was cut, though soon reverted to very high levels. Stress was placed on the realisation of short-term economic goals rather than on any long-term perspective and no five-year plan was to begin until the eve of the Cultural Revolution.

Combining the restoration of the planning system with the integration of industry and agriculture through the market has been succinctly described by Carl Riskin (1987: p. 82) as the opposite of the Great Leap strategy of dispersing authority from the top down while concentrating it from the bottom up. The provincial decentralisation measures of late 1957 were rescinded and moves, initiated in 1959, for the centre and provinces to negotiate shares of total revenue rather than relying on separate revenue sources were made more effective (Oksenberg and Tong 1991). Central planning was strengthened and local control was loosened. Thus, on the one hand, enterprises were gradually brought under direct central control. On the other hand, various industrial departments frequently held 'commodity exchange conferences' where contracts were signed one with another and with rural units for the supply of raw materials and the sale of industrial goods. At the same time, 'hook ups' were established between customers and markets. As a consequence local production teams, brigades or communes entered into direct dealings with urban consumer co-operatives or urban department stores.

Chapter 3 will consider the remedial measures taken in the rural sector. Suffice it to say that those measures generated considerable opposition in the subsequent Cultural Revolution, particular venom being directed by radical critics of Liu Shaoqi at what was called *sanzi yibao* – the extension of plots for private use, the expansion of free markets, the increase in the number of small enterprises with sole responsibility for their own profits and losses and contacting output to individual households. In his speech to the Ninth Plenum in 1961, Mao voiced opposition to what he felt to be general concessions to the development of 'petty capitalism' in the countryside (JPRS 1974: pp. 237–8, 244). His successor as head of state, Liu Shaoqi, however, at a conference attended by 7,000 cadres in January 1962, whilst expressing the Party line about the 'correctness' of the Great Leap, remarked that, in Hunan, peasants had told him that only 30 per cent of the difficulties in production had been caused by natural calamities, whereas the remaining 70 per cent had been caused by humans. Whilst he denounced Peng Dehuai's 'conspiratorial' activities, Liu endorsed some of Peng's comments and suggested that it might have been better had communes never been established (Joffe 1975: pp. 39–51). He went on, moreover, to criticise the campaign against 'right opportunism' which he equated with erroneous 'leftist' campaigns in pre-liberation days. In February 1962, Liu extended his criticism to current economic policies, which, he felt, had not solved most of the problems left over by the Leap.

At that time, the programme of retrenchment developed even further in the single-minded desire to restore production. *Sanzi yibao* was recommended as a general policy and Deng Xiaoping made his famous remark to the effect that it did not matter what colour a cat might be so long as it caught mice (*Current Background*, 874, 17 March 1969: p. 6; Joffe 1975: p. 24). Deng seemed to imply that one should not worry what the ideological implications of a particular policy might be, so long as it increased production. Mao, who had lashed out at various leaders during the 7,000 cadres conference, faced with a huge budget deficit, could only concede, advocating a five-year period of consolidation (Rice 1972: pp. 189–90), but was soon once again to go on to the offensive.

Continuous Revolution, 1962–76

Despite having gone along with remedial measures in the aftermath of the Great Leap, Mao saw everywhere the development of 'capitalist' tendencies, rationalised in Marxist language ('revisionism'). Reflecting on the problems of the Great Leap and what he felt to be the degeneration of the Soviet Union and Eastern Europe during his temporary retreat to the 'second front', Mao began to adopt a more pessimistic view· concerning the process of socialist transition. He rejected the idea that socialism was simply a positive model (or 'mode of production') in which most class problems were vestiges of the past or caused by external forces. Socialism was now seen as a process which could be reversed as vested interests grew into new classes. Those classes, moreover, were not simply the result of economic forces but might develop within the state structure and the Communist Party itself. Significantly he remarked that, since in less-developed countries revolution was prepared in the realm of culture (the weakest link in ruling class control), culture was an important site for the initiation of counter-revolution (Levy 1975). That tendency must be combated. Such were his first thoughts on cultural revolution.

Returning to the 'first front' at the Tenth Plenum of the Eighth Central Committee in 1962, Mao called for waging 'class struggle' which took the form of a Socialist Education Movement in the countryside. As Chapter 3 will discuss, the results were not satisfactory from his point of view. At the same time, he relied more and more on an army, politicised under Defence Minister Lin Biao, to restore the spirit of socialism and sought to turn literature and the arts in a more socialist direction. Failure to achieve this, as Chapter 6 will show, was a major cause of the Cultural Revolution.

Administratively, the period from 1962 to 1966, before the outbreak of the Cultural Revolution, was one of paralysis in the Party. No plenum was held and policy was worked out at various work conferences with shifting membership. While Mao pushed for waging class struggle and what was now called 'continuous revolution' (*jixu geming*), the formal state structure under Zhou Enlai's leadership operated routinely and the National People's Congress in 1965 endorsed what later became known as the 'four modernisations' (agriculture, industry, science and technology and national defence). Thus while Mao called for a radical Socialist Education Movement, many moderate economic policies continued and economic recovery occurred. Policy was ambiguous. On the one hand there were radical calls for a new 'leap forward' and new moves in 1964 towards administrative decentralisation. There was an affirmation of the self-reliant experiences and egalitarian payment of the model Dazhai production brigade in Shanxi and a move away from price planning in agriculture towards direct production planning (reliance on quotas). In industry, there was a stress on relatively self-reliant 'comprehensive' enterprises and an affirmation of a radical version of the experiences of the Daqing Oil-field, which had been led by many ex-members of the Army Engineering Corps and was said to exemplify discipline, worker participation, the integration of agriculture and industry and 'politics in command'. On the other hand, reform proposals were put forward which rejected the idea of 'comprehensive' enterprises in favour of greater division of labour and greater specialisation (belied perhaps by a system in which a viable market was absent and characterised by skeletal planning) (Riskin 1987: p. 219); in that light there were, of course, demands for greater market integration. At the same time central ministries devolved some of their powers to semi-autonomous vertically-integrated trusts, designed to operate more according to principles of profit (Lee 1987: pp. 73–96). There was also a small wage reform for industrial workers, a modest use of bonus payments and large-scale employment of contract workers which created intra-urban differentials. Yet, while vertical command in industry was stronger, workers and staff congresses were revamped and, in some enterprises, experiments were undertaken whereby factory general managers were elected (Richman 1969: pp. 255–6). Although 'one-person management' was occasionally revived, experiments were undertaken in 1964 to introduce a non-bureaucratic functional system of management which accorded well with the old Yan'an principle of 'concentrated leadership and divided operations'.

Economic policy was contradictory. Policies which might be considered to be 'revisionist' were still voiced and occasionally implemented. At the same time, impressive models had been put forward, though it was difficult to determine how to establish them in other areas. What probably preoccupied rural cadres were simply petty instances of capitalism and the lack of clarity in central policies. They were never quite sure whether the targets of their criticism ought to be their fellows or senior people in authority 'taking the capitalist road'.

The Cultural Revolution and the 1970s

Frustrated by cadres and senior leaders blocking his radical moves, in 1966 Mao launched the Cultural Revolution. During that revolution many leaders were persecuted by red guards and red rebels. Nevertheless, despite the fact that red guards and red rebels were encouraged to 'seize power' over their respective units, due to Zhou Enlai's efforts, it is said, one-half to two-thirds of the 366 ministers, vice ministers, heads and deputy heads of central commissions kept their posts during 1966–8 (Wang 1992: p. 117). During that turbulent period, while rebels attacked the Party organisation, loyalty to the Party as an abstract symbol remained.

Such was a consequence of Mao's failure to square his Leninist orientation with his views on 'continuous revolution'. If 'new bourgeois elements' were likely to develop within the Communist Party, then why should one have any confidence in that Party? Indeed, Mao lost confidence in the Party and endorsed attacks on it by red guards and red rebels. Yet, while the radicals attacked, they chanted the first quotation of Mao in his 'little red book' to the effect that the core force leading the cause of socialism was the Party. Eventually Mao proved to be sufficiently a Leninist to see that only a reconstructed Party could restore the damage done by the Cultural Revolution.

Mao's views on continuous revolution not only contradicted Leninist norms but were also patchy and inconclusive. Mao's early ideas were added to by a host of writers and writing groups (often anonymous). During the Cultural Revolution years there co-existed a hotch-potch of views ranging from those which discussed the spontaneous generation of new classes to the old idea of remnant classes seeking a come-back and the view that a 'capitalist super-structure' could grow on a 'socialist base'. Most of the contributions were not coherent and, while politically significant and dangerous, were not particularly interesting.

The preferred form of organisation, which emerged out of the turbulent years of the Cultural Revolution was, at all levels, the 'revolutionary committee' based on a triple alliance of revolution-ary rebels, old cadres and People's Liberation Army (a variant of a 1949 model). At first quite radical, these later often reflected the army's desire to prevent disorder. Under military guidance, many cadres were sent to the countryside or retrained in what were known as May Seventh Cadre Schools and some died in sometimes violent circumstances. From the 1970s, as many were rehabilitated, politics became that of revenge.

The end of the turbulent period of the Cultural Revolution was marked by the Ninth Party Congress of 1969, convened in a hurry to establish stability, prompted in part by Soviet pressure on the northern border and reflecting the importance of the military. Yet for all that it promised regularity, reflected in its insistence that Party congresses should be held every five years (thirteen years had elapsed since the first session of the Eighth Congress and eleven since its second session). The size of the Central Committee doubled to some 170 and the top leadership consisted of Cultural

Revolution activists headed by Chen Boda (formerly head of the Central Cultural Revolution Group), Jiang Qing, Zhang Chunqiao and Yao Wenyuan (three members of the subsequent ultra-left 'Gang of Four'), senior Party members concerned with public security work, the central military leadership under Lin Biao, representatives of the regional military commanders who had been engaged in restoring order, senior administrators of the State Council, headed by Premier Zhou Enlai and Li Xiannian (Minister of Finance), and a few old worthies.

There were good reasons why the military had come to enjoy great power in the aftermath of the Cultural Revolution; and, whatever latent conflict existed between the Lin Biao group and the regional military commanders who had been entrusted with restoring order, the army was still the only really unified organisation in the country. But the army was gradually phased out of administration, particularly after the Lin Biao incident of 1971. Allegedly, Lin Biao had tried to become head of state but, fearing Mao was about to turn against the left after adopting more policies of stabilisation in 1970, plotted a coup and died *en route* for the Soviet Union. Before long, the military command system was reorganised, a purge of the central military apparatus was carried out and emphasis was placed on stabilising the Party. But was the Party any different? Reflecting previous radical policies, the Ninth Congress had abolished the Party Secretariat and the Party supervisory apparatus and adopted the principle of 'open Party building', whereby candidates for Party membership had to be accepted not only by Party branches but also by non-Party people they worked with. The Party also accepted, in principle, that its members with grievances could by-pass various levels of Party authority and, if necessary, appeal directly to the chairman himself, whose thought was given pride of place in the Constitution. But 'open Party building' proved too slow and too contentious to be effective and direct appeal to higher levels was often too perilous a course of action. The reconstituted Party was much the same as that of old.

Later chapters will consider the effect of the Cultural Revolution on the legitimacy of the régime. That revolution had persecuted one generation of leaders and was felt to have 'betrayed' another. Equally damaging in the long term, but less frequently discussed, however, were changes in economic policy and relations between the centre and provinces. During the height of the Cultural Revolution, when red rebels seized power, there was little economic policy beyond demands from different quarters on the one hand for egalitarianism and on the other for worker privilege. Yet there was a broader economic agenda. A major part of this was set by considerations of defence (Naughton 1988). First was the policy adopted in 1965, to develop what were called 'third line' industries in the mountainous terrain of the West. Those industries, which consumed the bulk of new industrial investment, were costly and often very inefficient. Once established, they were very difficult to remove when the fears of war had abated. The chaos of the late 1960s, moreover, led to the collapse of central planning. The response to chaos was the very opposite of that following the Great Leap Forward which combined macro-economic centralisation with greater reliance on the market. In 1970 the scope of central planning was reduced. Various central planning bodies were merged with their entire staff reduced to some 12 per cent of the pre-Cultural Revolution figure. At the same time, the country was divided into ten relatively self-sufficient 'economic co-operation regions' and 2,600 large scale industrial enterprises were handed over to local governments. With that decentralisation went a greater degree of local control of foreign trade – a harbinger of future developments (Kamm 1989). The fiscal system, moreover, was changed to allow for much greater provincial autonomy. Those measures, also taken as preparations for a possible war, were likewise very difficult to undo. Throughout the 1970s, there were repeated changes in central–local fiscal arrangements and some regions were still forced by the centre to subsidise others (Riskin 1987: p. 212). But localism and weak central control have remained a problem ever since.

One of the aims of the Cultural Revolution was to restore the spirit of the Great Leap and the atmosphere in 1969–70 bore some similarities to 1958, with the Soviet threat this time providing the external stimulus. This was immediately apparent in the renewed decentralisation of decision-making power to local areas, at first (until 1972) to the *xian* (Riskin 1987: p. 214). Stress was also placed on what were known as 'five small industries' (cement, chemical fertiliser, machinery, power and iron and steel). There was also constant reference to policies of the late 1950s, in particular the National Plan for Agricultural Development, an extreme emphasis on growing grain, a greater stress on production as opposed to price planning and ambitious programmes for agricultural development in a number of provinces. The term often used to describe the situation at provincial level was 'flying leap'.

But the 'flying leap' was short-lived. Throughout the early 1970s (during the Fourth Five Year Plan beginning 1971), political goals gradually gave way simply to increasing production. There was a new emphasis on sound economic management and scientific farming and eleven high-yielding agricultural areas were once again advanced as models, though this time simply for the application of modern scientific techniques rather that out of considerations of comparative advantage. Although field experiments were still advocated, those who had neglected the activities of central research institutes were also criticised. The ambitious plans for electrification and mechanisation, put forward in the late 1960s, moreover, were re-interpreted in a more orderly way.

By 1971–2, full-scale rehabilitation of the bureaucracy was under way, even allowing for a pay rise for cadres. Foreign relations were restored (with a re-orientation towards the United States). Foreign technology was imported and universities were reopened. In that period, radicals vied with restorationists and various compromises were struck, as exemplified in the Tenth Congress of the Party in 1973. That congress, representing 28 million Party members, re-elected most members of the Ninth Central Committee with the exception of a significant military component (39) said to be followers of Lin Biao. The congress highlighted Mao's statement in 1966 that revolutionary upsurges would occur every seven or eight years (in fact seven years had elapsed). The official account of the Lin Biao incident, now formally made public, was that it was a continuation of the struggle against 'revisionism'. Yet there was a contradiction between the radical policy statements and the cautious measures taken to strengthen Party leadership and to stabilise the state structure. It was announced, for example, that the National People's Congress would soon be convened.

At the same time, rehabilitated ministers received senior Party posts, thus diluting the influence of such radicals as Jiang Qing, Zhang Chunqiao and Yao Wenyuan. The Tenth Party Congress, like those of 1956, 1958 and 1969, was probably seen by many as an antidote to excessive radicalism and, again like the preceding congresses, was convened in a hurry, without even a preparatory plenum. Though the congress was said to be a direct continuation of that of 1969, the leadership formula was quite different. No longer did Mao make any attempt to nominate a 'close comrade in arms and successor'. This time, a collective leadership was to be formed consisting of 'the old, the middle-aged and the young'. Organisational conservatism, however, prevented young people achieving senior Party posts, with the exception of Wang Hongwen, later considered to be the fourth member of the 'Gang of Four', who was elected vice-chairman of the Party in his thirties. Wang was invited to give the address introducing the new Party Constitution (*Peking Review*, 35–6, 7 Sept. 1973; pp. 29–33).

While Wang held to radical themes deriving from the Cultural Revolution, Zhou Enlai was cautious. The stage was set for a new confrontation. The confrontation went on from 1974 to 1976. The 'Gang of Four' launched a series of movements to revive the spirit of the Cultural Revolution which will be outlined in Chapter 6. Revival was not forthcoming and a new attempt at compromise was sought at the meeting of the National People's Congress in January 1975 (the first in ten years). The spirit of compromise at that congress was reflected in the salience of both Deng Xiaoping and Zhang Chunqiao, both of whom soon received senior posts in the People's Liberation Army. Similarly, whilst the role of the State Council was given prominence, it was announced that the number of ministries and commissions had been reduced, in Cultural Revolution spirit, from 49 in the mid-1960s to 29. Compromise also permeated the major speeches to the congress by Zhou Enlai and Zhang Chunqiao. While stressing the importance of making China into a modern socialist state by the year 2000 and reiterating the 'four modernisations', Zhou also made mention of 'class struggle'. For his part, Zhang, whilst emphasising the theme of 'continuous revolution', also laid stress on the rights and guarantees in the Constitution which he introduced. Conveniently, it seemed, the Constitution of 1975 solved the question of who should be head of state, which had figured prominently in the Lin Biao struggle, by abolishing the post.

The spirit of compromise of January 1975 did not last for long. Within three weeks of the end of the Fourth National People's Congress, a movement to study the 'theory of the dictatorship of the proletariat' was launched which was to be much more divisive than the earlier campaigns. During that movement there was a major struggle between Deng Xiaoping and the 'Gang of Four'. Deng symbolised the drive to improve economic management and the more outward-looking trade policy of the early 1970s. That involved the importation of complete plants from overseas and the resulting balance of payments problem was used by the 'Gang of Four' in its polemic. By 1975, however, petroleum production retrieved the situation but that did not stop the radical attack on Deng Xiaoping's economistic position. Deng reacted against radical 'metaphysics' and put forward his 'three poisonous weeds' (or 'fragrant flowers') which called for renewed importation of foreign technology (within the limits of 'self-reliance'), seeking long-term loans, foreign involvement in resource development, the adoption of a 'rational' (non class-oriented) management system, opposing egalitarianism in wage payment, better schemes for promoting workers and the need for technical skills. His opponents, on the other hand, accused him of playing down 'class struggle'. Notable here was Zhang Chunqiao and Yao Wenyuan who argued that 'bourgeois right', which prescribed a single value metric in socialist society (work), was a source of inequality which had to be restricted. By extension one could argue that any notion of equal rights, granted to unequal people, was a source of new inequalities which could engender new classes. In the name of equality, therefore, it seemed, some people should be more equal than others. The extreme positive discrimination which followed from that analysis was resented and eventually attacked both by lawyers and economists, as we shall see.

The movements of 1975–6, discussed more fully in Chapter 6, led to a full-scale onslaught on Deng Xiaoping after the death of Zhou Enlai in 1976 and to demonstrations in Tiananmen Square in support of the late Premier. They caused much disillusionment and much obstruction. One is not surprised that the death of Mao in September was soon followed by the arrest of the radicals identified as the 'Gang of Four'. At this point an epitaph on the 'Gang of Four' is in order. Its members were inept politicians and out of touch with mass sentiment. Yet they were committed to what has been called 'revolution from above' which, while reliant on central direction, requires much mass participation. In their opposition to bureaucratism, they were as fervent as the democratic activists of later years. With all the talk of China's continuing 'feudal' culture nowadays, we tend to forget that. What we must not forget is that opposition to democracy in later years by rehabilitated senior leaders was predicated by fears of the Cultural Revolution which that 'Gang' promoted.

2

China After Mao

The two years following the death of Mao saw much confusion in the Party. Legitimacy had been damaged by the Cultural Revolution notion that the Party, rather than being a pure Leninist vanguard, was the arena of class struggle, that Mao's 'close comrade in arms and successor' Lin Biao had been branded a 'conspirator' and that arcane movements such as that to 'criticise Lin Biao and Confucius' could help chart the way forward (Young 1989). The 'Gang of Four' was targeted as containing the principal villains and attempts were made to disassociate Mao from that 'Gang'. To secure continuity, Hua Guofeng, who held the posts of Party chairman and Premier, strove to revive Mao's ideas on 'uninterrupted revolution' of the late 1950s which fitted in with his advocacy of a new great leap into modernity (known colloquially as the 'foreign leap' [*yang yuejin*]). Significantly Deng Xiaoping who was rehabilitated and confirmed in office by the Eleventh Party Congress in 1977, consistent with his arguments of 1975, was initially quite enthusiastic about the new leap.

Reflecting Great Leap thinking, the ten-year plan released by Hua Guofeng to the first session of the Fifth National People's Congress in February 1978 (Selden 1979: pp. 695–701) was compared explicitly with the original National Programme for Agricultural Development of the 1950s. By 1985, it was anticipated that grain production would increase from some 305 million tonnes to 400 million, with an annual increase in the agricultural growth rate from some 3 per cent to between 4 and 5 per cent. Twelve key areas for grain production were marked out (there were previously eleven). Steel production was to reach 60 million tonnes (in 1977 it was some 24) and capital construction investment was to reach an amount equal to the total capital construction investment for the previous 28 years. Once again, increased agricultural output was partly to be achieved by bringing new land into cultivation and increasing crop yields. The mechanisation drive was intensified since, it was believed at the time, the rural areas suffered from a general labour shortage. At the time the government revised its earlier target of 'full mechanisation' by 1980 (Stavis 1978: pp. 231–3), down to the still unrealisable target of 85 per cent mechanisation by 1985.

Press comments were not slow in pointing out the parallels with 1958–9. But there was a difference. This time the leap was to depend on technology imported from capitalist countries, costing perhaps some $70 billion (Riskin 1987: p. 259). The plans, furthermore, while highly ambitious in Great Leap vein, demanded a much greater degree of central control than had existed in the late 1950s. This time it was clear that plans for controlling the major rivers and diverting waters from the Changjiang to the North could only be implemented through national co-ordination. Economic logic, moreover, suggested the use of *xian*-level agricultural machinery stations, which had not all been dissolved in the preceding radical periods, rather than communal control of machinery.

But the centralising tendency in the years 1977–8 must not be overstated. Throughout the period, rural development was still seen within the context of Schurmann's 'decentralisation II' and the campaign to establish Dazhai-type *xian* was carried on according to the spirit of local 'self-reliance'. The emphasis on commune level industries, which in the early 1970s had replaced that on more costly *xian*-level industries, remained quite evident. Whilst focusing on the miracles which could be achieved by local initiative, however, official utterances in 1977–8, unlike those of 1958–9, played down the theme of class struggle. In his speech to the national conference on learning from Dazhai in agriculture in late 1975, Hua Guofeng had laid down criteria such as being 'united in struggle' against 'capitalist activities' and the 'determination to supervise and re-mould class enemies' (*Peking Review*, 44, 31 October 1975: p. 8). By 1977, however, Hua's aim to transform one-third of China's 2,100-odd *xian* into Dazhai-type *xian* by 1980 seems exclusively to have been seen in terms of output, and the 1985 targets, announced at the first session of the Fifth National People's Congress in February 1978, reflected the new view.

The ambitious agricultural targets of 1978 were based on a feeling of success. After the years of calamities of the early 1960s, grain production had resumed a healthy growth of 3.4 per cent whilst the area sown in grain had steadily declined. Such 'success' had been achieved, of course, by the 'green revolution' which doubled and trebled the yield of some crops. But there were limits to that revolution since it demanded ever-costly inputs (irrigation and chemical fertilisers). Continued success, therefore, depended not just on a leap to make those inputs available but a total change in relative costs and, therefore, productivity. Indeed, economists observe, such a change did realise Hua's targets for grain production by 1984. But could the targets have been reached according to Hua's strategy? Probably not.

Nowadays most economists concur that the success indicators, embraced by Hua Guofeng in 1978 were faulty. Up to 1978, they argue, the dimensions of China's rural problems were hidden from foreign observers and most Chinese. As noted in our Introduction, by focusing on output data, many contemporary observers saw the performance of Chinese agriculture as outstanding. Agriculture had grown by an average of 4 per cent per annum (with grain slightly lower), putting China near the top of the low-income countries. Whilst China still imported wheat, it exported the higher-value rice and multiple cropping had increased output significantly. The price of grain sold to the state since 1949 had doubled in relation to the price of industrial products sold to the rural areas. Agricultural tax and state procurement, in addition, had declined considerably in relative terms. After the Third Plenum, however, when more statistics (especially those dealing with the cost of inputs and the method of calculating the urban-rural terms of trade) became available, another picture emerged. Allowing for the distorting nature of comparative statistics, economists began to note that it took five or six times the amount of rice to buy a tractor in China than it did in Japan. Production expenses as a proportion of gross income had risen considerably (from 25 per cent in 1957 to 33 per cent in 1977) with a corresponding decline in the proportion of income distributed to peasants (from 58 per cent to 51 per cent). The marginal costs of multiple cropping exceeded marginal revenue. The urban-rural terms of trade, moreover, were distorted by the fact that key production costs were not included in their calculation. Meanwhile, the agricultural labour force had grown by 126 million (declining only from 84 per cent of the total in 1952 to 75 per cent in 1979). This meant that agricultural productivity was only 5 per cent higher than 1952 (compared with 400 per cent for industry). In addition, the marketed portion of grain had fallen from 30 per cent to 20 per cent and a policy of insisting on grain production had made moderately well-off areas poor and had stifled the development of other crops.

Overall, despite considerable agricultural growth, living standards in rural areas in the late 1970s were said to be much the same as in the 1950s and the amount of cash paid to commune members had declined. According to one estimate, per-capita availability of raw grain in 1977 was some 226 kilograms which was only slightly higher than the 1957 figure of 214 kilograms. But now there was insufficient grain to divert to grain-deficient areas. Cadres were often unwilling to seek relief grain when their units were entitled to it because of bureaucratic obstacles or because such action would cause them to be considered failures according to the rubric of 'self-reliance'. Nevertheless, 100 million peasants were in receipt of relief grain, each receiving 150 kilograms (Riskin 1987: pp. 244–8, 257, 261–3, 268–71; Watson 1984: pp. 110–11; Lardy 1983: pp. 46–88, 112–28, 146–89).

Better statistics also revealed major problems in industry. It became apparent that many commune-level industries, of which China's leaders were very proud, were just as wasteful as the *xian*-level industries of the late 1960s. Local industries in general had performed inefficiently. Decentralisation had allowed enterprises to be established by local authorities without any reference to macro-economic rationality. There was much wasteful duplication and a proliferation of small plants exacerbated an already serious problem of over-accumulation. In industry as a whole, the prolonged wage freeze had caused the average wage to fall in real terms by 17 per cent between 1957 and 1977. There was a crisis also in productivity. Productivity per capita had tripled since 1952 but per *yuan* productivity had declined. Phasing out the policy of rusticating youth, moreover, revealed significant urban unemployment. The accumulation rate was also felt still to be exceptionally high (due to a concentration on heavy industry); it depressed consumption and caused dissatisfaction. Energy production (with excessive consumption) and the development of transport also lagged behind economic growth. There was a neglect of investment defined as 'non-productive' and also of trade and services. The over-centralised (and vicariously decentralised) system, which took as its basis the view that the economy as a whole was a 'natural economy', analogous to a single workshop, also gave considerable power to the arbitrary whims of top leaders and ignored the complexities of 'circulation'. With such a view, production was divorced from demand (Riskin 1987: pp. 264–82). A new strategy was called for.

Post-1978: The Development of a Reform Agenda

During 1978, the foreign leap was tempered by a new mood of sobriety which was hinted at in a new state constitution. The leap was eventually rejected by the Third Plenum of the Eleventh Central Committee late in that year. Changing tack, Deng Xiaoping, who triumphed over those who sought to persist with Mao's policies, was now seen as the symbol of sobriety. The official position, adopted after the Third Plenum, was that the battle lines were drawn between what were called the 'whateverists' (*fanshipai*) who, according to their opponents, wished to abide by the letter of Mao's instructions, and the 'practice' faction which felt that 'practice was the sole criterion for evaluating truth'. The reality behind that caricature was bitter disagreement between those who still inclined towards the increasingly obscured class struggle theme and those who sought to recapture the more technological orientation of 1956 – a time when Party intellectuals were relatively secure, particularly those in the fields of science and technology.

The plenum met amidst what became known as the 'Democracy Wall movement' when hitherto unknown or lesser-known activists erected large character posters, urging a more pragmatic orientation and calling for democracy. Their proposals, echoed in part by a number of intellectuals in the Party at an unprecedented theory conference and elsewhere, will be considered in Chapter 6. Suffice it to note here that, when Deng Xiaoping felt that the proposals had gone too far, democratic aspirations were circumscribed by 'four cardinal principles' – maintenance of Marxism-Leninism Mao Zedong Thought, the socialist path, leadership of the Communist Party and the dictatorship of the proletariat. A cynic might remark that Deng had used the 'democratic movement' to regain power and, having won, had no more use for the democratic activists. With the help of Hu Qiaomu, who had emerged as what in the

Cultural Revolution might have been called an ideological 'tsar', Deng could contain the proposals of reform intellectuals. One should be wary of such explanations. It might have been the case that Deng genuinely believed in his stated commitment to democratic reform but had become concerned by what he felt to be 'anarchist' turmoil which could take on Cultural Revolution dimensions. While, at one stage, he could approve 'large character posters', when their originators talked of his 'metamorphosis into dictatorship' (Goldman 1991) he may have become alarmed.

One should remember also that the constituency Deng could call on was very broad and very unstable. It included disillusioned red guards who at any time could extend their disillusion to him. It included ex-Youth League leader, Hu Yaobang's group of loyal (at that stage) reform intellectuals which, in traditional mode, sought to persuade the ruler to move faster than he might have been inclined. There were also senior Party members, smarting with sorrow or humiliation, who wished simply to restore order. These latter, including such people as Chen Yun and Peng Zhen, having gained the chance to restore 1950s policies, had no desire to go any further. Those moderate (even mildly reformist) Party leaders of the mid-1950s came to be seen by some as 'conservative'. Such labels, used behaviourally, are misleading. The term 'conservative' has been used both to describe those who harked back to the golden age of the 1950s and those who still cherished the ideas of Mao with whom the former were at daggers drawn, and the term 'radical' might be used to describe a broad continuum ranging from those who still harboured beliefs in the ideals of the Cultural Revolution to the democracy activists of 1978 and those who sought a more liberal régime. The latter, by engaging in 'extensive democracy', allowed the 'conservatives' to accuse anyone, radical or liberal, of creating turmoil and sowing the seeds for another Cultural Revolution. Such became the theme for the politics of the next decade. In discussing it, let us lay aside misleading terms such as 'radical', 'liberal' and 'conservative' in favour of distinguishing those who cherished the ideals of the late Mao (a rapidly declining group), those who sought to return to the mid-1950s, and those who wished to go further. (On confusing taxonomies, see Bucknall 1989: pp. 37–42; White 1993b: pp. 61–8.)

The purge of the 'whateverists', culminating in 1981 in the removal of Mao's 'successor' Hua Guofeng, decapitated those establishment figures who harked back to Mao's ideas of 'class struggle'. In the campaign to eliminate the influence of the 'Gang of Four', most of their intellectual spokespersons were silenced (though some may have remained in the General Political Department of the People's Liberation Army). At all levels discipline inspection commissions purged the Party of Cultural Revolution activists, particularly those who had gained 'crash admittance' during the time of the 'Gang of Four'. Conversely the 1950s establishment was reinstated with considerable power, though Hu Yaobang, who was to replace Hua Guofeng as chairman of the Party, and later general secretary (as the post was redesignated in 1982), wanted to go further than most of them. He was joined in his efforts by Zhao Ziyang who became premier of the State Council in 1980. But 'go further in what?' Had the Party returned to the old views of the geneticists or was there a new *telos*? If the *telos* of the Party had shifted from communism to economic development, what were the parameters against which that development should be measured? Were they capitalist, which, Marx insisted, constituted the best method for developing the productive forces? Surely not, some said, who, in the spirit of Mao Zedong, were not willing to reduce politics to economics.

Over the next few years, a number of cycles occurred in which reformers would take the initiative, organise animated forums for discussion, then face opposition from the heirs of the 1950s and then either compromise or endure a campaign of criticism (Hamrin 1987). Five such cycles may be identified. Reform in 1979–80 was followed by limited repression in 1981–2. Renewed reform in 1982–3, after the Party's Twelfth Congress, gave way to a campaign to criticise 'spiritual pollution' in 1983–4. Even greater impetus to reform occurred again in 1984–6, followed by demonstrations, the ouster of Hu Yaobang and a campaign to combat 'bourgeois liberalisation' amid calls for political restructuring. Economic reform, after the Thirteenth Party Congress in 1987, however, led to a clamp-down the following year in the midst of economic crisis, the growth of a democratic student movement followed by the bloody suppression of 1989, the removal of Party general secretary Zhao Ziyang and his replacement by the Shanghai Party leader Jiang Zemin. Finally a new bout of reform began in the early 1990s which, according to the Fourteenth Party Congress of 1992, seeks to create a 'socialist commodity economy' (Jiang Zemin 1992), without any major political concessions being made by the Communist Party.

The First Cycle of Reform and Repression

In the first cycle from 1979 to 1981, the two operative slogans were 'implement the four modernisations' and 'emancipate the mind'. The first term, it will be remembered, had been put forward by Zhou Enlai in 1965, reiterated in 1975 but continually frustrated. One of those modernisations was science and technology. Technologists were inspired by Deng's reiteration of the theme that science was a 'productive force' (and independent of class struggle) at a National Science Conference in March 1978 and attempts were made to recruit them into the Party (against some opposition). Financial rewards were given to inventors and those who applied research to production (though these were often clawed back) and efforts were made to send students and scientists to study overseas. Indeed, great store was set on the promise of science and the restoration of régime legitimacy was to be couched in its language. Thinking more broadly, the development of science and technology was felt to depend on an overall strategy which required a shift in economic orientation to a more open system which tried to combine priority planning with market competition. To direct the process a major body was set up – the Economic System Reform Commission. More specific planning groups were also established to promote technology and rationally to deploy labour to serve the cause of modernisation and these were eventually to lead to the establishment of think-tanks.

Developing a more open system, of course, required integration into the international economy. The Chinese government joined the International Monetary Fund, the World Bank and other international agencies, deciding to take out international loans and to encourage foreign investment. It opened 'special' (originally export processing) economic zones in Guangdong and Fujian with favourable tax rates aimed to attract foreign investment and, in the case of two of the four initial zones, Shenzhen and Zhuhai, to create structures for the eventual incorporation of Hong Kong and Macao. It sent many people to study abroad, exported large numbers of workers to other third world countries (especially

Middle East states which could pay for them) and engaged in joint ventures with foreign countries. It developed, moreover, a thriving tourist industry. But the tension between the concepts of planning and market could be expected to cause problems which were not seen in 1978–9.

As noted earlier, the Third Plenum rejected the 'foreign leap' in favour of 'comprehensive balance' and price planning, long advocated by Chen Yun. Chen Yonggui, the founder of the Dazhai production brigade, was forced into retirement and soon the Dazhai experience in 'self-reliance' was declared a fraud. Policy now was to proceed according to two documents on agriculture tabled at the plenum, of which one was a modified version of the 'sixty articles on agriculture', promulgated in the early 1960s and denounced in the Cultural Revolution (*Issues and Studies*, 15, 7–9 July-Sept. 1987: pp. 102–19, 91–112, 104–15). In the new climate, a three-year programme of economic readjustment was proposed. There was a new stress on formulating targets realistically and, in early 1979, the targets announced at the first session of the Fifth National People's Congress were scaled down.

A more sober assessment of costs led the government to take measures to restore peasant incentives. The tax burden was not much of a problem. Tax had declined as a percentage of grain output since the 1950s and was only some 3 to 4 per cent by the early 1980s (one-fifth of the level of the 1950s). In very poor areas it could now be reduced and sometimes eliminated. More important was a renewed effort to close the 'scissors' – between the prices of agricultural and industrial products. Thus in 1979 there was a further 20 per cent rise in the price of quota grain, accompanied by a further reduction in the price of farm machinery. Similarly, there was a 50 per cent rise in the price of above-quota grain sold to the state and large rises in the official prices of a number of other agricultural products.

In industry, during the first cycle, reformers confronted the problems of excessive heavy industrial bias, gigantomania and lack of enterprise autonomy. The first problem was tackled by encouraging the establishment of small light industrial enterprises which mushroomed throughout the decade, with growth rates significantly faster than in heavy industry. But what did one do with existing large heavy industries? By 1981, it became clear that huge capital-intensive industries could not shift production nor, it seemed, could they redeploy labour. After initial experiments in readjustment which saw a decline in heavy industrial capital construction, the heavy industrial sector renewed its growth and took an increased share of capital construction expenditure at the expense of other sectors.

Achieving enterprise autonomy in state industry was more easily said than done. Moves were made in 1978, in the spirit of the early 1960s, partially to recentralise administrative control whilst giving enterprises much greater autonomy. Recentralisation was attempted by the central government appropriating a greater share of enterprise depreciation funds. Autonomy, on the other hand, was pursued first by attempts to separate government from economic management. This initially took the form of re-establishing vertically integrated trusts. Up to 1982, some 2,000 'specialist corporations' were established (5.5 per cent of all enterprises, 31 per cent in Beijing, Shanghai and Tianjin). These trusts were similar to those 12 established in 1964 and subjected to bitter criticism in the Cultural Revolution. But again was this autonomy? Enterprises complained that they were stripped of authority and just had a new boss. Some regions, moreover, protected their position by forming horizontally integrated trusts of unrelated enterprises. Predictably, the central government retaliated and imposed controls. Some people in business, however, realising that both central and local control impeded operations, founded industrial associations with elected boards. These were a kind of voluntary trade association designed to co-ordinate a particular industry without the rigid central controls embodied in the trusts. Unlike the trusts, associations were not state organisations. They acted ideally as a bridge between the state and enterprises and between enterprises. As one might expect, they became a site of conflict.

Autonomy was also pursued by allowing a growing number of enterprises to retain a larger proportion of profits and permitting the free marketing of above-quota production. It was soon clear, however, that such incentives would not succeed in a situation where profitability did not reflect economic performance. The system of fixed prices meant that, no matter how efficient, some industries (such as coal) could not make a profit and some (such as petroleum) could not make a loss. Though price reform was placed on the agenda in 1979, initial moves were cautious. There were also many regional impediments to profitability. Thus the profit retention formula had to be modified from industry to industry, which gave rise to arbitrariness, confusion and some corruption, exacerbated by allowing direct sales at varying prices.

Autonomy resulted in negative fiscal consequences. Since state enterprises were the major source of government revenue, greater retained profits led to a decline in that revenue precisely at a time when the state embarked on a huge increase in food subsidies to prevent unrest which could be anticipated if higher agricultural purchase prices were passed on to consumers. The budget was in deficit from 1979 to 1984, the peak year being 1979 when it reached 20 billion *yuan*. The deficit was one-sixth of total expenditure. State revenue fell as a proportion of national income from 32.4 per cent (1950s) to 25 per cent in the 1980s. This occurred at a time when reduced central control over the foreign trading activities of regions resulted in a surge of local and often wasteful imports and the deficit in China's external trade reached some $300 million in the final quarter of 1980. Since much of foreign trade, which increased four-fold in the eight years after 1976 (according to some figures reaching 19 per cent of aggregate product), was under the control of local governments and corporations, it was clear that China's dramatic 'open door policy' had exacerbated localism.

All this played into the hands of those who felt economic reform had gone too far. They reminded each other of Chen Yun's 'theory of comprehensive balance', and in December 1980 (at a central work conference) decisions were taken on a second and more cautious readjustment. The government made it clear that the market was subordinate to the plan and that economic reform should not precede but follow economic readjustment. Ministry of Finance spokespersons argued directly that the fiscal crisis was due precisely to a growing 'enterprise-based economy'. Relaxation of controls had led to blind production and blind construction. By the end of the year, Chen Yun was talking about the dominance of the plan over the market – a position ratified by the Party according to the slogan: 'the plan as the centre and the market as supplement'. A campaign, therefore, was launched to study the works of Chen Yun which resulted in the internal publication of a second volume of his writings in 1982. For a while, as reform receded, Chen Yun became a cult figure. Weakness in the central budget, the loss of control over investment and inflation resulted in the first cycle of reform being halted in late 1980 with renewed price controls imposed in 1981 and the suspension of some foreign contracts. At the same time the newly established Ministry of Foreign Economic Relations and Trade (MOFERT) imposed restraints on direct foreign trade, especially on the freewheeling province of Guangdong (Vogel 1989: pp. 364–5). Such action was once again to boost foreign exchange reserves.

The same cyclic pattern might be observed on the political front. At first, while Mao's 'mass line' theory of participation was reaffirmed, representative democracy was stressed. Revolutionary committees were abolished (in 1979) and replaced by direct elections to *xian*-level people's congresses (sometimes by secret ballot). Though often rigged, they were acclaimed in the euphoria of the time (Saich 1989: p. 45). Despite irregularities in elections, the role of local people's congresses and that of the National People's Congress was reaffirmed. The latter (consisting of some 3,000 members) met annually and, as we shall note in Chapter 5, promulgated a stream of legislation. Contrary to popular views, that body was to be more than a 'rubber stamp'; it was to investigate ministers of state and showed considerable independence after 1988. In the early 1980s, however, it had yet to feel its way. Because of its size, its main executive arm was its Standing Committee. That committee was not always enthusiastic about reform proposals and, under Peng Zhen, may have served as a check on the reformist State Council (Wang 1992: pp. 115–16). Also revived was the Chinese People's Political Consultative Conference, with a third of a million members, representing 1,600 different organisations and led for the most part by non-Communist Party members. The conference served to legitimate the principles of the old 'united front' and to participate in forging links with Hong Kong, Taiwan and Macao. One also saw once again the reappearance of the eight pro-Communist 'democratic parties', excoriated in the Anti-rightist movement and the Cultural Revolution. Mass organisations such as the Women's Federation, the All China Federation of Trade Unions and the Communist Youth League, disbanded during the Cultural Revolution, were also revived, convened their own congresses and appeared, for a moment, to be something other than Leninist 'transmission belts'. At a local level, political institutions were restored in 29 (later 30) provincial-level units, nearly 200 secondary units (prefectures [formerly special districts] and later metropolitan regions) and some 2,000 *xian*-level units.

As a theoretical backdrop for events, Su Shaozhi, head of the Institute of Marxism Leninism of the newly formed Chinese Academy of Social Sciences, coined the term 'undeveloped socialism' to replace the idea of 'uninterrupted revolution', the emphasis on class struggle (in the Cultural Revolution notion of 'continuous revolution') and even the line of the Eighth Party Congress (which highlighted the contradiction between the 'advanced socialist system' and the 'backward productive forces') (Su and Feng 1979). According to Su's formulation, 'leftist' policies in the past had been inappropriate since the state of China's productive forces did not allow for them. This was later taken as a theoretical formulation with which to justify the decollectivisation of agriculture (discussed below) and, at the time, more orthodox commentators objected to that formulation because they felt that it denigrated the great 'socialist' achievements of the mid-1950s. But some reformers questioned those achievements and went on to criticise the inherited Stalinist and Leninist structures. When Deng Xiaoping argued for 'full democracy', Liao Gailong (1981: 11, p. 93), who worked closely with him, argued that the Leninist model of Party organisation, appropriate for early-twentieth-century Russia, was not suited to China and this led to a reassessment of Rosa Luxemburg's criticism of Lenin (Cheng 1983). It seemed in 1979, despite the limitations imposed by Deng Xiaoping, that democracy was in the air, particularly when Liao Gailong called for institutional forms to support democracy, such as a bicameral system for the National People's Congress, a Central Advisory Commission (to remove old leaders while still maintaining their expertise), freely elected trade unions (to prevent a recurrence of the Polish crisis), free peasant associations in the countryside and workers and staff congresses in factories with real executive power. He demanded also that Communist Party members should be subject to the law. Perhaps most significant was Liao's (1981, 12: p. 81) insistence, against Mao (who saw democracy only as a means to socialism), that democracy was also an end in itself.

The outpouring of critical comment, discussed in detail in Chapter 6, caused various Party leaders to express paranoia about the possibility of another Cultural Revolution. Concerned with intellectuals 'usurping power', they felt that too rapid democratic reforms could cause another bout of chaos and impair the legitimacy they were trying so hard to rebuild. As Deng Xiaoping's 'four cardinal principles' were loudly stressed, some of the bolder democratic proposals were shelved. A bicameral system never eventuated nor did free peasant associations (though remnants of the 1960s variety survived in places). Significantly, in 1981, the Military Propaganda Department moved against one of its cadres, the writer Bai Hua. The Bai Hua incident demonstrated that one could expect opposition to reforms to emanate from the Army which Deng was trying to reorganise and bring to heel. Significantly also, when Hua Guofeng stepped down as Party chairman in 1981 and was replaced by Hu Yaobang, Hua's post as chairman of the Party Military Affairs Commission was filled not by Hu but by Deng Xiaoping (Hamrin 1987). As became clear later, the Army did not like Hu's open style. At the same time, as noted above, a number of serious economic problems had arisen which gave strength to the cautious. The fall in state revenues, a trade deficit and other general imbalances were exacerbated by smuggling and foreign currency speculation (facilitated for a time by a dual official exchange rate), especially in Guangdong province which made good use of its links with Hong Kong.

The period 1981–2, therefore, was one of reassessment and consolidation, reflected in moves to streamline the central bureaucracy and reduce the number of ministries and commissions. It was also one of hesitation, seen in the official 'Resolution on Party History', influenced by Chen Yun and drafted by the ever-orthodox intellectual 'tsar', Hu Qiaomu, which reached a verdict on Mao Zedong (CCP 1981) and set the parameters for the burgeoning study of Mao Zedong thought (Knight 1992). Mao was declared to be a great Marxist-Leninist who had made serious mistakes in his later years. The spirit of the mid-1950s seemed vindicated and, despite the wholesale rehabilitation of remaining 'rightists' after 1978, the status of the Anti-rightist movement of 1957 (of which Deng Xiaoping had been an advocate) remained unclear.

De-collectivisation of Agriculture

Hesitation on the political front and caution in macro-economic matters, however, stood in sharp contrast to developments in the Chinese countryside which, in a manner reminiscent of the collectivisation drive of 1955–7, may not be fitted into the periodisation apparent in other areas. In the years after the Third Plenum there were further moves to improve the prices peasants received for their produce and a dramatic increase in the proportion of state purchases at above-quota and negotiated prices. Eventually statisticians were to observe that improvement in the terms of trade in the period 1978–88 was equivalent to the entire 26 years prior to 1978 (Ash 1991: pp. 516–8). Peasant incentive was also stimulated by extending private plots. During the 1970s, these had constituted some 5 per cent of cultivated land and regulations forbade households to derive more than 30 per cent of their income from them. By 1981 the limit on size was raised to 15 per cent in areas where the person–land ratio was favourable. Permission was also given for private herds of livestock (Walker 1984: pp. 789, 795).

These expanded plots soaked up some of the underemployed labour (said to be 20–30 per cent of the labour force, contradicting earlier views about a labour shortage) and provided goods for sale on the burgeoning free markets. In 1979 even grain was allowed to be traded on private markets after quotas were met. There came into existence, therefore, three price levels – official prices, above quota prices set by the state, and free-market prices. As one might expect, peasants often engaged initially in considerable subterfuge to sell as little as possible at official prices and as much as they could on the free market, but this became less prevalent with a fall in the free market price for grain. To exercise some leverage over market prices, to provide incentives to keep peasants producing low-priced grain and as a response to quota evasion, the government found itself buying a higher and higher proportion of grain at above-quota prices to the point where it became possible to buy grain from the state at low official prices and sell it back to the state at higher prices. This was curtailed by restricting grain sold at negotiated prices to husked grain which could not be re-sold to state granaries (Oi 1986: p. 275). Another problem, however, was more intractable. Increased above-quota purchases put an enormous burden on the central budget which, for political reasons, subsidised urban consumers.

The new policies adopted after the Third Plenum gave much greater stress to zoning and agricultural specialisation. The former policy demanded that areas became self-sufficient in grain before they diversified their crops. In the past, an excessive concentration on grain had resulted in insufficient raw materials being available for light industry, pasture land being ploughed up and serious soil erosion. This was particularly important since the crop area had been declining by 1.7–2.4 per cent annually and land was at a premium. Now there was a steady reduction in targets, in the wake of local non-compliance, and their replacement in part by incentive sales programmes whereby agricultural products might be exchanged for a supply of scarce industrial commodities. Soon planned sown areas ceased to exist. Such a policy of decentralisation would seem to contradict the adoption of a national land-use plan which was not particularly concerned with comparative advantage (Walker 1984: pp. 785–6).

The spirit of the Third Plenum also demanded that much more attention be given to making 'payment according to work'. This was increasingly spelt out as a call for greater attention to piecework. Of course, the old communal system of awarding work-points was ideally a system of piecework but its usual form allocated work-points on an almost uniform basis. Now production teams were enjoined to make all payments, above the basic ration, according to the amount of work performed. Since it was often too difficult to determine the work-points of each and every individual in every team, piecework groups were formed and these sometimes turned out to be individual households. Though the 'Sixty Points' of late 1978 explicitly outlawed this manifestation of one of the elements of *sanzi yibao*, it had already been initiated in the winter of 1977 in Anhui, the very province where it had been pioneered in the early 1960s. This time it was said to have been most efficacious in ameliorating the consequences of severe drought. It was soon spread to many other areas and the prohibition of household contracting disappeared in the version of the 'sixty points' approved in September 1979. Rapidly 'contracting output to households' in return for work-points (*baochan dao hu*) was adopted and then replaced by making contracts for specialised tasks or 'contracting everything to households' (*baogan dao hu*) and allowing the household to keep everything above the contracted amount. As contracting to households became widespread, production teams started to disintegrate. By May 1983 such contracting covered 93 per cent of what was left of the basic accounting units. The policy of separating units of production from units of administration, moreover, led to communes being redesignated once again as *xiang* and brigade leadership as village government.

De-collectivisation proceeded as rapidly as collectivisation in the mid-1950s.

The de-collectivisation of the early 1980s is sometimes presented as a spontaneous movement from below and sometimes as a measure imposed from above. The argument for spontaneity is supported by the fact that household contracting was widespread before it was officially sanctioned at a national level for poor areas and where it had been already proved satisfactory, by Document 75 of September 1980. It had been officially endorsed in Anhui nine months before Document 75. In other areas sub-contracting land and hiring labour was evident before receiving official sanction in Documents No. 1 of early 1983 and 1984. Mass pressure seems confirmed by the fact that, before sanctioning, household contracting was vigorously condemned and cadres spoke about the possible restoration of landlords (Watson 1984: p. 100). But was this spontaneity? One is immediately reminded of the Great Leap Forward. As in 1958, the initiative for forming new agricultural units came from a particular province (then Henan and now Anhui), backed by part of the central leadership, whilst official policy stipulated that no changes should take place. It was then imposed at breakneck speed over most of the country. Support for de-collectivisation, it seems, was very strong in poor areas whilst there was often resistance in richer communes around Shanghai which derived a large part of their income from collective industry. The poor, it seems, were most enthusiastic about both collectivisation and de-collectivisation and the rich resisted both (White 1993b: pp. 104–5).

The results of de-collectivisation have been claimed as outstanding. In the early 1980s there was a spectacular rise in the gross value of agricultural output (9 per cent per annum). Great diversity developed, productivity increased, the marketed portion of grain rose from some 20 per cent to 30 per cent (gross) and per capita net income doubled between 1978 and 1983. Per capita consumption was said to have risen 50 per cent in the same period (reaching a per capita daily calorie consumption of 2,400 which was 200 higher than in the cities) (Aubert 1988: p. 121). The improvement cannot be doubted; but it is not certain that de-collectivisation was the prime cause since the 9 per cent growth rate dates from 1978, long before de-collectivisation took effect. It pre-dates also the effects of the dramatic change in the price ratios. Even when those price changes took effect, they probably only accounted for one-fifth in the increase in per capita income. Perhaps the increased growth was due to an anticipation of future changes. Or was it good weather, the better use of fertilisers, the simple reporting of production which actually existed before 1978 and had been concealed as a 'hedge', or perhaps the more rational use of resources after abandoning the 'grain first' principle? The latter factors are, of course, unconnected with decollectivisation and raise questions as to whether de-collectivisation was necessary (Riskin 1987: pp. 290–9). In the case of grain production, moreover, it is possible to argue that 1978 represents simply a sharp improvement of a trend begun in 1974 (Hussain and Feuchtwang 1988: p. 43). Perhaps, though, a spurt in the agricultural growth rate was maintained longer than it otherwise would because of de-collectivisation.

But whatever the causes, peasants became undeniably better off. One survey shows that in 1978 one-third of all households had annual per capita incomes below 150 *yuan*; in 1984 the figure was only 5 per cent. In 1978, 2 per cent of rural households had incomes above 500 *yuan*. By 1984 the figure was 15 per cent. But the policy of 'letting some peasants get rich first' resulted in inequalities and invidious comparisons being made, particularly since cadres and soldiers were disproportionately among their number (Riskin 1987: p. 308; Vogel 1989: p. 333). Most large surveys show inequalities to be small. One attempt to work out a GINI coefficient of income inequality showed a small rise from 0.237 in 1978 to 0.264 in 1985, while others even show a slight decline for the early 1980s (Riskin 1987: pp. 234, 306–7). But GINI coefficients are crude indicators. There appeared some very rich families which derived their income from activities other than agriculture. These '10,000 *yuan* households' were held up as national models but were often resented, and reports appeared of attacks being made on richer households, with the government responding by calls to 'respect specialised households' (Croll 1988: pp. 90–1). At the other end of the spectrum, the poor in mountainous regions were not making much money and beggars were soon to reappear.

The Second Cycle

Considerations of agricultural de-collectivisation, which cannot be fitted into the cyclic model outlined earlier, have led us to proceed ahead of our cyclic account. Before the results of de-collectivisation became apparent, a new cycle began at the Party congress in September 1982. In a small move towards democracy, the 1,500 delegates to that congress turned out to be the product of election by secret ballot, with the number of candidates said to be greater than those elected. The congress saw the retirement (to the new Central Advisory Commission) of a number of senior Party people and the new Central Committee of 210 members and 138 alternates (which allowed in theory nominations other than those on the Party 'ticket') contained less than half the members elected to the Eleventh.

By 1982, it seemed, the Party had decided to adopt a more vigorous policy concerning retirement. Initial moves taken to persuade older officials to retire had not been very successful, particularly in the face of official fears about the social wage elements which went with their jobs. Attempts to promote retirement in 1978 had removed a number of veteran cadres to 'advisory' status and these were followed in 1982 by an explicit recognition of age rather than infirmity as the main ground for retirement. Such was deemed essential since older provincial officials often constituted powerful obstacles to reform. At that time, a stratified system of retirement was adopted which exempted a few dozen very old revolutionaries and provided different status and pensions for groups according to the time they began 'revolutionary' (or 'post-revolutionary') work. The pensions of 'post-revolutionary' cadres, who probably constituted the majority after 1983, as a proportion of salary, were much the same as workers. Those cadres consequently often resented those ranked above them who received full salary on retirement, honorific posts and, at the very top, exemption from retirement altogether (Manion 1992).

The Party Congress of 1982 not only symbolised a new attitude towards retirement. It also set in train a process which removed many of the Party's younger members. Stressing adherence to Party rules and discipline, Party organisation and Party style (like the Soviet *Partinost*), and paying much lip-service to the 'mass line', the Congress accelerated the purge of people admitted during the Cultural Revolution years. Ordering the re-registration of all Party members, the Party inaugurated a major process of closed rectification which from 1983 to 1987 was to result in the removal of as many leading personnel as in the Cultural Revolution itself. Over 650,000 Party members were to be disciplined, though increasingly these were simply corrupt elements rather than Cultural Revolution activists. The Congress also reaffirmed the enhanced role of the Party Secretariat which had been re-established in 1978 and elevated in status when the post of Party chairman was redesignated general secretary. Until 1987 the Secretariat was to exercise some of the former functions of the Politburo.

In 1982 there were reforms not only in the Party but also in the state structure. In that year a new National People's Congress enshrined a few of Liao Gailong's proposals in a new state Constitution, the most important of which was the principle of 'equality before the law', which was supposed to apply also to Party officials. That Constitution defined the state as 'a socialist state under people's democratic dictatorship' rather than the earlier stronger term 'a socialist state under the dictatorship of the proletariat' (NPC 1982). The National People's Congress restored the post of head of state ('president'). It reduced the number of vice premiers from 18 to 3 and confirmed the reduction of the 98 ministries and commissions (employing some 50,000 people) by one half (employing some 30,000). More generally the congress stressed more firmly the separating of policy leadership, as the preserve of the Party, from operational management by state authorities. Thus it created a Central Military Commission (under Deng Xiaoping) to demonstrate the separation of Party and military affairs, though the Party Military Affairs Commission remained in existence (also chaired by Deng). The congress also took the formal steps to abolish people's communes, as noted earlier, replacing them by *xiang* and *zhen* people's governments, though the process took at least two years to complete. Yet for all that, it seemed that democratic reform would have to wait upon what Hu Yaobang called the development of a 'socialist spiritual civilisation' (Saich 1989).

The new reformist climate of 1982 resulted in some economic problems, generated during the first cycle, being tackled with vigour during 1982–3. One of these was over-investment. At root was the fact that the initial re-centralisation measures had proved defective. Local authorities had received an increasing share of funds such as revised depreciation funds, new loans, retained profits, extra-budgetary funds and foreign capital. They had ploughed much of these into poorly planned investment with the result that projects were sometimes not completed. The centre, moreover, had insufficient resources to complete key projects particularly in the energy sector. There was, additionally, much duplication and waste. In response the State Council made heads of provinces, ministries and banks responsible for cutting back capital construction and assuring adequate supplies of resources for key projects. A 10 per cent levy was placed on all non-budgetary funds. Local governments were required to make a 30 per cent down-payment on all projects and locally raised funds for capital construction had to be lodged with the State Construction Bank. By 1983 the measures to cut back local capital construction were moderately successful.

The employment problem was also tackled with vigour. Once the state gave up sending high school graduates to the countryside in 1979, large numbers of urban unemployed were recorded (maybe as high as one-fifth of the workforce). This was apparently reduced to an official (understated) figure of 3.8 million by 1982 (State Statistical Bureau 1990: p. 123). That was a considerable success, though many of the jobs into which youth went were provided by small co-operatives with very low wages and no social welfare benefits. Interestingly, once the state openly gave up the promise that everyone would be found a job, the private hiring of labour 'helpers' was allowed. By 1984 there were to be 3.4 million workers in the urban private sector and 32 million in urban co-operatives. Such development could not be planned. Nevertheless, official comment maintained, the state plan was uppermost.

With the plan uppermost, problems of enterprise autonomy were more difficult to deal with. The question of profit retention was tackled initially by the formulation of profit contracts between ministries and their units. Difficulties in determining the base for those contracts led to lower-level deception, higher-level intervention and much acrimony. But it was not just a question of two parties. Local governments were also concerned to enhance their revenue at the expense of higher and lower levels. One solution, which ignored local governments, was to replace profit delivery by enterprise tax. By 1983, a scheme was put into operation whereby large enterprises paid a 55 per cent profits tax and small enterprises a progressive tax. The government then claimed a share of after-tax profits, ostensibly as a way of adjusting for the vagaries of the price system.

By 1983, it seemed, a degree of economic stability had been achieved and remaining problems could be tackled. One of these was the economic relations between centre and provinces. Since the commencement of reforms, a number of revenue-sharing schemes were in operation, each generating their own problems. Perhaps the most popular was that of Jiangsu which vested budgetary authority with the province but established a sharing rate for four years. It thus avoided haggling and animosity between centre and province. An attempt was made to generalise this over the whole country (Oksenberg and Tong 1991). Yet problems remained. Some people in Shanghai continued to complain that the bulk of its revenue went to the centre and, without that drain, Shanghai could develop in the manner of Singapore. Some provincial-level units resented perhaps the fortunate province of Guangdong, which (along with Fujian) enjoyed the greatest fiscal autonomy and the greatest leeway and was developing at a very fast rate. The government responded to those problems with some initial success even to the point of requiring loans from some provinces which it had no intention of repaying.

In combining reform with stabilisation, the second cycle of 1982–3 appeared a remarkable success. But, despite the promise offered by the constitutions of 1982, not much was achieved in democratic reform. Nevertheless there was considerable intellectual ferment and attempts to revitalise Marxist analysis (considered in Chapter 6). Using Marx in the service of democracy to criticise Marxist orthodoxy, however, was to cause those in charge of ideological matters in the Party to react and promote a campaign against 'spiritual pollution' in late 1983 which crudely lumped together critical Marxism and imported pornography and halted the cycle. The campaign was short-lived, probably because of fears of adverse foreign reaction which might impede the acceleration of a new economic modernisation drive then being considered.

The Third Cycle

As we have noted, by 1983 the centre had the basis for some sort of control over the provinces, but renewed economic reform during the third cycle which commenced in 1984 caused a loss of that control. In 1984 the government embarked upon a new boom in which it surrendered control (Riskin 1987: p. 366). That boom generated both excitement and the conditions for considerable social unrest. Perhaps a window of opportunity was ignored. As some see it, the relative stability achieved by 1983 offered the best chance to carry out the key reform – that of prices. After a major decision taken to accelerate reform in 1984, the government seemed to embark on every conceivable reform except that of prices. Price reform remained on the agenda, but so long as the planning system was required to authorise every change, the calculations were immense and beyond the capacity of the most powerful computer. Of course, one school of thought maintained, one could shift completely to a market régime and incur the huge political cost of removing subsidies. Most leaders in 1984 were much too cautious to entertain that view except in the very long term. In the meantime, there was some piecemeal price reform (with Guangdong in the lead and always resented).

The absence of thorough-going price reform, many would argue, caused other reforms to fail. For example, in its major economic reform programme of late 1984, the State Council decided that, in its relationship with state-owned enterprises, it would move gradually to a pure tax collection régime on an objective legally defined basis. But, pending thorough-going price reform, enterprises, experiencing temporary difficulties caused by the price structure, were permitted to negotiate tax reductions. One supposes that almost any enterprise could claim 'temporary difficulties' and the scope for deception and argument was increased. A major problem was also the tension caused by the division of ownership between central and local government, both dependent on enterprise remissions. Local resistance led to much acrimony and eventually (in 1987) to the modification of the tax system by the addition of 'profit contracting' – a variant of the former system (Blecher 1991: p. 47). Meanwhile equitable division of revenue was bedevilled by attempts to enliven the economy in the mid-1980s, creating major macro-economic problems which exacerbated the conflicts between centre, region and economic unit.

Problems of ownership were perhaps even more acute at lower levels. During the third cycle the government intensified its policy of developing industries in small towns, which was complicated by the definition of what actually constituted a town and whether the enterprise was owned by a designated town, a rural township not yet designated as a town (for reasons of tax minimisation) or by private persons. What, moreover, constituted private ownership? Once enterprises began to issue tradeable shares instead of bonds, ownership relations became most complicated, blurring the distinction between public and private. There were even problems attending individual household firms (*getihu*). These had been legitimated according to regulations of 1981 which allowed employment of up to seven people and were extended by formal state regulations in 1986. Many were small independent family concerns, though others were run by state employees who took leave from their unit and paid it to maintain seniority and benefits (Gold 1990b). Private enterprises (*siying qiye*), defined as employing more than eight workers, had also come into existence in the early 1980s, though were still barely legitimate. Indeed, it seems, so long as both of these forms of private activity involved blurring the line between state officials and private entrepreneurs, they would be denied a degree of legitimacy and would be suspected of being sites of corruption. Indeed, by the mid-1980s the government became particularly concerned with corruption and economic crime. Discipline inspection commissions, mobilised to deal with that crime, it is said, were often less than enthusiastic about reform policies which were seen as among its major causes. Significantly reformers were to establish a new working group in 1986 under Qiao Shi to tackle corruption and perhaps curb the power of the Central Commission for Inspecting Discipline under Chen Yun. In 1987 Qiao was to be made head of the Central Commission itself (Wang 1992: p. 89).

The third cycle of 1984–6 revealed the complexity not only of price reform and types of ownership but also of unbalanced regional development. The government embarked on what became known as a 'coastal strategy'. This involved a general relaxation of controls on foreign trade which was felt especially by coastal regions. The cycle saw once again a huge rise in imports by local governments, a decline in foreign exchange reserves and the imposition of new controls in 1985. The government also decided to allow direct investment in a number of coastal cities (undercutting the 'special economic zones'). It also promoted Hainan Island as an eventual alternative to Taiwan (and had to face the consequent corruption, especially in a scandal over importation of vehicles) (Vogel 1989: pp. 291–4).

In the third cycle, there were also major problems associated with creating a labour market. To free up the labour market the government took a decision that from 1986 new workers would be employed on contract. Such contract workers did not enjoy much of the social wage component reflected in the income of regular industrial workers. Some of them, recruited from rural areas, only had temporary residents' permits (one-third of the population of Guangzhou). This was a major source of resentment and had caused much friction in the early Cultural Revolution. Fearing disruption, therefore, management often concluded bogus contracts and tried to subvert the official provisions (White 1993b: pp. 140–1). One suspects that all moves taken to free up the labour market will cause resentment and disruption. It is difficult to see how a free labour market can operate in remaining 'third line' industries, which are remote, unattractive and often unprofitable (but which have established opportunistic links with elsewhere, notably the 'special economic zones') Some of these 'third line' industries have been moved to medium-sized cities and the residence status of their workers changed; but some can never be moved. One wonders also how bankruptcy provisions (experimented with since 1985) and more market-oriented policies can ever be extended to them.

Yet perhaps the major problem was inflation. In retrospect, the most significant reforms of the mid-1980s consisted in the powers given to newly reconstructed specialised banks to increase credit. Since capital construction was increasingly financed by bank loans rather than direct allocations, enterprises were able to renew excessive spending on capital construction and local governments were able to go on a borrowing spree. In Leninist vein, the People's Bank should have been able to exercise some central control over such developments. Local branches of all banks, however, could not be freed from local considerations. The result was inflation and a loss of economic control (You Ji 1991).

During the third cycle, the government clearly failed to deal with inflation. It failed also to solve the problem of heavy industry bias. Reformers, it seemed, were locked into the heritage of the past. By 1987, large and medium scale industries, which constituted only 2 per cent of all industrial enterprises, still absorbed one-third of the country's industrial labour force and two-thirds of fixed capital stock, contributed 50 per cent to the gross value of industrial output and accounted for 65 per cent of state revenues (Kueh 1989: pp. 431–41).

Nevertheless, observers noted, industrial problems in the early 1980s were clearly offset by rural successes. Yet by 1985 a different picture began to emerge. China was faced with a grain supply problem. The new policies made it more profitable to engage in activities other than grain production and, predictably, the area sown in grain declined (from 121 million hectares in 1978 to 114 in 1983). Concerned about future grain supplies, the authorities tried to halt the decline, but found their efforts unnecessary as grain production actually increased (from 305 million tonnes in 1978 to 407 million tonnes in 1984) despite the decline in area under cultivation. This was undoubtedly due in good measure to increases in productivity and was taken as such by the authorities. By 1984, the government considered that the major problem was excessive grain supply and more active measures should be taken to develop what it called the 'commodity' (rather than the 'subsistence') economy. The three-price grain system had become quite uneconomic. The unified procurement system required the state to purchase all grain supplied by peasants at a low price, which led to the government printing money to pay for it. In response the government abolished the distinction between quota and above-quota prices for grain. A 'proportional' price was set equal to 70 per cent of the old above-quota price plus 30 per cent of the old quota price, with variations in different areas to control production. As well as curbing speculation, the new system was designed to remove inequities caused by uneven quotas. Second, to limit procurement, the government removed mandatory grain quotas in favour of contracted grain supplies and usually insisted that agricultural tax be paid in cash instead of grain. This radical move was moderated by establishing a safety net, whereby if the market price dropped below the basic state procurement price, the state would buy the contracted amount at that price.

In the aftermath of the decision, there was a shortage of grain to feed the cities. One suspects that, as in 1958, too great a confidence in increased productivity had caused neglect of climatic good fortune which came to an end in 1985 and resulted in grain output for that year falling to 379 million tonnes. But only half of the decline in grain output in 1985 could be attributed to bad weather. The new proportional prices, which turned out to be lower than the old above-quota prices, sent negative signals to producers. Reduced supply caused free market prices to rise once again and peasants were reluctant to fulfil their contracts and sign new ones. The immediate government response has been seen as the effective reimposition of compulsory grain quotas in 1986. This was not particularly difficult, since the contract system, though formally 'voluntary', had been worked out or imposed by work-teams of cadres which operated with contract targets often more detailed than the former quotas. Contracting could be a means of imposing procurement quotas by other means and did not fundamentally change rural power relations. There were also a number of indirect controls which could be applied under the policy of supplying inputs in return for adhering to the required contracts or by manipulating local subsidies from industrial activities (Oi 1986: pp. 284–90; Sicular 1988; Oi 1989: pp. 155–82). The state retained control, though the hopes of reformers for effective market integration were dented.

There were other rural problems. One was poverty (Vogel 1989: pp. 270–4), which became salient by 1985. In that year the Minister of Civil Affairs estimated that 8 per cent of the rural population (70 million) were still in poverty (a possible underestimate) (Riskin 1987: p. 308; Hussain and Feuchtwang 1988: p. 60). Prominent here were such regions as Tibet, Yunnan, Guizhou, Xinjiang and Qinghai, with high percentages of minority nationalities (Hussain and Feuchtwang 1988: pp. 62–3). This will be discussed in Chapter 8. But the problems were not just regional. The social problems in Han areas will be discussed in Chapter 3.

Considerations of an overheated economy, inflation, loss of rural control, poverty and much else was to bring the third cycle to an end. Before describing its termination, however, as in the case of other cycles let us consider its political dimensions. The cycle started with the retirement of ten of the twenty-four Politburo members, the retirement of 18 per cent of the Central Committee, and gave rise to a new 'hundred flowers' campaign of breathtaking proportions which reached a high-point in 1986 (Schell 1988). It saw another reorganisation of the military structure, with the eleven military commands reduced to seven (containing twenty-three provincial military districts and nine garrison commands), and a reduction of the army's formal strength by one-quarter. During that period, economists began to challenge Marxist economics and political scientists again raised pleas for democracy. Indeed, in 1986, the issue of political reform as a necessary accompaniment to economic reform was given great stress.

But, with almost a cyclic inevitability, the new 'hundred flowers campaign' turned into something resembling a minor 'anti-rightist movement', similar to (though much less extensive than) the one in 1957, promoted often by the same people (such as Peng Zhen) and sometimes directed at the same targets. Party fears about disorder combined with inflation and economic chaos to produce a reaction. The Sixth Plenum of the Twelfth Central Committee in September 1986 set a new tone. It passed a resolution warning against 'bourgeois liberalisation' (BBC, *Summary of World Broadcasts/* FE/8377/C1/1–10, 30 September 1986) and Deng shelved the 'hundred flowers' movement and blamed Hu Yaobang for the overheated economy. Hu had made many enemies, not only because of his policies but also because of his drive against corrupt officials and their relatives and his establishment of a power base to ensure his succession to Deng. With the aid of members of the Central Advisory Commission (who played a role far greater than merely advisers), Hu was removed from office three months later, after student protests sought to stem the tide.

Yet, all the time, the backlash was once again softened by fears about business confidence. Though there was talk of returning power from managers to enterprise Party committees and restricting the growing stock market 'craze', the main thrust of economic restructuring continued, with even bolder experiments being undertaken to create a 'socialist capital market' and new ministerial organs coming into existence to promote reform. The younger generation of economists, moreover, did not have to make too many concessions to the old-guard reformers who had dominated the debates in the late 1970s and early 1980s. Leaders stressed that criticism of 'bourgeois liberalisation' should be confined to the Party, particularly those Party members who doubted the efficacy of Party leadership. And Party leaders insisted that, although the movement should be tackled with deliberation, caution should be exercised. An attempt was also made to separate political errors from professional matters. Hu Yaobang was given an honorary post on the Chinese People's Political Consultative Conference and occasionally officials even spoke about possibly inviting dissident intellectuals to re-enter the Party if they changed their ways. In such an atmosphere, discussion of political reform remained on the agenda.

The question of political reform was, of course, closely tied to that of administrative reform or reform of the public service. As we have noted, official policy was to separate Party and government functions, though clearly the Party still continued to play a major role in controlling *bianzhi* (the equivalent of the Soviet *Nomenklatura*), vetting appointments and dismissals, engaging in performance appraisal and maintaining cadre dossiers. Reforms in staffing included experiments with open recruitment of professionally qualified people, contract appointments, a stress on merit defined to a greater extent in technical terms rather than family origin (though with insistence on adherence to Deng's 'four cardinal principles'), lateral transfers of talented people and much else. In a situation where by 1984 only 19 per cent of cadres were university graduates and 40 per cent had only a junior secondary school education, regular training was considered very important. There was a sharp increase in the number of Party schools, cadre institutes and specialised courses in tertiary institutions, resulting, it is said, in cadres with tertiary training reaching 32 per cent in 1990. Great emphasis was also laid on administrative science. And in 1985 there was a review of the salary structure and a pay increase. As in specifically Party bodies, attempts were made also to improve discipline, especially after the restoration of the Ministry of Supervision in 1986 (Burns 1989c).

But, of course, reform of the public service was no substitute for more democratic political reform. In the mid-1980s, such wider political reform was promoted by Deng Xiaoping who apparently supported the establishment of a Central Deliberation Group for Political-Structural Reform, which led to a division among those who feared change, those who wanted greater democracy and those who felt that China should emulate the 'four little dragons' of East Asia and promote what was called 'neo-authoritarianism' as the only political form which would allow transition to a commodity economy.

The Fourth Cycle

Neo-authoritarianism in the service of a commodity economy, it appeared, appealed to Zhao Ziyang who at the Thirteenth Party Congress in 1987 took over the post of general secretary of the

Party. A belief in strong leadership did not contradict the need to accelerate public service reform. Thus plans were put forward for a new 16–grade professional public service (now 15) and gradually to abolish Party fractions in state organisations, lower-level discipline inspection groups and political departments (Burns 1989b). A professional public service, separate from other branches of society, was to be created.

But how far was such separation possible? At first sight, the desire to separate Party and state and state and economy led to official legitimacy being given to explicitly private enterprises. By 1992 officially licensed family firms employed some 25 million people and 140,000 explicitly private enterprises were said to employ 2.32 million (BBC, *Summary of World Broadcasts*/FE/ W0279/B/1, 28 April 1993), though in reality the latter figure was probably significantly higher since many such enterprises were licensed as 'collectives' (S. Young 1989; Solinger 1992: p. 127). The designation as 'collective' might simply reflect a desire to minimise tax or to assuage bureaucratic opposition. But it could indicate an association of officialdom and business reminiscent of the nineteenth century. Consider the fact that many of the new entrepreneurs were former state officials who took advantage of their connections and were derided as 'capitalists without capital'. Evoking even stronger memories of the past, those 'socialist compradors' often turned out to be the relatives of government officials who used political connections to manipulate the dual or multiple price system. They might control 'briefcase companies' (those without capital which depend on connections), set up as agents for the burgeoning arms trade and much else. Such people were seen as major sources of corruption in the 1980s and were to be directly condemned by the protesters of 1989. A major source of corruption inhered precisely in the new forms of association between officials and business.

Furthermore, at the highest level of state power, did the prescribed separation of Party and state have any real meaning? Despite Zhao's commitment to separating Party and administrative functions, once elevated to the role of general secretary in 1987, which should have resulted in his leaving the State Council and practical matters of economic management in the hands of the new Premier, Li Peng, he still intervened to promote his economic agenda. Spurred on by the State Commission for Economic

Restructuring and inaugurating a fourth cycle, Zhao pushed for further economic devolution and the development of the 'coastal strategy' which would plug the coastal economy even further into the international system. He went on to promote further relaxations of control on foreign trade which in 1987–8 contributed to an inflationary situation and contradicted austerity measures urged by the State Council. He also supported a system where cities such as Shanghai could retain a greater proportion of their revenue after state quotas were met, causing the ire of those who feared for loss of control and further inflation. He presided, moreover, over a frenzy of officially sanctioned 'free' foreign exchange dealing. Then, at precisely the wrong time, when the economy was seriously over heating in 1988, he secured agreement on rapid price reform. As inflation accelerated, his patron, Deng Xiaoping, turned against him, and in late 1988 the government swiftly applied the brakes, causing runs on the banks, local governments to have insufficient cash, local enterprises to collapse and unemployment to mount. The crisis of 1989 has to be seen in the context of a massive programme of retrenchment and deflation which Li Peng was well placed to oversee.

The Crisis of 1989

By 1988 much ideological legitimacy had been lost. The old values, as many saw them, were crumbling in the face of nepotism, graft and repression, and many of the new values (both of the liberal and neo-authoritarian kind) appeared frightening. As Chapter 4 will note, workers feared for their position once the freer market threatened their position and inflation bit. As for students, while some welcomed the proposed demise of the system of job assignment on graduation, others were alarmed at the prospect of finding their own job or not having one, It was perhaps the case that bad living conditions and sporadic repression could be endured if there was the promise of élite status at the end. Now the Party seemed to have abandoned them, many students also doubted the legitimacy of the régime and repression was taken much more seriously. This is not to say that growing democratic sentiment was not genuinely felt, merely that there were solid material reasons for dissatisfaction (Macartney 1990).

Increasingly students looked for heroes to get China out of its 'predicament' and intellectuals could be found to provide inspiration, particularly in their search for alternatives to 'feudalism'. As the seventieth anniversary of the iconoclastic May Fourth Movement of 1919 approached, efforts were made to debunk what had been portrayed as China's 'glorious heritage', its cultural uniqueness and indirectly the recourse to patriotism which accompanied the insistence on orthodoxy. Such was the theme of a television series *He Shang* (Yellow River Elegy) which appeared in 1988, indicating that the Party had not broken with the past and the way forward demanded an alliance of intellectuals, managers and small entrepreneurs. By early 1989, various intellectuals were circulating open letters demanding reform, and think-tanks, associated with Zhao Ziyang, appeared to be fermenting dissent (Kelly 1990). This is not surprising when one considers that Zhao's economic strategy, which had caused severe inflation, had been overturned by the Party in late 1988 and Zhao's supporters feared he might suffer the same fate as Hu Yaobang.

At that critical moment (April 1989) Hu Yaobang chose to return to centre stage, and during or after an explosive meeting with his colleagues he died. His funeral sparked off renewed student demonstrations which were to culminate in the massacre of June Fourth. The events of the summer of 1989 will not be narrated here. Suffice it to note that the over-reaction by the authorities was in large part a result of what they perceived to be back-stage manipulation of the student movement by Zhao Ziyang, his associates and intellectuals. But most revenge was taken out on workers who had dared to defy a 'workers' state'.

For a time the ensuing repression was severe. We do not know how many hundreds or thousands died or were imprisoned nor can we assess the degree to which régime legitimacy plummeted. We do know, however, that various organisations were set up overseas to go beyond the ideals of 1989 (Leung 1993). Those bodies will certainly not be listened to by those in power in Beijing, despite general secretary Jiang Zemin's (1992: p. 22) somewhat hollow announcement that those who return from abroad will be respected despite their past political positions. But one can be sure that if the present government is as insistent on economic reform as the recent Fourteenth Party Congress (1992) declares it to be, similar voices will soon be heard more loudly in China itself.

The crisis of 1989, while resulting in repression, did see some measures taken to deal with the complaints of protesters. For example, further measures were taken to deal with the corruption of 'capitalists without capital'. Moves were made to recoup unpaid taxes to assuage popular outrage. In general, though, the more powerfully connected seem impossible to deal with (Chan 1991: pp. 115–17). We have yet to see whether the frenzied anti-corruption measures of August 1993 will make much difference.

The Fifth Cycle

In 1991 there was the promulgation of a new (eighth) five-year (1991–5) plan and a ten-year development plan. Concerned with stability and avoidance of the inflationary problems of the late 1980s, the plans set a target growth rate (6 per cent) lower than that achieved in the 1980s. Whilst the plans indicated that reform was still to be gradual and piecemeal, a new atmosphere was quite evident in early 1992 when Deng Xiaoping undertook a tour of South China and gave renewed legitimacy to the rapid development of market relations and special economic zones in the region. There followed the (often illegal) establishment of many quasi economic development zones which were often no more than instances of real estate speculation (since foreigners, Overseas and Hong Kong Chinese were now allowed to buy land). Local leaders also began deliberately to disregard planned growth rates and rapidly to remove price controls. The spirit of accelerated reform was confirmed by the Fourteenth Party Congress which met later in the year. A fifth cycle was clearly under way which in 1992–3 ushered in a new boom with a growth rate approaching 12 per cent and renewed inflation.

The Fourteenth Congress (with 2,000 delegates) elected a Central Committee (of 189 plus 130 alternates) and produced a Politburo (of 22) including a Standing Committee of seven. That Standing Committee dispensed with some of the old guard and attempted to present a new image. At last, it seems that the problem of retirement has almost been solved. By the end of the 1980s the 'voluntary' nature of retirement had in effect become mandatory for almost all but those at the very top (Manion 1992). At that level, it appears, the price of standing down was often the promotion of a client to one's official post. But recent events have shown that at the very top it is not necessary to hold any formal position in order to wield considerable power. An obvious case in point is Deng Xiaoping who in 1989 gave up his last official post – Chair of the Military Commission – but was still able to launch a new cycle in 1992.

Yet there is new blood in the top leadership. Some members of the new Politburo have good reformist credentials – for instance, Zhu Rongji, a reformer who made his name in Shanghai and who in 1993 became first vice premier and, as governor of the People's Bank, was in charge of reigning in the economy, and Li Ruihuan who may have softened some of the ideological backlash of recent years. One is less confident about some of the others. But to return to the above problem: is the old system, based on informal and semi-formal hierarchy, weakening and does the announced demise of the Central Advisory Commission (1992) signal a move away from gerontocratic manipulation?

Clearly the distribution of political power at the highest levels in the Chinese political system is still, in Max Weber's words, more traditional (based on informal hierarchy) than 'legal rational'. In practice, personal position in a hierarchy of clientelism is more important than institutional position. The crisis of 1989 reveals very clearly how personal connections in the military and elsewhere can be mobilised to effect a show-down (Burns 1989a: pp. 483–6). Yet the paradox is that a traditional patriarchal political leadership has attempted to promote a legal rational system. We shall remark on the problems this gives rise to in Chapter 5 which deals with law. Suffice it to note here that the image of a gerontocratic leadership, symbolised in 1988 by the replacement as president by 79-year-old Li Xiannian by 81-year-old Yang Shangkun, responsible for more and more stringent and 'rational' retirement provisions, did not generate confidence. But things change fast. Jiang Zemin has replaced Yang Shangkun and Yang's relatives have been removed from senior positions of power.

Gerontocratic manipulation, one might surmise, will become more difficult as Party members become more educated. By the time of the 1987 congress, whilst the majority of Party members had only a primary school education, the intellectual component of the 46 million Party members was stronger than ever before. That trend was confirmed at the time of the Fourteenth Congress of 1992 by which time Party membership stood at 51 million. Yet, since entry into the Party was increasingly an opportunist choice rather than a choice based on ideological commitment, reform endeavours have still foundered in the face of 'networks of relationships', characteristic of a patriarchal society, and those have engendered considerable corruption.

Of all state institutions perhaps the army is the most patriarchal. All armies depend on reputation and male 'networks of connections'. Loyalty networks in the Chinese military are probably not much different from those in any other army and one would expect loyalty to the ideals of Mao, forged in war, to be particularly strong there. But there is an added complication. Of the four modernisations, that of defence has received the lowest priority and there has developed a technocratic as well as a traditional hostility to reformers. Deng Xiaoping has tried his best to create a loyal military command structure but the events of 1989 and the consequent courts-martial and removals (especially in 1992) indicate a problem which has not been fully resolved. The fact that the military budget has been increased repeatedly after the events of June 1989 could indicate a concern with possible disloyalty. Nevertheless, bearing in mind the record of an increasingly professional and disciplined army (even after the courts martial and reorganisation after 1989) (Jencks 1991), any prediction of a new warlord era seems far-fetched in the extreme.

Fears about the military, factional struggle in the Party and general ideological scepticism have led several scholars to speculate that China might enjoy a fate similar to the Soviet Union. Such scholars must face up to the fact that, whereas the Soviet economy suffered years of stagnation, China has one of the fastest growing economies in the world (an average of 9 per cent per annum in the 1980s with a planned rate of 6 per cent in the 1990s). China could achieve the 1981 target of quadrupling gross national product by the year 2000. In some forty years it has become officially the sixth largest in industrial output, the seventh largest in gross national product and the eleventh largest in volume of trade. From 1952 to 1990, the contribution of industry to net material product is said to have increased from some 20 per cent to some 48 per cent and agriculture to have declined from about 58 per cent to 32 per cent (State Statistical Bureau 1990: p. 26), a rate of transformation rarely equalled. In certain sectors imported technology has been successfully absorbed and copied, though by the year 2000 the general level of technological development is only planned to reach that of developed countries in the late 1970s and 1980s.

Yet, for all that, China is said to have a gross national product per capita of US $370 (1990) which puts it among the poorest twenty-five countries in the world. The paradox is glaring and for some scholars simply not credible. In terms of life expectancy, the provision of physicians, food consumption patterns and the like, China looks more like a middle-income country than a poor one. Ma Guonan and Ross Garnaut (1992) feel that the export share of output (15 per cent in 1990) is too high to be credible for a poor country, and actual per capita gross domestic product is probably three times higher than official figures, making China the fourth largest economy in the world (coming just after Germany). Considering that the World Bank revised its estimate of China's per capita gross domestic product downwards from US $410 in the late 1970s and since then the economy has been growing at 8 per cent, Ma and Garnaut suspect that a distortion of official figures has taken place in order for China to qualify for special credits available only to poor countries. But underestimation of China's gross domestic product probably has a much simpler explanation. The International Monetary Fund has recently decided that the problem lies in basing calculation on international exchange rates. If calculation is based on purchasing power at home compared with other countries' purchasing power at home ('purchasing power parity'), the Chinese economy is probably four times the size of official and World Bank calculations, making China the world's third largest economy. Extrapolating recent growth rates, China will have the largest economy in the world by 2010.

We will not go into the technical arguments here. Suffice it to say that even if Ma and Garnaut and the International Monetary Fund are wrong, even if growth turns out to be more extensive than intensive and even if problems of population pressure (discussed in Chapter 7) increase, the Chinese economy is not as crisis-ridden as that of the former Soviet Union. Dynamism, however cyclic in nature, suggests a different future. There are, however, obvious problems. It may be the case that external debt, which increased ten fold from 1980 to 1991 to US $52 billion, will reach serious proportions though at the moment there is no debt servicing problem. A more immediate concern is that, in the first half of

1991, some 37 per cent of state enterprises operated at a loss (Cheng and Wang 1993: p. 4.9) and the number of enterprises in debt was increasing. Inefficiencies are still very marked and the improvement in total factor productivity of state enterprises, noted in the early 1980s, has slowed down (Yeh 1992: p. 530).

It is clear also that the euphoria attending agricultural de-collectivisation has evaporated. The government has seemed to oscillate between *de facto* direct procurement and indirect control according to 'a two-tier operational structure'. Meanwhile, with better (though still inadequate) prices and intermittent controls, grain production has risen. But many economists feel that purchase prices could not rise much more unless more of them are passed on to consumers. Accordingly there have been government moves towards a freer market régime (Watson 1993) and these may result in tension. Consider also the limits on grain production. Grain output in 1992 was some 440 million tonnes and the current target for the year 2000 is 500 million tonnes. By that time, however, the population will probably reach 1.3 billion, meaning that per capita grain consumption (the major element in diet) will remain roughly at current levels.

Clearly the initial spurt in agricultural production has come to an end. Some economists speak now of agricultural stagnation and official comments in 1988 spoke of the agricultural situation as 'grim' (White 1993b: pp. 107–17). Some observers even talk of peasants changing from the major beneficiaries of reforms to the 'victims', though their conclusions are somewhat exaggerated (Wu-Beyens 1990). We recall the problems of the mid-1950s. If the aim is to be development rather than simply (extensive) growth, a new rural strategy which may promote productive investment is required. Meanwhile some 70 per cent of peasant investment goes into housing (Yeh 1992: p. 535). Vigorous strategies are also required to absorb the large number of persons displaced from agriculture if extensive unemployment is not to occur with disruptive consequences.

Problems have also been generated by foreign investment. Direct foreign investment has taken the form of joint ventures or the establishment of wholly foreign-owned enterprises. Both of these have given rise to arguments about the hiring and control of labour and, in a situation where the 'social' component of wages of state workers is several times their money wage, its remuneration. Major problems have occurred also in the relationships, both legal and practical, between the state and the foreign sector and between national planning and co-ordinating bodies such as the China International Trust and Investment Corporation (CITIC) and local government units in charge of investment decisions. The role of the Ministry of Foreign Economic Relations and Trade (MOFERT), established in 1982 (and renamed in 1993), in regulating specialist corporations has fluctuated widely. Predictably there have also been problems concerning multiple administered prices.

We must look also at the performance of the 'special economic zones'. That of Shenzhen, at least, has been more spectacular than observers of other similar zones might have predicted in the early 1980s and overall foreign investment has been significant, if not as great as China's leaders initially hoped. Nevertheless, a major problem remains. The zones were originally designed to be export-oriented, but a significant proportion of their production is directed to the domestic market. When we consider investment we must evaluate also the later establishment of cities 'open' to direct foreign investment. The 'open city' experiment, though subject to fits and starts, has attracted substantial amounts of overseas Chinese investment. Will that experiment lead to unbalanced growth?

Investment policies have contributed to problems of local bureaucratism. Decentralisation of authority has led to swollen local bureaucracies and ineffectiveness in personnel planning. Recognising the immense financial burden imposed by those bureaucracies, in 1992 the government designated a number of experimental sites for the reform of local administration and in 1993 proposed to extend the experience. Under the rubric of 'small organisation but big service', measures were put forward to surrender official control over some local enterprises and to transfer some government functions to non-government organisations (Cheng and Ting 1993).

Reform of the central bureaucracy also remains a problem. Despite the reforms of 1982 and 1987–88, the central government is not simpler and leaner. Marketisation and a degree of privatisation was to reduce the micro-economic functions of the state; yet there has been increased pressure to enhance the role of the state as macro-economic manager. By 1993 the central ministries, commissions, offices and bureaux with overlapping functions grew again to some 60 employing much the same number of people as in the period prior to the reforms of 1982. From 1978 to 1991, personnel employed in the state administration increased 127 per cent from 15 million to 34 million (Cheng and Ting 1993: p. 4.11). The reasons for this are first that victims of the Cultural Revolution have been rehabilitated and that many of those who replaced them remain in employment. Second, the fact remains that agencies with large pay-rolls are the most prestigious. Following the expansion of tertiary education, moreover, there has also been pressure to find jobs for graduates in the bureaucracy. The myriad tasks of administrative reorganisation and judicial reform have also required more and more personnel, and therefore increased expenditure (18 per cent per year compared with 7 per cent in 1978) (Blecher 1991; pp. 35–40). All that has occurred when there has been a squeeze on state income. One understands why Li Peng announced to the Eighth National People's Congress in 1993 that he intends to reduce the central bureaucracy by one-quarter, though memories of 1982 and 1987–88 cause scepticism.

The problem of a growing central bureaucracy, however, pales into insignificance beside the general problem of regionalism. We must note that growth rates in the Pearl River Delta are twice the official 9 (later 12) per cent. Special economic zones (especially Shenzhen) belong to a different order of economic development. Some regions (such as Guangdong which produced some 21 per cent of China's exports in 1991) are said to be 'one step ahead'. They eliminated rationing much earlier than other areas. They have carried out radical price reform, have most enterprises operating outside the plan, have implemented 'user-pays' principles and are seen by some as sites of depravity (Vogel 1989), whilst others (the North West and the South West) are several steps behind. Though policies of centralisation and decentralisation alternated throughout the 1980s, seeing partial reversals in 1981, 1983, 1985 and 1988–91, the tendency towards administrative decentralisation, begun in the late 1950s and greatly accelerated in 1970, has continued through the reform period. Some coastal areas, able to participate in international trade, favoured with regard to taxation in the early 1980s and by other aspects of positive discrimination under Zhao Ziyang, have snubbed the centre and some other areas. They have sometimes engaged in trade blockades and, in the quest for foreign exchange earnings, have exported raw materials in short supply elsewhere, requiring other areas to import the same materials at higher prices (Yeh 1992: p. 529). Measures taken to counter such activities, such as re-registering local trading companies in 1988–91 have not been particularly drastic (Lardy 1992: p. 702). Perhaps most significant here, in the context of economic reform, is that the state, whilst surrendering its monopoly over economic life has also surrendered its monopoly over the 'circulation of protection'. As we shall note in Chapter 4, successful resistance to the separation of Party and state bodies in local areas shows that the central government has not been able to protect its own economic units from local networks of dependence dominated by local Party machines which are reluctant either to bow to central dictates or to surrender independent power to enterprise managers (Chevrier 1990: p. 123). The fact that local cities could adopt measures different from Beijing in the aftermath of the 1989 June Fourth incident shows that local government has achieved a degree of autonomy unprecedented in previous years.

But a stress on 'local government' may be misleading. There is increasing evidence that in economic matters, administrative boundaries are becoming less important. This has partly been acknowledged in the creation of 'metropolitan regions' to replace 'special districts'. Yet there are wider implications. We have seen the development of growth nodes around major cities which extend beyond provincial boundaries. For example, the shares of the gross value of industrial production of Beijing and Tianjin have declined but that of nearby Hebei has grown. Similarly, while Shanghai's share fell during the 1980s, there have been considerable industrial developments in nearby areas of Jiangsu and Zhejiang (Kueh 1989: p. 428). Because of the availability of skilled labour in that region, some feel this could become a growth area rivalling Guangdong (Murdoch University 1992: p. 114). Such a development was foreshadowed in Jiang Zemin's (1992) report to the Fourteenth Party Congress and manifested in the recent attention given to developing Pudong in Shanghai.

Regionalism is developing rapidly. Not only have local bureaucracies grown excessively, as we have noted, but their interests often run counter to the state. Can we make any intelligent prediction on that issue beyond noting that local government reform will be very difficult? Economic forecasts can be made but politically we can say little. Perhaps all that may be said is that rather than political fragmentation, we see the future as further national economic devolution, with different strategies for different regions (suggested by the division of China once again into ten economic regions in 1991) and the orientation of some Southern and Eastern regions to nearby engines of growth (particularly Hong Kong and Taiwan). Indeed, events in 1992 point to a revival of Zhao Ziyang's 'coastal strategy', though we hope that he (if rehabilitated) or whoever conducts it has a better sense of timing. As things stand, the central government can accommodate, for the time being, 'one China' and several systems, providing that the dominant political formula is adhered to. The death of the present, very small, stratum of senior leaders might prove the crucial test of that formula.

Part 2

Themes

3

State and Countryside

The Introduction to this book put forward several questions concerning agriculture. Two of those were explicitly economic. What is the best method of extracting a rural surplus for industrial development and is collective agriculture necessarily wasteful? We saw in Chapter 1 that the approach to the first question adopted by the Chinese government in the three decades after 1949 was to manipulate urban–rural trade by buying agricultural goods cheaply and selling industrial goods to the peasants at a high price. Politics during those years centred on the degree of permissible extraction and the method to achieve it (through price planning or through extraction at the point of production by new forms of rural organisation). This chapter hopes to deepen that analysis by looking at the social consequences of various policy shifts. Chapter 2 noted also that the successes of collectivised agriculture, recorded in the 1970s, proved to be illusory once the cost of inputs in relation to outputs was examined more fully. That observation, however, should not necessarily be taken as an indictment of all collective agriculture.

We saw earlier that the Chinese government shifted tack during the 1980s, embarked upon greater degrees of price planning and, of course, undertook a high degree of de-collectivisation. Again enthusiasm for initial success (this time real rather than apparent) gave way to pessimism. In the 1990s, the problems of procuring grain and other crops and the negative consequences of individual farming mean that the same questions remain salient. We shall not attempt to give any definitive answers to those questions but we shall analyse measures taken to deal with them and the social consequences of such measures.

The Introduction also posed an important socio-political question. Do we need to go beyond conventional analyses of the relationship between the Chinese state and countryside? These often depict coercive policies which, when found unproductive, give way to manipulating interest groups in a growing market environment. But is Jean Oi (1989) correct in seeing the Chinese state as not particularly Stalinist nor pluralist? According to Oi's analysis, a better model is clientelism. Rural politics are those of patron–client relations. The state has sought to extract a surplus at low cost without sacrificing legitimacy. For their part, at various times, village elder, team leader and village cadre have all been concerned with distributing resources and opportunities in return for compliance and have pushed peasants into a dependent relationship. Rarely have any of those leaders been part of formal government. Instead they are gatekeepers, engaged both in extracting the surplus and buying favour. Sometimes they have been complicit in harsh central policies and sometimes have concealed the size of the surplus from the state. They have incurred the wrath of central government, have been visited by work teams and have been punished for survival strategies which are seen as 'corrupt'. But also they have formed the core without which any social transformation would have been impossible. Both praised and vilified, they have provided the best models of devotion either to social transformation or personal enrichment or have appeared the epitome of cunning and sloth. The focus of this chapter is agrarian policy. It is inevitably also about the point at which state and peasant meet.

The Early Twentieth Century

As in all the thematic chapters of this book we shall proceed chronologically. We noted in Chapter 1 that, contrary to the myth of isolated villages, in early-twentieth-century China, where some 30 per cent of agricultural produce was marketed, the horizon of peasants' existence was bounded by markets larger than individual villages. The basic unit was what G. W. Skinner (1964–5) has referred to as a 'standard marketing area', consisting of a group of villages oriented to a market; beyond that there were larger marketing areas around market towns. The lowest level of government, the *xiang*, was largely informal and consisted of local dignitaries at the head of networks of dependent relationships. Within the villages might be found lineage organisations (more common in South China) and secret societies. The former, usually dominated by those members who had larger holdings of land, provided a site for group worship, a primitive system of social welfare and a forum for the settlement of disputes. The latter, based on simulated kinship, might duplicate the functions of lineages and serve as mechanisms for resisting forces felt to be alien. Both offered some sense of security for families dislocated by the economic crisis considered in Chapter 1. Responding to that crisis, as Friedman (1974: p. 118) points out in his study of revolutionary movements after 1911, peasants took up arms to restore traditional values which had been massively undermined. A revolutionary party may perhaps not have in mind the restoration of old verities but it may respond to that yearning by offering restitution and a fair deal. Both nationalists (until 1927) and communists held out that promise in their programmes of land reform. In the Jiangxi Soviet such reform was quite radical, distributing the land of rich peasants as well as that of landlords. Hostility generated at that time was borne in mind by the Communist Party based in Yan'an in the late 1930s and early 1940s. That and considerations of the united front strategy caused the Party to turn officially to the simple measure of rent reduction. The rent ceiling was set at the old *Guomindang* figure of 37.5 per cent of crop, and work teams would descend on the villages to ensure that that figure was adhered to. Habituated to clientel relationships, peasants initially regarded those teams as alien. They were supplemented, therefore, by peasant associations (*nonghui*) and traditional forms of labour organisation were incorporated into their structure.

To prevent associations being taken over by traditional organisations and to counter the influence of those landlords and members of the old rural élite whose power had increased following the cessation of land reform, a programme of rustication of urban residents was introduced. That policy facilitated the extension of administration into many natural villages (*cun*). Some rusticated personnel, however, detested rural life and had to confront hostility from the former rural élite and local cadres who felt that the movement was aimed at usurping their position. Officially cadres, whether new or old, were required to carry out policies according to the 'mass line', to be responsive both to central directives and the leadership of local Party committees (dual rule) and to tread the narrow line between 'tailism' and 'commandism', the major deviations identified in Party rectification movements. They were to play a major role also in fostering rural 'people-run' (*minban*) schools, necessary in a region where the literacy rate was some 3 per cent. Those schools were required to be both educational and productive and indeed military units and civil offices were obliged to engage in production and achieve a degree of self-sufficiency. At least that was the ideal, which varied in implementation from place to place depending on the quality of local cadres and their degree of flexibility.

The above 'Yan'an way' demanded the 'unity of work and arms'. The co-operatives were frequently identical with units of the people's militia and soldiers not in combat might return to farm work or at least help train the local militia units which were also engaged in political work. With the onset of civil war after 1946, that became impossible. Increasingly the Party had to rely on village activists (*jijifenzi*) to instigate rural reforms and those were not always reliable.

Land Reform

As noted earlier, the onset of civil war inaugurated a new approach to land reform (Hinton 1966). Rapidly the Party moved from purchasing land for redistribution to a much more radical Land Reform Law in 1947. Cadres were now required actively to mobilise peasants but were often found to be 'slothful and bureaucratic'. Such attitudes were wrongly diagnosed as the products of an 'impure background'. Thus, in the process of rectification, many poor peasant cadres remained lazy while active cadres suffered from 'commandist' persecution. During land reform, moreover, work-teams were enjoined to form peasant associations and poor peasant bands (*pinnongtuan*) to carry out the struggle. In practice, the teams all too often descended upon the village and imposed policies from above without much heed to mass line techniques.

Such action was a response to frustration. Institutions such as lineages or secret societies usually contained both landlords and poor peasants and, as in the past, clientel loyalties often frustrated any attempt by an outside organisation to penetrate the villages. Peasants, moreover, fearing *Guomindang* reprisals, were often reluctant to get involved. Thus the Party sought to create an emotional climate through 'struggle meetings' where landlords were denounced, land deeds were destroyed and where peasants announced once and for all their repudiation of clientel loyalties. In such a situation passivity could often change into recklessness, leaving cadres and activists perplexed and open to the charge of 'tailism' (following the masses without regard to the Land Reform Law). The Party responded with more rectification but again policy was unclear. Leaders were still not sure whether the targets were to be cautious cadres or those from 'impure backgrounds' or whether priority should be given to combating 'ultra-leftist' indiscipline resulting from inviting ordinary peasants to criticise cadres ('open rectification'). Eventually the Party was forced to switch to enforcing discipline from above. Such, as we have seen, was intensified after March 1949 when the Party turned its attention to urban areas and passed a new more moderate Land Reform Law. In mid-1950, land reform was temporarily suspended in the interest of maintaining production, an attempt was made to regularise trials, the land of 'rich peasants' was declared protected and 'enlightened gentry' were invited to participate in a new united front (Liu Shaoqi, *Collected Works*, 2: pp. 215–33). To implement what became known as the 'rich peasant line', a new and complex method of 'class analysis' was adopted. The category of 'small rentiers' was introduced, being defined as those who had been compelled to rent out their land but who had supported the revolution, and the new term 'prosperous middle peasant' became current. It was frequently the case that several of these different categories might be found in the same family and implementing the new scheme of categorisation became confused (Selden 1979: pp. 218–25; Shue 1980: pp. 47–56).

A cautious agrarian policy, therefore, pertained as land reform was extended to the 'later liberated areas' of south China in the autumn of 1950. In those regions, the class structure was much more complex than in the North, with some landlords doubling as businessmen. Many of them had transferred ownership to their relatives and were disguising tenancy arrangements. Lineage organisations were much stronger and there was a much larger number of local cadres who were related to landowners. The leadership of the Central-South Region in Wuhan did not appear to appreciate that complexity and northern cadres were often resisted the further south they went. While famine relief was surely welcomed, other policies such as purging the militia of 'opportunist elements' were not. Nor perhaps were the *ad hoc* taxation measures carried out by military cadres who simply appropriated what they could from the rich. Very quickly, therefore, a regular system of progressive household taxation had to be established, which, pending renewed land reform, discriminated against income derived from renting out land. The use of village quotas, moreover, persuaded peasants to reveal unreported ('black') land. There was also some rent and interest reduction, though such measures were not always successful since some people believed the reforms would be short-lived.

In 1950 it seemed that land reform in the South would be very gradual, proceeding from a few 'key-point areas' (usually controlled by the Communist Party before 1949) to the whole region. Yet there were pressures to speed up the whole process. One source, as we have seen, was China's involvement in the Korean War in late 1950. Another was simply cadre frustration at the defensive tactics of landlords and cadres not being able to proceed quickly enough to demonstrate to very cautious peasants what they felt to be the material benefits of reform. Before long, the authorities took radical action, despite what were felt to be immature conditions. They denounced local cadres, locked into clientel relationships, who tended towards conservatism and 'localism', and hardened their attitude to landlords who claimed to be 'national capitalists'. The movement was conducted with much speed and many deviations. There was some landlord 'sabotage' (usually destruction of their own property to maintain a sense of 'dignity') accompanied often by violent mass reaction. By the end of the movement in 1952–3, landlords, estimated nationally at some 4 to 5 per cent of the rural population, had lost their former land with some 400–800 thousand killed (one in six landlord families), and 44 per cent of cultivated land had been distributed (Vogel 1969: pp. 53, 95–124; Stavis 1978: pp. 23–32).

Consolidating the Countryside

With the exception of the small state farm sector (mainly in newly opened up areas), land reform divided the country into small plots of land individually owned and individually farmed, with poor peasant households holding on average some 0.8 hectares, middle peasants 1.3 hectares and rich peasants 1.7. Some of those plots were often not large enough to supply an adequate calorie intake much less provide a surplus for investment, although some household investment did take place (Riskin 1987: pp. 51, 60, 67). In such a situation, the Party was quite clear that its ultimate policy was to promote co-operativisation. It was left, however, without local village governments with which to do it. With the end of land reform, a shortage of cadres caused the Party to retreat from the village, making the *xiang* the basic level of administration. The boundaries of *xiang*, which at that time contained some two to three thousand people, were redrawn and peasant associations were formed into *xiang* people's congresses and *xiang* people's governments which operated largely through permanent and *ad hoc* committees (Schurmann 1966: pp. 438–42). In the villages which were left much to their own devices, power still rested with a stratum of 'rich' peasants. As noted above, such peasants were not particularly rich, owning only two to three times the amount of land of poor peasants and some two draught animals and one plough compared with the poor peasant's one animal for every two families and one plough for every three. They could, however, make loans to poor peasants with high rates of interest (5 to 10 per cent per month) due to high risk and might buy out peasants who hit upon hard times (Riskin 1987: p. 67).

The government responded with taxation policies designed not merely to appropriate the rural surplus but to inhibit the private concentration of land. It also promoted mutual aid teams, organised according to traditional forms of labour exchange but including new features such as elected heads and a work-point system for evaluating contributions of labour. Those teams were given preference in bank loans. At the same time attempts were made to establish credit mutual aid teams and credit co-operatives to short-circuit money lenders. Reflecting the impending demise of the 'rich peasant line', rich peasants were generally forbidden to join the mutual aid teams and when they formed their own organisations were not allowed to call them 'mutual aid teams' (Bernstein 1968; Shue 1980: pp. 99–191). The initial mutual aid teams, however, were not always successful and many dissolved after disputes about work-points. Credit co-operatives only extended to *xiang* level, were often badly managed and frequently collapsed. Even less success attended the initial larger elementary co-operatives.

As we saw in Chapter 1, a more immediate problem concerned grain supplies. Following land reform the government induced peasants to cultivate economic crops to support light industry and the amount of land given over to producing grain declined. At the same time the new state-led supply and marketing co-operatives were only able to control a portion of the grain supply; low-quality grain passed into state granaries and granary maintenance was revealed as inefficient and corrupt. Consequently the urban grain supply barely kept up with the growth of population and rationing was introduced in the cities. To rectify the situation and also to act in the spirit of the 'General Line for the Transition to Socialism' (1953), the government imposed a unified purchase system for grain in November of that year – the first step in the extractive system which was to last for three decades. At the same time the government accelerated the formation of mutual aid teams as the units which would conclude purchase contracts with the state-organised supply and marketing co-operatives. As in land reform, the movement proceeded from 'key-point' areas to the country at large but this time much more use was made of model experiences.

We have seen that in her detailed treatment of the period, Vivienne Shue (1980: pp. 176–91, 213–27) is at pains to demonstrate remarkable mass compliance with the movement to implement the unified purchase and marketing system because of its appeal to peasant incentive in the provision of loans and advanced payments and in pricing policy, with state prices at that point not much different from free market prices. Yet, as those who adhere to the coercive model (noted at the beginning of this chapter) have pointed out, 'commandism' was a serious problem and generated dissatisfaction. In 1954 grain quotas were too high. Cadres sometimes applied quotas uniformly to areas both where there was a surplus and where there was a shortage and did not account for local natural calamities. To counter arbitrariness, misclassification and disorder, a 'three fix' (*sanding*) campaign was inaugurated in March 1955 whereby quotas were set for each *xiang* with regard to output, surplus and sale of grain and later in the year the assignment of quotas was extended down to households. In that campaign, some work-teams forced peasants to give up what was arbitrarily defined as 'surplus'. Others denounced 'tailist' leadership and the influence of 'bad elements' and 'counter-revolutionaries'. Soon, quotas were reduced and more concern was shown for the livelihood of peasants. The movement revealed considerable commandism, yet it perhaps also demonstrated the characteristic approach of the Communist Party to rural transformation at that time, noted by Shue – swift assault followed by rectification in line with maintaining peasant incentive.

Accelerated Co-operativisation

We have observed that the state grain monopoly was not sufficient to cream off a greater surplus from agriculture, demanded by the First Five Year Plan. Nor, the government felt, could taxation check class polarisation in the countryside. Both problems were tackled by accelerating co-operativisation. The prescribed initial co-operatives – subsequently referred to as 'lower-stage' (*chuji he-zuoshe*) – were four or five times the size of the mutual aid teams and consisted of some two to three dozen households. Members pooled most machinery, draught animals and all but about 5 per cent of their land ('private plots'). They received a share of the harvest after the co-operative had paid land tax and had made its compulsory sale of grain to the state and were paid a rent for land pooled. Such institutions were not 'co-operative' in the Western sense of making payment according to a dividend based on shares (though some compensation was made for resources pooled). Nor were they 'socialist', since rent was still paid and payment was not based entirely on labour contributed. They were referred to, there-fore, as 'semi-socialist'.

Such co-operatives were not formed easily. Whilst much progress had been made in transforming mutual aid teams into permanent teams, attempts to speed up the process of co-operativisation, in the spring of 1953, met with little success. Many of the co-operatives which did form collapsed or were dissolved as inefficient. In 1954, however, there was a renewed drive and the number of co-operatives reached 114,000. Progress was still felt to be too slow and in March 1955 the Party shifted its focus in recruitment back to rural areas to speed up the process. But still a shortage of personnel meant that responsibility for co-operativisation rested at *xiang* level. Cadres were sent down to the villages and attempts were made to ensure that one of these was attached to each co-operative. At least one co-operative existed in each *xiang* as a model for the formation of others (Schurmann 1966: pp. 442–7). Soon attempts were made to ensure that the heads of co-operatives were Party members, and frequently meetings of *xiang* Party committees consisted simply of such co-operative heads.

There were, however, considerable difficulties. Cadres were not sure how to handle tension between middle peasants who enjoyed a privileged position and poorer peasants unable to negotiate loans to provide capital for entering the co-operatives. Though credit facilities were provided at *xiang* level, it was not always clear whether they could generate funds quickly enough. Once the co-operatives were formed, there were also endless disputes over the amount of rent payable, since this was calculated according to figures dating from the earlier 'three fix' period when peasants understated their holdings. Land could also still be withdrawn. The situation became even more complicated as rich peasants, wishing to join the co-operatives because of inability to hire labour and because of discriminatory treatment in taxation and credit, demanded higher levels of compensation than cadres were prepared to provide. Cadres also found it difficult to persuade both rich and middle peasants to put their wealth into the co-operative rather than spending it on their houses or business ventures and both were discriminated against. There was wrangling also about the method of work-point allocation, the care of animals and much else (Shue 1980: pp. 287–308). Such difficulties seemed to suggest caution, and apparently a cautious line triumphed in May 1955 when a rural work conference cut back 20,000 co-operatives (Liu Shaoqi, *Collected Works*, 3 (1968): p. 366).

In response, Mao Zedong, faced perhaps with peasants who refused to invest in their land due to fears about co-operativisation, decided to intervene directly in rural policy. On 31 July, one day after the National People's Congress had endorsed a gradualist plan to organise one-third of farm households into co-operatives by 1957, he delivered his famous speech 'On the Co-operative Transformation of Agriculture' which set the tone for the whole movement (*Selected Works*, 5 (1977): pp. 184–207). In the speech, Mao revealed that the original target for co-operativisation had been one million co-operatives. Now the figure was set at 1.3 million. At a plenary session of the Party Central Committee in September–October 1955, Mao outlined his long-term strategy (JPRS 1974: pp. 14–26). He put forward a series of very ambitious targets to be achieved within twelve years, anticipating an increase in grain output from some 184 million tonnes in 1955 to 300 million tonnes by 1967. By 1967, the area under mechanical cultivation was to be increased to some 60 per cent of the total. Quite clearly, if those targets were to be achieved, a 'leap forward' in agriculture and industry was called for and the first step in that process was the rapid transformation of agriculture. As guide-lines for that 'leap', a number of documents were issued which were incorporated into the National Programme for Agricultural Development (1956–67) discussed in Chapter 1. The eventual document, put forward in January 1956, was less ambitious than Mao's original proposals but it did signify China's first attempt at a 'leap forward' and was to lead to even more rapid co-operativisation.

Following the Plenum in October 1955 and the formulation of detailed plans in local areas, the co-operativisation movement reached its 'high tide'. Without any regard for the old policy of forming co-operatives by stages, quotas and targets were constantly revised to the point that, by the end of the year, 75 million peasant households (63.3 per cent of the total peasant population) had joined co-operatives. The sheer pace of change found many cadres wanting and sometimes resulted in 'formalism' where mutual aid teams were transformed into co-operatives with very little other change. Once the breakthrough had been made, however, the process of strengthening and consolidation could proceed. Those richer peasants who had resisted the tide came under all sorts of pressure, even to the point of co-operatives demanding amalgamation to rid the richer peasants' land of pests and assuming responsibility for collecting grain from the non-co-operativised sector.

As pressure mounted, once again cadres decided to deal swiftly with arguments over rent payments and difficult problems concerning things such as fish ponds, tools and fruit trees. The answer was to move to a new 'socialist' form of organisation where payment was made exclusively according to work (plus initially a small amount of compensation). The model for a new type of co-operative – the 'higher-stage co-operative' (*gaoji hezuoshe*) – was clearly the Soviet *kolkhoz* (or collective farm). Those formed in 1955 varied considerably in size from a few lower-stage co-operatives to collectives as big as a whole *xiang* though soon they were reduced in size according to a standardised pattern.

De-radicalisation, 1956

We noted in Chapter 1 the decision in April 1956 to de-radicalise policy and that one factor in the decision was the recklessness of the 'little leap forward'. However accurate Shue's account might be overall and although incentives were offered to peasants to join the co-operatives, some were coerced. Livestock was killed prior to collectivisation (State Statistical Bureau 1990: p. 359), a cavalier attitude was adopted towards private plots and peasants' sideline activities showed a marked decline. 'Small rentiers', who had rented out their land because they were incapable of working it and had lived on the proceeds, lost their land and often constituted a collective welfare burden which could not adequately be borne. Provincial authorities, moreover, escalated production targets beyond realistic levels and used coercion to achieve them. They imposed central policies upon peasants, who knew that such policies could not work; for example double cropping and the forced use of Soviet model plough. By April, there was much talk of the need to 'seek truth from facts'.

The 'socialist high tide' of 1955–6 involved extravagant targets, some economic chaos and much coercion. Yet the authorities hesitated to adopt the extractive policy which had characterised Soviet agriculture – the direct assignment of planned quotas. Indeed, it was not only chaos but fears about direct production planning which led to the reopening of markets and the shelving of Mao's twelve-year plan for agriculture. But, as we have seen, collectivisation could not be stopped and all the government could do was establish a regular framework for the formation of collectives. The 'Model Regulations for Collectives', promulgated in 1956, specified the division of collective income. The collective retained amounts of grain for seed and fodder (which rose over the years as they were diverted to other uses) and made direct payment to peasants. That payment consisted of a small amount of cash which had accrued to the collective from the sale of grain and other goods plus a share of the harvest in kind. The calculation of individual income, however, was by no means an easy task. The ideal was a piecework system but it was extremely difficult to work out equivalents between different types of farm work and between farm work and work in subsidiary industries set up by the collective. Perhaps the most intractable problem was assigning work-points for capital construction projects which would only yield a return in the long run – a problem which provided an incentive to concentrate only on short-term projects. Such difficulties often led to arguments as intense as those over rent payments had been and were exacerbated by the fact that, whereas the collective determined distribution, the smaller brigade usually assigned work. In practice, however, most members received a nominal daily amount of work-points. But even when that was the case, problems arose in adjusting annual accounts to deal with members who had drawn rations in excess of their entitlement.

The collectives were run by an administrative committee of nine to nineteen members, which was elected by a members' council or members' delegates' council and was monitored by a supervisory committee similarly elected. Wherever possible, a Party committee was also set up in the collective, the membership of which overlapped the management committee. Ideally, leadership should include a significant number of younger people, but often young cadres were considered to be too inexperienced. Experience, however, was not very useful in a situation where Party policy was not clear on how to draw the line between maintaining production and fostering a 'capitalist' mentality, particularly as the 'high tide' policy changed to one which fostered rural markets. In a confused situation, some cadres continued to discriminate against the private sector while others did little to restrain peasants who wished to leave the collectives. Occasionally, rural leaders permitted the contracting of production to individual households (*baochan dao hu*) or ignored what was happening provided that grain quotas were met. They permitted peasants to spend an increasing amount of time on their private plots and were even said to act like 'rich peasants' themselves.

To help retrieve the rural situation, assist the ideological remoulding of urban youth and solve the problem of urban employment, a process of *xiafang* (sending down) was once again employed. At the same time, in the wake of the Anti-rightist movement, Mao called for a Socialist Education Movement to clean up 'unhealthy tendencies' in the countryside. That movement, led by work-teams, while somewhat limited, had a significant impact. In August 1957, the State Council moved once again effectively to restrict rural markets. Soon rural Party rectification could be undertaken in earnest and work was begun on collectives with the most serious problems (the so-called 'third category' collectives) (Vogel 1969: pp. 204–9). Aiming to reduce the size of collectives to about 100 households, the work-teams were able to bring the average down from 246 households in 1956 to 169 in 1957. The official purpose, however, was not to promote new radical change but to consolidate the collective structure. Indeed, in September 1957 a Party directive declared that once the size of the collectives and brigades had been fixed, there should be no further changes for ten years (Schurmann 1966: pp. 456–7). Mao Zedong was not to be so easily satisfied.

The Great Leap Forward

As Chapter 1 described, The Great Leap Forward was launched at the Third Plenum of the Eighth Central Committee, less than one week after a gradualist policy was adopted. Abandoning caution, the government decided both to decentralise authority and engage in direct production planning. There was nothing that was not to be pressed into the service of the leap. The policy of 'walking on two legs' (combining the old and the new) was reaffirmed. Light industry and intermediate technology was promoted with a 'cable-drawn plough' replacing the old Soviet model plough as the new miracle tool in a mass campaign to produce and use new tools. Self-reliance in rural and semi-rural areas was extolled in accordance with a policy known as 'get the best out of each area' (*yindi zhiyi*). The programme of extending water-works, begun in late 1957, was extended, requiring the labour of several collectives to combine, particularly in Henan at the junction of several major rivers. That campaign led to a further reduction in the size of private plots, the amalgamation of collectives and eventually the appearance of communes which organised labour on a quasi-military basis. The upshot of such developments, was the generalisation of the Henan experience in the Beidaihe meeting in August 1958.

The Beidaihe communiqué was in many ways quite cautious. Cadres were instructed not to disturb the villages too much and to take existing collectives as communal sub-units. Ideally, the commune was to replace the *xiang* as the basic level of rural administration and the former collectives would become its brigades and the former brigades its teams. In addition, specialist teams might be formed to undertake light industrial or special agricultural work. The system whereby Soviet-style machine tractor stations had leased tractors to co-operatives in return for a high fee was denounced as an oppressive method of extracting a surplus from agriculture and tractors were handed over to the communes. The *xiang*-level school system and marketing co-operatives were merged into a single organisation under the leadership of a Party committee and an elected management committee. Though central directives appeared cautious, many of those local leaders, with increased powers, were excited. To them, the commune represented a fusion of state and society and the beginnings of a process whereby the state would begin to wither away. As noted earlier, some expressed the intention of initiating a transition from the 'socialist' principle of 'payment according to work' to the 'communist' principle of 'payment according to needs'. Opposing the piecework system of work-points as individualist, they preferred to award peasants a daily supply of grain, which differed from the old basic ration in that it did not form part of annual accounting. In theory the old basic ration was added up and subtracted from the amount of grain due to peasants at harvest time, calculated according to work-points. If the resulting figure was negative, the peasant was in debt to the collective. If it was positive, the peasant received a share of grain plus cash. Rationing, however, plus removal of up to 20 per cent of grain for reserves often led to collective units having no grain to distribute. In that case, richer units which earned more cash could distribute it, whilst those which had no cash could only credit unredeemable work-points (Oi 1989: pp. 33–7). Such a policy, it was later felt, acted as a disincentive to hard work. With the 'communist sprit' of 1958, however, that was far from people's thoughts. Free supply was deemed possible and so was the introduction of ideological factors in determining wage-grades.

Local leaders interpreted the Beidaihe resolution permissively in a whirlwind process whereby 90 per cent of the Chinese rural population was organised in communes within a few months. Sometimes, over-zealous cadres confiscated personal property such as radios, bedding and watches. Domestic sideline operations were suppressed and instances of excessive egalitarianism were frequently noted. One particular practice, which later merited official con-demnation, was known as 'one equalisation and two transfers' (*yiping erdiao*), where the income of each peasant was equalised, the property of wealthy brigades above the average was transferred to other brigades and the labour force from brigades was transferred elsewhere without compensation (Chang 1975: pp. 98–101). Local cadres also disregarded official prescriptions on the size of communes. The Beidaihe resolution had decided that communes should consist of about 2,000 households. In practice the initial communes became bigger and bigger. The largest commune embraced a whole *xian*, though, in general, the size of most communes was roughly equivalent to the *old qu* (or intermediate level between *xiang* and *xian*) with some 5,000–11,000 households. As such, they may have cut across the old 'standard marketing areas' and contributed to rural dislocation. Indeed, with power decentralised to commune level, there were severe dislocations in the supply and marketing network.

Local cadres once again mobilised peasants to undertake tasks for which they were unprepared and which later proved worthless. They mistakenly considered that now there was a labour shortage, the old problem of rural underemployment had been solved permanently, with the result that the farm labour force declined from 192 million in 1957 to 151 million in 1958 and, as we have seen, left insufficient peasants to get the harvest in in its entirety. Most serious of all, a better harvest than usual combined with inflated statistics for grain production (believed to be 375 million tonnes, later scaled down to 250 and reassessed in the 1980s as 200) led to the view that the problem of food supply had been solved. Over-confidence caused authorities to believe they could implement swiftly a ten-year plan to reduce the area sown in grain by 30 per cent. In fact, the area planned for 1959 was 10 per cent lower than 1957 (Walker 1965: pp. 444–5; Lardy 1983: p. 42).

By November 1958 it was quite evident to most members of the Party leadership that urgent corrective measures were necessary. These were put forward at a conference in Zhengzhou in November and at the Sixth (Wuchang) Plenum in December. In his speech to that plenum, Mao admitted that a number of problems had arisen with the formation of communes and that cadres had exaggerated production statistics (JPRS 1974: pp. 140–8). He felt, however, that only some 1 to 5 per cent of cadres were guilty of violating discipline and had resorted to 'commandism'. In his view, the original aim 'basically to transform the country within three years' was over-optimistic. The transition to communism was off the agenda. Here Mao was responding to reports by investigation teams which had discovered massive problems, not the least of which was that planning had broken down and many communes were operating on a day-to-day basis.

Though Mao wavered between recognising the need for consolidation and hoping for a revival of the Great Leap, early 1959 was characterised by remedial measures. Limits were imposed on mass mobilisation, and houses, personal items and bank deposits were handed back to their owners. Formal administrative structures (such as commune management committees) were strengthened and dislocations in the supply and marketing network were dealt with by the partial revival of free markets. In February and March 1959, the Wuchang decision to make the production brigade the basic unit of account was interpreted as the brigade becoming an independent unit of ownership with the right to allocate its own resources. In effect, this meant that the old property status of the higher-stage collective was restored and the commune returned property formerly owned by the collective. Relationships both among communes and within communes, moreover, were to be regulated by means of contracts and attempts were made to work out a system of responsibility at all levels. This new stress on tightening up the planning system was reflected at a national level in the new policy of 'taking the whole country as a co-ordinated chess game'. The new stress on planning, the still prevalent view that China's rural areas faced a long-term labour shortage, plus the lesson that mass mobilisation would not solve everything led Mao to introduce in 1959 a ten-year plan for the mechanisation of agriculture. That plan was much more carefully formulated than anything which had appeared in 1958 (Stavis 1978: pp. 126–31).

Although policies concerning rural organisation constituted a retreat from the Great Leap, the commitment to production planning was maintained; the ambitious targets approved by the Wuchang Plenum were not scaled down and an enlarged Politburo conference in late March resisted any such attempt, revealing an extraordinary ambivalence in policy. Mao, it seems, supported the maintaining of targets yet had become even more critical of unrealistic exaggeration (Teiwes 1979: pp. 393–4). We cannot be sure of exactly what Mao's position was since for every cautious statement he made there was another which proclaimed adherence to the impending revival of the Leap. The Leap was, in fact, to be revived after Peng Dehuai's negative evaluation of the 1958 experiences at the enlarged Politburo conference at Lushan and Mao's bitter reaction. There followed a campaign against 'right opportunism' which, while treating senior leaders mildly, censured large numbers of lower-level cadres (Teiwes 1979: p. 432). Though the targets for struggle were exaggerated, there seemed no doubt that continuing problems in the rural areas resulted in quite strict organisational sanctions. This was perhaps the case because the 1959 harvest had been poor and peasant ardour had declined in the face of sheer exhaustion. According to one estimate, the labour days spent in agriculture increased by 14 per cent in 1958 and by another 23 per cent in 1959 (Riskin 1987: p. 119). 'Tailism', therefore, became a major deviation.

But although organisational sanctions at lower levels were quite strict, the overall policies of the revived Great Leap were much more modest than those of 1958. The Lushan Plenum scaled down the targets for the Leap, requiring some 275 million tonnes of grain. That was still unrealistic and it appears that statistics as well as targets were still not reported accurately; in fact corrected statistics worked out in the 1980s show a figure for 1959 of 165 million tonnes. Nevertheless, the twelve-year plan for agriculture was, once again, given a new lease of life, but its final form in early 1960 only reflected the targets specified at the Third Plenum and not those agreed to at the second session of the Eighth Party Congress in May 1958 (Chang 1975: pp. 243–62). These, of course, were still too ambitious. In the communes, the principle of decentralisation (according to the three-level ownership formula) was still officially endorsed. In the field of rural trade, although free markets were restricted once again, they were not totally abolished, the policy being 'freedom but not disorder, control but not strangulation'. Whilst cadres who had permitted the large-scale restoration of private plots were branded as 'right opportunists', moves to restrict private family activities were cautious. In short, the Great Leap of late 1959 and early 1960s was but a pale reflection of that of 1958. But, given the bad climatic conditions, could it have been anything else?

Economic Crisis, 1959–62

The natural calamities endured by China in the early 1960s were massive. By 1960, average per capita food grain availability had declined to some 160 kilograms, compared with 200 in 1957. Put another way, rural daily calorie intake fell to some 1,500, compared with some 2,000 in 1957 which was, according to some estimates, about the same figure for the early 1930s. As commented on earlier, from 1959 to 1961 there was a net loss of population of between 14 and 28 million. But even as late as 1961, newspaper accounts were boasting about grain reserves. Such 'reserves' might simply reflect the growing practice of local cadres to evade official regulations by calculating reserves in terms of grain entering granaries and not subtracting grain covertly removed subsequently in the form of loans to poor teams or for other purposes (Oi 1989: pp. 12–24). The Great Leap had demonstrated the dangerous consequences of cadre collusion to distort information – a problem which was to remain for many years. Clearly human errors were a prime cause of the disaster, as Liu Shaoqi insisted, but one has also to consider the vagaries of climate.

Whatever the major causes of the crisis, there was no doubt in leaders' minds that human errors should be rectified, but these were the errors of lower-level cadres. Singled out for criticism were what were known as the 'five styles' (or 'five winds'). These were 'the communist style', 'the style of exaggeration', 'the commandist style', 'the privileged style' and 'the style of leading production blindly'. Cadres were denounced for exceeding the spirit of directives from above, pushing too far the idea of mess halls, collectivising too much private property and being insufficiently concerned with the livelihood of the masses. The rectification movement of 1960–1 had much in common with that of 1947–8 which had also been designed to curb 'leftist' excesses though it was clearly more moderate. In 1961, Mao called for the formation of peasant associations, and sometimes what were known as 'poor and lower-middle peasant core groups' (*pinnong xia zhongnong hexin xiaozu*) assisted work-teams in denouncing cadres. Mobilisation, however, was not always carried out and was beyond the capacity of regular work-teams organised by local government. Sometimes, therefore, special work-teams, organised at higher levels, descended on the villages and did little more than subject local cadres to humiliation before meetings of peasants. Punishments seemed to depend less on a particular cadre's mistakes than on the record of the particular province in 1958. In short, more punishments occurred in provinces with a leftist reputation, including some which suffered badly from natural calamities (Teiwes 1979: pp. 459–60, 465, 470).

But punishment would not solve the food crisis. The initial response in 1960 was to hand over what remained of private plots to commune and brigade canteens in order to keep the supply of public meals going. There was little surplus to distribute to peasants much less feed animals. Once the grain earmarked for animal fodder was consumed by humans, animals were killed (see State Statistical Bureau 1990: p. 359), and thus the supply of fertiliser was reduced which adversely affected output. A decline in land devoted to industrial crops, moreover, led to a paralysis of light industry. Local leaders, therefore, were forced to conclude whatever deals they could, which impeded the official policy of restoring central control. To restore control and ease the food crisis in the cities, *xiafang* was intensified. At the same time administrative cadres were required to spend greater amounts of time at lower levels. In some areas, *xian*-level cadres were given administrative jobs within the brigades, but the problems were immense and often beyond the abilities of newly retrenched cadres. Cadres were unsure, for example, about the unit of account. After the decentralisation of some powers to brigade and team levels in 1959, further moves seem to have been taken towards the end of 1960 to transfer the bulk of decision-making power to the now much smaller teams. With the publication of a twelve-article directive on rural work towards the end of the year, *de facto* decentralisation to team level took place and this move was confirmed at the Ninth Plenum of the Eighth Central Committee in January 1961. Teams (which usually corresponded to the old lower-stage co-operatives) were now given full rights over the use of labour, land, animals, tools and equipment. Those teams, reduced in size to some 24 households, were usually run by a leader, a deputy, an accountant, a militia leader, a treasurer and a custodian of tools, animals and granary (Riskin 1987: pp. 70–2).

As noted in Chapter 1, the new rural structure was formalised in a sixty-article document issued on 12 May 1961 and revised in 1962. This endorsed the reduction in the size of the communes from units of some 5,000 households in 1959 to units of some 1,600–1,800 in 1961–2. On average the communes now contained some 10–11 brigades and 65–75 teams. At the same time, the role and rights of the teams, as basic accounting units, were affirmed. Brigades were instructed to guarantee to the teams a fixed amount of labour power, land, animals and tools. The teams' production targets were to be arrived at by consultation between various levels and incorporated in contracts. Under no circumstances were targets to be imposed from above. As a production incentive the ratio of 'basic grain' to 'work-point' grain which the team might distribute changed from 5:5 to 3:7 (Oi 1989: p. 39).

But all that was easier said than done so long as quotas existed and brigade leaders were required to negotiate the contracts. However relaxed policy might be, brigade cadres were always caught between the requirement to implement quotas and the interests of the teams from whom they received work-points. In those troubled times, they usually let the teams do what they wanted, for which they were later to be censured. Ceding temporarily to team autonomy, brigades, consisting of some seven teams and 150–180 households, did very little except manage some rudimentary enterprises, a clinic and perhaps a primary school. For its part, the commune, which usually contained a grain management and tax office, still maintained formal authority over some agricultural and industrial activities according to the 'three-level system of ownership'. It might also run a supply and marketing co-operative, a hospital or clinic and a secondary school. Before long, communes were also able to revive some of the rural industries which had been closed down. The regulations, however, guaranteed team autonomy and the commune was supposed simply to assist in persuading peasants to continue cultivating grain by incentives such as sales at above quota prices according to principles of price planning; direct production planning did not extend lower than *xian* level. But soon communes and brigades came to use more coercive measures; they also drafted team labour and infringed on team rights.

There were also conservative violations of official policy. The extent of private plots was now set at some 5 to 7 per cent of total cultivated land, with peasants allowed to derive 20 per cent of their income from private business. Income earned from those plots and from land privately reclaimed was tax free. At first, some 5 per cent of land was reassigned for private cultivation. By 1962, however, reports appeared that 20–50 per cent of land in some areas was under private cultivation. Once peasants were allowed to sell the produce of their private plots there inevitably developed thriving rural markets, and the new regulations specified what goods might be privately traded. Although 'free markets' were officially sanctioned, they were required to be under some kind of official control. But it soon became difficult for local leaders to know exactly what kind of transactions were going on and they were later castigated as abetting *sanzi yibao* which, it will be remembered, consisted in the extension of plots for private use, the expansion of free markets, the increase in the number of small enterprises with sole responsibility for their own profits and losses and, most serious, 'the fixing of output quotas on individual households'. As noted in Chapter 1, the latter policy was adopted in a few provinces, notably Anhui where it was embraced as part of a 'responsibility system' designed to restore production after the bad summer harvest of 1961.

All the above were desperate measures adopted out of immediate practical necessity. There was, however, a long-term strategy. The key slogan of the Ninth Plenum was 'agriculture as the base and industry as the leading factor'. But, as we have seen, 'agricultural priority' proved to be vacuous. In the meantime, though, to facilitate Mao's ten-year plan for mechanisation, tractors were handed back to the state to be leased to peasants by agricultural machinery stations. The sudden removal of Soviet assistance in 1960, however, halted tractor deployment and before long the ten-year mechanisation plan was shelved. By 1964 only 10 per cent of the cultivated area was ploughed by tractors (Stavis 1978: pp. 95–6,

144–51). In the early 1960s, other forms of investment also fell off sharply.

The Socialist Education Movement, 1962–6

Though various leaders differed in their attitudes to policies aimed at rural reconstruction, few could deny there were major problems. Official documents spoke of a general 'spontaneous inclination towards capitalism'. Many peasants were devoting an excessive amount of time to their private plots and privately reclaimed land or had abandoned farming to go into business. Some cadres were corrupt and had appropriated public funds for their own use. Speculation and gambling were rife and there had been a revival of 'feudal' practices such as religious festivals, bride-purchase and witchcraft (Chen and Ridley 1969). To remedy those particular problems and more generally the problem of evasion of government policies, Party-led work-teams were sent to the countryside to join up with 'poor and lower-middle peasant associations' which had begun to reappear in the rectification movement of 1960–1.

Initial work in trial areas (notably Hebei and Hunan) were bedevilled by ineffective leadership, and attention focused on improving the leading group within brigades and promoting cadres from poor and lower-middle peasant backgrounds (Chen and Ridley 1969: p. 151). By early 1963, reports were mixed. Some economies in administration had been effected and a few private plots had been restricted, but some cadres were still insisting that the amount of money available for peasants to spend in the free markets should be increased. The spirit of Yan'an was referred to, both to promote radicalism and to curb what were felt to be excessively radical actions – in Mao's words of 1942, to 'develop the economy and safeguard supplies'. At that time, newspapers carried both articles by radical army cadres to propagate the spirit of socialist education and pleas by some leaders for caution (Vogel 1969: pp. 302–4). To speed up the movement and quell opposition, central work conferences were held, resulting in May 1963 in a 'Draft Resolution of the Central Committee on Some Problems in Current Rural Work' (Baum and Teiwes 1968: pp. 58–71). This document, commonly known as the 'Early Ten Points', said to have been compiled under Mao's personal supervision, stressed the importance of class struggle. The notion 'four clean-ups' (*siqing*) was introduced which signified cleaning up accounts, granaries, property and work-points and ending cadre corruption. Cadres were to participate in productive labour and, most important of all, the Party proposed to re-establish poor and lower-middle peasant associations at commune, brigade and team levels to lead the movement.

The 'Early Ten Points' were not clear about operational details. How exactly were the poor and lower-middle peasant associations to be established and how did their functions relate to work-teams? When the first 'poor peasants' representative groups' were set up after the directive, they were charged with fostering the collective economy under the leadership of the Party and being assistants to management committees (Baum and Teiwes 1968: pp. 16–7). But what were they to do when a local Party branch was corrupt? How were Party committees to submit to supervision by the peasant associations and yet also lead them? In September, the Party Centre attempted to provide more specific guidelines – 'Some Concrete Policy Formulations . . . in the Socialist Education Movement' (Baum and Teiwes 1968: pp. 72–94; Baum 1975: pp. 44–59). The aim of those directives, commonly referred to as the 'Later Ten Points', was to clarify a number of general issues enunciated in the 'Early Ten Points'. But in clarifying certain issues, did the 'Later Ten Points' actually negate the spirit of the earlier document? Instead of 'struggle' (which was now confined to a very limited number of people), the later document preferred to speak of 'appropriate criticism'. Contradictions were to be seen as 'among the people' and 'non-antagonistic'. People were not to be branded as 'rightists'. 'Prosperous middle peasants' were not to be considered 'rich peasants'; more important still, the work-teams were to control the peasant associations and were not to disrupt existing organisations in the countryside. The detailed class analysis in the document, moreover, must have left cadres unsure of exactly what the movement's targets were to be.

Cadres participating in the movement were now required to 'squat on the spot' (*dundian*) in specific areas, and many, faced with intractable problems, became passive. They were worried by the extension into the countryside of the movement of February 1964 to 'learn from the People's Liberation Army'. Army cadres, transferred to help militia units, began to propagate more radical policies. They helped peasants hold meetings, compile their 'three histories' (personal, family and village) so as more easily to compare the present with the past and to strengthen peasant associations. In that atmosphere, Mao demanded struggle against 'bad elements' who resisted the movement. The 'Organisational Rules for Poor and Lower-Middle Peasant Associations' (Baum and Teiwes 1968: pp. 27, 95–101), formulated at that time, however, still placed the peasant associations under the leadership of local Party committees but warned cadres not to 'strike retaliatory blows'.

No mass movement, of course, could proceed without a model and, as we have seen, the Dazhai production brigade in the poor loess lands of Shanxi was chosen. Dazhai symbolised 'self-reliance' in the face of natural calamities, triumph over a cautious work-team, the priority of collectivisation over mechanisation and the 'living application of Mao Zedong Thought'. In practical terms, it symbolised the spirit of the Great Leap, particularly in its group appraisal of work-point allocation which incorporated political attitudes rather than more economistic methods of payment. Dazhai was later said to have made fraudulent claims concerning self-reliance though these date from 1967. It was, however, taken very seriously at the time, remaining a symbol of radical rural development.

By September 1964, it seemed, a more radical approach to the Socialist Education Movement prevailed. The 'Later Ten Points' were replaced by another document known as the 'Revised Later Ten Points' (Baum and Teiwes 1968: pp. 102–17). Now the Socialist Education Movement was seen not as a moderate closed rectification movement but as something which required long and bitter struggle and which might perhaps last five or six years or even longer. The document warned against superficiality, called for the re-registration of Party members and demanded that action be directed against those cadres who had degenerated into becoming class enemies. The 'Revised Later Ten Points' required mass mobilisation to criticise errant cadres at all levels. At that point, effective leadership of the movement passed to Liu Shaoqi. Liu, it appears, had come to see the need for a much more radical process of mass mobilisation after his own and his wife Wang Guangmei's experiences in the Taoyuan production brigade in Fuhing *xian*, Hebei (Baum 1975: pp. 83–101). He inaugurated, therefore, a new stage in the campaign known as the 'big four clean-ups' (politics, economics, ideology and organisation) in which huge work-teams descended on the countryside and engaged in disciplining up to one million basic-level cadres. Though the primary initiators of the new intensified campaign were the work-teams, the poor and lower-middle peasant associations were also strengthened, often through the militia. As work-teams and militia-backed peasant associations went into action, those who were found to be guilty of 'unclean practices' were denounced, fined or dismissed from office (Teiwes 1979: p. 545; Baum and Teiwes 1968: p. 33). At first struggle was directed against obvious (and usually harmless) targets such as old 'counter-revolutionaries' and unregenerate landlords, but gradually extended to include most cadres. Many of those cadres were not slow to retaliate.

One of the major criticisms during the more radical period of the Socialist Education Movement of late 1964 was that cadres had permitted or even encouraged the earlier 'spontaneous development of capitalism'. There was now pressure for the restriction of free markets in the countryside, and by December, Mao Zedong was once again using the term 'Great Leap Forward' to describe future policy (Schram 1974: p. 231). By that time food grain output had returned to pre-Great Leap levels (though per capita availability did not regain that level until the late 1970s). That achievement was due both to increased price planning and to the use of new high yielding seed strains. Radicals, of course, ignored the former and emphasised the superior ability of a collective system to develop the necessary irrigation support and to supply chemical fertilisers. The perceived need for further massive irrigation works and more local fertiliser production fuelled hopes for a new 'leap'; and these were exacerbated once rural enterprises (particularly chemical fertiliser plants), abandoned after the Leap, went back into production. In Great Leap spirit, a new decentralisation of authority was occurring (Riskin 1987: p. 159). At the same time, there was a move once again away from price planning in agriculture towards direct production planning. In that process, the commune, shorn of many of its powers in the early 1960s, came to serve as an important link in determining the types of main crop and sown acreage, according to a 'two down and one up procedure' whereby targets were sent down from the centre to the basic level, adjusted and then sent back up again. The return to production planning, however, should not be seen exclusively in terms of a Stalinist 'command economy'. There was considerable negotiation and argument among teams required to sign quota pledges, the brigades and higher levels. Here, Oi argues, legitimacy was purchased by a degree of democratic discussion and flexibility, though in a zero-sum bargaining situation where the structure of quotas dictated that one team's gain would be another's loss. To gain more control over the harvest without increasing procurement quotas, a flexible system of grain reserves was built up. Such a process was clearly open to clientelist manipulation (Oi 1989: pp. 55–65, 70–6). More to the point here, it looked like a return to Great Leap policies without the coercive errors of that time. One may understand why Mao was excited.

Yet whatever excitement Mao may have entertained was cooled by the obvious fact that initiative was still in the hands of work-teams, rather than peasant associations. Mao soon came to the view that the movement had been mishandled and its 'leftism' had generated too much local hostility. The disciplining of basic-level cadres had not brought much new vitality to the countryside. The fault, therefore, must lie with more senior members of the Party who had failed to provide the conditions for the peasant associations to play a more constructive role. In late 1964, therefore, policy switched away from disciplining cadres. This was evidently to the taste of those who feared local instability. Thus in his report on the work of the government to the Third National People's Congress in December 1964, Premier Zhou Enlai made it clear that the focus was now on the 'big four clean-ups' (*Peking Review*, 1, 1 Feb. 1965: p. 13) rather than the earlier narrower concentration on things like accounts, granaries, property and work-points. He demanded also that the movement should not confine itself to petty misdemeanours.

The theme of antagonistic contradictions at a national level was taken up in a new policy document which was to govern the Socialist Education Movement. This document, 'Some Problems Currently Arising in the Course of the Rural Socialist Education Movement' (commonly known as the 'Twenty Three Articles') (Baum and Teiwes 1968: pp. 118–26), was said to have been written by Mao himself. At the level of policy, the document made the extremely radical demand that the Socialist Education Movement focus its attention on 'persons in authority taking the capitalist road' at all levels up to and including the Central Committee itself. At an operational level, however, the 'Twenty Three Articles' suggested merely that peasants combine with basic-level cadres and work-teams in a 'triple alliance', which as we saw earlier was reminiscent of that organisational form which characterised the immediate post-liberation period. In the villages the stress was on patient persuasion, and what was left of local rectification focused on *xian*-level Party leadership. Gradually, therefore, the Socialist Education Movement wound down in 1965.

The stability of 1965 (which proved to be temporary) was seen as a prerequisite for what Zhou Enlai announced as the 'four modernisations'. One of those modernisations was, of course, agriculture, and significant moves were made in 1965–6 to promote agricultural mechanisation, semi-mechanisation and, once again, miracle tools (for example rice transplanters) (Stavis 1978: pp. 204–14). There was much dispute, however, as to how mechanisation should proceed. As we have seen, after 1963, proposals had been put forward for establishing agricultural machinery trusts, developing into a China Agricultural Machinery Corporation to handle the production and leasing of farm equipment. Mao came to oppose that policy. He felt that to set up huge surplus-extracting corporations, operating according to the profit motive, would negate both Party leadership and mass activism. Although a few pioneer trusts were established in 1964, as noted in Chapter 1, the general plan was reversed. After 1966, machinery stations were required to sell machinery to communes and the latter were given two years to pay. Their personnel, moreover, were removed from the state pay-roll and made to receive work-points. Needless to say, there was some opposition which went on until 1968. Cadres could drag their feet on the grounds that no action should be taken until the massive convulsions of the early Cultural Revolution had ended (Stavis 1978: pp. 183–201, 237–8).

The Cultural Revolution and 'Flying Leap'

In 1966, as the Cultural Revolution erupted in urban areas, rural residents were urged not to launch the Cultural Revolution in villages 'where original arrangements for the socialist education movement are appropriate and where the movement is going well'.

But not long after the beginning of 'revolutionary exchange', urban-based red guard units acted as the catalyst for the formation of groups of suburban peasant red rebels which sought resolution of economic and other issues left over from the Socialist Education Movement. Like their urban counterparts, peasant red rebels were subject to splits and came into conflict with the still active work-teams which responded characteristically by branding many rebels 'counter-revolutionary'. In turn those rebels denounced basic-level cadres in suburban villages, particularly those who had escaped the pre-1965 'small four clean-ups', and who were now required to answer for their 'economism' and other deviations (Baum 1969: pp. 99–101).

As conflicts began to occur in the suburban countryside, the central leadership, worried about the harvest and red rebels requisitioning or stealing from granaries, issued a directive on 14 September 1965 stipulating that the Cultural Revolution in rural areas should be conducted in communes and production brigades 'in association with the original "four clean-ups" arrangements', effectively calling a halt to the rural Cultural Revolution. Not long after the directive, however, the central Party journal *Hongqi* (Red Flag) interpreted the directive as saying that urban-based red guards were only forbidden to 'make revolution' in rural units 'where the "four clean-up" provisions were considered appropriate by the masses' (Baum 1969: p. 103). In that climate work-teams ceased to operate; though, until December, policies adhered to the slogan 'grasp revolution and promote production', with a very clear emphasis on the second part.

The Socialist Education Movement was formally brought to an end on 15 December 1966, whereupon poor and lower-middle peasant associations were urged to form their own Cultural Revolution committees. Together with special groups formed to promote production, the peasant Cultural Revolution groups could now intensify action against local cadres. The situation, however, was highly confused, since large numbers of peasant rebels, branded as 'counter-revolutionary' by the work-teams, demanded the removal of that invidious label but were joined in their demands by rightists, ex-landlords and people said to be 'genuine' counter-revolutionaries. The peasant Cultural Revolution committees were to find new evaluations extremely difficult. Once attempts were made in January 1967 to recall the original work-teams to undergo criticism, the central leadership, fearing that proscribed elements would take the initiative, endorsed once again the defunct Socialist Education Movement and prohibited the reversal of any previous judgements, at least for the time being. Peasants were forbidden to take any action against members of the former work-teams, leniency was stressed during the spring planting season and factional struggle declined in suburban communes.

Some violence, however, was to occur in suburban areas in 1968 when 'five category elements' were sometimes killed by fanatic 'ultra-leftists' (*Survey of the China Mainland Press*, 4225, 25 July 1968: pp. 12–13; Baum 1971: pp. 448–9), but in the deep country-side the Cultural Revolution had little effect. In general, the winding-down of the Socialist Education Movement in late 1966 had left the old administration intact. Certainly, the reports of ex-red-guards who went to the rural areas do not suggest a high level of peasant activism (Bennett and Montaperto 1971: pp. 220–4). In such a situation, the ideals of the Cultural Revolution were often imported into the countryside by the army which set up Mao Zedong Thought propaganda teams and 'front-line committees' to replace the existing administration, to safeguard production and to promote the Dazhai model. Those committees were soon replaced by revolutionary committees at commune and brigade level. With the stress on consolidation, the main cadre deviation was seen to be excessive 'tailism' and cadres were denounced for failing to prevent feuds (Baum 1971: pp. 447–53).

We noted in Chapter 1 the 'flying leap' which followed the active period of the Cultural Revolution. In that short-lived 'leap', particular attention was devoted to the qualities of local Party secretaries who were to take over from the army the leadership of poor and lower middle peasants and to foster younger leaders. Those secretaries were bereft of clear-cut policies but on a few questions there were clear directives. For example, Party secretaries were instructed to make provision for the *xiafang* of large numbers of former red guards. Cadres were also enjoined to propagate the idea of 'storing grain everywhere' (at household and collective levels) both as a safeguard against dislocations caused by possible war and to prevent a recurrence of the hardships of 1959–61, in the aftermath of the original Great Leap. In 1969, huge reserves were built up in the collectives and, contrary to the Sixty Articles of 1961 and the flexible policy of 1964, such reserves could not be used for loans to overdrawn households which were denounced as profligate. By insisting that teams store grain, the government could reduce its own growing expenditure on storage and, it hoped, exercise control over the 'surplus' whilst giving peasants the impression that grain was under their control. In fact, it simply transferred costs, led to peasant dissatisfaction and caused local leaders considerable trouble preventing spoilage – in which task they were frequently deficient (Oi 1989: pp. 76–82). Of course, storing grain everywhere meant growing grain everywhere at the expense of other crops, contradicting the former concentration on specialised 'high and stable yield areas'. Instead there was 'self-reliant' production of grain which, as we have noted, made inter-provincial grain transfers extremely difficult. At the same time, cadres praised high-cost and environmentally damaging double cropping and directly imposed production targets, considering any talk of price planning 'revisionist'. To secure over quota grain at less than the prescribed price, they sometimes invoked 'loyalty to Mao' and the need for war preparations (Lardy 1983: p. 154). At the same time, the mechanisation drive received added impetus and pressure was brought to bear on machinery stations which had been reluctant to follow the decentralisation policy. In retrospect, that policy had deleterious effects on agricultural costs.

On other questions, however, cadres had to make their own interpretation of official policy on the basis of material criticising the rural policies in the early 1960s. Take for example the question of corruption. The state had to make peasants grow more grain and had reinforced a procurement system which forced local leaders to engage in practices which were technically corrupt. Team leaders, without sufficient grain to distribute, were forced to meet quotas, provide brigade expenses and arrange for public works projects which took labour away from the teams and required compensation which devalued work-points. They might under-report production, conceal ('black') land, bribe tractor drivers and granary managers and falsify accounts in order to survive. One might also expect brigade cadres, as 'gatekeepers', caught up in a web of conflicting interests and personal connections, to favour some teams over others and to be complicit in 'corruption'. During the turmoil of the Cultural Revolution, when central control had been paralysed, local leaders enjoyed much latitude and many teams did not even pay tax. One is immediately reminded of complaints made during the Socialist Education Movement of the early 1960s (Oi 1989: pp. 104–30).

Perhaps most serious was lack of guidance on the appropriate unit of account. Officially, the team was to remain the basic unit of ownership in the rural sector at which work-points were allocated and the harvest divided but the brigades now enjoyed a degree of authority far greater than at any time since the early 1960s. They could supervise team activities and most rural industry was administered at brigade or commune level. In addition, the decentralisation of educational facilities and the commercial network provided the brigades with new administrative responsibilities (Bastid 1973: pp. 177–80). It seemed clear, therefore, in the radical atmosphere of 1969–70, that it was only a matter of time before the brigade acquired more power over the production of basic food grains, and it is worth bearing in mind that Dazhai (the model) was a brigade (if only a small one) and not a team. How quickly, therefore, should the rural cadre proceed with the task of upgrading the unit of account? The cadre was similarly beset with a host of problems concerning the private sector and the free markets. The 1965 rules on the amount of land allocated to private plots were still in force and yet, since that time, there had occurred the Cultural Revolution, aimed, amongst other things, at countering privatism. Officially, provision was made for rural markets, and yet the extension of rural markets had been one of the 'crimes' of which Liu Shaoqi had been accused. What attitude should the cadre take? How, moreover, were cadres to combat 'economism'. The ratio of 'basic grain' to 'work-point' grain was shifted from 3:7 in the early 1960s to 6:4 on the eve of the Cultural Revolution. But even that was considered as 'putting work-points in command', and in the late 1960s the ratio sometimes reached 7:3. Since basic grain was allocated on the basis of family size, a hard-working peasant might earn less than a peasant who did not work as hard but had many children (Oi 1989: p. 40).

In such an atmosphere it is not surprising that rural cadres began to commit many of the old errors of the Great Leap. They inflated production goals beyond realistic limits and then used coercion to achieve them. They arbitrarily collectivised private property, prematurely upgraded the unit of account and even considered the restoration of a partial free-supply system. Sometimes, they interpreted the Dazhai model as a blueprint for rural policy to be put into immediate effect over the whole country, despite the fact that certain of its features ran counter to general policy towards the countryside (Woodward 1978: pp. 161–5).

Consolidating the Rural Sector and Echoes of the Leap

During the 'flying leap' of 1968–70 there was much talk of leadership by the poor and lower-middle peasants. After 1970, however, as the Party was rebuilt in the rural areas, though the poor and lower-middle peasant associations remained in existence, there was more talk of leadership by the appropriate level of Party committee. As far as the revolutionary committees were concerned, more and more authority came to be exercised by Party secretaries and the mass representatives found themselves spending less time in decision-making than in performing productive labour. It would seem, however, that rebuilding the rural Party network was deemed insufficient to establish the balance between public activity and privatisation, and in 1970 a major rectification campaign, known as *yida sanfan* ('one strike and three antis' – 'strike counter-revolutionaries, oppose corruption, oppose speculation and oppose extravagance and waste') was extended into the rural areas to point cadres in the right direction (Woodward 1978: pp. 161–2). It was aimed at combating deviations both from the right and the 'ultra-left' yet, as time went on, it was to be the latter deviation which earned the most attention. It was, of course, no use conducting a rectification campaign when the criteria for what constituted a deviation were constantly changing. Thus, to establish such criteria, teams of senior Party cadres were sent to the rural areas to monitor the current balance between productivity and mass activism and between public and private activity. There was much that those teams had to decide and many contradictions which had to be resolved. They had to see that the new stress on adequate grain reserves was being implemented and that peasants were not consuming too much. This sometimes involved putting quantitative ceilings on the distribution of per capita basic grain and, in the spirit of the Campaign to Criticise Lin Biao and Confucius, denouncing what was referred to as 'dividing all and eating all'. They were required to promote local mechanisation and tool production yet at the same time ensure that rural units did not set their accumulation targets too high. They had to monitor a renewed birth control campaign which got under way in 1970 and yet promote a system of rural distribution which still discriminated in favour of those with large families. They were enjoined to propagate Mao's call for equal pay between the sexes and yet foster a system of 'payment according to work' which favoured brute strength. They had to see that the peasants' standard of living was maintained and yet prevent peasant households obtaining advances greater than their annual income entitlement. They were expected, moreover, to see that the large numbers of 'educated youth' who had been sent to the countryside in the wake of the Cultural Revolution were treated properly.

In retrospect, it would seem that the campaign to resettle educated youth in the countryside in the years after the Cultural Revolution left much to be desired. Though some youth managed to integrate successfully with the local peasants and got married, most lived in segregated quarters or even segregated villages. Only occasionally did those educated youth who did integrate with the peasants attain positions of authority in the communes. Frequently they complained that the peasants had no confidence in them and they were assigned to low grades in the system where work-point assessment was based on a hierarchy of skill. Sometimes they were welcomed by commune leaders so long as the initial resettlement subsidy from the *xian* lasted; after that they were regarded as a nuisance (Bernstein 1977).

The task of local cadres in the early 1970s was not enviable though the rural situation gradually stabilised after the Fourth Five Year Plan went into effect in 1971. With the new stress on orderly production, the programme of 'learning from Dazhai' was reassessed in a movement to emulate Xiyang *xian* (in which Dazhai was located). This, as time went on, was held up less as a model of social experimentation than as an example of how to improve production techniques. Soon 'success' in this campaign was recorded, in that North China had, for the first time, become self-sufficient in grain and no longer depended on imports of grain from the South. As noted earlier, as improved production techniques were stressed, it became even clearer that China's ability to profit fully from the development of new seed strains depended on better irrigation and more chemical fertilisers. Political goals receded. According to the new five year plan, those who, in the 'flying leap', had committed the Great Leap error of advocating a reduction in the cultivated area were denounced and those who had collectivised the private property of peasants were told to hand it back. Private activity was once again fostered, markets were reopened, peasants were encouraged to keep their own pigs, family handicraft production developed and greater liberality was shown in determining legitimate sideline activities. The emphasis was on stability and to achieve it there was a renewed emphasis on the integrity of the production team. Back in the early 1960s, Mao had maintained that the point at which the unit of account might be upgraded was when a greater degree of income was generated at the higher level than at the lower. Since very few communes or production brigades were in that position in 1970, the reiteration of Mao's criterion consigned most of the attempts at upgrading during the 'flying leap' to the category of 'ultra-leftist'. In any case, upgrading was becoming progressively difficult as all collective units increased in size. Communes increased on average from 1,600–1,800 households in 1961–2 to almost 3,300 in 1976, brigades from 170–190 to some 250 and teams from 24 to 36 (Ash 1991: p. 494). Brigades, moreover, were enjoined not to encroach on the rights of teams, not to take labour away from them without due compensation and not to draw on the teams' 'public accumulation funds'.

But during the 'foreign leap', after Mao's death, there was still talk of upgrading and achieving massive increases in agricultural output, reflected in the speeches of Hua Guofeng. We have seen, however, that the data on which Hua based his assessment was faulty. Output was impressive but costs had risen disproportionately. Taxes, independently of production, had to be paid equally in the bad years as well as in the good. Because they were required to be made in grain, grain-deficient teams would sometimes purchase grain on the black market to pay their taxes. Procurements likewise depended on whether a team was designated 'grain-deficient' or 'grain-surplus' (with per capita availability of 'basic grain' above 15–17.5 kilograms per month, a figure lower than international standards of adequacy). Such designation had remained unchanged for years, resulting in the state failing to receive its share of rich teams' production and surplus teams which had become deficit still having to sell to the state. Grain-rich teams, in debt, moreover, often preferred to sell their grain on the black market at lower prices than to the state because payment had to be made through credit co-operatives which might garnish the proceeds (Oi 1989: pp. 17–26, 46–9). We have seen that overall, despite considerable agricultural growth, rural living standards were much the same as the 1950s.

The case against continuing the existing strategy was strong. In its own terms, that strategy had not markedly improved living standards. Some 10 per cent of the population was in dire poverty and decentralised power had prevented adequate transfers of food to poorer areas. Sudden changes and reversals of policy had sapped peasant morale. Despite Mao's insistence, urban bias had not been corrected. Although housing space was more adequate in the rural areas than in the towns, urban residents were much better off and urban incomes were 2–2.5 times higher than rural ones. That being said, among less-developed countries, China enjoyed a very high degree of equality and its record in meeting the basic needs of 90 per cent of the population was impressive. There were, of course, wide disparities of income between the richest peasants near Shanghai and those in the deep hinterland (perhaps 1:40) but the World Bank's estimate for 1979 shows a GINI coefficient for rural personal income of 0.26 (before subsidies). Another survey for the same period shows a figure of 0.237. These compare well with figures for South Asian countries with coefficients of 3.0–3.5 (Riskin 1987: pp. 232–42, 306–7). If change was to come, therefore, could one be sure that it would not be at the expense of equality and basic needs?

The Consequences of De-collectivisation

Chapter 2 has described the shift from the moderate policies of 1978 to close the 'price scissors' to radial de-collectivisation. Initially most peasants were much better off. GINI coefficients still showed a high degree of equality though indeed some peasants became quite rich. By 1984 it seemed to most commentators that China's leaders had made an accurate diagnosis of the problems attending the former system and that the new market-oriented strategy was the most appropriate. If we consider the questions raised at the beginning of this chapter, however, one is not wholly convinced that it was de-collectivisation which was primarily responsible for the increase in growth and peasant incomes. After all, Chapter 2 noted, accelerated growth dates back several years before de-collectivisation took effect. Secondly while strenuous efforts were made to close the notorious 'price scissors', the old extractive policy remained and by the late 1980s improvement in the urban–rural terms of trade appears to have been reversed. Clearly the switch away from production planning to price planning was of enormous benefit, but this could surely have been achieved without the radical de-collectivisation which took place and the disruption it caused.

Riskin (1987: pp. 299–311) and others have highlighted many of the practical problems to which the new strategy gave rise. Since agricultural activities yielded a worse return than some others, land was taken out of production for industrial activities and for an unprecedented housing boom. This sometimes led to a shortage of vegetables, though eventually the situation was rectified by free market determination of their price. The new system, could not deal adequately with forestry and many trees were illegally felled before (and probably after) the Forestry Law of 1984. There was also predatory use of land by peasants who, noting cadre opposition, feared the household contracting system would not survive and did not bother to replace soil nutrients. With this in mind, and with their short leases, they were unwilling to invest in their family farm. The government responded, in Document No. 1, 1984, by extending contracts for fifteen years for ordinary crops and longer for others and later by allowing them to be inherited.

The problem of investment in agriculture was, of course, much more complicated than that and credit co-operatives were strengthened to supplement the reconstituted Agricultural Bank to mobilise savings for agricultural investment. The bank soon became the major source of rural investment but it was interested mainly in mobilising funds for rural *industry*. Meanwhile state investment, which in the 1970s had kept pace with agricultural growth, declined markedly. In June 1979, the government announced that state investment in agriculture was to increase from 11 per cent of budgeted investment in 1978 to 14 per cent in 1979. It was supposed to increase to 18 per cent in 1981–2. Because of budgetary problems (generated in good measure by reforms which allowed enterprises to retain a proportion of their profits), however, it actually fell in absolute terms. In the period 1976–80 state investment in agricultural capital construction constituted some 10.5 per cent of overall capital construction investment; in the period 1981–5, it was only 5 per cent. There was a decline also in investment in agricultural support industries. Short-term support for agriculture and the provision of subsidies to improve peasants' living standards and tax concessions, however, were maintained, which probably served to generate enthusiasm while production subsidies declined and the agricultural infrastructure deteriorated markedly. The decline of state investment could not be offset for long by local investment nor by the rapid increase in peasants' savings so long as more profitable sources of investment continued to appear and the peasant consumption boom continued. Communes, moreover, the institutional basis for some investment in capital projects such as waterworks, had been removed and replaced by cash strapped *xiang* governments. The result of all that was a plethora of disputes over water-rights, government directives in response (1982), but overall a decline in the irrigated area and perhaps an increase in the impact of natural calamities (Kojima 1988: pp. 496–509).

At a lower level, land division itself led to problems. A parcelling-out of land, reminiscent of the European feudal system (Watson 1984: p. 98), was car·ied out to ensure that each peasant obtained a mixture of good and bad land. By the mid-1980s each family held an average of nine to eleven plots (compared with six in the 1930s). Land, therefore, was wasted by digging ditches and there was a decline in the machine ploughed area in nine provinces. It was not until 1989 that the area ploughed by tractors regained the level of 1979 and the irrigated area has still not regained the level of that year (State Statistical Bureau 1990: p. 333). Pest control suffered and erosion was caused by the provision of good and bad land in vertical strips running up hillsides. Time was wasted travelling between plots. And the allocation of plots was often not according to the number of people in a family who actually worked in agriculture, but either according to the number of people it had regardless of skill or according to the number of labour force units it contained, regardless of where they worked. Thus some parcels of land were not farmed (because of lack of labour) or left fallow for part of the year. Some families with abundant labour power wanted more land to farm and others wanted to get out of farming into more profitable non-agricultural pursuits. Land therefore began to be transferred and sub-contracted, after Document No. 1, 1984 permitted a quasi-renting arrangement, paid for until 1985 in grain at the low official price. Many methods were employed here, leading to tendering for rental agreements and eventually to a *de facto* leasehold land market, though this was smaller than one might have expected. Increase in land-holding, moreover, demanded the use of non-family labour and the growth of a hired labour force. A maximum of nine 'helpers' was set but often disregarded. Some economists wished to go further and called for *de jure* private ownership and a regular land market. To clarify the situation the government set up a State Land Management Bureau in 1986, established regulations for the transfer of land and rejected private land ownership as a means of land concentration.

With the collapse of the collective structure, it was not always clear just which organisation owned collective land. There was also some destruction of collective assets before new forms of co-operative (share-owning) management could be instituted. We have noted above the problem of water-works; the same applied to other collective assets and some schools closed. Once the burden for rural education fell on *xiang* governments, those bodies were authorised to levy education taxes but these often proved insufficient. Thus school enrolment dropped. The percentage of the rural labour force that was illiterate rose from 21 per cent in 1984 to nearly 23 per cent in 1989 and, due to the decline in school enrolments in the 1980s, may be expected to rise further (Yeh 1992: pp. 510–11). The number of 'barefoot doctors' also declined and was not matched by an adequate increase in the regular medical network. This must have contributed to the slight rise in the rural mortality rate. In 1980, China's mortality rate was the lowest in the third world but thereafter began to rise (until 1990). That rise was underscored by the growth of female infanticide, discussed in a later chapter. That chapter will consider also the glaring contradiction between the household contracting system and policies to restrict the birth rate.

Problems occurred also in the growth of the free market system. Whilst peasants near to towns prospered, those in the deep countryside could not avail themselves of the new opportunities. The search for markets led to long-distance trade (permitted after 1982), re-selling and speculation. And because peasants were unused to dealing with state agencies they were often fleeced by the latter, who took advantage of their monopoly position and demanded kick-backs. State agencies were sometimes unwilling to deal with peasants (especially in providing chemical fertiliser) and banks were not always willing to trust peasants with loans. Of course, village cadres soon stepped in and in the process enriched themselves.

The Changed Role of Rural Cadres

The Introduction to this book and the first section of this chapter raised the question as to whether power relations in the Chinese countryside should best be seen in terms of cycles of coercion and relaxation in a market direction, or in terms of local cadres manipulating clientel relationships. Adopting the former approach might lead to the conclusion that the power of local cadres has weakened. A strong case may be made, however, that rather than weakening the power of local cadres, de-collectivisation has given them new roles as 'gatekeepers' between peasant and state. In the 1980s, they manipulated grain sales as surely as they controlled procurement in the past. In the early part of the decade, it will be remembered that, contrary to expectations, grain supplies increased. Granaries could not cope. Cadres in charge of granaries often classified grain as 'sub-standard' and rejected it or took bribes to make a favourable classification. Since peasants did not know the official procurement price, granary cadres might buy grain at a low price and keep the difference. Middle persons also appeared who bought grain from peasants at very low prices and used their connections to sell it to the granaries at a profit. Peasants might have to wait a considerable period of time to get their grain into granaries; they went into debt, awaiting payment, and a considerable portion of their grain went rotten. Recourse to the free market, moreover, became unattractive as increased supply depressed prices there. The state, officially obliged to buy grain, sometimes purchased what peasants said they had produced and allowed them to store it themselves for a fee. Some of this grain turned out not to exist, either because cadres had not time to make appropriate checks or because they were corrupt. Other grain was turned over to households which negotiated a storage contract – which added costs to the procurement of grain, subsidised increasingly from general revenue.

By the mid-1980s, therefore, the government had to devise a new system which would reduce speculation, reduce subsidies, promote a more rapid diversification of agricultural production and guarantee a supply of grain to the cities and grain-deficient areas. The reforms of 1985, which appeared to remove controls and then reimposed them, exacerbated the tension between authorities and peasants. At first sight, the reforms were to establish more direct links between state purchasing authorities and peasants without the intermediary of village (formerly brigade) cadres. In reality, village government became active in reimposing control and limiting the market. Local government, furthermore, sometimes imposed block-ades to ensure contract fulfilment. We see here the classic contra-diction between what Schurmann called decentralisation I (to economic units) and II (to local areas). Planning has meant different things at different levels and contradictions between levels have hampered economic activity.

Decentralisation of power to local areas in a situation where local government has inadequate funds has resulted in a plethora of local levies made upon peasants. Local cadres believe this to be permissible because of the very low relative tax burden of peasants. Local levies, however, have intensified the hostility between peasants and cadres and have resulted in peasants taking revenge against them (Ash 1991: p. 510; Burns 1989a: p. 492). More generally, cadres are continually suspected of corruption. Such suspicions are surely inevitable in a system where cadres have been responsible for distributing land, have used clientel criteria in turning the village, in Oi's words, into a 'franchising company', and have demanded profits from or shares in lucrative enterprises. They have run the only employment agency; they still influence access to the use of tractors and play a major part in companies which serve as market brokers. Cadres have been the major allocators of state-supplied and rationed farm inputs (priced lower than the free market) and have created artificial shortages to jack up prices (a major source of unrest in 1987) though the government has tried to change the situation either by specifying alternative sources of rationed items or reducing the scope of rationing. The role of cadres has changed, and ultimately they cannot prevent entrepreneurial peasants with sufficient will escaping their control, but more commonly they form alliances with entrepreneurial peasants who do not seek an independent path and they still exercise considerable power over the majority. Now basic grain supplies are no longer guaranteed, a vulnerable peasant, exposed to market competition, might be more disposed to turn to the cadre for patronage. Some of these cadres have 'become prosperous first' and, like most in that category, are envied by local people. Indeed, observers remark, cadres or former cadres seem to have done very well out of the new system, though some challenge that observation (Odgaard: 1992). One survey of 21,000 prosperous families in Shanxi province in 1984 shows that 43 per cent of them were headed by brigade and team cadres or former cadres; this brings into a question the charge that the bulk of commune and brigade cadres in the past were incompetent. Another 42 per cent were rusticated educated youth (formerly considered incapable of assimilation) and demobilised soldiers. Skilled industrial workers were 9 per cent. Only 5 per cent were skilled peasants (Oi 1989: pp. 183–226; Riskin 1987: p. 308).

Rural cadres are still very influential. Though the source of envy and resentment, they have been instrumental in reviving the old institution of village compacts, designed to promote harmony and commitment to the existing order. Yet the new compacts have a new function. They are designed not just to maintain law and order but to counteract the divisive effects of the introduction of market relations (settling questions of land claims and the like). Little has been written on their operations but pioneering work by Anagnost (1992) points to questions of vital relevance. Do such compacts simply represent new forms of control exercised by a coercive state or organisations mid-way between the state and an emerging civil society, reflecting new forms of adaptation by clientel relationships to the realities of the market? It is too early to say whether or not a civil society is emerging in rural China. While groups of self-organised specialist producers abound, one cannot be sure as to whether state control is any less (White 1993b: pp. 227–8). We shall return to the vexed question as to whether a civil society is emerging in China in the next chapter.

Taking account of the fact that local cadres still enjoy considerable power, we must return to another question raised in our Introduction. If it can be demonstrated that cadres are not simply the agents of a coercive state, have been successful in acting as brokers between state and society and still continue to play that role, then is there any reason to believe that continued economic reforms are resulting in a freer, much less a democratic, society? The evidence presented in this chapter is mixed. Land reform was imposed by work teams sent down from higher levels but was twisted in particular directions by local activists. The unified purchase and marketing of grain was sometimes achieved through coercion yet was always modified by local networks of dependency. Collectivisation and the Great Leap Forward were surely exercises in coercive mobilisation, yet over the long term, cadres could rectify the excesses of their successor campaigns (such as the Socialist Education Movement) and blunt their impact, if only to be accused later as 'corrupt'. The Cultural Revolution, moreover, was never a specifically rural phenomenon. Its policies were eventually imported into the countryside, resulted in the 'flying leap', but eventually receded in the face of dependent relations of power. The new policies of the 1980s and 1990s promise perhaps the same scenario. The market is bounded by networks of dependency which might subvert the best intentions of China's leaders. Such should be borne in mind when we consider the new forms of co-operation which have developed in the late 1980s and 1990s.

Initially, cadres were to supervise a three-stage process, consisting of land allocation, taking measures to ensure land concentration, and developing new forms of co-operation. Some of the resulting forms of co-operation are not all that new, with mutual-aid teams reappearing and loosely structured 'agricultural groups' taking on some of the functions of the old production teams. Sometimes collective labour can be obtained for infrastructural projects in return for extra allocations of land and a supply of land may be retained for the needy (Judd 1992). The momentum of change, however, has been such that local cadres often do not have the wherewithal to achieve effective co-operation, nor to preserve elements of the old welfare provisions such as help for the poor and 'five guarantees' for the aged (though this latter category covered only 0.3 per cent of the rural population in 1981) (Hussain and Feuchtwang 1988: pp. 39, 70–1). Land concentration has been continually frustrated by peasants' unwillingness to abandon the security of land even if they could not farm it, and by rising tenancy fees, no longer paid in grain at low official prices. Meanwhile some 180 million farms remain which need support services. Sometimes cadres have set up service stations which provide aid for specialised handicraft enterprises and play a major role in the formation of a wide variety of economic associations in the countryside. Some of these organisations offer shares and in many ways echo the early co-operatives of Yan'an times. Others are much more modern in attempting to provide collectively run forward and backward linkages to support essentially private agriculture. As Kojima (1988: pp. 723–6) notes, an obvious model which China could follow is Japan, though initial moves in China are rudimentary indeed.

The Situation in the Early 1990s

While most peasants, though not rich, have done very well, the decline in agricultural infrastructure has become obvious to all and official documents of 1991 urged the development of socialised 'collective' services. They indicate perhaps a desire on the part of the leadership for more collective organisations. The question of agricultural investment, moreover, must have become a major topic of local debate. Some scholars argued in the mid-1980s that to maintain the spurt in growth, investment during the last fifteen years of the twentieth century should be some 1,000 to 1,500 billion *yuan*. For the first few years of this period (1986–9) it was only a small fraction of that. Indeed, in 1990 the official proportion of state investment in agricultural capital construction was less than half that of the late 1970s (White 1993b: p. 91). While not everyone might be conscious of the precise figure, the effects are glaring and plans for 1993 call for raising investment by one-third over the previous year (BBC, *Summary of World Broadcasts*/W0266/A/4, 27 Jan. 1993). It also seems that one of the major achievements of the early 1980s, the further improvement of the urban–rural terms of trade, may have been halted. The official prices of farm inputs rose markedly in the late 1980s and have been exacerbated by free and black-market activities (Sicular 1988: pp. 696–700).

Also apparent by the second half of the 1980s were the long-term implications of land contracting. Since plots of land are so small further sub-divisions have been forbidden. This means that if young people get married they cannot usually get a share of land, and women marrying into peasant families, characterised usually as half labour force units, often do not appear in calculations of land allocation. The official answer is that those people will be absorbed into non-agricultural pursuits, and examples have been given where rural industry is most successful. In the long run, however, it is unlikely that those successes will be generalised and a new landless class may come into existence. A lot depends here on the speed with which rural industry may develop. Chinese optimists predict that the proportion of the rural labour force employed in agriculture will decline to 30 per cent by the end of the century. In the decade up until 1991, 100 million people have been moved out of agriculture. Many have sought jobs in the (newly defined) towns. Current policy is to make non agricultural jobs in the countryside for a further 100 million in the next decade. Few consider that this may be achieved, and the way there will be fraught with massive convulsions. Another problem which will undoubtedly arise is that, like Poland, the peasant class will get older and older whilst the labouring or landless class will be young. This could be explosive if adequate jobs are not found; and an aged peasantry does not augur well for efficiency.

Conclusion

As noted in our Introduction, Western scholars (including ourselves) have frequently been excessively optimistic or excessively pessimistic about China. After the Great Leap some pessimists saw China locked in a 'downward spiral', at the end of which was an economic disaster even greater than that endured in 1960–1. To many in the mid-1970s, Chinese agriculture had vindicated socialist planning and provided a model for the third world. When better statistics became available, China's socialist model was seen as defective. There followed exaggerated enthusiasm for the reforms of the early 1980s which saw unprecedented growth rates and increase in income. Greater income inequalities were tolerated because, in GINI terms, they were small and seemed to justify a Rawlsian 'difference principle' where inequalities may be tolerated if they help those at the bottom of the pile. By the same Rawlsian logic, however, there was no equal parcel of liberties, as is manifest by the new forms clientel politics have taken. Nor can there be fair equality of opportunity so long as rural areas continue to be discriminated against with regard to everything except calorie intake; one thinks here of things like terms of trade and educational opportunities. For all his advocacy of ending the 'major differences', Mao failed to close the urban–rural gap and one expects that current 'trickle down' theories will achieve no better.

Scholars are still not all agreed on why socialist agriculture in China achieved much less than we once thought. Most people of a liberal economic persuasion blame collectivisation. But whilst collective agriculture was deficient in providing some foodstuffs, the current view that there are no economies of scale in agriculture is far from proven. In this chapter we have found arguments about replacing price planning by production planning and failing adequately to tackle the price scissors more pervasive. Of course, collectivisation was seen as a necessary condition for production planning. But surely a collective sector is capable of responding to price planning also. Clearly, collective leadership often proved incapable of effective management. But the effectiveness of current village leadership in managing a quasi market economy is still an open question. What little evidence we have seems to indicate that local leadership has proved quite effective in reproducing patron–client relationships at the expense of the non-clients. Those non-clients are usually much better off than before, but are they secure?

Security aside, there was a tremendous improvement in the livelihood of rural people in the early 1980s and to some extent that continued in the second half of the decade. As we have seen, however, agriculture has lost its dynamism. Market reformers fervently hope that further liberalisation will improve the situation and moves toward a more market-oriented pattern of appropriation in 1993 have given them heart (Watson 1993). But every move in a market direction has led to unforeseen consequences and dramatic reversals of policy. We still see, it seems, what Shue described as bold moves followed by rectification. In the meantime, massive contradictions exist between political imperatives (maintaining subsidies) and market incentives, between government, central and local, and unit economic activity. And China's arable area declines. In 1978 it was 99 million hectares. In 1986 it had declined to 96 and in the year 2000 it is forecast to be 91. Due to sensitivity about the costs of multiple cropping, moreover, this has not been compensated for, as in the past, by an increase in the sown area; indeed the sown area declined faster than the arable area, from 151 million hectares in 1978 to 144 in 1986 (Walker 1988: pp. 593–9) though official accounts in 1993 speak of it being some 149 (BBC,

Summary of World Broadcasts/FE/W0270/A/3, 24 Feb. 1993). And lurking behind the economic and political debate are massive ecological problems – the whole gamut of problems labelled 'sustainable development' – so important for a small and declining arable land area. Faced with those, pessimism and optimism are luxuries we can do without.

4

State, Enterprise
and Town

Over the past few decades, scholars have analysed sprawling third world cities and the growing inequality within them. Observing towns in general, they have noted the decline of community and growing anomie. What is remarkable about China in the 1960s and 1970s was that effective policies were adopted to prevent urban sprawl and inequalities remained small. Measures were taken to create urban communities. Yet, we have noted, the industrialising strategy perpetuated considerable urban bias despite Mao's injunction to close the urban–rural gap. The nature of urban communities, moreover, left much to be desired. Community feeling certainly developed but so also did coercion. This chapter will consider the questions raised in our Introduction, the most important of which is the extent to which urban anomie might be the price of urban freedom? We question also the Chinese approach to urban community building which often fused together units of production, administration and residence. Did that fusion lead inevitably to major economic problems, particularly in the more market-oriented 1980s? What specific problems arose from considering an enterprise sometimes as an actor on the market, sometimes as a community and sometimes as a bureaucratic outpost? How was it possible to reform those enterprises? In the absence of a universal welfare system, we asked in our Introduction about the dangers of welfare provision depending on the resources of various enterprise-based and non-enterprise based communities? Is the result envy, a fractured larger community and the entrenchment of a labour aristocracy not always attuned to economic reform? What are the benefits and costs of the considerable subsidies provided for urban consumers, in particular in the field of housing? Finally, as grey monochrome towns begin to display the colour of Chinese towns elsewhere, would we be rash in concluding that the change has always been for the better? Are the new class relations which are developing universally acclaimed?

Early Twentieth-Century Towns

The Chinese word for town is *chengshi*. The *cheng* character originally referred to walled towns which were essentially bureaucratic outposts, whilst the *shi* character referred to market towns. Market towns, however, developed without any of the independence one usually associates with such structures in the West. This was simply because, whilst economic development occurred, there was no indigenous bourgeoisie. Many reasons have been put forward for this, the most important being that despite the comparatively low status given to merchants, those who engaged in commerce could move into the landowning classes and then into the bureaucracy and did not form a stratum insulated from access to power as in the 'feudal' West and Japan. The town, therefore, whilst a site of wealth, did not become an alternative site of power. With no relatively independent towns in China and with an élite drawn in large part from rural landowners but required to study and work in the towns, the dividing line between urban and rural life was less clear-cut than in the West. As administrative centres, moreover, contrary to the West, towns were the site of orthodoxy.

By the nineteenth century there were some two thousand administrative towns at *xian* level and a national capital with a population of about one million. Linked to the rural areas by bi-directional mobility, those towns maintained associations of local people drawn from particular rural areas and these might specialise in certain trades and form guilds. The guilds, containing both rich and poor members, were integrated by complex patron–client relations which, like the secret societies with which they were often linked, might take the form of quasi-kinship relations. Those guilds, in addition to organising apprenticeships, disciplining members and fixing prices, organised worship and were responsible for the provision of many urban services such as local policing and fire protection. They might also arrange for their deceased members to be sent back to their rural place of origin (Whyte and Parish 1984: pp. 9–13).

The impact of the West, however, produced a new kind of town – the treaty port, of which there were over 90. In those ports, there were special areas for foreigners (subject to foreign law and policed by foreigners). In many of them, modern forms of organisation developed, together with chambers of commerce, trade unions and political parties. Where modern institutions replaced traditional ones, the organic link between rural and urban areas was severed, resulting in the appearance of large numbers of rootless beggars and prostitutes. Migration, moreover, resulted in an excess male population. In such a situation, new forms of quasi-kinship organisation sprang up, usually linked even closer with secret societies. Among these were the labour contracting networks, which offered a minimum of security for migrants into the towns in return for a substantial portion of their wages once the contractor had found them a job. Those organisations might be looked on favourably by some of their members, but they were highly exploitative and there were clear links with crime.

As one might expect, the Communist Party opposed the foreign domination of significant parts of the industrial sector and 'comprador' capital. It opposed also what it called 'bureaucratic capitalists'. That class owed its origin to the fact that provincial administrations had promoted industry in the nineteenth century by the initial use of state funds and had then sold all or parts of those industries to individual shareholders, many of whom were foreigners or 'compradors', but a significant number might be government officials. In such a situation the relationship between the state and the private sector was extremely complex. With the change of régime, it was relatively easy to eliminate that class. What is striking, however, is that, forty years later, a return to the market seems to be producing a new complex network of bureaucratic capital in which state and private ownership merge, producing, in Solinger's (1992: p. 122) controversial words, a less sharp distinction between state and civil society than under Mao.

From the perspective of the late 1940s, however, the task of establishing macro-economic control seemed simple. We have seen that heavy industry in the North East was already in state hands. As for small business, socialisation was not part of the 'new democratic' agenda. At that time, the Communist Party's target for reform was not so much small business but what was felt to be the depraved nature of urban life. From a Marxist viewpoint, the Party wished to transform 'consumer' cities into 'producer' ones. As the Party swept to victory in the late 1940s, it was determined to change what it felt to be the 'parasitic' nature of cities. The rural leaders, moreover, suspected the Party's urban underground of collaboration with all sorts of unsavoury elements, as we have noted, and that hostility remained right through until the Cultural Revolution, when a large number of former urban leaders found themselves the object of struggle.

Establishment of Control

In 1948–9, military control commissions took charge of organisations and enterprises run by the former régime and, after making inventories, handed them over to newly formed 'people's organisations'. Though varying in composition at different levels, these consisted of personnel retained from the old régime, representatives of mass organisations ('red' labour unions, worker picket organisations etc.) and Party-military personnel (Barnett 1963: p. 340). At the same time, local activists registered the urban population (through controlling grain supplies), rounded-up 'vagrants' (*youmin*), employed them on construction tasks at low wages and extended inventory work. By controlling financial institutions, the government brought down the inflation rate and established consumer co-operatives. At the same time, local authorities published a stream of regulations to control and restrict private service organisations.

At first sight the establishment of control appears to have been successful. Figures, published in 1980, claim that the crime rate was reduced from 9.3 per 10,000 in 1950 to 4.2 per 10,000 in 1952, though we do not know to which crimes these referred nor how they were calculated (Whyte and Parish 1984: p. 249). We do know, however, that control was bedevilled by weakness in leadership. Some Party branches, out of enthusiasm or distrust, took everything on to their own shoulders whilst others appeared passive in the face of routine. This latter deviation was particularly marked in the newly formed labour unions which, once jerked into action, began to pursue policies which Party leaders considered to be 'economistic' and even worse. In response, unions were effectively subordinated to Party leadership. But rapid recruitment made the Party itself seem weak; factories at that time showed increases in Party membership from some 3 per cent to between 10 and 30 per cent, of whom large numbers were skilled workers and technicians retained from pre-liberation days. One can understand why Party leaders were concerned that these new recruits may not have been as keen on the goals set by the Party leadership as it would have wished. There were problems also of old cadres resting on their laurels and accusing their critics of 'taking a rural viewpoint' (Brugger 1976: p. 87).

Inexperience and laziness were not the only problems. Some Party branches had been infiltrated by the old simulated kinship structures, such as secret societies and the gang-boss network. To eradicate them, a 'democratic reform movement' was launched immediately after taking over North East China with apparently much success. In other places, particularly in the construction industry, former gang-bosses still practised extortion and often infiltrated or took-over Party committees. Various secret societies such as the notorious Green Gang and the *Yi Guan Dao* were still in existence, as were *banghui* (mutual aid groups which were often protection rackets) (Brugger 1976: p. 105).

In response, the 'democratic reform movement' was intensified in June 1950, though that response was sluggish. Cadres were unsure how to eradicate the gang-boss system without harming production, how to distinguish gang-bosses among skilled workers or how to deal with the informal structure within factories. With the advent of the Korean War, however, official attitudes hardened and a major campaign against 'counter-revolutionaries' was set in motion with ruthless consequences. At the same time, greater pressure was placed on foreign firms and businessmen and large numbers of foreigners were persuaded to leave. A nation-wide propaganda network was established to eradicate foreign culture, drugs, prostitution and gambling. *Guomindang* textbooks were removed and there was a general campaign against 'cultural imperialism' in education and foreign control of religious bodies. Churches were forced to adhere to a new policy which, contrary to the beliefs of Catholics and Jehovah's Witnesses, demanded an oath of loyalty.

By August 1951, the various movements under way merged into one to 'increase production and practise economy' and later a 'three anti movement' which, as we have seen, took as its main targets graft, waste and bureaucratism. The movement widened in January 1952 to take in businessmen. Former capitalists now employed in the state sector, it was argued, were using economic information to help their relatives and colleagues in the private sector and government officials were taking bribes to treat former capitalists leniently. The 'five anti' movement, aimed at the private sector, took as its targets bribery, tax evasion, theft of state property, cheating on government contracts, and stealing state economic information (Gardner 1969). Selected businessmen were required to confess their misdemeanours, though predictably most tried to defend their position. Responding in February 1952, the Party imposed regulations such as being confined to one's place of work and being forbidden to go out of business, to conclude deals with certain people in the public sector, to dismiss employees and to withhold or lower wages. Labour unions also mobilised industrial and shop workers to investigate and denounce their employers. When the movements got out of hand and production suffered in March 1952, the movements were terminated. They had succeeded, however, in the sense of laying the basis for an orderly system of administration – the Soviet model.

The Soviet Model

We described the broad features of the Soviet model and its patterns of vertical administration in Chapter 1. It rested on a 'stick and carrot' policy. The latter awarded material incentives (piecework and managerial bonuses) and designated model workers. The 'stick' policy was initiated by a top-down rectification movement, resulting in a tight system of responsibility and a system of 'one-person' management which subordinated all staff functions to line management. The education system, moreover, became highly specialised and technocratic, with the old liberal universities, modelled on a Euro-American pattern, supplemented by the Soviet system of technical academies. Education was equated with *schooling* and obviously the children of the urban well-to-do did better than others. The children of cadres, however, were the objects of active positive discrimination.

The Soviet model required that all social organisations be classified and their organisation specified. Obviously, therefore, there had to be an official demarcation of what constituted 'urban' and 'rural'. In 1955 officially designated towns included seats of *xian* government and settlements with a population of over 2,000 at least half of whom were not agricultural. Larger settlements with a higher proportion of the population in agriculture were denied classification as towns (Lee Yok-shiu 1989).

The Soviet model also required specifications for urban organisation. By the time of the three and five-anti movements, parts of China's urban population had been organised in street committees which, in turn, were divided into residents' groups (Schurmann 1966: pp. 374–80). Those organisations, which were nominally elected but usually in practice appointed, undertook such tasks as settling disputes, sanitation, literacy work and, of course political mobilisation. Though not formally part of government, the residents' committees' did in fact constitute the farthest reach of the state. Formally, however, the lowest level of government administration in the towns, introduced after the five anti movement, was the street office (*jie gongsuo*) which was articulated to ward (*qu*) and municipal (*shi*) government and which maintained links with the urban police force.

Those parallel bodies were responsible for continued urban registration which was made extremely difficult by the massive increase in urban population (40 per cent between 1950 and 1953). They replaced the multiplicity of *ad hoc* committees set up after 1949 and, by 1954, had stabilised to the point that formal regulations could be issued governing them. Street offices became mandatory in towns of more than 100,000 people and optional in towns of between 50,000 and 100,000. Their area of jurisdiction was exactly coterminous with local police stations (*paichusuo*) which maintained a system of permanent 'household register policemen' (*hujijing*) within each residential area. Each street office supervised a residents' committee which consisted of the representatives of some 100–600 households and was subdivided into a number of residents' groups of 15–40 households.

In the early 1950s, therefore, the urban population was organised in a dualistic structure of residents' organisations and work units. The provision of welfare reflected that division. Rather than a universalistic welfare system, there developed a hierarchical one with employees in the state bureaucracy or in state enterprises at the top. Most of those state employees received lavish sick and maternity leave provisions. They qualified for generous retirement benefits, paid for by their units, and perhaps superior housing and other services. They could receive hardship allowances or special allowances for crisis situations. Outside that sector, however, provision was minimal, the state expecting families to take care of their sick and aged. Whilst 'homes for the respect of the aged' and relief provisions existed, the really impoverished were old people who had never worked in a state unit and who had no children.

Clearly both work units and residents' organisations played a major part in social control. Most of the larger work units maintained a security office, which played the same role as the local police station in the residents' organisations. They might also impose administrative sanctions upon members, provide information and education and mobilise workers and dependents for the various movements. Since they controlled workers' livelihood, they had much more powerful coercive means at their disposal than residents' organisations. They could both coerce and reward more effectively. But here we return to the problem raised in our Introduction and the beginning of this chapter – the relationship between control and a sense of community. In the retrospect of the 1990s, we recall the greater importance of the surveillance function and the loss of privacy. Yet it is fair to say that the dualistic structure of urban organisation managed to prevent many problems characteristic of urban centres in developing countries. Though there was undoubtedly considerable resentment at the myriad eyes which checked on the urban resident, there was less anomie, reflected in a low crime rate. Again, citing the unexplained 1980 figures referred to earlier, the crime rate stabilised at some 4.5 per 10,000 from 1950 to 1963. This, according to Martin Whyte and William Parish (1984: pp. 231–73), reflected greater solidarity, greater fear and also greater opportunities for upward mobility. It was only later that the third of those conditions disappeared and generated major problems.

The Socialisation of Industry and Commerce

The 'five anti' movement of 1952 left some 30 per cent of China's total production in private hands. With the 'General Line of

Transition to Socialism' in 1953, however, it became clear that the private sector would soon be brought under state or joint public–private control. In September 1954, the State Council passed temporary regulations on joint state–private enterprises which established 'joint public–private' (or 'joint state–private') as the prescribed form of operation for formerly private concerns. Small traders or service concerns, however, would be co-operativised rather than socialised. The normal method of joint public–private operation was for the state or local government to take over ownership of a concern, paying the former owner 1 to 5 per cent per annum 'fixed interest' (*dingxi*), while still employing him or her to manage the concern at a fixed salary. Most capitalists in this category did not do much better than skilled workers, especially since they might be urged to spend their fixed interest payments on government bonds. Indeed payment to state capitalists between 1956 and 1966 amounted to some 1.2 billion *yuan*, roughly US $44 per recipient per annum (Riskin 1987: p. 97). From a Marxist view, however, those capitalists were still exploiters. But before it could worry about such problems, the Party had to ensure that the socialisation process was achieved without too much disruption of production.

Between 1952 and 1955, the state had achieved some socialisation but, at that time, planning was the major preoccupation. Controls imposed over the distribution of certain goods effectively turned many private shops into agencies of the state marketing organs which had already come to control the bulk of wholesale outlets. Since price controls often left retailers small profit margins, a guaranteed 5 per cent per annum began to look attractive. There were a number of problems, however, which suggested that the pace of socialisation should be forced. Shopkeepers, faced with eventual socialisation, were often unwilling to invest large sums of money in their businesses. Insufficient goods were purchased from wholesalers which led to stockpiling and waste. Private industry tended to neglect quality as it sought to make as much money as possible before the axe fell and private entrepreneurs seemed unwilling to share technical knowledge with people in the public sector.

By early 1955, the problems in the private sector were such that the government found itself supporting all sorts of conservative policies just to keep trade and industry moving. Trade fairs were organised which by-passed the state marketing organs. State banks made loans to private businessmen who were unwilling to continue investing capital in their concerns. Goods were redirected from co-operatives to private concerns and regulations governing some goods were relaxed. Senior cadres were so concerned that production and distribution would be disrupted by a lack of business confidence that, once the rural sector radicalised after Mao's speech of 31 July 1955, they tried to convince businessmen that a similar radicalisation would not occur in the urban sector. They soon, however, set about making sure that it did, in fact, occur.

By August, plans were being actively pursued to effect socialist transformation. Investigation teams were formed. United Front-type organisations of businessmen, such as federations of industry and commerce, became active in preparing the ground and shops were reorganised according to specified lines of work (often through existing guilds). As in the rural sector, there was a need for more and more cadres to supervise the work. Some might be found in the labour unions but many were businessmen themselves who were retrained in numerous study courses. By October 1955, Mao called for a speed-up and in December revised the original plan for completing the transformation by 1962 to 90 per cent completion by 1957. Progress was even quicker. Meetings of businessmen were hastily organised to petition local government to reorganise their concerns into joint public–private enterprises and the target dates were progressively brought forward. Chen Yun, far from the cautious man often portrayed in the literature, took the lead. But he was outpaced by Beijing's mayor, Peng Zhen, who managed to convert all private industry, commerce and handicrafts in the capital within the first twelve days of January 1956 (MacFarquhar 1974: pp. 23–4). This pattern was soon copied in other cities, where United Front bodies, reminiscent of the five anti movement, busied themselves in assisting the reorganisation of whole lines of business and attending parades to celebrate the successful 'completion' of the task.

But what was implied by completion? It could not have meant that reorganisation had resulted in stable forms of management. Since inventories were often made before the State Council Regulations for Inventories and Assessments were promulgated, they were frequently quite inaccurate. Cadres were unsure, therefore, about the assets they were to reallocate. Nor had cadres any guidelines on how the process of amalgamation was to proceed and firms often got bigger and bigger to the point where management became most confused. Faced with such a situation, Mao was somewhat critical of the Beijing experiences. Yet socialisation could not be stopped and the period of consolidation which occurred in 1956 was used to sort out the problems.

We have seen that a second aspect of the socialisation campaign of the mid-1950s was to reorganise large numbers of shopkeepers, hawkers and service providers into collectives. The word 'collective' is a very loose one, covering huge firms indistinguishable from state organisations to a handful of service providers. What theoretically distinguished a collective from a state organisation was that it was responsible for its profits and losses and could go out of business. Notionally it could generate incomes higher than in the state sector, though in practice the collective sector was discriminated against in taxation policy and the like. Bearing responsibility for losses, moreover, only seemed to apply to the small collectives.

The Reassertion of Party Control

Party control was reasserted with accelerated co-operativisation and the socialisation of industry and commerce. We described above the implications of 'one person' management for Party control. As early as 1954, there were clear signs of dissatisfaction with the system (Schurmann 1966: p. 263). Presumably under the protection afforded by the new principle of 'collective leadership', adopted after the death of Stalin, press articles showed that factories indicated their implementation of the principle of 'responsibility of the factory general manager under the unified leadership of enterprise Party committee' *despite* current policy. Other articles described opposition to one-person management and the fact that the Party committee in some enterprises had been reduced to merely 'staff' status. Contrary to normal practice, little attempt was made to refute the critics and by 1955 articles appeared criticising the extent to which the system had, in the past, been introduced too precipitately (Schurmann 1966: pp. 272–8). Finally, in 1956, as we saw earlier, the system was formally abolished. Critics of the rigid Soviet system might, of course, be both relatively liberal or radical. Clearly though, it was the latter who triumphed in the political economic debates of the mid-1950s and vertical administrative control was diluted by local political mobilisation by a Party which was none the less vertically organised. The Anti-rightist movement, discussed in other chapters, saw increasing radicalisation along those lines. The effect of that movement on urban life was quite considerable. The intellectual world was most obviously affected but so also were trade unions which were locked into one of the most vertically-integrated of structures. Such bodies were brought under specifically Party control. Party leadership in state enterprises, furthermore, led to a revaluation of the relationship between virtue (*de*) (later called 'redness') and expertise (*cai*) and to the relationships among politics, policy and operations. These were major themes in the Great Leap Forward.

The Great Leap Forward

Problems of urban planning were exacerbated by the drift of rural people into the towns. Since the Korean War, official policy was to shift resources to smaller interior cities and discourage the growth of the very large cities, in fact to restore the relatively even distribution of urban areas which had existed before the impact of the West. But unlike the situation in former times, moves were made to prevent the relatively free flow of people into urban areas and, in particular, large cities. As we have noted, however, control of population was at first not successful. It was to be implemented by the household register system which was extended to most of the rural areas in 1958, but, given the production-mania of the time, was still not effective in stemming the tide in that year. The single-minded stress on production, moreover, reduced expenditure on urban housing from the 9 per cent of basic construction funds allocated in earlier years to under 3 per cent (Lee Yok-shiu 1988: pp. 388–90). Apparently urban residence and expenditure on urban housing was 'revisionist'.

We have seen that the establishment of residents' committees in the 1950s and the take over of industry had produced a dualistic structure. Ideally the orientation of employees should be to their work-unit (*danwei*). This was more than just a place of work. Work units might run residential compounds, organise services, distribute goods, perform policing duties and much else, depending on the resources at their disposal. Many of their members, however, would also be members of residents' groups which were organised usually by non-employees. The Great Leap spirit was to integrate the two types of organisation by creating urban communes. The urban communes were supposed to serve the social goal of creating new communities and the economic goal of rapidly expanding the opportunities for town employment.

The model put forward in 1958 was the Zhengzhou urban people's commune, where a factory became the nucleus of a people's commune which took in the entire surrounding population of 10,500 people (Salaff 1967). New satellite factories were set up around the core factory to employ dependants and process waste. All commercial and service facilities in the area (formerly run by the city) were taken over and organised by the commune. A 'red and expert' university was set up together with elementary and night schools. The entire neighbourhood was organised into a militia unit and, perhaps most significant, two agricultural production brigades and one sheep milk station were attached. The Zhengzhou commune was, of course, just a model and most of the communes formed in late 1958 fell short of its ideals. This was inevitable where funds were inadequate and the relocation of housing was difficult (as in Shanghai). Most communes, therefore, were simply amalgamations of the former network of street administrations which, although useful in generating employment, were nothing like as comprehensive as the Zhengzhou type and in some cities it seemed that no attempts were made to establish communes at all. Even the model Zhengzhou commune fell far short of its ideals. For example, the core factory was technically provincially-owned whereas the other property was collectively-owned. There were thus conflicting lines of authority. Second, there were wide disparities in wage structures; the workers in the core factory were paid at a much higher rate than those in satellite factories and the peasants still operated according to a work-point system.

As the economy worsened in the wake of the leap, urban communes came to be less the product of organisational inspiration and more an attempt merely to solve the problems of food production and distribution and to keep small industry in the towns alive. Wherever possible, suburbs were combined with agricultural production brigades to produce communes more or less self-sufficient in food. Most of the 1960 communes were not combined with regular industrial enterprises and consisted largely of house-wives and family dependants, with many of the male residents leaving the commune every day to work in regular factories. These later communes tended to be huge. The original Red Flag Commune of Zhengzhou expanded seven fold from 4,684 house-holds in 24 streets to 150,000 people and consisted of sub-divisions each larger than the original commune (Salaff 1967: p. 108). Thus many of the urban communes, which continued in existence throughout the 1960s, were little more than synonyms for urban wards (*qu*).

Although the 1960 urban communes were not very successful *qua* communes, various policies with which they were associated were revived later in the 1960s. Many of the locally run child-care centres and service points set up in 1960 obtained a new lease of life, and the urban commune policy, whereby urban residents combined and pooled their own funds to set up small industries, continued. In the really critical years of 1960–2, their activities were limited, but in the period immediately prior to the Cultural Revolution, there were many urban small industries in operation. Yet, as in so many areas, the 1960s saw a return to old forms of organisation. The old network of street offices with parallel street committees was revamped, even though the name 'commune' might be retained. At the same time, the state once again licensed individual service providers, though the service sector remained very small.

In the early 1960s, urban policy in general and industrial policy in particular was *ad hoc*. As we commented in Chapter 1, with the breakdown of the planning system, industrial departments frequently held 'commodity exchange conferences' and direct links were often established between producers and consumers. Rural units, for example, might enter into contact with particular consumer co-operatives or shops in the towns. In a desperate situation, 'black-market' dealings were often tolerated or simply countered by allowing government shops to include off-ration goods at higher prices. In industry, while central control was strengthened, especially over finance, and a number of closures, transfers and stoppages were ordered, enterprises were allowed much greater economic independence. For this managers were castigated for being unduly driven by the profit-motive and, indeed, as the bad times receded there was much discussion of shoring up the 'red' side in the 'red–expert' dichotomy and restoring 'politics' to a position of 'command' in industrial work, as exemplified in Mao's 'Anshan Constitution, which called for mass movements, cadre participation in manual labour, worker participation in management, the reform of irrational and outdated rules and regulations, the close co-operation among workers, cadres and technicians and a fostering of the movement for technical innovation (*Peking Review*, 16, 17 April 1970: p. 3; 14, 3 April 1970: p. 11). As we noted earlier, some of that spirit was implemented after 1962 (Andors 1974), though one gets the general impression that industrial management returned to a more technocratic mode, according to the seventy-point document for industry discussed in Chapter 1. Policy in the early 1960s called for the development of contractual relationships, the creation of networks of specialised enterprises, and some semi-autonomous vertically integrated 'trusts'. There was also much more concern for workers' health and safety.

It was clear by the early 1960s that the strict policies of rural registration introduced in 1958 had failed adequately to stabilise the urban population. By the spring of 1962, as a last-ditch measure to solve the urban food problem, the government had no course but to transfer physically large numbers of the urban population to the rural areas. A campaign was launched in April 1962 known as *huixiang* ('back to the village') whereby people were urged to return to their native areas (even if they were 'ancestral homes' with which their connection was purely historical) (Schurmann 1966: pp. 399–402). Assessments of the result are mixed. On the one hand, it can be argued that, though the Great Leap failed to prevent the drift of people into the cities and resulted in drastic transfers of population in the early 1960s, policies inaugurated at that time eventually brought about a situation where mobility from large cities to small ones and from urban to rural areas was encouraged (particularly by the *xiaxiang* of urban youth) whilst movement in the opposite direction became extremely difficult. That policy clearly served the purpose of preventing the polarisation characteristic of other third world countries and the growth of a peripheral group of impoverished migrants which is characteristically difficult to control. It could also serve the socialist purpose of developing stable urban communities which integrate work and residence. On the other hand, the enforcement of household registration policies reflected the fact that one of the conditions identified earlier for relative urban harmony no longer applied. Reducing the surplus urban population might shore up urban solidarity and deterrence of crime might be strengthened but the opportunities for upward mobility (especially for youth) were curtailed. This was to have an impact on growing urban anomie and crime. We return to the question posed at the start of this chapter. Whilst restricting urban freedom for older urban residents was accompanied by less anomie, restricting the freedom of youth actually increased theirs.

Concern with limiting migration resulted in 1963–4 in a re-designation of the criteria for being considered urban. Towns were now specified if they had a population of whom more than 70 per cent were non-agricultural or a population of 2,500–3,000 where more than 85 per cent were non-agricultural. Thus many seats of *xian* government lost their 'urban' status. At the stroke of a pen, the number of officially designated towns declined from 4,429 to 3,148, and the official urban population was reduced by 25 million (Lee Yok-shiu 1989: p. 778).

Though policy in the early 1960s was aimed at reducing the urban population (if in large part only statistically) and de-emphasising the allure of the towns, amidst the contradictory propaganda of that time there were calls to emulate the economic achievements of cities such as Shanghai (*Current Background*, 731, 11 May 1964). But Shanghai was always contradictory. It was economically the most advanced city in China and the most 'bourgeois', yet it also had the most radical leadership and the one most enthusiastic about the Great Leap. Shanghai, moreover, like most cities, was pursuing policies which were considered in the Cultural Revolution to be 'reactionary'. For example, there was an enormous growth in the number of temporary contract workers recruited from the rural areas, in the spirit of the 'seventy articles'. In 1958, there were about 12 million such workers, whereas in the early 1960s that figure increased to some 30–40 per cent of the total non-agricultural workforce. One might argue that the employment of cheap labour actually served to close the urban–rural gap but it also created sharp *intra-urban* differentials which were potentially very divisive and militated against a sense of community.

For all its radical leadership, Shanghai, like other cities, was considered to be experiencing 'revisionism' and in need of reform. For inspiration Mao looked elsewhere. As we saw in Chapter 1, after 1963 Mao endorsed his version of the experiences of the

Daqing oil-field. He stressed the participation of cadres in manual labour and other features of the, as yet unpublicised, Anshan Constitution. Most significant was the military theme. Thus, paralleling the Socialist Education Movement in rural areas, another 'five anti' movement was launched in the cities and urban economic departments were re-established according to the rubric of 'learning from the People's Liberation Army'. Urban political departments were established and even street committees sometimes employed (military-style) 'political instructors' (White 1972: p. 342). Such were felt to be necessary because of 'revisionism' but also because of palpable problems such as the appearance of 'social youth' (hoodlums and petty criminals) who had somehow managed to avoid being sent to the countryside.

The Cultural Revolution

The Cultural Revolution, in addition to paralysing educational institutions throughout China, had a severe impact on industry and commerce in the cities. Joint public and private enterprises were early objects of criticism and the interest earned by 'national capitalists' was suspended. There was also a massive outpouring of all kinds of grievances concerning conditions of work, bonuses, piece-rate systems (sometimes labelled as 'economism'), participation in management, the role of the labour unions (Esmein 1973: p. 174) and the fact that the job assignment system was manipulated in favour of those who came from official backgrounds. As one would expect, a major bone of contention was the status of temporary workers recruited on contract from the countryside. Some advocated that the wages and working conditions of those workers should be raised to the level of regular industrial workers whilst others could not see how job opportunities could be created to accommodate such a demand. Consider also the factionalism in the workers' movement, of which the case of Shanghai is the most famous. There revolutionary rebels demanded workers 'seize power' and run the factories themselves. Before the end of 1966, Jiang Qing echoed their demands and endorsed an attack on the All China Federation of Trade Unions. The Federation collapsed amidst chaos, with different red rebel groups seizing power one from another and various authorities fabricating 'power seizures'. Radical experiments such as the attempt to reorganise cities (notably Shanghai), along the lines of what people believed the Paris Commune of 1871 should have been, failed, and the despatch of troops to 'support the left' often resulted in repression as the army took over public security duties.

This chapter will not narrate the ebbs and flows of radical activity in the tumultuous period of the Cultural Revolution. Suffice it to repeat that, in the wake of the 'January Revolution' of 1967, Mao's preferred model of organisation was clearly that of 1949, now known as the 'revolutionary committee' based on a triple alliance of revolutionary rebels, old cadres and People's Liberation Army. These were set up at all urban administrative levels and units of production in 1967 and 1968. Throughout that period, there was considerable criticism of street cadres (White 1971: p. 339; Salaff 1971: pp. 295–8), exacerbated in many cases by the return of young people from the countryside or the frontier regions where they had been despatched during the Socialist Education Movement. As urban residents' committees organised themselves into 'newspaper reading groups' to formulate criticisms, they made frequent contact with red guard organisations but do not seem to have been greatly influenced by 'ultra-leftism'. The main problem in the residential areas seems to have resulted from the breakdown of the public security network; and occasionally residents' vigilante groups or 'worker pickets' were formed to deal with petty crime (Salaff 1971: pp. 304–8).

The first task in reconstruction was to persuade residential organisations and work units to form revolutionary committees and to help in the decentralisation of urban services. Medical services were reorganised on a local level and integrated with neighbourhood administration. In the spirit of the Great Leap Forward, the stress was on producing more medical workers rather than specialists. Large numbers of paramedical workers were trained who, after a short course of one or two years, could deal with routine medical cases and were responsible for spreading China's medical network to areas where it had hardly existed before.

The decentralisation of services in the towns was part of a general process of urban reorganisation. Here, as elsewhere, the problem was to improve the quality of local cadres. To achieve this, a particular institution was utilised known as the May Seventh Cadre

School (Salaff 1971: pp. 298–312). Such schools were, at first, temporary creations designed to reorient cadres criticised during the Cultural Revolution. They soon became regular institutions. Cadres, at various levels in administration and education, were required to spend a period of time in them, not just studying and discussing their orientation but also engaging in productive labour.

A major task of the newly rehabilitated cadres and propaganda teams was to rebuild neighbourhood committees (street committees and residents' groups) according to the triple combination and the old Yan'an slogan of 'simple administration'. The first residential committees were established in Shanghai as early as March 1967, though it took a whole year before neighbourhood revolutionary committees were set up over the whole city. In other areas, the establishment of street revolutionary committees appears to have been undertaken a little later, though by the second half of 1968 progress was quite rapid. As street revolutionary committees were articulated first to military control commissions and later to higher-level revolutionary committees, the number of rehabilitated urban cadres increased and their street-level mass component decreased.

By the end of 1968, many towns had established revolutionary committees at municipal, ward (*qu*), sub-ward (*fenqu*) and street level. Below that level, the old residents' groups had been reorganised into Mao Zedong Thought study groups. Local public security was in the hands of 'citizens' public security enforcement teams', revived 'worker picket organisations' or bodies known as 'teams for the dictatorship of the masses'. These were soon subordinated to the regular police force but often remained in existence throughout the early 1970s. In many ways, this was a revival of the 1949 system which had been changed once the Soviet model of vertical rule had been adopted. Clearly, residents' committees were service providers and played a role in generating employment. Such was probably one aim of merging neighbour-hood co-operatives with street administration (Bastid 1973: p. 174). Yet that action and many others has been seen by most to reflect the role of residents' committees as mechanisms of control. Half of Whyte and Parish's (1984: pp. 281–90) sample remember them negatively as dominated by aged people of an officious nature, though a quarter spoke of them in more positive light. Perhaps in some cases they served as a buffer between the individual and the state, but never to the same degree as in some rural production teams. In general, they enhanced the reach of that state. We return once again to the relationship between community and coercion.

The 1970s

As the Cultural Revolution wound down after 1969, order was restored in industrial enterprises, cadres were rehabilitated and attempts were made to restore the morale of both workers and management. In the industrial sector, moreover, fears about importing technology were overcome and, as Chapter 1 described, once again complete plants were imported from overseas. In the towns in general, old forms of organisation began to reappear. Illegal peasant hawkers were occasionally seen on the streets. Old doctors started once again to charge fees for private patients and participation in the 'black economy' increased. Yet, according to Whyte and Parish's (1984: p. 30) sample, people who engaged in such practices were only about 3 per cent of the total, presenting a picture very different from the Soviet Union. In the early 1970s, moreover, one saw the revival of semi-legal private activities, such as the 'putting out system' employed by various factories, but these did not amount to much.

Other chapters in this book deal with the political ebbs and flows of the 1970s and the attempt to preserve the 'socialist new things' of the Cultural Revolution. Suffice it to repeat here that after his return in 1973, Deng Xiaoping was eager to see that few 'socialist new things' were retained in industry. As we noted earlier, his 'twenty articles' on industry of 1975 aimed to strengthen discipline (in the face of railway stoppages and the like). The articles stressed orderly planning, inter-enterprise co-ordination, the strengthening of managerial roles (under Party committees), the production responsibility system, incentives 'according to work', and the importance of technology. As we saw in Chapters 1 and 2, the apparent neglect of politics in those articles led to the document being branded a 'poisonous weed' in 1976, though, with the restoration of Deng Xiaoping in 1977, it was elevated to the status of 'fragrant flower' and eventually replaced by another document known as the 'thirty articles' (1978). At the same time the Daqing experience was rewritten in more economistic vein. At the level of high politics there was much drama, and in low politics there was some unrest and even strikes. Yet the overall trend in the early 1970s was towards a reaffirmation of the industrial policies of the early 1960s and, with the removal of the 'Gang of Four' and the shelving of the subsequent 'foreign leap', China's achievements in urban organisation were assessed positively by Western observers.

What had China achieved in urban organisation? As noted in our Introduction, China seemed unique among third world countries in reducing the size of most of its biggest cities and achieving an equal urban spread. There was also a great degree of equality amongst urban residents. According to Whyte and Parish's (1984: pp. 44–5) survey, the poorest 40 per cent of China's urban households received 25 per cent of total income, compared with 15 per cent in twenty-four developing market states. China also did better than other socialist states. Around 1970, the ratio of the highest-paid decile to the lowest was 2.3, similar to Romania and much more equal than the Soviet Union (3.2). Most conspicuous was the absence of an urban 'culture of poverty', characterised by early sexual relations, 'common-law' marriages and shifting residence. Whilst that absence was surely explicable in part by cultural characteristics, since the same pattern may be found in Taiwan and Singapore, much was surely due to the policies of the Chinese government concerning restriction of migration (Whyte and Parish: 1984: pp. 192–4).

Whilst the 80,000 or so high officials (*gaoji ganbu*) above grade 13 in the then 24-grade salary scale for cadres had considerable perquisites (for example housekeepers, access to chauffeur-driven cars and, most significantly, more adequate news and information), their privileges were less marked than in some other socialist states. And their official perquisites were not particularly resented, though many complaints were voiced about unofficial 'back-door' activities (such as getting one's son into college or a good job). Marked privileges extended only to a very few. Middle-level cadres and professionals did not enjoy much better living conditions than others (Whyte and Parish: 1984: pp. 91–3). Of much more significance at that time was continued urban bias – the fact that Mao's attempt to close the urban–rural gap had merely achieved a 3:1 income ratio, comparable to other developing countries, due in part to official restrictions on rural-urban migration (Whyte and Parish: 1984: pp. 51–4). The drive to convert 'consumer' cities into 'producer' cities, moreover, had failed to generate enough jobs, and the *xiafang* system, adopted as a remedy, was increasingly unpopular. Despite impressive rates of growth, a large inefficient labour force eating from the 'iron rice bowl' (state) or 'wooden' one (collective) was resented by those who could not do either. Yet, however privileged they might have been, workers, by 1975, had experienced a 20 per cent drop in real income and resented factory favouritism: the strikes of that year and of 1976 were partly a result.

Relative equality in income was paralleled by relative equality of purchasing power. Despite rises in farm prices over the years, the retail prices of grain and oil remained stable. This subsidy was a 10 per cent addition to every non-agricultural wage by 1979 (Whyte and Parish: 1984: p. 89). Rationing, extended throughout the 1970s, also achieved equity of distribution. On the other hand, subsidizing food and oil imposed severe burdens on the state budget. The rationing system was highly complex, varied from place to place and inevitably gave rise to envy. It was also seen increasingly as a mechanism of control. It imposed severe limits on movement, allowed for discrimination against 'bad' elements and was open to corruption. The latter could take many forms, from supplying information concerning scarce items to forgetting to ask for ration coupons. Butchers apparently were well placed, as they were in wartime Britain. In Guangzhou, it was said, one was fortunate to have good relations with a doctor, a sales clerk and a truck-driver (Whyte and Parish: 1984: p. 97).

The major question, asked by all students of development in the 1970s, was whether basic needs were being met. The answer is a qualified yes and that is no mean achievement. Despite the fact that food expenditure consumed some 55 per cent of average family income (64 per cent for the poorest), which was much the same as capitalist countries with similar levels of income, basic food-grains were adequate and equitably distributed. Vegetables could be obtained, though these were poor in variety and condition. With the exception of Beijing and Shanghai, however, meat and fish were insufficient. Chicken and eggs were difficult to get, a fact which led to some urban dwellers keeping chickens in their often cramped houses (though that practice was forbidden in Beijing and Shanghai). In line with converting cities from centres of consumption to centres of production, the number of retail outlets had declined considerably. In Beijing, for example, despite a large increase in population, the number of retail shops declined to some 10,000, compared with 70,000 in the 1950s. This involved travelling long distances frequently (because of the dearth of refrigerators) and queuing. Some people complained that the work they had to do every Sunday to obtain supplies was much harder than that done at their regular place of employment. And when they reached the shops, sales personnel were frequently surly or lazy.

The supply of non-food items was worse. Although most urban households managed to obtain a watch and a bicycle, repair centres declined in numbers. Furniture was difficult to obtain and of low quality. Radio receivers were easy to purchase but a television set typically had merely a small black and white screen and was beyond the means of all but a tiny minority of individuals (it cost the equivalent of a year's average worker's wage). In general, according to Whyte and Parish's (1984: pp. 85–106) informants, the situation had deteriorated since before the Cultural Revolution and consumers were losing faith with the centralised distribution system.

The education system appeared much better. National figures (rural and urban) showed an adult literacy rate comparable with middle-income countries (70 per cent). Egalitarian policies were said to have resulted in widespread primary school education. The provision of education at higher levels, however, declined sharply, resulting in only 1 per cent of the population enjoying higher education (a significantly lower figure than most low-income countries). Yet the stress on quantity had been achieved at the expense of quality. Since it was very difficult to fail at school, parents constantly complained that they could not make their offspring work hard. The prospect of rustication on graduation from secondary school, moreover, dampened motivation. The abolition of examinations in favour of recommendation led to complaints that cadre children were favoured. We return here to Whyte and Parish's observation that one of the conditions for urban social order – legitimate opportunities for youth – had disappeared. Whether out of considerations of motivation or recognition of sheer logistical problems, major modifications were made to the *xiaxiang* programme after 1974. But by despatching youth simply to camps near the cities rather than to distant areas, the problem of illegal return became more serious and added to social disorder.

The perception of blocked opportunities was exacerbated by former red guards returning illegally from the countryside. They had learnt to distrust authority, had once enjoyed power and now felt betrayed. It is not surprising that the official crime rate rose from the pre-Cultural Revolution figure of 4.5 per 10,000 to 6.5 in 1977–9. These figures, it will be recalled, were unexplained and the rise may simply reflect the fact that after the Cultural Revolution many more things were included under the rubric 'criminal'. Nevertheless, the appearance of street gangs (much the same as in other countries), specialists in magical practices, black marketeers and the like, and the increase in gambling and similar activities are backed up by more than mere anecdotal evidence. That being said, the problem of youth crime in China in the early 1970s was probably significantly less than in most other countries (Whyte and Parish: 1984: pp. 58–62, 246–73).

The contradiction between quantity and quality applied also to health care. Quantitative statistics are very impressive. Nationally the ratio of doctors trained in Western medicine (1:2,470 in 1979) was double that of middle-income countries and four times that of low-income countries. In addition there were large numbers of Chinese herbal doctors, semi-integrated into the same system (1:872) and semi-skilled 'secondary doctors' (1:1,172). The ratio of hospital beds to population was 1:503 (higher than middle-income countries and over three times higher than low-income countries). Life expectancy at birth (68) was significantly higher than middle-income countries. These were national figures. In the larger cities, the figures were, of course, even more impressive. The (Western) doctor/population ratio in Beijing was 1:700 and in Shanghai 1:1,040. The urban provision of hospital beds was 1:206 in 1978 (Davis 1989: p. 586). While registration and medical fees were charged, these were very low. The three-tiered urban medical system, moreover, was superior to anything found in societies with a comparable level of economic development. All this might support Ma and Garnaut's (1992: p. 4) and the International Monetary Fund's claim that China is really a middle-income country in disguise.

Of course, as any critic of socialised medicine will note, there were problems of quality. Medical personnel were not always as up to date and skilled as they might be. Secondary medical practitioners sometimes made wrong diagnoses. Cheap provision of services and generous sick-leave provisions for state workers facilitated malingering and there were major problems in servicing out-patients. Pressure resulted in consultations being brief. Supplies of medicine were often inadequate and connections were used to by-pass official strictures. While routine medical expenses were low, those not covered by unit provision or insurance schemes might pay very high hospital fees. All those problems were compounded by the fact that China had to bear the cost of rapidly achieving a first world level of life expectancy with a much less developed economy. That being said, the achievements were remarkable. Of particular note were developments in preventative medicine (which could be undertaken by secondary medical personnel) (Whyte and Parish: 1984: pp. 62–71).

As for the provision of housing in cities, China compared well with other countries with a similar level of economic development, though housing provision had declined since the 1950s and was not exactly a socialist triumph. There were, of course, wide variations across the country. In smaller towns, some two-thirds of housing stock remained in private hands, though in major cities only 6 to 10 per cent was private; a national survey of 200 cities in 1981 gave a figure for private ownership of some 18 per cent (Lee Yok-shiu 1988: p. 398). Owners might have to endure sharing with families allocated housing by local housing management bureaux. Housing allocation was relatively egalitarian, with lower-level bureaucrats enjoying housing only slightly better than ordinary workers. Rents were subsidised and, therefore, low; they ranged from 2 to 3 per cent of total income and only 5 per cent when one added charges for water and electricity, much less than the 1950s (Whyte and Parish: 1984: p. 79; Lee Yok-shiu 1988: p. 392). Yet annual repair and maintenance costs, being double that of rents, resulted in almost one-third of the housing stock in some towns being considered dilapidated. Rising construction standards added considerably to the cost of subsidies. Though the provision of housing was relatively egalitarian, privilege was accorded to Overseas Chinese and top-level cadres. And subsidies were given according to existing housing space rather than family needs (Lee Yok-shiu 1988).

There was, of course, a housing shortage, with some 36 per cent of urban households deemed to have insufficient housing space in 1978 and 31 per cent in 1982 (47 per cent in Beijing in the same year). In 1978 Guangzhou had as little as two square metres per capita, compared with a 3.6 national average for urban areas (State

Statistical Bureau 1990: p. 310), a significant decline since the 1950s (Lee Yok-shiu 1988: pp. 389–91). There was a degree of over crowding due to insufficient investment, and wide variations existed between town-owned housing stock (29 per cent in 1981), stock controlled by enterprises and government units (54 per cent) and that owned by individuals (18 per cent). Overwhelmingly more investment flowed into state-enterprise-owned housing (whose employees were already more privileged) than into that owned by collective enterprises. Provision of electricity was good, by third world standards, yet plumbing was inadequate and sewage disposal posed major problems (and gave rise to ingenious contractual schemes for providing 'night-soil' to rural units). As we have noted, maintenance was bad and the bureaucratic allocation of housing gave rise to all sorts of exchange arrangements (which opened up areas of corruption). Squatting occurred, which might be legitimated by urban authorities, and young married couples complained continually about lack of space.

Even less impressive was the selective social security system, which discriminated in favour of state employees. Those inside the system (which allocated some 17 per cent of its budget to welfare provisions, not including pensions) were well-served. State units might provide subsidies for a wide range of goods and services. Outside there were major problems. The very poor families (with per capita income of less than 12 *yuan* in major cities and 8 *yuan* elsewhere) might be helped, but the moderately poor endured real hardship. This is a problem also encountered in countries with more centrally controlled welfare systems. In mitigation one might note that the Chinese system was exempt from the charge made by some critics of Western welfare systems. There was no welfare bureaucracy. But there was no profession of social worker either.

Conventional wisdom has it that the negative features of the above system outweighed the positive, despite the fact that many of the remedies advocated by Western theorists to solve urban problems had been tried. No judgement will be made at this point. Suffice it to say that many Chinese migrating to Hong Kong found life in that territory cold. They remembered a situation in China where control was pervasive, where speech had to be guarded and where it was too difficult to associate with kin except on a few festivals. While neither work units nor neighbourhoods produced strong communities of choice based upon freedom, there was little sense of isolation. In Hong Kong, access to the telephone allows for closer kinship ties, but the pressure of work has destroyed many neighbourhoods (Whyte and Parish: 1984: pp 332–56). It is not altogether clear that greater access to one's kin greater negative freedom (plus anomie) is always better than constant proximity to sometimes helpful, but sometimes tiresome and even hostile, neighbours in an atmosphere of oppressive state control. We rehearse once again a consistent theme of this chapter

Reform in the 1980s

The economic reforms of the late 1970s and 1980s have brough about major changes in the towns (and in the definition of 'towns') Soon after Mao's death, as we have seen, the education system wa changed, followed by an end to the programme of rusticating youth The advent of a partly private economy greatly augmented th number of retail outlets (surpassing the levels of the 1950s) (Stat Statistical Bureau 1990: p. 569). After the Third Plenum of 1978 'national capitalists' were given compensation and, together with formerly suspect intellectuals, had their housing restored. A Chapter 2 remarked, enterprises were accorded a degree of auton omy and some market relations were tolerated. At first tha autonomy took the form of greater profit retention and a degre of direct sales to consumers. The result was a decline in centra government revenue, a capital construction spree and the growth o corruption. We noted also that economic problems, exacerbated b social protest and demands for autonomous trade unions, cause the reform programme to stall in 1981. But in the following two years, remedial measures were applied, only to be abandoned in 1984.

Having outlined the broad contours of economic change, we must discuss overall social trends as they affected urban areas. First let us consider the criteria for 'urban'. In 1982 there were 2,66 officially designated towns. This was less than 1964. It was even les than 1981 since incentives at that time favoured enterprise designated as 'rural'; urban enterprises were taxed at a higher rate than rural ones. The number of towns rose to 3,200 in 1983, 5,69 in 1984, 9,130 in 1985 and to some 10,000 in 1987. On the face of it much of the huge increase in 1984 is simply explained by official relaxation of the criteria for 'town' status in that year.[1] Part of the large increase before November 1984 might also be explained by provinces adopting more lenient standards before the official national designations were promulgated (though some provincial regulations were stricter).

The degree to which 'towns' are officially designated is crucial to an understanding of the official figures concerning the size of China's urban population. During the 1960s and 1970s, this stood at some 17 per cent. It reached 20 per cent in 1981, some 32 per cent in 1984 and some 47 per cent in 1987. Yet, Lee Yok-shiu argues, official re-designation only explains a part of the dramatic rise in apparent urban population. Migration of villagers into small towns also only explains a part. Perhaps the most important reason for the dramatic growth is simply that 'towns' enlarged their boundaries to take in surrounding villages in order to revitalise the rural economy. In that process, prefectures often became 'metropolitan regions' – a separate level of government. In such a situation officials maintained two measures of urbanisation. All that means is that a very large number of 'urban' dwellers are actually peasants (Lee Yokshiu 1989; Vogel 1989: pp. 248–50).

A huge problem in the 1980s was that of social order. A major characteristic of Chinese cities in the late 1970s and 1980s was growing unemployment following the end of the policy of rusticating youth. The return of educated youth together with dashed aspirations in 1979–80 led to considerable urban disorder and resulted in legislative measures discussed in a later chapter. Though official comments in the early 1980s speak of a decline in the crime rate, it was probably the case that petty crime increased throughout the decade, peaking in 1978–81 and after 1985. We are not convinced by Whyte and Parish's (1984: pp. 269–73) comment that progress was made in providing greater legitimate opportunities (a prerequisite for

[1] In November 1984, 'towns' were re-designated as seats of *xian* government, seats of *xiang* government where the *xiang* population was below 20,000 but contained 2,000 non-agricultural persons in the *xiang* seat or where the *xiang* population was more than 20,000 and the number of non-agricultural persons residing in the *xiang* seat was more than 10 per cent. Furthermore, some seats of *xiang* government, in remote or minority nationality areas, might be designated as 'towns' even when they did not meet those criteria.

urban harmony). The criminal element was, of course, very small and large numbers of educated youth found employment. This, as we have seen, was usually in small collectives, with low wages and minimum services. Probably because they were thankful to have any job, those employees, like the employees in rural sweat-shops, were not a major source of unrest in the 1980s. But, as a consequence of the credit-squeeze of 1988–9, when large numbers of small firms ceased operation, some tens of millions of former peasants, it is said unable to go back to the land, roamed the country, creating major logistical problems and social disorder. Even more important, the unemployed, the employees of small collectives and private firms together with large numbers of migrants from rural areas who (usually illegally) have found work in the cities, represent a growing underprivileged stratum. Among them there has been increasing poverty and (illegal) incidence of child-labour. Prescribed state relief for the needy, moreover, has usually not been forthcoming (Chan 1991: pp. 121–2).

At the other end of the spectrum one can identify a 'monied élite' owners of private enterprises, lessee-managers of state and collective enterprises and 'socialist compradors' (state officials engaged in private business). In 1988, 10 per cent of the 12 million industrial and commercial workers earned over 10,000 *yuan* per year and 1 per cent earned up to 100,000. We considered the development of private firms in Chapter 2. These have been both envied and resented. Envy came simply from their success plus the ability of their owners to get fast entrance into the Party. Reportedly some 15 per cent of private entrepreneurs were Party members by 1988 and by 1989, Party branches appeared in private factories (Solinger 1992: p. 131). Private entrepreneurs were resented, partly because of their ability to evade taxes prior to the Enterprise Law of 1988 Indeed, self-employed workers, who earned about double the amount of those in state enterprises, were also suspect prior to the tightening-up of personal income tax regulations in the late 1980s. Most resented, however, were the lessee managers of state and collective enterprises who, as we noted earlier, were seen by many as corrupt in the protest movements of the late 1980s. To answer the question posed at the start of this chapter, the new class relations are not universally acclaimed.

As for workers in large state enterprises, there has been what social psychologists call 'aspirational relative deprivation' – increasing aspirations that are dashed. But though this may be the perception, a case might be made that in the early 1980s in some places at least, greater rather than less equality has accompanied the reforms (Walder 1990: pp. 135–56). As commented on above, at first the wages and working conditions of regular workers improved far quicker than for those employed in education or the public service. They tripled over a decade and allowed for a degree of consumerism, with housing space increasing markedly (average 6.9 square metres per capita in urban areas in 1991) (Lau Kwok-yu 1993: p. 24.3), ownership of televisions increasing 38-fold, electric fans 12-fold, refrigerators 131-fold and washing machines beyond calculation (Guojia tongjiju 1988: p. 836). Wages, moreover, as noted above, were cushioned from the effect of the rise in agricultural prices by very large subsidies. In 1978, it was estimated that subsidies to urban state workers doubled the value of their wages and in 1987 unit-level subsidies alone averaged 85 per cent of monthly pay (Davis 1990: p. 106). At the same time, workers were offered greater participation in workers and staff congresses which were supposed to be the supreme decision-making bodies in enterprises (Brugger 1985). Hopes were also expressed about the development of a freer market in labour. In addition, 1978 had seen the introduction of more generous retirement benefits and the popularisation of a system whereby a retiring worker could nominate one of his children to take his place. There was a predictably a large increase in retirements with many retirees expressing satisfaction that their offspring could return from the countryside to a secure job.

The policy of allowing retiring workers to be replaced by their children created such confusion in job allocation that it was officially curtailed in 1983 and replaced by new contract provisions in 1986. But better retirement provisions caused financial problems for units. They therefore began to share the burden with other units as a first step towards removing provision for retirement pay from enterprises and particular government units altogether (Ikels 1990: pp. 222–3). Clearly, when a more universal system eventuates, many privileged workers will be worse off. It soon became clear, moreover, that labour market reform was not occurring and that the centralised system of assignments had only been slightly modified. Those skilled people who would benefit directly from a freer labour market, took advantage of more flexible leave arrangements and the establishment of 'talent centres' for labour exchange. Yet they were continually frustrated by units which did not want to lose their investment in skill. Managers, constantly fearful that workers might be poached by other enterprises, sometimes imposed a 'training levy' as compensation. At other times they and their immediate superiors just refused requests for transfer. Indeed, their ability to do this had been enhanced by decentralisation of power which ironically had been implemented to enhance flexibility (Davis 1990). Of course, for many workers who enjoyed considerable benefits and did not have to work very hard (referred to earlier as a 'labour aristocracy'), the lack of a labour market was seen as an advantage. But those workers resented being castigated for being lazy and 'eating out of the big pot'.

Realising that managers earned greater bonuses than themselves, regular state workers voiced dissatisfaction and, more dangerously, envy (Walder 1991: pp. 477–8; Burns 1989a; pp. 488–90). Some came to feel that workers and staff congresses were 'empty shells'. Workers were often subjected to a labour discipline which consigned them to working for a 'labour service company' (which, for a few, generated significantly higher incomes and, for many, much lower). Others were consigned to lay-offs dignified by the word 'reorganisation'. Inflation, furthermore, ate into their incomes. National figures claimed that wages increased by 50 per cent in real terms over ten years, though in places this, in practice, boiled down to 1 per cent per year up to 1986 when inflation really took off (Walder 1991: pp. 471–2). Nevertheless, aspirations rose far beyond the perceived indices of prosperity, particularly housing space. Enterprises had given subsidies to workers to help them compete on a freer market, but confronting real market prices was a shock and to avoid the adverse consequences of that shock local authorities often defied State Council regulations and set house prices simply as a multiple of family income (Lau Kwok-yu 1993: p. 24.12). The bulk of public housing, however, was still allocated in the old way, but this time relatively openly and naturally gave rise to acrimony, when one could actually see the perquisites of leaders (Walder 1991: p. 480). Disappointed with the state union structure, workers began to form lateral linkages with other workers, which the authorities tried to subvert in the crack-downs of 1981, 1983, 1986 and 1989. Through such lateral linkages, workers learnt more and more about the apparent success stories of individual entrepreneurs and (although inequalities were possibly not as bad as in the past) envy increased. Whilst welcoming reform, at first, many workers were suspicious of a technocratic leadership which sometimes made democratic noises but which seemed to threaten their privileged position. It was probably not the case, however, that many supported the old 1950s-style leaders who were seen as benefiting from corruption. Responding to worker dissatisfaction, the All China Federation of Trade Unions managed to win some concessions from the government and for a time to subvert the drafting of a bankruptcy law which workers feared.

As we have noted, experiments in bankruptcy date from 1985 in Shenyang and experimental closures and lay-offs occurred in 1986. The question was, who was to blame – the government, the price system or whoever? The problem of unprofitable firms could be tackled by mergers which were carried out throughout the late 1980s and early 1990s, with some 10,000 enterprises being merged in 1992. The issue of how to implement bankruptcy provisions, however, remains (Blecher 1991: pp. 48–50) and, as of 1992, only a few dozen bankruptcies of state enterprises per year have been recorded (BBC, *Summary of World Broadcasts*/FE/W0272/A/2, 10 Mar. 1993).

Modification of the bankruptcy law in the late 1980s won some support for reform through official channels but disaffected workers engaged in sporadic go slows, absenteeism and strikes and began to form independent trade unions once again. These appeared in a number of cities, though the Beijing autonomous union, which figured in the 1989 movement, was the best known (Chan 1993: Walder and Gong 1993). Such unions were to be more bitterly persecuted than the student organisations.

Worker dissatisfaction was clearly a major factor influencing the behaviour of management in the state sector in the 1980s. On the one hand, managers had to respond to state policies to promote productivity, local pressure to fulfil political and social goals (from political education, planting trees to birth control) and on the other they had cultivate better labour relations. Calculating the costs of workers disliking participation in community services (which violated the principle of separating government and economic functions), they might reduce the bonus fund to employ other people to perform them – an action which could bring about worker opposition. They had to respond to a growing belief among workers that, with greater enterprise autonomy and the transformation of ministerial branches and municipal bureaux into corporations, higher levels did little but syphon off tax and interfere in the lives of workers, whilst at the same time cultivating those higher levels upon which they were dependent for promotion. They had to respond to a workforce which could not see why in a freer 'commodity economy' they had to seek permission for everything. Managers, moreover, continued to deceive state authorities in negotiating profit (and tax) quotas, making sure that they did not greatly exceed planned profit for fear of a new assessment. They continued to take more than a fair advantage of direct sales and cultivated non-market supply and sales connections. And as the equivalent of 'mayors' in charge of a community, they ploughed large sums into 'non-productive' investment (especially housing, in violation of the 1988 State Council regulations) and genuinely tried to cultivate worker support (Yang 1989; Walder 1989). We can now see more clearly the deleterious effects of fusing units of production, residence and administration – a problem noted in our Introduction.

The fact that large state factories were, in Phillip Selznick's (1957) words, 'communities' inserted into larger local communities rather than organisations (geared to a single task), meant that it was virtually impossible to separate Party and management. From 1984 to 1986, the central government proclaimed that policy most loudly under the rubric of the 'factory director responsibility system', whilst local community leaders (Party) strengthened the dependency of enterprise communities upon them, both in an exploitative and protective sense. Local government was, in Charles Tilly's (1985) words (applied to Europe centuries ago), a 'protection racket'. Occasionally managers broke loose and when charged by local authorities with excessive individualism or worse 'economic crime', they sought the protection of central auditing agencies. Frequently they attempted to establish their independence by legal contracts. But of course those often just represented a formalised statement of dependency relations. More commonly they (usually Party members themselves) remained loyal to local networks, awaiting a shift in central policy back towards a greater recognition of dependency on the local Party. This occurred in 1986–7 and the Enterprise Law of 1988 reflected both the new factory director responsibility system *and* Party leadership. Conflict was institutionalised (Chevrier 1990).

Throughout, managers and Party secretaries vied for worker support. Occasionally, managers might dominate those secretaries but the latter usually continued to exercise a major role in decision-making and, in particular, personnel management. Party secretaries, castigated in the Cultural Revolution, were not eager to lose their authority once again (Blecher 1991: pp. 40–4). Whilst officially denied for a time a direct policy-making role, they strove to maximise their power by appealing to workers' grievances and contributed to forging an association between 1950s-style leadership and maintaining workers' interests (Walder 1989). Yet, over the period, enterprise Party organisations lost prestige. In the light of events of the late 1980s, one suspects that, overall, neither management nor Party secretaries were all that successful in cultivating worker support. We have yet to see whether new regulations governing enterprise operations put forward in 1992, which stress once again separating political and economic tasks, will change the situation.

A later chapter will consider the complaints of intellectuals and students. Suffice it to note here that one of the first areas to experience reform after the death of Mao Zedong, long before the Third Plenum of 1978, was education. In a major reversal of priorities, the system of élite schools and nationwide examinations was introduced. Over the 1980s, nation-wide, primary and secondary school enrolment dropped. Surveys in the 1990s show that 33 million children between the ages of 6 to 14 do not attend school and of these 5 million are in urban areas (Lo 1993: p. 22.9); universality is now set as the goal for the year 2000. There was, however, a dramatic increase at the tertiary level. To some extent the decline in primary school enrolments reflects demographic factors, but not secondary enrolments. Decline at both levels was obviously greatest in rural areas as a consequence of the household responsibility system, a factor which exacerbated the urban–rural welfare gap. Urban areas, however, were affected by falling rates of completion in an increasingly competitive environment and by higher charges. While fewer urban parents keep their children out of school for financial reasons, much anger has been generated by 'miscellaneous expenses' (*zafei*), levied to provide bonuses for teachers in a cash-strapped sector (Davis 1989: pp. 581–5). The dramatic expansion of the tertiary sector, moreover, has not been matched by a commensurate allocation of funds – a fact admitted to by Deng Xiaoping and a major factor in the student disturbances of 1989. Indeed, teachers have been most vocal concerning the decline of working conditions. Some have resigned and gone into private business. Some university departments have set up their own businesses (from high-level consultancies to running a lowly campus fruit stall) and have supplemented their expenses by taking on a quota of full-fee-paying students (the offspring of the 'monied élite' who had failed the national examinations and who paid fees amounting to almost a year's average wage); in 1992 these students were to constitute some 15 per cent. By 1988, some 15 per cent of ten million academics and professionals had taken second jobs. For all that, as Anita Chan (1991: pp. 109–10) points out, we are once again often dealing with perceptions of relative inequality rather than reality. While academics earn less than most of the self-employed, they do not earn less than average workers. They are predisposed to think they do because they are now allowed to promote the 'superiority' of mental labour. In any case, in the climate of the late 1980s when inflation was eating into all incomes, the perception, real or otherwise, became particularly acute.

Reforms in the health care system have also widened urban–rural differences for much the same reason as reforms in education. While the numbers of medical centres and doctors trained in Western medicine have increased significantly and there has been an improvement in the provision of rural hospital beds (Davis 1989: p. 586), the provision of basic health care in rural areas has lagged behind the cities, a process exacerbated in the early 1980s by urban hospitals poaching rusticated medical personnel at the expense of rural clinics. In urban areas, faced with an aging population and escalating costs, efforts have been made to make patients pay a share of expenses according to various schemes. Sometimes workers are paid a fixed sum for medical expenses each month; if they are not sick, they keep the money, but if they are, they are expected to pay any extra expenses themselves. Some enterprises operate insurance programmes, with co-payment schemes for contract workers. Enterprises increasingly have to cover all their medical expenses; this has not adversely affected large enterprises but has forced smaller collective enterprises to cut services or charge higher fees. While the health-care system has performed better than the education system, it has become more stratified and unfair (Davis 1989: pp. 585–90; Henderson 1990).

We noted above the improvement in urban housing space. That improvement will continue if the government carries out its intention to double annual investment in housing during the 1990s (Yeh 1992: p. 515). But housing shortages, some economists feel, can only be remedied by further commercialisation of rents. The regulations of 1988 would eventually have increased rents per square metre seven or eight-fold, offset by a subsidy equal to 22 per cent of basic salary (resulting in an effective 500 per cent increase) (Chan 1991: p. 120). Such a move was politically dangerous and was treated with caution but since 1989 radical action has been taken in some areas. One anticipates severe divisions as the wealthy buy larger flats and an underclass is squeezed into less and less space. We have yet to see if the usual problem of reforming socialist states occurs, whereby the best housing remains in public (bureaucratic) hands and it is the poorer housing which is sold off. In a wider context, the question of land ownership remains a problem, though the crisis of recent years has not prevented land sales to foreigners and a frenzy of real estate speculation by Hong Kong Chinese (Lau Kwok-yu 1993: pp. 24.22–8).

The Development of Civil Society

Are there any general conclusions one may draw from the above? One pessimistic scenario is that we are seeing the collapse of one welfare system without any alternative being offered. We are also seeing, some claim, the failure of a statist system to develop genuine social ownership, despite calls to develop joint-stock enterprises and the like. Trading shares, they claim, smacks too much of real capitalism and will be limited. Yet such experiments continue and have resulted in riots on the new stock market of Shenzhen. More positively, some commentators argue, we are seeing the development of an embryonic civil society which the events of 1989 may retard but not suppress (Whyte 1992). The greatly abused term 'civil society' may mean many things in the Chinese context (see White 1993a). At its broadest, the development of civil society means simply that there are more areas not directly under the control of the state, as the legalisation of the informal sector of the economy makes clear. The problem here is to define exactly what state control actually means, as we hinted at in our brief mention of rural village compacts. More specifically, civil society could mean that there is more of a pluralist structure. Interest groups (of businessmen, workers and intellectuals) have indeed gained a stronger voice but those 'social groups' have to be registered by the state. Some 150 business guilds were revived in 1989 as 'non-official' bodies, yet they are tied to the All China Federation of Industry and Commerce. Does the appearance of such groups represent a diffusion of power? Solinger (1992) is clear, civil society is even further away than under Mao. Rather than a diffusion of power at higher levels, there is probably a destabilisation of power at middle and lower levels. As we have seen, units of production often remain units of administration, units of welfare and education and centres of Party control. One can, however, speak of growing contradictions among those functions (Yang 1989).

Conclusion

With the advent of the 1990s, we are confused about what the term 'urban' signifies; it also seems less and less meaningful to speak of Chinese cities in general. Rather, following the decentralisation measures, policies which favour modernisation with particular cities as the basis and a strategy which deliberately favours the better-endowed coastal cities, one should talk of different types of regional cities and their surrounding networks. Clearly Shenzhen, the centre of the predominant special economic zone, and the Pearl River Delta have developed in a manner totally different from city networks in the hinterland, despite the decision to open up some other cities. Those southern areas are the most modernised of urban areas and yet, as we have remarked, reveal an interweaving of state and private ownership reminiscent of the situation before 1949. The involvement of the China Merchants' Steam Navigation Company in the Shenzhen special economic zone makes this apparent (Vogel 1989: pp. 125–60). Clearly also, local autarchy has resulted in inter-regional rivalry. We return to the point we made at the end of Chapter 2.

This chapter and the proceeding one have clearly shown that urban bias continues despite the fact that a more salient fault line is between suburban peasants able to profit by new market relations and those in the hinterland who cannot. In particular this chapter has depicted both a partial breakdown of urban communities and less coercive policies – more freedom and more anomie. It has noted, however, that anomie amongst youth was quite prevalent under the old system of the 1970s. Continuing anomie may be overcome by more opportunities for their upward mobility; but current data on that issue is inconclusive. Of course, communities based on the old policy of fusing together units of production, residence and administration remain and are often resented by less secure economic units. Perhaps policies designed to commercialise more services will gradually destroy those communities, but not without considerable friction. Perhaps too the removal of urban subsidies, while a more universalistic provision of welfare facilities remains rudimentary, will also create further urban unrest. We remain open-minded as to the development of a civil society but incline towards Solinger's view. Consider here the return to a phenomenon which was once denounced as 'bureaucratic capital'. Of course, that 'bureaucratic capital' can exhibit economic dynamism. Indeed, when combined with small-scale business ventures, operating across various communities, bureaucratic capital can be a powerful engine of growth, as other Asian economies have demonstrated. It can, however, generate social division, as we have seen. Such social cleavage will surely be exacerbated by conflict between those who observe it from the perspective of 1950s nostalgia and those who observe it from the naive perspective of free-market economics.

5

Law and Policing

The Introduction to this book posed questions concerning the general conditions for the 'rule of law', the relation between law and policy determined by a teleologically informed vanguard Party, between formal law and informal notions of proper behaviour (propriety) and between formal and informal law. It also asked questions about the relation of law to a particular economy (or mode of production), the functions of the police and the 'universal' nature of human rights. Such a complicated agenda requires an introduction more detailed than for other chapters.

A popular view of Western liberalism is that its prime achievement has been the 'rule of law', built upon the inviolable natural rights of the individual and founded in a struggle against absolutism. An opposing non-liberal communitarian view might protest that formal law is only necessary when community breaks down. Standing outside the philosophical struggle, some sociologists, moreover, might note that modern law arose before liberalism, indeed at a time of absolutism. It is the product of what Max Weber called the 'rationalised' state and may be expected continually to discipline us. Thus we find in the Chinese People's Republic admirers of the West who bemoan that country's failure to explore 'natural' individualism, and others, unconvinced about the existence of any trans-historical notion of rights, who maintain an official view which sees law and rights as no more than the product of the state. We also find those of a sociological bent who see their task as redirecting discipline away from class struggle towards the 'four modernisations' and promoting (or destabilising) an unproblematic rationalised 'modernity'. The first group bemoan the absence of a Chinese 'rule of law' (*fazhi*); the latter two affirm that one exists now that the 'lawlessness' of past years is over. But obviously a single-minded stress on natural rights, legal positivism or the belief in a single 'iron cage of modernity' serve the cause of ideology more than balanced scholarship.

The problem lies in good measure in the translation of the Chinese word *fazhi*. As Richard Baum (1986) points out, that could either mean the 'rule of law' or 'rule by law' or simply the legal system. The 'rule of law', according to Roberto Unger (1976), arose out of a desire of competing estates to prevent any one of them using the state for its own ends. Its universality and inviolability, moreover, stemmed from the notion of a personal creator. Eventually it came to mean a system of law which protected (however imperfectly) a pluralist civil society against the state. What Baum calls 'rule by law', however, simply means using a non-arbitrary system of rules to govern and might be found in all societies with a regular bureaucracy. Whilst the 'rule of law' was a liberal notion, 'rule by law' was not necessarily liberal. Nor was it particularly communitarian. Those communitarians who see the state as embodying social ethics might look askance at a 'rule of law' which requires laws to protect civil society from that state, or more generally regard rule essentially by law as ethically deficient. The attitude to law which has informed the Chinese tradition reflects both communitarian and bureaucratic concerns but not pluralist ones.

The two and a half thousand years old Chinese debate on this question is expressed in terms of *li* and *fa* (see Schwartz 1968; Bodde and Morris 1967). Far from exotic, the Chinese debate reflects universal concerns and has important contemporary relevance. Confucian cosmology held that there was a natural moral order governed by eternal principles geared to a goal of harmony. The concept *dao* (the way) was equivalent to the Greek *logos*. *Li* consisted in behaviour in the human world appropriate to cosmic order and that behaviour, in turn, helped fashion cosmic order. In practical terms, *li* specified the 'natural' behaviour appropriate to a role in the network of social relationships which constituted the community. Those who embodied *li* possessed a moral force superior to any physical force. The best government, therefore, was government by example – example which required no formal rules nor formal courts to reconcile conflicts of interest. Indeed, Confucius castigated those who established written rules as fostering conflicts of interpretation and disharmony and held the best judge to be one who did not have to deal with any cases. Those who grasped *li* would make the necessary concessions to self-evident principles of harmony without the aid of rules and forums for adjudication. Ideally, then, *li*, as 'propriety', subsumed many aspects of what in our society is covered by civil law and extended to the whole field of ritual behaviour. It embodied 'rights' as entitlements due to social role but rendered meaningless any notion of 'rights' as claims against a legitimate social order (Nathan 1986b). A person who embodied *li* would know when to yield; to resist in the name of inviolable interests would be to violate *li*. In its ideal form, therefore, *li* was a communitarian notion which could not conceive of the 'rule of law'.

But could exponents of *li* conceive of rule *by* law? Clearly one does not need to be a follower of Michel Foucault (1979) to realise that any system of social regulation, even one which explicitly repudiates formal policing, itself needs to be policed. The policing of *li*, therefore, might be rationalised in terms of restoring *li* which had broken down (Dutton 1992: pp. 21–54). Indeed, the dominant ideology maintained that after the mythical 'golden age' the community was always somewhat deficient in *li* and required an alternative (though subordinate) regulating principle. This was *fa* – the maintenance of order by the state by the threat of punishment (rule *by* law). Practical necessity forced Confucians to make concessions to *fa* whereas the less practical retreated to *Daoism* and withdrew from the community. Some scholars and leaders, however, made *fa* into a virtue, seeing it as the only way of creating and preserving a strong empire and perhaps providing social welfare. Such was the ideology which supposedly informed the Qin empire which united China in the third century BC. Though the harshness of that empire has been castigated by Confucians for two millenia, a strong legalist element had to remain in Chinese thought and informed the various legal codes promulgated over the centuries. Confucianism kept regulations vague and relegated legal scholars (hardly lawyers) to inferior positions, yet the 'rationalisa-tion' of the bureaucratic state (which, contrary to the Weberian interpretation, should not be tied to 'modernity') demanded an affirmation of legalist principles. Indeed Jiang Jieshi, for all his Confucian pieties, had explicit recourse to the Chinese legalist tradition and the 'Gang of Four' sought a rehabilitation of the

First Emperor of Qin during the Anti-Confucius campaign of the 1970s (though hardly with Weber's 'rationalisation' in mind).

We have cast the debate so far in terms of a communitarian tradition and supplements to it. It could also be seen as similar to that carried on between traditional natural law theorists and utilitarians in the West. Clearly there is a crucial difference between Christian natural law which depends on a divine creator (legislator) and the Confucian natural order given by an impersonal 'heaven' (*tian*), and Unger (1976: pp. 86–109, esp 100) makes much of the distinction. Yet even the Thomist tradition differentiates divine law and natural law. There is a difference also between the particularistic and concrete postulates of *li* (embracing loyalty, kinship bonds and the like) and the abstract universalism of Western natural law. Yet *li* applied particularistic concerns universally and could be seen as having some influence on those who regarded Marxism as universalising the values of a particular class (the proletariat). Indeed, many scholars speak of a modern Chinese Marxist version of *li*, where 'socialist morality' has replaced Confucian morality and 'comrade' has replaced 'the superior man' (*junzi*). They see this communal, societal or, in Victor Li's (1971: pp. 221–55, esp 223; and 1978) words, 'internal' model of law permeating and sometimes conflicting with an 'external' (or jural) model of law deriving from *fa* and supplemented by foreign imports. With Victor Li (1978), they might agree that the former model was particularly suited to Chinese conditions under Mao – a situation where there was 'law without lawyers'.

But Mao's position was ambivalent. In pursuing strong government and social welfare in the tradition of *fa*, he admitted he was a utilitarian (though a 'proletarian revolutionary' one) (*Selected Works*, 3: p. 85). Here he reflected the Chinese anti-individualist version of that doctrine which, in the spirit of rule *by* law, placed welfare rights on a par with political rights (Nathan 1986b). Mao clearly had recourse to the pleasure and pain calculus and saw rights as the product of the state subject only to the test of social utility. Yet, at the same time, Mao and the Party affirmed the old communitarian idea that utility was shaped by communal values and ought to be geared to a communal *telos* which could only be hampered by hard and fast rules. Thus, in the tradition of *li*, he showed distaste for the proceduralism (characteristic of utilitarianism) which could encourage litigiousness, commodify justice and favour 'an enemy' with resources at its disposal.

Mao and the Communist Party, of course, saw the litigiousness and commodification of law as products not of rationalisation but of capitalism. Here they reflected Soviet legal thinking. The most sophisticated of Soviet legal theorists, E. Pashukanis, had argued that the essence of all law was contract in commercial exchange. Rights and duties derived from exchanges with other bearers of rights and duties both in civil law and criminal law (where punishment is seen as 'payment' for a crime). Law, therefore, was as old as commodity economy and, like commodity economy, reached its culmination in capitalism. The transcendence of capitalism, therefore, meant the transcendence of law. But what was law to be replaced by? Surely the answer could only be by some modernised and socialist version of communitarian values – by a new *li*. But once one gives up the conservative essence of *li*, one is left merely with teleological policy in which both duties and rights are programmatic expressions of policy; 'policy is the soul of law'.

So long as the pre-communist régime needs a state, however, it is subject to the dictates of rationalisation. Thus the celebration of the Soviet socialist state in 1936 saw the institutionalisation of formal law of a long-standing nature, unlike the laws of the New Economic Policy period which the commodity school could accept as necessary due to temporary concessions to capitalism. Of course, Stalinist law, which consigned large numbers of people to death or labour camps, produced the very antithesis of the predictability of the modern rationalised state and the law was frequently violated. For that it was attacked by liberals. But it also could be attacked from the left for producing a non-bourgeois version of the 'bourgeois dictatorship' which Soviet caricatures (and occasional perceptive analyses) detected in certain Western countries. Thus, though one might criticise the ideas of people such as Pashukanis for abetting lawlessness, the consequences of 'socialist law' might be said to have been much worse, informed as it was by a crude class-reductionism (Kamenka 1965).

The Chinese Communist Party's view of law, therefore, was utilitarian rather than resting on fundamental rights yet it also demanded a new form of *li* which could be pressed into the service of combating capitalism. Indeed, the Party's case against capitalism could be seen in terms of there being no clearer manifestation of the breakdown of *li* than private articulation of claims against the community. Socialist morality demanded a new *li* but both simple class justice and the needs of a rationalised state required *fa*, expressed in class-reductionist terms.

Modernised *li*, however, could lead to élitism (the entrenchment in power of the interpreters of a new propriety) and to arbitrariness in the interpretation of vague principles. It could cause resentment particularly when it inverted the class hierarchy of the previous variety. *Fa*, on the other hand, could lead to a utilitarian disregard of legitimate minority interests, debasement of morality and again a hostile reaction. *Fa*, moreover, with its utilitarian underpinnings could result in what some Party members considered either as 'bureaucratism' or as 'bourgeois' litigiousness. Oscillation between those views has been considered to result in 'lawlessness'. Indeed, during the early 1950s and the Cultural Revolution there is some force to that charge. At other times, however, a system of *fazhi* was maintained – rule by law but, in the absence of a pluralist civil society, not the 'rule of law'. Law was always seen as an instrument of state.

In recent years some aspects of procedure have come to resemble Western practice and when scholars talk of *fazhi* they sometimes refer to what might accurately be translated as 'the rule of law'. More generally, though, jurists are referring to rule *by* law. Their methodology, moreover, is positivist in the sense of law meaning nothing more than rules legitimately made by the sovereign power. Such is clearly the mood behind those drafters of various Chinese constitutions who insert after a statement of rights the words 'according to law' (Nathan 1986a), implying that law makes rights rather than rights shaping law. Surely a prior question is what rules might legitimately be made. Whilst an adherent to the liberal notion of 'the rule of law' might seek an answer in safeguarding civil society from the state, Chinese communitarians (traditional or socialist) turn to modernised versions of *li*. *Fazhi*, as simply rule by law, satisfies neither. Should one be surprised that many of the radical communitarians of the Cultural Revolution are now upholders of the 'rule of law', once denounced as 'bourgeois' Brugger and Kelly 1990: pp. 139–69)? Though their way of thinking has changed dramatically, they are still opposed to *fa* being used in the interests of utilitarian autocracy and *li* in the interests of an old elite.

Traditional and Transitional China

Formal government in pre-twentieth-century China did not exten
below the two thousand or so *xian* (counties). The *xian* magistrate
who was both the basic administrative and judicial official, as th
embodiment of *li*, did not wish to deal with many legal cases, whic
is just as well because his other duties left him little time to do so
Legal cases were minimised by the general atmosphere of dread i
which people held the courts and by the time-consuming process o
criminal adjudication which ideally had to be both punitive an
educative. Indeed, the educative function of *fa* meant that it had t
be exemplary and a conviction was not considered legitimate in th
absence of confession. Torture, therefore, which was quite common
increased dread of the courts, kept people away from them an
helped convince magistrates that the paucity of trials was a sign tha
they embodied *li*. As untrained educators, moreover, judges, dealin
with cases not covered by law, had no reservations about the use o
analogy and promulgating regulations which might be applie
retrospectively. The only safeguard offered by the system wer
formal provisions for the review of serious cases by highe
authorities (which could order acquittal or punish a magistrat
for wrong acquittals), though poor communications did not rende
that safeguard very valuable.

   The number of cases dealt with by magistrates was als
minimised by the fact that most law was informal and communa
or in Li's words 'internal'. Most civil and minor criminal cases wer
settled informally by local leaders and might be referred to loca
bodies by officials (despite the provisions of the Qing legal code)
At most times the magistracy was content to play only a super
visory role over the institutions of customary law. A concern fo
security, however, resulted in the creation of a system consisting o
groups of ten and one hundred households known as *baojia*, whic
waxed and waned under several names over the centuries. In it
various forms *baojia* required the head of each of its constituen
units to be responsible for the conduct of the group's members an
that person might be punished if a crime occurred. Indeed, by
extension, the idea of collective security could result in th
punishment of those who had offered guarantees of particula
persons' good conduct. As one might imagine, people were ofte
reluctant to serve as guarantors and to carry out the forma

provisions of the *baojia* system. In general, most scholars concur, that system was very ineffective during the close of the empire and remained ineffective when it was reintroduced by the *Guomindang* government in 1932. Though that régime claimed that it had reintroduced *baojia* to prepare the people for democracy, *baojia* was designed to fulfil its old functions of tying together policing and customary patterns of mutual aid. As before, it was concerned with collective security, or more particularly with linking the family with the patriarchal state by opening the family to social policing in a manner which gave the impression of strengthening family order (Dutton 1992: p. 35). It signified an attempt to fuse bureaucratic and communal concerns and judicial and executive functions. Regarding the law simply as an instrument for enhancing state power and disciplining people to carry out state policies, *baojia* was far from any 'rule of law'. With rule *by* law in mind, it is not surprising that Jiang Jieshi looked for guidance on establishing a legal framework to Japan and continental Europe. The result was the 'six codes' of the early 1930s which were ineffectively implemented.

For its part the Chinese Communist Party derived formal legal models from the Soviet Union, inspired by the same European source. Thus in 1931 the Jiangxi Soviet separated formally the functions of courts (*renmin fayuan*), procuratoral authorities and police. In practice, however, the exigencies of land reform and war led to the use of a number of *ad hoc* people's tribunals (*renmin fating*) which dispensed a kind of rough popular justice often at mass trials. During the Yan'an period, whilst mass trials were still used against people accused of collaborating with Japan, the united front dictated a softer line and parts of existing *Guomindang* legislation were combined with new laws and decrees. During that period extensive use was made of people's assessors (ideally elected) who joined the formal bench and of mediation committees to solve disputes outside the courts. The renewal of civil war after 1946, however, saw a return to the earlier combination of regular proceedings, conducted by courts, procuratoral organs and people's assessors, informal processes of mediation plus summary justice dispensed by people's tribunals, public security organs and the military. The procedure used depended on the nature of the case and the intensity of the revolutionary struggle at any particular time (Leng 1967: pp. 1–26).

The 1950s

Unlike the revolutionary government in Russia, the new Chinese government in its Common Programme of 1949 abolished all legislation of the 'reactionary *Guomindang* government which oppresses the people' (Blaustein 1962: p. 41). At the same time, regional government, exercised by military control commissions and assisted by military courts, had perforce to retain a number of personnel employed by the old régime, including police and some members of the judiciary. Such people, obviously suspect, were placed in an even more precarious position in the absence of legal guidelines and in light of the fact that they were instructed only to adhere to Party and government instructions in the spirit of 'new democracy'. Most of these fell foul of the major movements of the time, in which new versions of the people's tribunals of the old liberated areas played a major part. Land reform was usually conducted by *xian*-level tribunals of which half the members were supposed to be elected. Those tribunals tried landlords and handled problems of land demarcation. Similar bodies played a major role in the three and five anti campaigns of 1951–2, which amongst other things exposed major deficiencies in the operations of courts and security and legal personnel. They operated also in the Judicial Reform Movement of 1952–3. That movement accused many former lawyers of crimes, removed some 80 per cent of judicial personnel retained from the former régime and launched an attack against 'black lawyers'. It resulted in the massive transfer of Communist Party activists and ex-army personnel to legal and security duties (Leng 1967: pp. 27–44, 132–4).

Though there were regulations governing those tribunals, stipulating procedural safeguards and allowing for defence, they usually presumed guilt in their exercise of a kind of martial law and disregarded stipulations governing capital punishment. Traditional disdain for people who offered their services to the public in litigation was reinforced by suspicions of abetting 'the enemy' (Leng 1967: pp. 127–32). For their part, the formal courts, faced with an enormous backlog of cases, shortage of qualified personnel and hastily recruited people's assessors, made extensive use of circuit sessions to arrive at decisions which were not always well-informed even by Party policy. New laws did appear covering such matters as the punishment of counter-revolution (1951–2), corruption (1952), the undermining of the monetary system, and narcotics (Blaustein 1962: pp. 215–39), but only some time after mass movements to deal with those matters were well under way. The laws either prescribed directly, or were interpreted to prescribe, retrospective judgement and judgement by analogy, which left much room for arbitrary interpretation. Procuratoral and public security authorities, furthermore, relied on an informal, diffuse and unreliable supply of information, provided by 'correspondents' and 'denunciation boxes' (Leng 1967: p. 104).

Lack of established procedure and reliable information led in some cases to the violation of express commitments. For example, leniency was promised to 'counter-revolutionaries' who registered with the authorities but was often not granted. Lack of clear procedural rules resulted also in the administration of criminal justice oscillating between secret administrative trials and the mass educative trials associated with the various movements. In 1951, there were almost 30,000 of these in Beijing alone, attended by some 3.4 million people (Leng 1967: p. 31). They have been referred to as a form of 'terror'. During the early 1950s, as we have seen, many hundreds of thousands of landlords and 'counter-revolutionaries' were executed. Most persons judged to be 'counter-revolutionary', however, were consigned by the courts, the *ad hoc* tribunals or the public security organs to 'control' though labour and deprived of the rights to vote, be elected, hold administrative office in a state organ, join the armed forces or people's organisations and to demonstrate. They were specifically denied freedom of speech, association, correspondence and movement of household. Formally the period of 'control' was set at three years though the term might be extended or reduced (Blaustein 1962: pp. 222–6).

Though such 'control' would seem to be a criminal sanction, it was often formally defined as 'administrative', since court proceedings were not undertaken. Administrative sanctions were also applied to large numbers of vagrants, loafers, prostitutes and other 'anti-social elements' who were simply rounded up and sent to what were first called 'new life schools' and later schools for 'rehabilitation through labour'. The educative spirit here was reminiscent of the early utilitarian reformers, though, as Michael Dutton (1992: pp. 14–15) points out, it was geared not to produce the individualised and disciplined subject of early-nineteenth-century England but a class of proletarians. Yet surely the old utilitarians would have discerned in China a classic problem of the cost–benefit calculus. Long-term re-education in labour camps strained administrative resources to the limit and created pressures for early release; yet early release might exacerbate chronic problems of urban unemployment. The greatest good of the greatest number, moreover, demanded urgent measures to clean up the cities but the administrative means used gave great scope for arbitrariness and left little opportunity for rectifying a mistaken classification. Such Benthamite dilemmas were as relevant for proletarian utilitarians as they were for the 'bourgeois' variety.

Despite the capricious nature of justice in the early years of the régime, attempts were made, in utilitarian spirit (though never described as such), to create the rudiments of a formal structure of security and adjudication, governed by rules. Three hierarchies were constructed. First was the court system headed by the Supreme People's Court. Second came the procuracy, headed by a Supreme People's Procuracy, no longer subject to dual rule, responsible for conducting formal prosecution, seeing that state officials adhered to the law and collecting information on illegality. Third was the public security system headed at national level by the Ministry of Public Security, charged with directing the police, the secret police and the public security armed forces (known after 1955 as the People's Armed Police). At provincial level there was a public security department, a higher people's court and a higher people's procuracy. At city (*shi*) or special district level came a public security division, an intermediate court and intermediate procuracy, whilst at *xian* or urban ward level there existed a public security bureau, basic court and a basic procuracy. That basic court was empowered to set up people's tribunals. These were not the same as the old tribunals created for the specific purpose of conducting a mass movement but were regular delegated courts established in various local areas to replace the old circuit courts. Each level of court might establish judicial committees to review judgements, sum up experiences, select model cases and organise people's reception offices to handle letters, settle simple cases and prepare petitions. In addition there were special military courts and procuracies solely concerned with water and rail transport (Leng 1967: pp. 77–126). For its part, the People's Procuracy built up a regularised network for collecting information (with the continued use of 'correspondents' and denunciation boxes') and mechanisms for supervising the courts. In that system, procurators had the power to protest against court judgements and the head of the Supreme Procuracy could even protest against decisions of the Supreme Court directly to the National People's Congress (Leng 1967: pp. 102–19).

As we have seen, the lowest public security organ, the local police station, worked in parallel with a street office. Below that came 'mass organisations' with informal sanctioning powers. We noted in Chapter 4 that these consisted of residents' committees each with a mediation committee (of three to eleven members) and a security defence committee, which might be sub-divided into teams, or failing that an individual charged with security. All such bodies were supposed to be elected. The smallest unit of informal organisation was the residents' group, supervised by a 'household register policeman' who kept files on the residents (Cohen 1968: pp. 139–41). Such was the beginning of the contemporary household register system which by the mid-1950s extended into rural areas and, as the key to entry into the welfare state, was an effective method of control (Dutton 1992: pp. 189–245).

Security defence and mediation committees, teams or persons might also be found in economic enterprises, offices or government organs where they were sometimes joined by representatives of the state apparatus responsible for economic control or by 'comrades' adjudication committees'. Those committees had existed since the days of the Jiangxi Soviet but clearly those introduced in 1953 were copied from the contemporary Soviet Union. They dealt with absenteeism and other questions of labour discipline and, without punitive powers of their own, might refer cases to management for the imposition of sanctions (Leng 1967: pp. 93–4; Cohen 1968: pp. 170–9). In general, sanctions in economic units were largely characterised as 'informal' or 'administrative', a fact which raised knotty problems once one took literally the slogan of 1953, noted in Chapter 1, that 'the state plan is law'. Within those state organs sanctions included demotion.

To handle disputes among enterprises, arbitration committees were set up. In theory, a collective enterprise as a 'juridical person' could sue and be sued and contracts involving change of ownership (with the state as one party) could be the subject of litigation. In practice, however, to conform with the state plan, disputes seem to have been settled by financial and economic commissions and by administrative agencies responsible for particular enterprises outside the formal legal structure (Hsiao 1965: pp. 115–18). Contracts, moreover, were a means of ensuring compliance with the plan and contained few understandings as to what measures might be taken should a party default. Particularly when private businesses were involved, such contracts might be registered by public notaries, who were less concerned with legality than controlling enterprises in the interests of the plan (Lubman 1970: pp. 233–7). There is a dearth of information on this whole issue and we have access only to a few specific governing procedures (covering statutory bodies responsible, for example, for maritime casualties). Lack of information is, no doubt, due to the desire to present a picture of harmony (Blaustein 1962: pp. 495–506; Dicks 1989: p. 561).

In the countryside below *xian* level, there were *xiang* or village security defence and mediation committees and teams (subsumed later by collectives and communes), or at least a person entrusted with that task. Because the security apparatus in the countryside was thinly stretched, members of security committees usually held prominent positions in the basic militia which could be used for policing duties. Clearly mass involvement in security had an important educative function as well as one of control; that, it will be remembered, was one of the rationales for *baojia* (Cohen 1968: p. 119). Indeed, one might ask, was the new system merely a return to a form of *baojia* under another name? Surely not when one considers that this time the system was geared to the values of the work group rather than the family (Dutton 1992: pp. 15, 189–245). We return to the problem, discussed earlier, of the nexus of community and control.

Legislation establishing all of the above bodies appeared in the early 1950s and culminated in a spate of acts in 1954 at the time of the new state Constitution (Blaustein 1962: pp. 1–33, 115–71; Leng and Chiu 1985: pp. 253–68). The legislation created a vertically integrated hierarchy of economic control headed by a Ministry of Supervision (Schurmann 1966: pp. 327–46). It affirmed that the courts were the main bodies responsible for implementing criminal justice and forbade public security offices to impose the death penalty and other serious sanctions (an occurrence of the early 1950s which was by no means rare). It specified the organisation of trials. It gave people's congresses powers to elect presidents of courts (for a term of four years), to investigate legal organisations and to call meetings to handle complaints. It once again made provision for the election of lay assessors who were ranked equal to judges and stressed the need for judgement to be a collegial product rather than that of a single judge. Those assessors were elected for a term of two years and were required to serve for ten days per annum. The legislation went on to affirm the need to revamp the legal profession, to provide what were known as 'people's lawyers' and made provision for law schools, cadre schools, training classes and other means of supplying defence counsel.

Yet for all that, the basic-level administration of justice, as specified by the legislation, was still held to be informal. An attempt made in 1953 to replace arbitration and mediation bodies by the formal courts under the anti-bureaucratic rubric of 'five too many' had soon been abandoned once it was seen that courts could not handle the strain. Thus, in 1954, the informal and formal sanctioning powers of the police were regularised and the roles of security defence committees and mediation committees were affirmed. Though questions of security were the responsibility of the former, mediation committees (largely staffed by women in the larger cities) did handle minor criminal matters involving censure or 'voluntary' labour. Their main function, however, was settlement of civil cases, matters of divorce and, in general, saving the time of the formal legal apparatus. Thus legislation stipulated that no dispute should be submitted to a court until after mediation had been tried.

That the formal powers of mediation committees were limited and that they relied on voluntary submission and could not compel a disputant to appear before them (Cohen 1971: pp. 29–50), gives the impression that their role was changing from an alternative to the formal justice system to merely a supplement (Palmer 1988b: pp. 236–8) and by the mid-1950s some doubts were expressed as to their continued utility (Lubman 1970: p. 240). The change reflects what Kamenka and Tay (1971) (after Tönnies) call a shift from Yan'an-type *Gemeinschaft* (community) law to bureaucratic rule by law with the infusion of a modicum of *Gesselschaft* (bargaining) law. Put another way, such committees were seen increasingly as a popular supplement to a system of adjudication by experts, to a régime based on science mediated by popular will.

But clearly the experts and the formal structure could not cope with eventualities in rural areas. They could not handle the numerous cases thrown up during a mass movement and once again *ad hoc* bodies were convened by local authorities to implement 'mass justice'. Such was the case during the *sufan* campaign and the collectivisation drive, which in 1955 was said to have dealt with over 81,000 'counter-revolutionaries' and to have persuaded 190,000 other 'counter-revolutionaries' to give themselves up (Leng 1967: p. 61). With de-Stalinisation in 1956, however, as the Soviet Union moved closer towards some Western norms, there was a new emphasis on legality and regularity, and Dong Biwu, President of the Supreme Court, complained to the Eighth Party Congress that a small number of officials did not pay attention to the new legal system (Leng 1967: p. 52). The first task was to rectify irregularities in the *sufan* movement and *ad hoc* bodies were established by public security organs, Procuracy and courts to investigate cases of prolonged detention (Cohen 1968: pp. 385–6). As the excesses of *sufan* were rectified, the definition of counter-revolution became more narrowly circumscribed and there was much discussion as to exactly which political rights should be denied following conviction. Demands were made that the extensive deprivation of counter-revolutionaries' civil rights should not be extended uniformly to those convicted of other crimes. More attention was given to limits on the confiscation of property and there was a move also to restrict the use of the death penalty which had previously been imposed for crimes as minor as swindling. In 1957 all death sentences were required to be approved by the Supreme Court. In his political report to the Eighth Party Congress Liu Shaoqi even spoke of the future abolition of the death penalty (Leng 1967: pp. 50–1, 167), though in the meantime much was made of the 'humane' practice of sentencing people to death with execution suspended for two years if the convicted person did not reform; needless to say a very high success rate was recorded in such cases (Scobell 1990: p. 505; Cohen 1968: pp. 535–41).

At the same time the use of extra-legal sanctions became less frequent. Since 'control' through labour was now specified as the prerogative solely of the courts, there was a need more clearly to specify the different standards for administrative and criminal sanctions, though, in effect, this seemed to boil down to the authorities considering whether or not an accused person should have to bear the burden of a criminal record. There was much discussion on what constituted a 'criminal' offence and on concepts such as 'hoodlum' and 'criminal negligence'. Those discussions led to various actions such as adultery being declared 'not criminal' in contrast to earlier periods where they were so designated, simply because complainants had appeared before the courts. There was debate also about the use of judgement by analogy which was defined as a temporary measure to be abolished once the system was consolidated (it was formally abolished in the Soviet Union in 1958) (Cohen 1968: pp. 336–41). The debates were characterised by much confusion, yet they did reveal a sensitivity to the injustice of severe sanctions of a purely administrative nature.

An attempt was also made to implement that section in the Constitution which specified that trials should be public in a regular sense, rather than secret or public in the manner of the earlier mass trials. According to legislation of 1956, the only exceptions were to be cases relating to state secrets, those which required the disclosure of intimate personal details or ones involving juveniles (Cohen 1968: p. 442). Defence in public trials could be conducted by any relative (regardless of class status [*jieji chengfen*]) or by any other person specified by the accused who had not been deprived of civil rights and, of course, official defence counsel (charging fees in many cases) could be appointed by the courts or provided by lawyers' associations attached to local legal advisory offices. Those lawyers might be professionals, university lecturers, people's congress delegates working part-time or various other officials or ex-officials. The right of the accused, moreover, to challenge any member of the adjudication panel was affirmed. There was even discussion of the presumption of innocence and the right of the accused to remain silent, though that was a matter of considerable controversy (Leng 1967: pp. 127–46: Gelatt 1982: pp. 269–74).

In practice, however, public trials were more the exception than the rule and the use of defence counsel was rare. In the mid-1950s defence counsel were often regarded by judges as an inconvenience and, in the spirit of rule *by* law rather than rule *of* law, were always considered to be auxiliaries to the state rather than agents of the accused. A few model trials were reported mainly for propaganda reasons and, in Jerome Cohen's words, often resembled 'morality plays' (Leng 1967: pp. 140–6; Cohen 1968: pp. 13, 429–60). Their educative function was highlighted by the fact that the president of the court might invite spectators to voice their opinions. Yet, despite their rarity and often unusual procedure, their very reporting signified a new spirit, a willingness to strive for new standards of due process and an invitation for scholars to debate controversial legal issues with the aid of Soviet advisers. Here the role of the press was crucial as it also was in rectifying court injustices. The aim was to inform those who were drafting a Criminal Code (under the leadership of Peng Zhen) and working out experimental rules of criminal procedure.

By 1956, therefore, it seemed that full-scale attempts were under way to establish in China something like the Soviet legal system, reformed after the death of Stalin. In criminal law, procedure was regularised and in civil law consideration was given to Soviet-type state arbitral machinery. Yet, for many, the process of regularisation was too slow. With reform in the air during the movement to 'let a hundred flowers bloom and a hundred schools of thought contend', criticism arose. Complaints were voiced that the system of reform through labour could be more punitive than educative, as exemplified by the increased death rate in institutions which had tried to be self-sufficient (Dutton 1992: pp. 274–5). There were even hints that some eminent people wanted something like the 'rule of law' when the Chief Justice of the Criminal Division of the Supreme Court complained that whereas the formal criminal system talked of an independent judiciary, the judiciary in practice fell short of any genuine independence and judges were under the control of executive or legislative organs. Disquiet was also felt concerning the fact that if a conviction could not be obtained, a trial might be interrupted and the case set back to the Procuracy to collect further evidence. And many legal scholars voiced their concern that the Party might intervene in legal proceedings on an *ad hoc* basis. Those scholars complained loudly about what seemed to them to be reluctance by the authorities to promulgate the proposed Criminal Code (Leng, 1967: pp. 54–63).

The Anti-rightist Movement, the Great Leap and After

The draft Criminal Code, said to consist of 261 articles and released to lower courts for trial implementation, was not to be promulgated, it being a casualty of the Anti-rightist Movement (Leng, 1967: p. 54). As we have noted, both that movement and the 'hundred flowers' which preceded it were prefigured by versions of Mao Zedong's speech 'On the Correct Handling of Contradictions Among the People'. That speech specified different kinds of contradiction which required different kinds of legal treatment. We have already discussed problems of distinguishing an 'antagonistic contradiction' (between 'the people' and 'the enemy') from one 'among the people'. Advice given to lawyers, moreover, to the effect that not all criminals should be classified as 'the enemy' and that crimes could occur 'among the people', was not always clear about over whom 'dictatorship' was to be exercised. One had to include among the enemy counter-revolutionaries who 'had the intention of overthrowing the régime'; but how should one treat hoodlums and habitual criminals who, according to such advice, deserved 'dictatorship'. To make it even more confusing, classification depended not only on the laws of the state but on Party policy at a given time – policy which was going through rapid change and reversal (Cohen 1968: pp. 89–96; Leng 1967: pp. 154–7).

Suffice it to say that during the Anti-rightist movement, the focus was on an expanded notion of 'enemy' and there was much talk of renewed 'frenzied' attacks of counter-revolutionaries. As the class nature of law was reasserted, exponents of the presumption of innocence and the right of the accused to remain silent were accused of 'bourgeois' leanings. Feudal thought, it was argued, presumed guilt, bourgeois thought presumed innocence but now a materialist analysis held that one should presume nothing. Those who believed that some legal principles could be inherited from the past were charged with supporting the 'dictatorship of the bourgeoisie' and the spirit of Jiang Jieshi. Those who felt that the Judicial Reform Movement of 1952 had deprived China of competent lawyers were assured that 20 per cent of former lawyers were retained. Though the educational level of new legal personnel was not all it might be, such legal personnel were said to have had a 'firm class stand'. Complaints about incomplete legislation were met by the argument that over 4,000 pieces of legislation had been passed. And those who had insisted on the need to separate more clearly the functions of courts, Procuracy and police and had complained about Party interference were accused of 'negating the dictatorship of the proletariat' (Gelatt 1982: pp. 274–81; Cohen 1968: pp. 495–506; Leng 1967: pp. 54–63). At the same time, moves were made to replace the functions of the Ministry of Supervision by specifically Party organs and to restore the old practice of 'internal control'. As Party leadership and the non-neutral character of court procedure were affirmed, non-Party personnel were removed from judicial organs and official utterances proclaimed that a model judge should consult the Party at all times. The Procuracy, moreover, was accused of disobeying the Party in the guise of 'learning from the Soviet Union' (then affirming a more independent role for the law). In short, contrary to the provisions of the 1954 Constitution, moves towards a more independent judiciary were curtailed. Vanguardism had triumphed over procedure.

Despite the stipulations of 1956 on the administrative imposition of 'control' through labour, the Anti-rightist movement led to a large number of sanctions being imposed by administrative organs without any recourse to the courts. According to regulations of August 1957, persons with no proper employment, anti-social elements, loafers and those who did not obey work assignments were once again sent in increasing numbers to undergo 'reform through labour' for indefinite terms (Cohen 1968: pp. 249–74). This time, however, rather than relying simply on camps, such people were often despatched to collectives (and later communes) which had facilities for their supervision. The same fate attended many of those who flocked into the cities without permission. Many people, also, were branded as 'rightists' by Party organs, sent to the countryside and/or simply expelled from the Party (which for some might be worse than the imposition of criminal sanctions). Indeed, sanctions were imposed on the Chief Justice of the Criminal Division of the Supreme Court, mentioned earlier. During that period experiments in conducting regular public trials were discontinued. Lawyers collectives were reduced to skeleton staff as defence lawyers became redundant after they had been warned not to favour the defendant and to act in the interests of the state. More generally, it was felt, a return to an internal model of law had no place for lawyers, not so long before denounced as 'tricksters'.

This process was exacerbated during the Great Leap Forward, which concentrated on administrative simplification and speed. In the interests of simplification, the ministries of Supervision and Justice (the latter in charge of the staffing and administration of courts), which were under a cloud for being 'rightist', were abolished (1959). People's reception offices were decentralised and legal personnel were sent down to the grass-roots to conduct summary trials with local Party personnel. The prescribed mechanism for implementing speedy justice was a team of representatives of public security, procuratoral and court personnel under Party leadership. That team, combining personnel in administration, justice and education, might convene *ad hoc* mass meetings in conjunction with a trial to ensure the maximum propaganda effect, might take pride in settling a case in one day and take part in manual labour in its 'spare time' (Leng 1967: pp. 65–6; Cohen 1968: pp. 17, 413–4, 474–83). Needless to say, officials often expressed exasperation with appeals (Cohen 1968: pp. 555–63).

As we saw earlier, the Great Leap stress on simplification and speed was joined by a single-minded focus on production. Thus, institutions in charge of reform through labour were forced once again to become self-sufficient, with a consequent rise in the death rate within them (Dutton 1992: p. 275). A fourth theme was 'popular justice'. Thus the use of adjudication committees declined and new experiments were conducted to extend the powers of mediation committees, now seen once again as alternatives rather than as supplements to the formal process. Those committees dealt with anti-social conduct through what were known as adjustment committees, blurring the line between security and conflict resolution. Pacts (reminiscent of traditional China) were also concluded among local residents to deter frequent petty crime (Cohen 1968: pp. 179–88). Some of the practices introduced during the Great Leap, such as holding on-the-spot-trials conducted by teams under Party leadership and replacing formal channels for voicing complaints by provisions for visits and letter-writing, continued well into the 1960s, though with the collapse of the Leap there were calls for greater regularity. In the meantime a deteriorating economy began to require emergency measures and the army sometimes imposed its own rough justice (Leng 1967: p. 126).

Even before the Leap came to an end, a more relaxed attitude was beginning to prevail. One considers here the general amnesty granted at the time of the tenth anniversary of the foundation of the People's Republic in late 1959 (which amongst other things released the former emperor, convicted as a war criminal). In the early 1960s, as in so many other areas, the class struggle theme was played down. At that time many 'rightists' were released and in some cases the period of reform through labour was limited to three years. Throughout the early 1960s the use of the death penalty declined as did the overall number of criminal cases (which might simply reflect the greater use of administrative sanctions). For their part, public security personnel were obliged annually to engage in a 'love the people month' to restore good relations with the masses (Leng 1967: pp 68–71; Cohen 1968: p. 269).

Yet Mao's call of 1962 'never to forget the class struggle' and the ensuing Socialist Education Movement acted as a counter-current. After 1962 there was, on the one hand, a renewed stress on class struggle, on the plans of landlords to 'stage a come-back' and the need for unrestrained policy to prevent 'revisionism'. Yet, on the other, the very denunciation of Soviet 'revisionism' caused legal scholars to look to foreign systems other than the Soviet, to examine past traditions of law and to reinterpret *li* and *fa*. The general attitude towards foreign systems and the past was uniformly critical, but, as Leng Shao-chuan (1967: pp. 74, 124) sees it, the very fact that they were discussed was a significant advance on the Antirightist movement and the Great Leap. As one might expect, Soviet spokespersons became more and more vocal in denouncing Chinese criminal procedure.

Increasing leniency, however, was not paralleled by large amounts of new legislation. In 1957, 195 laws, decrees and regulations had been enacted; in 1958 there had been 147, and in 1959 143. In 1960 the figure declined to 50, falling to 20 in 1961 and 24 in 1962. The 1963 figure was 36. Consequently the *Zhonghua renmin gongheguo fagui huibian* (Compendium of Laws and Regulations of the People's Republic of China) ceased to be an annual publication in the 1960s and before long ceased altogether. According to one Chinese legal authority, it was the 1959 campaign against 'right-leaning' elements which hampered legislative work (Wu Jianfan 1986: pp. 12–13), though one has doubts about this considering that in 1962, allegedly on Mao's instructions, work on the various codes, interrupted in 1957, was resumed and in 1963 drafts of a criminal code (the 33rd), a code of criminal procedure and a civil code were distributed to judicial departments for trial use. Though those drafts were not approved by the National People's Congress they were said to have been referred to by the courts in reaching verdicts and meting out punishment (*Beijing Review*, 2, 12 Jan. 1979: p. 26). Whilst effects of the Great Leap Forward might have been a major factor in the general decline in legislative activity, the Socialist Education Movement was surely the most important reason why the draft codes were not enacted.

There was, however, a need for some economic legislation to clear up the chaos after the Great Leap Forward and to deal with *de facto* changes in property relations. A number of regulations were issued governing industry, agriculture, education and much else. The moderation of central planning by the use of contracts required a new set of regulations in 1962–3. In theory, contractual disputes might be settled by the courts, though observers such as Barry Richman noted no such instance (Liang 1985; Richman 1969: pp. 385–9). Once again, it seems, contractual disputes were handled by administrative agencies, often by means of conferences, with penalties being imposed by the banks (Lubman 1970: pp. 249–50). Civil law, therefore, continued to maintain its informal character and a wide variety of persons might appear in informal discussion of cases, even during the appeal stage of the court procedure. But, of course, the vast majority of civil cases (which consisted in large measure in marital disputes) never reached the courts and were settled by mediation committees (Leng 1967: pp. 169–74).

The Criminal Sanctioning Process in the Early 1960s

Having described the various changes in criminal law through the 1950s and early 1960s, let us sum up the criminal sanctioning process which existed prior to the Cultural Revolution (Cohen 1968: pp. 20–53). As we have seen, sanctions were classified as administrative or criminal. Administrative sanctions might be informal or formal. The former ranged from private criticism and warnings, group criticism, public censure, to forms of public struggle', imposed by residents' committees, enterprise or commune/brigade security defence committees (or their 'special agents') with or without the recommendation of the police.

Formal administrative sanctions, imposed by the police, were governed by the Security Administration Punishment Act of October 1957 (Leng and Chiu 1985: pp. 235–48) which specified warnings, fines (from 0.50 to 30 *yuan* and ideally geared to pecuniary status) and detention (up to 15 days), covering what in the West are termed misdemeanours and providing compensation to victims. That Act might impose detention even for such minor offences as 'spreading rumours', making loud noises after due warning, using obscene language and acting indecently with women, polluting drinking water, dirtying other people's clothes, urinating and dumping rubbish in the street, violating traffic regulations, throwing stones at trains or failing to keep a register of guests in hotels. Whilst detention for such offences might seem harsh to Western eyes, it is fair to say that the provisions of the Act were often ignored (Cohen 1968: pp. 200–37). Some of the sanctions, applied according to the Security Administration Punishment Act, might also appear to Western eyes as criminal rather than administrative and as violating the state Constitution. One should remember, however, that the Constitution was seen more as a programmatic document than as a legal bed-rock; its terms were frequently disregarded after 1957.

For more serious offences, defined officially as 'criminal', the police might impose 'supervised labour' within society and confinement in a rehabilitation camp (perhaps for an indefinite period). The latter involved not only labour but psychological techniques of group 'study' which, as we have seen, were designed not to individuate in Benthamite manner but to bolster a regime of mutuality – to create a new selfless individual. To this end everything, including family visits, were pressed into service (Dutton 1992: pp. 258–62, 310). Though these actions of the police were carried out under the jurisdiction of the Procuracy, infrequent reference was made to that body, particularly after 1957.

The Procuracy and the courts were concerned with the imposition of more serious penalties, ranging from 'control' (a stricter form of 'supervised labour'), serving a sentence outside prison under someone's else's guarantee (for the sick), various periods of imprisonment (which employed the same techniques as labour reform), to a death sentence suspended for two years and an immediate death sentence. The formal criminal provisions, however, like those of the Security Administration Punishment Act, were not strictly adhered to and decisions as to whether a crime had been committed depended on reference to changing Party instructions and policies more than formal laws. That is not to say that detailed regulations, instructions, interpretations and syntheses of judicial decisions did not exist. Indeed there were many. The point is they were rarely published (including those covering vital matters such as murder, rape and arson), it being felt sufficient to provide information to the public on correct and incorrect behaviour through the mass media and small group discussions. At one level one could say that *li* was still superior to *fa*. More bluntly one could also say that Party policy, commitment to the 'internal' mode and flexibility in applying different standards to different classes and 'bad elements' were better served by details not being made public. Because it was difficult to keep up with changing policies there was frequent recourse to judgement by analogy and to retrospective regulations.

Yet, for all that, there was a conception of proper administrative process and of formal rule *by* law. A case submitted to, or initiated by, the police could earn an immediate administrative sanction or be handed over to an informal body such as a mediation or security defence committee in the interests of 'curing the patient' rather than 'pushing her or him over the cliff' (Li 1978). If a case was sufficiently serious, the police could detain a suspect for interrogation, which might be authorised by a public security sub-bureau at ward level. There were formal regulations specifying a maximum period for such detention without formal arrest but these were often circumvented by declaring prolonged detention necessary for interrogation itself an administrative sanction. During interrogation, the accused was allowed no contact with persons outside the detention centre; any evidence, including hearsay, was permitted and there was no privilege against self-incrimination. Usually the accused was initially not charged specifically with an offence and a general confession was sought, which entailed writing countless self-incriminatory drafts. A confession, however, was not required for conviction, as in traditional practice, though clearly the doctrine of applying leniency to those who confessed resulted in more confessions than otherwise. After 1954, the application of physical coercion to solicit a confession, long prohibited, was said to have played only a minor part.

Interrogation might be followed by formal arrest. Warrants for arrest were the prerogative of the Procuracy or basic courts though were often issued by public security sub-bureaux without seeking permission. Arrest signified that an investigator had broken the case. Up to that point cases might be discontinued but, after formal arrest, termination of proceedings became most unlikely. Upon formal arrest the case was then handed over to a procurator who might question the accused and then decide on whether to prosecute, the speed of deliberation depending on whether a mass movement was in progress. If a decision were taken not to prosecute, the case might be handed back to the police who could release the accused or impose an administrative sanction. If prosecution were recommended, the bill of prosecution was handed over to a basic level court (usually at urban ward level in the towns) which might negotiate with the procurator on appropriate action or seek advice from a higher court. Usually the accused did not appear in court.

After the verdict, a draft judgement was submitted to a higher court (in the case of the death penalty the Supreme People's Court) for approval or modification, following which the verdict and sentence was made public. An appeal period was prescribed and if, on rare occasions (5 per cent in 1960), appeal was made (Leng 1967: p. 152), the case was handed over to the appropriate intermediate people's court. That appeal was not limited to the grounds given by the appellant or the procedures of the first trial and, in effect, constituted a complete re-adjudication, revealing what R. Randle Edwards (1986: p. 47) calls the 'principle of non-finality' according to which any aggrieved party may expect further review. The court might indeed impose a harsher sentence or grant an acquittal. In the latter eventuality, compensation and apology was rarely given and then only to persons of impeccable class background. Officials who had been found to have made errors in the process were usually subject only to the administrative sanctions of the authority for whom they worked. Indeed, Party personnel were often subject only to their internal Party disciplinary apparatus.

At any stage following sentence, the sentence might be modified for reasons unrelated to the original trial. This might be because the culprit had been deemed reformed through labour or perhaps because an adjudication committee had come to a new conclusion after the investigation of a superior court official or after Party or mass pressure (Cohen 1968: pp. 572–3). In such a case a convicted person might be returned to his or her original place of work or residence (conditionally or unconditionally) where that person usually remained under a stigma, or might be employed as a free worker in the labour institution to which he or she had been sent. After 1958, the latter became more common in accordance with policies aimed at restricting the growth of the urban population.

The above description shows that some administrative checks existed among police, Procuracy and courts, that the process was ideally (though not always) geared towards re-education rather than retribution and that the system was open at various stages to appeal. Safeguards existed but these were administrative and not what we usually understand as procedural (avoiding self-incrimination, hearsay evidence and the like). At no stage was the accused given ample scope to defend him or herself and defence counsel rarely appeared. There was also considerable scope for arbitrariness in deciding among the various sanctions available. Nor could appeal be made to precedent since past cases were presented for reference only and there was no acknowledgement of the part judges played in making law (Leng 1967: p. 86). Above all, despite the complaints of 1956, Party intervention continued to occur at all points. Such Party intervention might prevent sufficient time being devoted to a case. More frequently the problem was the excessive length of proceedings, with one writer complaining that whereas one needed much money to survive the old *Guomindang* courts, to survive the new ones one needed a long life (Li 1971: p. 234). The number of bureaucratic hurdles which had to be gone through resulted in people spending long periods in detention awaiting the next stage. Chinese criminal justice, therefore, was either too swift or more usually painfully slow. It was the latter problem which preoccupied the radicals of the Cultural Revolution.

The Cultural Revolution

With the onset of the Cultural Revolution in 1966, dissatisfaction with the bureaucratic nature of rule by law resulted in a large number of legal officials being dismissed, including the President of the Supreme Court and the Chief Procurator. Late in that year, Jiang Qing called for the 'revolutionary seizure of power' over the public security system and the courts and the 'revisionist' collaboration of these organs, and the Procuratorate (*gongjianfa*) became a butt of red rebel attacks. Despite the fact that leading persons in public security, such as the minister Xie Fuzhi, were prominent on the radical side, particular venom was directed at the public security apparatus which, far from obeying the Party, was said to have placed Party leaders (including Mao) under surveillance (Li 1971: pp. 248–50). Institutions charged with 'reform through labour' also were attacked for their economistic concern with 'self-sufficiency' resulting in a virtual collapse of that system in 1968 (Dutton 1992: pp. 278–9).

Red guards and red rebels differed in their opinions. Some focused on bureaucratism, complaining that 'dictatorship' had been replaced simply by 'administration'. Others went to the extreme of dismissing all law enacted before 1966, declaring that people who believed that legal ideas could be inherited were venerating feudalism, the *Guomindang* and 'revisionism'. Such people claimed that Mao Zedong had insisted that one should depend on the 'rule of persons' rather than the 'rule of law' and often extolled hasty judgements based on an interpretation of Mao Zedong Thought. In emotionally charged situations, the most extreme red rebels made what might be termed 'sacrilege' the cause for conviction and cases are on record of prison sentences being given for unintentionally defacing Mao's portrait. Populist fervour, moreover, led on occasions to a reversion to the traditional practice of punishing whole families for the actions of one of their members (Dutton 1992: p. 235).

As we noted in Chapter 4, the functions of the police at the basic level were sometimes taken over by vigilante groups with such grandiose titles as 'dictatorship of the masses teams' and, when those failed, by the army. As military control commissions came to wield executive power, military tribunals passed judgements necessary for restoring order. Under military aegis, a savage movement was launched in 1968 known as 'clearing the class ranks', guided by a 'six point decree on public security' issued in January 1967, it is said, in the name of the Party Central Committee by Kang Sheng, adviser to the Central Cultural Revolution Group on security. According to that decree, targets for struggle and imprisonment included those who opposed Mao and Lin Biao, hidden counter-revolutionaries, criminals, 'bad class elements', 'black hands' and 'bad leaders' of the Cultural Revolution. Indeed, the directive was a licence to pursue any of the old targets, plus anyone who was felt to be too disruptive in the Cultural Revolution, or simply anyone who had the wrong attitude and who maliciously attacked top Party leaders not already under attack by the Central Cultural Revolution Group (Baum 1986: pp. 81–4). In that movement some persons were killed and many (including red guard leaders) were imprisoned in makeshift gaols (commonly known as 'cow sheds'), dispatched administratively for re-education or simply relocated in the countryside (Li Zhengtian 1985). The worst excesses of the campaign were curtailed in 1970, though a new campaign got under way in 1970 known as 'one strike and three antis' (*yida sanfan*), referred to earlier, which prevented the revival of regular judicial processes. Those campaigns were attacked in the late 1970s as examples of Lin Biao and the 'Gang of Four's' 'feudal fascist rule', which subjugated tens of thousands of innocent people to cruel persecution.

Yet name calling is no substitute for analysis. As one would expect, there was a dearth of legal theory in the Cultural Revolution but it is possible to tease out some sort of rationale behind the radical position. That rationale represents an extreme version of the contradictions outlined in the introduction to this chapter. On the one hand, it will be remembered, Zhang Chunqiao argued that the commodity system fostered capitalism, and one might infer that law, being the manifestation of that system, had to be transcended. After all, did law not affirm 'bourgeois right' – applying an equal standard to unequal people and, therefore, entrenching inequalities? Though Zhang Chunqiao, Yao Wenyuan and their followers denounced the élitist Confucian notion of *li* and extolled the values of a proletarian version of Qin legalism, the various 'models' of correct behaviour put forward for emulation suggested the desire to promote a new socialist *li*. While, in practice, there was a merciless use of fa against what was felt to be the wrong kind of *li*, the impression was that the punitive techniques of a rationalised state (police and army) were being bent to the service of a new *li* which repudiated rationalisation. The result was not the transcendence of rationalisation, nor the achievement of a new kind of rationalisation, but irrationality. Eventually the only way to end that irrationality proved to be a return to the old forms of rationalisation.

In the meantime, as the Cultural Revolution wound down in the early 1970s, there was resistance to the return of the old mechanisms of the rationalised state. Renewed stress on the 'internal' model of law resulted in the appearance of new institutions, such as 'red sentinels' to maintain order in factories, 'May Seventh Cadre Schools' to re-educate cadres through labour, and 'three in one' bodies (public security, residents' committee and mediation committee) to resolve disputes. The new mediation committees, however, revived many of the functions of the old ones, even though in previous years mediation committees had been attacked as pernicious promoters of 'class harmony' (Palmer 1988b:

pp. 220, 238). The new committees, it seemed, differed only in their more intensified promotion of the study of Mao Zedong Thought. Indeed, many of the 'socialist new things' of the Cultural Revolution turned out not to be so new after all and gradually even the major elements of the old formal order were restored. As military control came to an end, an attenuated court system was re-established and a considerable degree of power gravitated to the public security apparatus.

The demise of military control and of Lin Biao, however, did not satisfy those who felt that the 'Lin Biao system' continued. This was the complaint of the famous hundred-metres-long poster put up in Guangzhou by three people whose abbreviated names became Li Yizhe. That poster, combining Cultural Revolutionary activism and liberal reformism along the lines suggested at the beginning of this chapter, denounced a system which exercised feudal rites, maintained magical spells, in which the 'little red book' was used, and allowed the rule of a 'new noble clique'. The answer, the poster argued, lay in a new system which enshrined legal safeguards and constitutionalism. The authors were subjected to struggle meetings in 1975 but allowed to debate their case at those meetings perhaps because their attack on what became known as the 'Gang of Four' met with some sympathy from Zhao Ziyang, then in a leading position in Guangdong province. They were eventually imprisoned in 1977 and not released until 1979 after the democracy movement had campaigned for their rehabilitation (Chan, Rosen and Unger, 1985).

The efforts of the Li Yizhe group to sway the National People's Congress did not meet with any success. As remarked on in Chapter 1, when that body finally met in 1975, it passed a new short Constitution of 30 articles, compared with 106 in 1954. It reduced the 12 articles covering the judicial system in the 1954 Constitution to only one and removed many of the rights enshrined in the earlier document including the immunity of members of the National People's Congress to criminal action without the consent of that body or its Standing Committee. In Cultural Revolution vein, however, it added the right to strike, to engage in mass debates and to put up large character posters. In short, the new Constitution, which deleted even programmatic reference to judicial independence, affirmed the primacy of class struggle and implied direct Party control over the judiciary. What was left of the judiciary was reduced to a bare minimum, people's assessors disappeared and the People's Procuracy was abolished. Procuratorial functions and powers were 'to be exercised by the organs of public security at various levels'. The 'mass line' was to apply to procuratorial work and mass mobilisation was required in the case of major counter-revolutionary criminal cases.

By 1975, the participatory enthusiasm of the Cultural Revolution had long been dissipated both because of its excesses and because of Party repression. Control by a restored Party over a restored judiciary, as specified in the new Constitution, had resulted in a situation subsequently referred to as 'judgement by Party secretaries'. Authorisation by relevant Party secretaries of all verdicts resulted in much delay and miscarriages of justice. The very opposite of delay, however, occurred in the revived mass trials of the period in which the masses deliberated on selected evidence designed to produce a predetermined result and which produced even greater miscarriages of justice. During those trials, sentencing was geared to maximum propaganda effect. Thus a thief might be executed in a drive against theft whilst another might receive a mild sentence once the drive was over (Leng and Chiu 1985: pp. 19–25). The virtues of the ideal mid-1950s legal system, attacked in the Cultural Revolution, had been regularity and predictability. The virtues of the radical ideal of the Cultural Revolution had been popular access to the instruments of justice. The former had degenerated into bureaucratism and the latter into thuggery. By 1975, the system revealed both bureaucratism and unpredictability with some thuggery, without the excuse of spontaneous mass enthusiasm.

The Post-1978 Situation

The arrest of the 'Gang of Four' in late 1976, albeit illegal, was followed by condemnation of that 'Gang's' 'lawlessness' and 'legal nihilism' (*falü xuwu zhuyi*), attributed to the residual influence of 'feudalism' or more specifically to ideas about the 'rule of persons' (*renzhi*) rather than 'rule by law'. Soon a debate developed amongst scholars who were said to have divided into three schools affirming each of the above positions with a third seeking compromise. As one might expect from the earlier discussion concerning the translation of *fazhi*, there was much confusion, with *fazhi* at some times meaning simply the legal system, and at others 'the rule of law' or, yet again, 'rule by law' (which could be a means to ensure the 'rule of persons'). There was debate also between those who took the orthodox Marxist view which stressed the class nature of law and those who affirmed its 'social' nature, which raised once again the notion that elements of law might be inherited from the past. Those debates continued throughout the 1980s with ever more stress on rule by law and less emphasis on class reductionism (Keith 1991; Lo 1989: pp. 1–109).

On a more practical plane, efforts were made to return to the 'golden age' of the 1950s. Thus, even before the Third Plenum, there was a new stress on 1950s-style legality which was reflected in the new Constitution of March 1978. That Constitution reintroduced some features of the Constitution of 1954 which had been omitted in that of 1975. It restored the rights of the accused to a public trial and the participation of people's assessors. It also re-established the People's Procuracy which was once again required to authorise police arrests (*Chinese Law and Government*, 11, 2–3 (1978): pp. 115–74). In mid-1978 some 110,000 'rightists', 'capped' in 1957, were released and their civil rights were restored in 1979. By 1980, over one million cases dating from the 'ten years of turmoil' were investigated, a quarter of which were judged as miscarriages of justice. In 1979 the Ministry of Justice was also re-established to supervise adjudication, arrange for the training of legal cadres and promote legal education.

There followed a spate of legislation, hastened by the need to set new limits on permissible behaviour in the wake of the democracy movement and mass demonstrations of late 1978 to early 1979. Such legislation was facilitated, no doubt, by the fact that some of the new laws were based on their predecessors of the 1950s or had been on the drawing board since the Anti-rightist Movement of 1957. First came the 'seven major laws' of 1979 of which four had a direct bearing on criminal law. In the spirit of Li's 'external' model, legislation once again stressed judicial independence, public trials, the right to defence counsel and a two-stage appeal system and were supplemented by statutes governing the provision of lawyers (1980) (Leng and Chiu, 1985: pp. 271–6). The seven laws were introduced by Peng Zhen who had been in charge of drafting a Criminal Code in the 1950s and was now chair of the Legal Affairs Commission of the National People's Congress (Potter 1986), signifying that that commission rather then a specifically Party body was to take the initiative in drafting legislation.

Indeed, as we have noted, the 1982 Constitution, which culminated law-making in the early reform period, whilst adhering to Deng Xiaoping's 'four cardinal principles', which affirmed Party leadership, explicitly placed Party members under the law. In united front spirit, it went on to restore more of the rights of the 1954 Constitution but did not advance on that Constitution's view that rights were programmatic and the gift of the state. Explicitly specifying that the exercise of citizens' rights must not infringe upon the interests of the state, it could not restore the right of freedom of residence. The Constitution also affirmed the separation of Party and state and restored immunity from criminal prosecution of National People's Congress deputies without the sanction of that body's praesidium or Standing Committee. The spirit of positivism and 'rule by law', however, was too strong for it to create mechanisms for judicial review. Geared to current resentment against the Cultural Revolution, moreover, it abolished the right to strike.

The revival of law in China has met with a mixed response in the West, ranging from the cautiously enthusiastic to outright condemnation in cold war vein or regret at the eclipse of mass justice (Gellhorn 1987; Copper, Michael and Wu 1985; Wu *et al.* 1988; Brady 1982). The reminder of this chapter, we hope, will fall into none of those categories.

Criminal Law in the 1980s

Two of the 'major laws' of 1979 dealt with the organisation of the Procuracy and the courts. Courts were organised in much the same way as in the 1950s with people's assessors, adjudication committees and people's reception offices. The special courts which had disappeared in the late 1950s were revived and provision was made for regular military courts. The Supreme People's Court, whilst not a constitutional court, could give 'explanations' on the application of laws and decrees. For their part, branches of the Procuracy, declared independent once again, were now made responsible both to their own hierarchy and to local congresses (the old dual-rule system). In supervising state cadres, they were empowered only to deal with matters concerning the criminal law, non-criminal misdemeanours of Party members being the responsibility of 'discipline inspection committees' and, later, as moves were made to separate Party and state functions, the re-established Ministry of Supervision (1986) (Leng 1982: pp. 205–11; Leng and Chiu 1985: pp. 62–84; Kolenda 1990; pp. 219–21). In general, therefore, the institutional structure governing criminal law resembled that of the 1950s, though in 1983 a new body was created. This was the Ministry of State Security, linking public security and intelligence, with powers similar to the Soviet KGB. That ministry controlled a new version of the People's Armed Police, was responsible for border guards, guarding foreign missions and general surveillance of foreigners who were said to have exercised a corrupting influence.

The two most important legislative items, the long-awaited Criminal Code and Code of Criminal Procedure (Leng and Chiu 1985: pp. 192–235), were again a codification of 1950s practice, modified by certain elements drawn from similar codes of the RSFSR (1960). Like the Russian codes, they continued to stress the educative role of law but were more concerned with the effect on certain categories of criminal than on either the specific criminal acts or the personality of the criminal. They were also more moralistic, less concerned with the rights of the accused and the need to mitigate the stigma of a criminal record, less concerned to limit the power of the police by procuratoral involvement at an early stage and less worried about procedural matters such as the use of hearsay evidence. In this they reflected the different historical experiences they had to confront. The Chinese codes had to establish the role of law in a situation where the very notion of legality had been under challenge, whereas the Russian codes had to deal with Stalinism where legal formalism had been used for arbitrary ends. The Chinese government, therefore, was more concerned to entrench the function of law than was the Russian government, which was preoccupied with correcting the past misuse of law and particularly that directed at certain social categories (Berman, Cohen and Russell 1982).

Though vague on many crucial points, the Chinese codes gave more detail than before on what constituted 'counter-revolutionary crime' and on 21 offences for which the death penalty might be imposed (14 of which were 'counter-revolutionary'). Retrospectivity was abolished but judgement by analogy was retained, though limited by Supreme Court approval. Obviously with the Cultural Revolution in mind, torture, forced confessions and libellous attacks (amongst other things in large character posters) were expressly forbidden. The appeal procedure, though still limited to one appeal, was now changed to prevent a court of the second instance aggravating the original punishment, which led to an increase in cases appealed from some 5 per cent prior to the Cultural Revolution to 22 per cent in 1980–1 (Woo 1989: pp. 134–5). A procurator, however, could still protest about the lightness of a sentence and require a new trial and probably only some 2 per cent of appeals resulted in acquittals (Copper, Michael and Wu 1985: p. 111). Perhaps most important, the new codes stressed 'equality before the law'. Such was also a feature of the 1950s legislation, though this time, whilst there was a greater focus on social categories than in Russian law, efforts were made to oppose adjudication based on the principle of class status earned as long ago as the land reform of 1950 (Blaustein 1962: pp. 291–324). The reverse also held: the legislation of 1979, anticipating the Constitution of 1982, insisted that 'no special privilege' (such as Party status) was allowed before the law.

Formally abolishing the privilege of Party membership must have raised hopes, as indeed did the gradual removal of the time-honoured slogan 'policy is the soul of law' and the affirmation of a new division of labour among Party, court, procuratoral and police bodies, though official statements went to great pains to explain that this was not the 'bourgeois' separation of powers. Yet, at a popular level, there was at first more cynicism than hope as public order deteriorated at a time of growing unemployment. Increasingly public security authorities found themselves unclear as to what was now permissible and could not handle those who exercised their new-found freedoms (which, of course, included obvious criminals). Frequently they had to bear the brunt of popular resentment dating from the 'ten years of turmoil' and in 1979 the army was frequently called out in cities to assist the public security authorities (Dreyer 1980: pp. 57–65).

In response, efforts were made to restore the structure of urban residents' committees with their security and mediation adjuncts and frequent use was made of 'reform through labour' which was reaffirmed as an administrative rather than simply a criminal measure. Regulations governing such action were revived in November 1979 (limited this time to four years) and proved a convenient way of dealing with dissidents (Leng 1982: p. 235; Copper, Michael and Wu 1985: pp. 94–5; Leng and Chiu 1985: pp. 251–2). The 'democracy movement' of 1979–80 had thrown up many of these, encouraged by official utterances concerning the need to institute a democratic system. As noted in Chapter 2, fears that the democracy movement was getting out of hand, however, resulted in the removal of Beijing's famous 'democracy wall', followed by a crack-down on unofficial publications and finally by the arrest and trial of those who campaigned against the power of a new 'dominant class' (including Wang Xizhe, one of the Li Yizhe trio). It took some two years to bring dissident intellectuals to heel, though by 1980 normal crime was less overt. Nevertheless, disturbances erupted from time to time and, despite some official denials noted earlier, crime seemed to increase throughout the decade, especially after 1985.

One response to public disorder was to increase criminal penalties and speed up criminal proceedings. Thus, in 1981, under Party pressure, the National People's Congress changed the terms of the Criminal Code to allow higher courts (rather than the Supreme Court) to authorise the death penalty. In 1982 the Code was amended to deal with corruption and mounting economic crime (Townsend 1987), prescribing the death penalty for 'serious' cases of smuggling, speculation, habitual theft, swindling, drug trafficking, bribery and the theft or illegal export of precious cultural relics. In 1983, a number of resolutions were passed specifying seven additional capital crimes, including gang warfare, pimping, trafficking in human beings and passing on criminal methods. Those resolutions speeded up trials and shortened the period of appeal for a death sentence. Indeed, one capital case was recorded as lasting only six days from arrest to execution. Another case described execution being carried out before the covering legislation was passed. And reports exist indicating that the old practice of specifying quotas for executions may have occurred and that summary executions were reviewed and approved by higher people's courts in advance (Woo 1989: pp. 146–7). In 1988, the scope of the death penalty was extended yet again to include more smuggling offences and cases of theft, embezzlement and bribery involving large amounts of money. In 1989 the offence of revealing 'state secrets' was added. The military also might impose the death penalty on its members for passing secrets to foreigners, for 'spreading rumours' which undermine morale and for harming civilians. By the end of the decade there were 48 capital offences compared with 21 in the Criminal Code (Scobell 1990: pp. 507–11; Copper, Michael and Wu 1985: p. 50; Copper 1988: pp. 56–76).

Indeed, it seemed the more legality was stressed the more widely was the scope of the death penalty extended and the more frequently was it employed. Such action contradicted earlier Chinese government pronouncements and also the 1977 resolution of the United Nations General Assembly calling for progressive restriction of the number of offences for which the death penalty might be imposed, with a view to its eventual abolition. Whilst that resolution was non-binding, it was one in which the Chinese government had participated (Davis 1987: pp. 332–3). There are no official statistics of the number of people executed but estimates during the period 1983–6 range from 10,000 to 30,000. That number of executions is, of course, very small compared with killings by extra-legal means during the Cultural Revolution but is probably over ten times higher than legal executions carried out during the decade from the mid-1950s to the mid-1960s, despite the Anti-rightist movement and the speedy justice of the Great Leap Forward (Scobell 1990: pp. 513–15). Of particular concern to human rights advocates is not only the scope of the death penalty but also, despite the new concern for legal precision, the vagueness of the relevant statutes.

Particularly vague are statutes governing corruption, state secrets and serious 'counter-revolution'. With growing economic reform, the definition of corruption, the penalties prescribed for it and guidelines concerning the burden of proof have undergone continued change but not in the direction of greater precision. (Townsend 1987: pp. 239–42). For their part, state secrets were defined until 1988 according to revived regulations of 1951 which included 'all state affairs which have not yet been decided on or which having been decided have not been made public'; and, if anything did not fall within the prescribed definitions, 'all other state affairs which should be kept secret' (Leng and Chiu 1985: pp. 130–1, 182–87). In 1988, however, new regulations attempted to make more precise what might or might not be revealed. There was also talk at that time about replacing the term 'counter-revolution' with more legally definable concepts such as 'sedition' or 'harm to national security' though the events of June 1989 delayed progress on that score (Gelatt 1989: p. 320). Nevertheless, however defined, the number of people detained for 'counter-revolution' in China's two largest cities had declined by the mid-1980s to some 2 to 3 per cent of all criminal detainees, compared with some 40 per cent prior to the Cultural Revolution (Baum 1986: p. 97).

Vagueness in legislation may perhaps provide the flexibility that allows for reeducation rather than simple punitive action – in Mao's terms, to 'cure the sickness and save the patient'. Education in the 1980s, however, serves the much cruder purpose of deterrence. Such deterrence is defended on utilitarian grounds, though Jeremy Bentham, who maintained that a penalty should only be slightly greater than the benefit to be derived from getting away with a crime, would have been shocked at the severity of penalties. Utilitarian deterrence is still achieved by 'mass sentencing meetings' and those sentenced to death are still humiliated and paraded around the streets in trucks to 'assuage the anger of the masses'. Though legal scholars and anyone who takes human rights seriously must be disturbed, the 'greatest good of the greatest number' appears confirmed by mass preference for the increased use of the death penalty and the spectacle which goes with it (Scobell 1990: pp. 506–7). The popularity of such measures is no doubt due to public fears about increasingly visible youth crime (at least half of those executed seem to be under 25) and resentment at those who have abused their position to make money (half of all crime is classed as 'economic' and some 10 per cent of all people executed are 'economic criminals'). One can also imagine there would be popular support for the imposition, through illegal, of the death sentence for holding 'dancing and sex parties' and 'showing pornographic films'. Yet one wonders whether those measures would have been so popular were everyone aware of the fact that proportionally far fewer Party members have been executed than non-Party members (Scobell 1990: pp. 515–19).

The 'equality' of Party members 'before the law' remains questionable. So also does the Party's willingness to allow for the development of an atmosphere of regularity. Not long after the 1982 Constitution, the Party was swift to amend the law to meet the needs of a mass movement, to adopt high-handed measures when under provocation and to violate the law. Thus the crackdown on crime in 1983 was carried out simply on the basis of a Party decision which resulted in violation of legal codes before the necessary amendments were passed (Leng and Chiu 1985: pp. 103, 136). Recourse to the codes, moreover, was not made when demonstrators were shot; in those cases one is not aware of procuratoral investigation nor the Procuracy handling any protest by relatives of the deceased (Dicks 1989: p. 548). Perhaps most notoriously, when the Party came under intense pressure in mid-1989, the Military Commission was quite capable of disregarding legal procedure, bringing about speedy trials and persuading the Supreme Court to support it after the event. One doubts, however, the stories about secret executions in 1989, for such action would defeat both the purpose of deterrence and of public retribution which have featured in the recent exercise of *fa* in its old legalist sense (Scobell 1990: p. 514).

Still, it seems, for the Procuracy to be truly effective in difficult and tense cases it needs Party backing, and prudent legal officials seek Party advice before making decisions. The Party has also been reluctant to remove its own structures set up to control legal institutions. At the highest levels the Party retained its Central Commission on Political and Legal Affairs, and moves to abolish political-legal committees at all levels of administration, linking Party and state institutions, were halted by the events of June 1989 (Kolenda 1990: p. 230). Party bodies at all levels continue to vet elections to the bench and might remove presidents of courts and coerce verdicts. A discrete Party structure, moreover, has often resulted in the Party imposing internal disciplinary sanctions on its members rather than having recourse to normal legal channels (Woo 1989: pp. 144–5; Kolenda 1990: pp. 219–21). Structure, it seems, is not conducive to the implementation of a policy which emphasises judicial independence and which has abolished (in 1979) Party review of serious cases. Yet, continually in calmer times, propaganda has stressed the courage of legal officials who dared to oppose Party leaders' usurpation of law. Numerous accounts have appeared in the press complaining about the exercise of Party cadres' privileges and apparent immunity before the law, and the prosecution of Party cadres has been designed to create a new legal spirit. Given the structure of power, the fact that collective Party bodies may not be brought to court and the fact that Party members have been less likely to be convicted than others

(Copper, Michael and Wu, 1985: p. 115), however, those prosecutions, far from improving confidence, led to complaints about those who were not convicted. Such was a major element in the student demonstrations of the late 1980s, the aftermath of which did result in greater attention being given to punishing Party members (Kolenda 1990: p. 224). Even more attention was given to the offences of Party members in August 1993 but we have yet to see what verdicts result.

Despite all the abuses of power which the structure has allowed, the imposition of formal restraints on the Party and the abolition of judgement according to class status, it would seem, was the first step in the affirmation of 'human rights'. Yet the Chinese government has offered merely general and philosophically unsatisfying statements on that score. For all that, the government's white paper on human rights of 1991 (State Council 1991), whilst clearly a ploy to regain international legitimacy, has elevated human rights to a major position in state policy (He 1992). Though it adhered to seven international conventions of relevance to human rights (more than the United States), the government still clings hesitatingly to the belief that rights are merely the product of a particular state. The Chinese government, of course, rejects the unacceptable 'natural' variety of human rights, inappropriate in a 'people's democratic dictatorship'. But, of course, 'natural rights' are not the only universal form. There are constructivist alternatives (Rawls 1985), or simply the more common notion that rights may be acknowledged to be artificial whilst serving the universalistic purpose of limiting the scope of all states' actions (a position argued by the now-dissident Yan Jiaqi). Perhaps more important, however, in the calculations of the Chinese government, has been its unwillingness to tolerate what might be seen as foreign interference, particularly since patriotism has continually been invoked to repair damaged legitimacy and since the work of Amnesty International and Asiawatch has been cited by foreign leaders and media. Thus, even though the Chinese government acceded to the International Convention on Racial Discrimination, it voiced reservations concerning the compulsory arbitration of the International Court of Justice (Dicks 1989: p. 549). More recently, in 1992, it lobbied successfully against attempts by the United Nations Human Rights Commission to conduct investigations in China. Apparently several other countries represented in that commission maintained similar views on sovereign inviolability. In such a situation one is left with arguments that China has its own notion of 'human rights', as the official 1991 statement makes clear. Surely, while rights may be specific to a situation, 'human rights' must, by definition, be universal.

One may perhaps be convinced by official Chinese interpretations of 'human rights'. But the government can mount no excuse for violations of its own legislated rights laid down in the 1991 statement. It will be recalled that, although there was no procedural code in the 1950s, regulations governing the treatment of persons under detention, time limits for such detention and the general 'administrative' provisions of the Security Administration Punishment Act were frequently violated. This was also true of the early 1980s when that act was revived and used to evade new stringent regulations on time limits prescribed for criminal cases (in, for example, the revised Arrest Act of 1979) (Leng and Chiu 1985: pp. 187–91). As in the 1950s, detention might be prolonged by declaring it 'administrative', and search might be carried out without the specified warrant by having a security administration committee actually conduct it. Suspects, moreover, might be held incommunicado by reference to an escape clause in Article 5 of the Arrest Act which allows authorities not to release information which would hamper the investigation (Leng and Chiu 1985: pp. 78, 89–90). Indeed, all sorts of irregularities might be covered by administrative detention on the grounds of 'undermining stability and unity'. Of course, most nations have legislated similar catch-all clauses and most police forces routinely violate their own legislated rights by administrative sleight-of-hand. But that can be no excuse.

Violations have not been rectified by any statement in the Chinese codes about the dignity of the accused which is supposed to apply to Western notions of *habeus corpus* (even if frequently violated there too). There have been amendments, however, to the Security Administration Punishment Act (1986) to allow for judicial review of administrative sanctions imposed by public security authorities (Woo 1989: pp. 142–3) and there is now much less reluctance than in the 1950s to publicise violations of citizen rights. Many of those violations have been due to traditional attitudes and considerable efforts have been directed to educating public security officers. Indeed the old practice of designating periods for public security personnel to 'love the people' has been revived together with the conferring of 'Lei Feng-type awards' (named after the selfless soldier Lei Feng who was praised in the 1960s as a 'rustless screw' in the service of the people and the revolution) (Leng and Chiu 1985: pp. 78, 91–2).

Violations of legislated rights and indeed penalties are revealed also in official records of trials. They show that even the model trial of the 'Lin Biao clique' and the 'Gang of Four' resulted in detention much longer than prescribed limits, involved interested parties in the judgement and manifested very dubious trial procedures (Leng and Chiu 1985: pp. 214, 17). The implementation of the sentence was also irregular. On the expiry of their two-year suspended death sentences in January 1983, the Supreme Court's collegiate bench ruled that Jiang Qing and Zhang Chunqiao 'did not in any flagrant way resist reform'. There is no evidence that Jiang Qing ever changed her position and the court's ruling that culpable resistance has to be in an 'odious manner' was arbitrary (Scobell 1988: pp. 159–60). The trial of the 'Gang' was supposed to provide an important lesson. It was perhaps a lesson in leniency, but surely not in legality. Accounts of other famous trials, such as that of the dissident Wei Jingsheng in 1979, leaked unofficially, show that they were 'kangaroo courts' to say the least. That trial, like many others, compromised the principle of open trial by requiring admission tickets, distributed to approved organisations (Copper, Michael and Wu 1985: pp. 47–8; Leng and Chiu 1985: p. 91). In more routine trials it is clear that violation of rights must occur so long as there is a shortage of personnel to handle cases properly. Local officials are often quite frank in arguing that they have neither the facilities nor the money to conduct proper public trials. In the early 1980s there were only some 3,000 lawyers in China (the same number as at the time of the Anti-rightist movement). By 1991 the number of full-time lawyers had increased to some 50,000, though that was only one per 20,000 people (BBC, *Summary of World Broadcasts*/FE/ 1082/B2/6, 27 May 1991). One might compare that with the United States figure in 1974 of one per 500 (Li 1978: p. 9).

It was probably because of resource constraints that the Code of Criminal Procedure stipulated merely that the court *may* appoint defence counsel rather than imposing an obligation. Such defence counsel as there were, however, have often been unsure of their duties. In general they have been precluded from pre-trial proceedings (unlike the system in Russia) and have been prevented from making available to the accused all the accumulated evidence on the grounds that such would impair the voluntary character of a confession (Berman, Cohen and Russell 1982: p. 245). Hampered procedurally, defence counsel, required to be both independent and loyal to the state and socialism, have been faced with a long-standing prejudice against legal defence and are still mindful of the fact that in the past they were accused of 'siding with the enemy'. Even in model trials attended by foreigners, defence counsel have generally been passive, with most questioning conducted by the presiding judge (Leng 1967: pp. 214–21; Leng and Chiu 1985: pp. 92–6; Gellhorn 1987: p. 18). They have remained passive throughout the 1980s despite the fact that their numbers have increased substantially and that they have appeared more and more regularly.

Defence counsel have been particularly ineffective in a situation where the presumption of innocence has been an alien belief. Such is reflected in the language of the Criminal Code and Code of Criminal Procedure and the continued denial of the right to silence. Consider Article 28 of the Code of Criminal Procedure, which stipulates that 'the responsibility of a defender is, on the basis of the facts and the law, to present materials and opinions proving that the defendant is not guilty', rather than seeing the onus of proof as resting with the prosecution and requiring defence counsel to refute charges. There has been renewed debate on the presumption of innocence, however, taking off where the Anti-rightist movement interrupted it. Whilst some have claimed that 'seeking truth through facts' embodied the presumption of innocence, others argued, in the manner discussed earlier, that the concept is unscientific and hampers law enforcement agencies. A third group has echoed the old argument that one needs to go beyond the 'feudal' idea of presumption of guilt and the 'bourgeois' idea of presumption of innocence to something else. Once again, that group affirmed the positivistic idea that 'seeking truth through facts' suggests neutrality. All three arguments seem to miss the point that the principle has nothing much to do with truth or 'science' but with procedural equity (Gelatt 1982: pp. 291–316; Edwards 1986: p. 47).

Still another group has argued that, in practice, there can be no pre-trial presumption of innocence and that the principle applies only in court procedure. Such a view is disturbing, since most of the work is done before a case ever gets to court, and certainly most Chinese court proceedings focus not so much on innocence or guilt but on the nature of the punishment (Gellhorn 1987: p. 18). Indeed, in criminal cases currently only one person in 200 is found 'not guilty'. One should bear in mind, however, that restriction of the presumption of innocence to court procedure often reflects the actual practice of Western law in dealing with less serious matters and a view which has found support in the United States Supreme Court (Gelatt 1982: pp. 312–15; Pfeffer 1970: pp. 261–81).

Civil, Economic and Administrative Law

Apart from rectifying 'leftist excesses', one of the major purposes of reviving law in the 1980s has been support for the 'four modernisations'. This has given rise to volumes of civil and economic legislation (Rui Mu 1986: pp. 61–76) and detailed treatises on those subjects, discussing the relationship of economic law to civil law and administrative law (Jones 1989). Each economic department has been responsible for drafting laws and the State Council set up an Economic Law Centre in 1981 to co-ordinate such activities. Major acts promulgated by the central government covering joint ventures (one of the 'seven laws' of 1979), income tax, inheritance, land appropriation and compensation, special economic zones, trademarks and much else have been published, though at local levels, it is difficult to gain access to detailed legislation. Some local governments have expressly prevented regulations from being disseminated (Dicks 1989: p. 540).

Such restrictions are probably due to bureaucratic inertia and it is fair to say that there has been a growing recognition that modernisation in a capitalist direction produces conflict of interests and requires more extensive use of mediation committees and arbitration tribunals both in domestic matters and between Chinese and foreign parties. This became clear once the reversal of criminal verdicts was seen to imply the reversal of financial verdicts. It became even clearer as the contract system replaced mandatory planning, with the status of economic enterprises as 'juridical persons' more clearly specified and when foreign investors expressed caution about the legal machinery necessary to ensure safety. The result was the enactment of an Economic Contract Law (1981) and a further series of contract laws in the years which followed, specifying the nature of economic contracts, provision for mediation and arbitration and allowing final recourse to ordinary or special people's courts. Such contract law, which can not cover every eventuality, leads, of course, to new self-generated non-statutory law (Gellhorn 1987: pp. 13–14). That is significant when one considers the reluctance hitherto in China to admit judgement by precedent.

It was clear also that changing notions of property (including, by 1985, 'intellectual property') and consequently inheritance (now required both to reflect new contractual arrangements and to shift the burden of welfare on to the family reconstituted as an economic unit – Palmer 1988a) demand quite complicated legislation both of a civil and criminal nature. Thus distinctions in ownership among rights of possession, use and disposal, customary in some other socialist countries, have been enshrined in civil law (NPC 1986). Changes in the line between legality and the grey and black market have given rise to much dispute and much anguish. One only has to consider the strictures on 'speculation' in Article 117 of the Criminal Code to realise that that word has undergone a rapid transformation in meaning and required special regulations in 1987 (Kolenda 1990: p. 216). Significantly here the recent tripartite division of courts into civil, criminal and economic chambers assigns both a criminal and civil role to the third category.

Yet even that tripartite division is insufficient to deal with a new phenomenon – disputes between the government and the governed. A body of administrative law is appearing and courts have also set up administrative chambers. The former practice of claiming that accountability existed simply because of administrative bodies' willingness to answer letters and 'receive complaints from the masses' is no longer sufficient. Accountability is now strengthened by a State Audit (legislated for in 1982 and strengthened in 1988) and by the re-created Ministry of Supervision (1986). And the draft Administrative Litigation Law (NPC 1988) which allows citizens and organisations to file suits in court against the actions of administrative organs and personnel, seems to offer some hope of more formal accountability. Here, Anthony Dicks (1989: pp. 567–8, 575) believes, is the greatest test for the new legal system if the famous jurist Dicey is correct and the 'rule of law' replaces simple 'rule by law' once the state itself becomes simply another party to a dispute, subject to the same rules as any other party. The events of

June 1989 cast a shadow here, though in 1991 some 25,000 cases were considered under this law with one-third of plaintiffs winning and being awarded compensation and another third being settled by out-of-court mediation. Of note has been the case of Guo Luoqi, a philosophy teacher, who filed suits against his university, the head of the State Education Commission and his local branch of the Party. Here the court ruled, significantly, that the Party, not being a government organ, could not be sued. The famous dissident journalist Wang Juntao (an associate of Zhao Ziyang) recently also filed legal suit against the authorities of his prison. Though one is mindful of the Party's defence, such developments are very important.

We saw earlier that in the 1950s regulations governing civil disputes were rarely published. In the 1980s, however, a civil code began to emerge. Notable here was the Code of Civil Procedure (For Trial Implementation) (1982), the revised Code of Civil Procedure (1991) and the General Principles of Civil Law (1986). These were based not on 1950s precedents but on European models torn out of context. As many commentators have pointed out, China has reverted to the thinking of the early part of this century which also drew ideas from Europe (especially Germany) rather than Anglo-American law. Thus, as in Europe, the power of the bureaucracy impinges on the law more than in the Anglo-American system but the writings of legal scholars carry more weight. This latter point is worth bearing in mind in view of the large number of legal journals and books which have appeared outlining arguments about the new legislation and the philosophy behind it. These have not just been aimed at members of the new law schools, departments and classes but have also informed a major campaign for mass legal education and have provided a channel for legal appeals (Dicks 1989: pp. 560, 571; Jones 1989: pp. xv–xviii; Woo 1989: p. 149; Sidel 1987).

Civil law has been the responsibility of a number of specialised judicial or quasi-judicial agencies and the complex machinery for arbitrating economic contracts. There are still major areas, however, where dispute settlement depends on *ad hoc* bodies. This is particularly noticeable in disputes between regions which, as we have seen, have multiplied with economic decentralisation and which often involve fierce and sometimes violent resistance to particular decisions (Dicks 1989: pp. 559–63).

The development of formal institutions responsible for civil law has been spectacular but the bulk of civil cases are still dealt with by mediation committees. By the mid-1980s 90 per cent of civil cases were handled by almost one million of those committees, involving nearly five million mediators. The aim, apparently, is eventually to have one mediator for every ten households, eliciting memories of *baojia* and reflecting perhaps more a concern with social control than dispute settlement. The committees are active in initial divorce proceedings (in practice preventing divorce), in the increasing disputes associated with housing and, of course, in the myriad disputes associated with land demarcation and other problems of the household contract system in agriculture. Having forsaken their old role of fostering class struggle, they are said also to have played a major part in the dissemination of legal knowledge. Once again the committees are active in forming and monitoring rural compacts, reminiscent of the late 1950s, and noted in previous chapters.

We return here to a problem noted earlier in this chapter. Are these mediation committees an alternative (*Gemeinschaft*) form of justice or merely supplements to the courts? A move to a more formal system of justice would suggest the latter, though much has been made of the Chinese tradition of popular dispute settlement and the continuing role of mediation in 'socialism with Chinese characteristics' – an alternative to law based on European codes. Indeed, there has been talk of the development of a separate science of 'mediology' (*tiaojiexue*) which suggests that they are much more than stop-gap measures pending the full development of the court system. One should note also that in the 1980s there were five times as many mediators as in the 1950s which again indicates a long-term role. The 'internal' model of law still thrives. Yet, as in the mid-1950s, legal professionals stress the role of mediation committees as adjuncts rather than alternatives. Those professionals often look down on the committees as not sufficiently professional. They note cases of illegal mediation where committees take over functions which properly should be handled by the courts, the improper use of coercion, the manipulation of questions of 'face' and actions taken by committees to gloss over serious misdemeanours or minor crimes. Such legal professionals are influenced, no doubt, by the old image of a mediator as an untrained housewife and entertain a sexist bias, confronting a situation where sometimes

80 per cent of mediation committees consist of women. They are clearly mindful of the fact that, in many cases, the low esteem in which mediation committees are held has resulted in cases being brought to public security offices and workplace authorities rather than to the committees. Thus attempts have been made to place mediation committees more firmly under the control of the Ministry of Justice and the courts, to ensure the registration of mediated agreements, to provide lawyers for hire in mediation cases and to appoint lawyers as part-time mediators. Above all, major efforts have been made to improve the skills of mediators, to recruit younger ones and especially Party members, to employ professional full-time mediators and to award payment for their services commensurate with employees in civil offices (Palmer 1988b: pp. 219–77).

Prospects for the Future

The events of June 1989 and violations of human rights at that time silenced temporarily those who entertained a hopeful view concerning Chinese legal developments. After June Fourth, any attempt at a sober assessment, it seemed, evoked the protests of cold warriors. Though the events of that time were followed by a renewed drive against corruption, to 'pacify the masses', new and harsh regulations controlling demonstrations and curbs placed upon the media throttled an important vehicle for monitoring accountability (Kolenda 1990: pp. 221–8). One should point out, however, that there is no evidence that the development of civil law and economic law was set back too far. In 1991 a revised Code of Civil Procedure was promulgated which inhibited administrative interference and obstruction in civil cases. There has also been a stream of new legislation governing stocks and shares, patents, copyright, taxes and the rights of enterprises as juridical persons. The question of administrative law is perhaps more difficult though reform continues, particularly with regard to providing compensation for those who have suffered damage by state action. Criminal law, however, remains perhaps the most stubborn branch of law. But legal awareness cannot easily be squashed. At the time of martial law, there was much discussion as to the constitutionality of that action particularly since it seemed to have been promulgated without reference to the National People's Congress or its Standing Committee. Such discussions of constitutional legality still continue in a manner which would have been unthinkable in the mid-1950s or 1960s. There is also continuing debate on human rights, despite the fact that the government still takes the relativistic position remarked on earlier (Gelatt 1989).

The achievement of the 'rule of law', some feel, is inevitable so long as economic reform remains the prime concern. In the light of the debate about 'neo-authoritarianism', however, this is open to question. Though economic reform must inevitably affect civil and economic law, one is not so sure about its effect on criminal law. Clearly a more stable approach to criminal law developed during the 1980s once leaders began to question the effectiveness of generalising ideas about the carceral management of reform to society as a whole. The rapid growth of recidivism, however, led to severe doubts about the reformative potential of the carceral system itself, and the spectacular growth of transient crime (particularly on trains) has led to questions about the social milieu in which re-education might effectively be undertaken. As we have seen, there was a rapid shift in emphasis from reform to deterrence as exemplified by the increased use of the death penalty. Deterrence required much more than the use of regular legal mechanisms. As Deborah Townsend points out, economic crime generated in large measure by economic reform, has often been dealt with by extra-legal institutions, often on an *ad hoc* basis. She wonders whether the dichotomies of 'internal' and 'external' and *li* and *fa*, discussed above, are adequate to encompass the role of the Party which still resolves criminal problems by campaigns in an era of supposedly formal legality (Townsend 1987: pp. 250–8). The problem of transient crime, moreover, escalating in a period of rapid social mobility, has contributed to the imposition of a new and ever-tighter system of social control which, one suspects, is too pervasive to be dented significantly by the guarantees promised by the new administrative law. Dutton refers to this latter development as the growth of a 'carceral society' – hardly one which holds out much promise for the 'rule of law' (Dutton 1992: pp. 325–40).

Returning to the questions raised at the beginning of this chapter and in our Introduction, it seems that the recent moves towards stability might simply result in continued 'rule by law', punctuated by repeated mass campaigns and supplemented by continued reliance on 'internal' mechanisms of law with weakened educative potential. It is clear that Party policy still supervenes, though less so than previously, that informal law still plays a major role and there is still scepticism concerning universal legal values. What is beyond doubt, however, is that impaired legitimacy cannot be repaired by economic progress and patriotism alone. One expects further protests both in the interests of communitarian values and those of the 'rule of law'. It is rash to say anything further than that.

6

Intellectuals and Struggles

The term 'intellectual' is culturally-specific. The Chinese term *zhishi fenzi* (one who knows things) is defined much more broadly than in the West (it includes teachers, technicians and sometimes all people with a secondary school education) and this causes much difficulty when Chinese Marxists try to translate the Stalinist usage of the concept as a 'stratum' distinct from specific classes. Indeed, a decade ago, Deng Xiaoping revised the Stalinist legacy by defining intellectuals as part of the 'working class'. Deng's reasons for doing this were clearly political rather than analytical; he wished to cancel the bad image of intellectuals fostered during the Cultural Revolution. One should note, however, in response to the question posed in our Introduction, that, despite the efforts of Marxist theorists such as Gramsci, the connections and lines of demarcation between intellectuals and class are hard to draw.

Some observers of Marxist régimes in Eastern Europe, however, have defined 'intellectuals' as forming a class in itself or at least a grouping striving to become a class (Konrád and Szelényi 1979). This is because the leaders of a teleological redistributive state define their legitimacy to rule by the articulation of a *telos* and intellectuals are instrumental in that endeavour. Party leaders, as teleological redistributors, feel the need to define themselves in intellectual terms and the various writings of such leaders are the object of study. Those of a more academic bent assist them in their writing and help provide authoritative interpretations. Yet there are problems with such categorisation. The Marxist formulation cannot accommodate the view of intellectuals as a class since the 'intellectual class' may not be defined in terms of a necessary exploitative relationship with any other class (a failing which

225

applies also to the Stalinist position). The Weberian definition of economic class in terms of groupings in receipt of similar allocations of life-chances fails when it is seen that some intellectuals are ministers of state or their equivalents and some are isolated writers. As for the Weberian concept 'social class', one can only conclude that whereas the process of rationalisation might accord privilege to certain intellectuals (and certainly most of those considered in this chapter), the elements of rationalisation are too varied to provide any basis for unity (such reasoning also applies to more recent 'new class' theories).

We have no choice, therefore, but to use the term 'intellectuals' somewhat loosely and this chapter will avoid discussion of demarcation. Let us adopt an essentialist position. An intellectual is someone concerned to discuss universal values rationally in a publicly accessible form. Such applies even to those who deny there are any universal values; at least they are forced to discuss them. One might note, moreover, that such a rejection usually accords privilege to what often become new universal elements, be they elements of discourse, determinants of the technology of discipline or class determinations. We shall leave open the thorny question as to whether this is inevitable. All we need to consider here is that, repeatedly over the past forty years, those in China who seek universal values are attacked by those who see universal concepts as reducible to class. Yet the attackers then proceed to evoke a 'scientific method' which adopts class categories which come to transcend history. A rejection of the universal employs universal values.

Science, of course, is seen as the pre-eminent universal discourse. A régime which professes 'scientific socialism' needs scientists and the social sciences are bent in a scientistic direction. Considerations of science, therefore, have come to dominate official discourse and, we argue, inform much of an emerging civil discourse (Buckley 1991: pp. 18–19). Yet many observers claim that China has traditionally been characterised by an absence of civil discourse outside official parameters. Two millenia of rule by a scholar-bureaucracy has resulted in the suffocation of civil discourse by official discourse, based on textual authority and patriarchal rule. All that has changed is the 'scientific' language which justifies that rule. The old *ti* (body) remains with Western or Soviet elements incorporated for their usefulness (*yong*). In such a situation, the overwhelming majority of intellectuals, as employees of the state, continue to be treated instrumentally as advisers to those who rule and are seen as disruptive if their views break though the ever-changing official boundaries prescribed for advice (substantive and formal). As our Introduction noted, state officials depend for ideological support upon those they are prone to despise and baulk at theoretical analysis which goes beyond support. But is there a fall-back position? Can there be a civil society?

This chapter focuses not on intellectuals *per se* but on struggles. It is concerned, therefore, not with all academic debates but with those academic debates which generated a hostile response from the political authorities – with debates which broke through the officially prescribed boundaries. It shows how official boundaries have changed back and forth. We are not convinced, however, that all is variation on an ancient theme. In the process of changing boundaries the régime has lost much legitimacy. One is not certain whether legitimacy may be recovered by simple economic develop-ment. Perhaps there is a parallel with the process of economic development itself. We have considered the argument that Stalinism is very effective as a strategy of 'extensive' development, but when the economy moves to a phase of 'intensive' development, where the quality of inputs is seen as more important, there is a need to develop and tap the quality of civil discourse which openly flaunts official norms. We cannot say whether the present régime will adequately meet the challenge but at least this chapter offers the background for intelligent speculation.

The Early 1950s

The early years of the People's Republic saw the entrenchment of a new scientific discourse as massive efforts were undertaken to restore production after years of war. Scientists were recruited and trained in ever-increasing numbers as the Soviet model of economic planning was imported and consolidated. An Academy of Sciences was set up on Soviet lines and, when this was seen to be tardy in promoting applied research, was joined by a Scientific Planning Commission to pursue what were clearly utilitarian goals. At that time the régime employed a number of Marxist and leftist scholars who had previously been sympathetic to the struggle of the

Chinese Communist Party against the *Guomindang* and, as we have seen, many of those people now look back on the period as a golden age. Yet even then there were serious ideological struggles. In 1955 there was a major rectification campaign directed at intellectuals (Lee Ta-ling 1988: pp. 160–8). In the first few years of the new régime, the famous scholars Hu Shi (the Westerniser), Liang Shuming (the traditionalist) (Chi 1970), and Yu Pingbo (the commentator on the famous eighteenth century novel *The Dream of the Red Chamber*) (Bonner 1976) were denounced and Mao himself occasionally intervened to criticise works, such as the films *The Story of Wu Xun* (1950) and *The Inside Story of the Qing Court* (see *Chinese Law and Government* 11, 4, Winter 1978–9).

In the early 1950s the régime relied upon what Carol Hamrin and Timothy Cheek (1986) call 'establishment intellectuals' who became part scholar and part bureaucrat. The veteran novelist Mao Dun became Minister of Culture. Others such as Ai Siqi, Guo Moruo, Chen Boda, Hu Qiaomu and Zhou Yang played important roles either behind the scenes or in occasional public utterances. There was later to be much animosity among those people but we cannot say whether this may be dated back to the early 1950s, nor whether the animosity extended to Propaganda Chief Lu Dingyi and Mao's later Party policeman-cum-'theoretical authority' confidant Kang Sheng. Ever since Yan'an days, it seems, Mao had been dependent on theorists to establish Mao Zedong Thought. Indeed, after Mao's death much effort has gone into showing that Mao Zedong Thought was not simply the creation of Mao 'the only philosopher' but was a collective product.

In the People's Republic, little positive may be said nowadays about Chen Boda who played a major role in shaping Mao Zedong Thought but who is castigated for his 'leftist' sins in the Great Leap Forward and the Cultural Revolution. Much, however, has been made of the role of Ai Siqi, the editor of the Party's theoretical journal *Xuexi* until it was replaced in the Great Leap Forward by the more radical *Hongqi (Red Flag)*, edited by Chen Boda. Ai is celebrated for providing Mao with material for and amending some of his popular essays as well as being perhaps the most popular writer of philosophy after Mao himself. As Joshua Fogel (1987) sees him, Ai was a Chinese version of the Soviet theorist Mark Mitin who provided Stalin with much ammunition after Stalin broke with Abram Deborin in the 1930s. Another pivotal figure and close ssociate of Mao was Guo Moruo, who acted as a bridge between cademia and the Party. Under his protection, leftist historians ianaged to accommodate their research to the régime, seeing at hat time no major contradiction between the national struggle and uestions of class struggle.

For his part, Zhou Yang kept a watchful eye over literary figures. "hese were more constrained than other intellectuals both by Mao's 942 'Talks at the Yan'an Forum on Art and Literature' (*Selected Works*, 2: pp. 69–98) and the strictures concerning 'socialist ealism'. The former distinguished between an artistic criterion nd a political one in evaluating literary works but laid major stress n the latter. Indeed the 'Talks' had been given to curb certain inds of political criticism and were followed by the disciplining of vriters such as Wang Shiwei and Ding Ling (Goldman 1964). Back n 1942 Wang had pointed out that literature was like a 'Wild Lily' (he title of his famous essay). It could be beautiful yet bitter to the aste but, for all that, medicinal. Whatever Mao had intended in his Talks', it was clear that later they would be used to brand many uch lilies 'poisonous weeds' (Rubin 1987: pp. 33–4). Socialist ealism, for its part, stressed the bright features of socialist abour, painting characters sharply in terms of black and white. "he original version of this had been established under Stalin's egis in the 1930s. The Soviet formulation was amended in 1954 hough the Chinese Communist Party did not endorse the more iberal amendments (Chan 1980: pp. 185–6). The prescribed model or writers was to be a 'cog and screw' in the revolutionary nachinery. Typical here was Zhou Libo's *Hurricane*, narrating and reform through the eyes of a work team. Party guidelines nformed the writing and the finished work was used by cadres to einforce faith in those guidelines (Wagner 1987). The medium was he message.

This model was very different from the critical reform literature vhich may be traced back at least to the late Qing period or the iting sarcasm of Lu Xun's essays (*zawen*). For all that, Lu Xun vas celebrated as the major leftist writer of the early twentieth :entury. The model contrasted also with the more heroic genre used)y leftist writers in the days of *Guomindang* rule. Typical here, as Rudolf Wagner (1987: p. 186) sees it, is Guo Moruo's *Qu Yuan*, the egendary hero who protested to King Huai of Chu about evil ;overnment, committed suicide in 278 BC, and finally had his warnings confirmed as the state of Chu was swallowed up by Qin. Guo's 1942 version of this was clearly an allegory of United Front policies at that time and was directed at the *Guomindang* government in Chongqing with Japan cast as the state of Qin. Such was an example of polemics by historical analogy which was to characterise the whole period of the subsequent People's Republic.

A major crack in the unity experienced by leftist intellectuals occurred in 1955. This was the Hu Feng case. Hu Feng might be cast as a critical reformer in the spirit of Lu Xun who objected to the 'saccharine optimism' of the socialist literature promoted under the aegis of Zhou Yang. In 1954 he wrote a letter to the Party Central Committee protesting against restrictions on literary activity. After much academic discussion, the Hu Feng debate became openly political as Zhou Yang mounted a full-scale attack against him. By January 1955, Hu had confessed his errors, but his confession was considered inadequate and a nationwide campaign of criticism unfolded (Goldman 1962). In May, Hu Feng began to be denounced not merely as a 'petty bourgeois' writer but as a 'counter-revolutionary' and a number of documents appeared, annotated by Mao, which subjected him to severe criticism (*Selected Works*, 5, pp. 172–83). It has been claimed that this was the origin of *sufan* which, as we have seen, soon enlarged its scope to investigate other people.

The Hu Feng case, instigated by Mao Zedong, occurred in the radical climate of 1955 just prior to the acceleration of rural co-operativisation and the socialisation of industry and commerce, and, as noted earlier, *sufan* may have been designed to clear the way for those movements. The movements themselves generated criticism in the Party along the orthodox 'scientific' Marxist lines that Mao was pursuing too 'volontarist' a path and was disregarding the objective constraints of political economy. Such seems to have been the position of Yang Xianzhen, head of the Central Party School who had joined in the denunciation of Hu Feng and was certainly a potential dissident of a very different stripe. Yang's comments at that time were made behind closed doors, though a train of thought was set in motion which culminated within two years in a debate on the 'identity of thought and existence', noted in Chapter 1, in which Yang affirmed the priority of material existence over thought. Over the next decade, what seemed to be an obscure philosophical point was seen to have important practical relevance. Theorists recalled that the official Soviet *Concise Dictionary of Philosophy* (1954) had criticised Mao's 'On Contradiction' as Hegelian. Though Yang was to defend Mao as materialist, there is no doubt that he too came to see the interpretation of 'the identity of thought and existence', promoted by certain of Mao's followers, as excessively idealist, with disastrous economic consequences. The debate, at first, was scholarly, though, by moving to this position, Yang incurred the opposition of Ai Siqi and the enmity of Kang Sheng who strove to remove him from his role as head of the Central Party School (Hamrin 1986).

Though Yang Xianzhen's position was orthodox Marxist, it represented a marked gradualist and reformist strand of thinking which coexisted with the radicalism of the 'little leap' of 1955–6. After following the Stalinist model of administration, in line with the Soviet 'thaw' after Stalin's death, a new and more flexible Soviet way of thinking had been imported (but not the revised guidelines on socialist realism). The class struggle motif which informed many fields of scholarship, and certainly the arts, gave way to a new formulation culminating in the line of the Eighth Party Congress of 1956 which, as we have seen, declared that the principal contradiction in society should no longer be seen in terms of class but as that between the 'advanced socialist system' and the 'backward productive forces'. Demonstrating their flexibility, philosophers such as Ai Siqi provided Party ideology with material establishing distance from Stalin and, with the prompting of Premier Zhou Enlai, more and more leaders came to stress the role of intellectuals in developing those productive forces.

As we saw in Chapter 1, the new formulation in economics gave rise to a wide-ranging debate about the shortcomings of the Stalinist command system, with Chen Yun appearing as a major reforming element in the central leadership (Bachman 1985). Mirroring Soviet debates, the economist Sun Yefang began to argue that the 'law of value' should play a major role in planning, implying careful attention had to be paid to costs and accounting and making allowance for a capital charge in calculating production prices. This was a bold proposal at the time since it could be seen as opposing Marxist-Leninist orthodoxy which held that capital could not create value (Naughton 1986: pp. 131–7). In politics new stress was laid on the evils of bureaucratism which was a major disease of the Stalinist system. Prominent here were those associated with the Communist Youth League under Hu Yaobang. They included people such as Liu Binyan and Wang Meng who were cast as 'scouts of the Party', eager to point out bureaucratic errors and to seek rectification (Wagner 1987: pp. 197–203). They were joined by older campaigners against bureaucratism such as Wang Ruowang (a critic of Yan'an vintage) who opposed hypocrisy, élitism, dogmatism and blind faith in the Soviet Union manifested by many senior Party leaders. He noted that intellectual critics were kept separate from the Party by the latter branding them as 'privileged'. They were frequently given political labels – a process which alienated the Party from the people. Wang spoke as a Party member who did not criticise the Party as such – but that did not save him from later persecution (Rubin 1987: pp. 238–40).

The Anti-rightist Movement and the Great Leap Forward

As remarked on earlier, the high point of anti-bureaucratic criticism was the movement of 1957 to 'let a hundred flowers bloom and a hundred schools of thought contend' (see MacFarquhar 1974). Mao had called for such a movement back in 1956 but it was only after the Hungarian incident and Mao's speech 'On the Correct Handling of Contradictions' (*Selected Works*, 5: pp. 384–421) that it really got under way. Faced with considerable bureaucratic opposition, the movement turned in mid-year into an Anti-rightist movement, in the initial stages of which critics of bureaucratism were often capped as 'rightists' and sent to the countryside. In the universities and among cultural bureaucrats there was much alarm. Some, such as historian Jian Bozan, vacillated but managed to reach an accommodation between scholarship and policy (Edmunds 1987: p. 68). Others lost their jobs and retreated into obscurity for a number of years. From its inception, the 'hundred flowers' movement was to have been accompanied by a rectification movement, though originally this had been seen by critics as a movement to rectify the errors they pointed out. Although the thrust of the Anti-rightist movement turned on those very critics, some of the old targets remained and it is interesting to note that even such a safe thinker as Ai Siqi was labelled a 'dogmatist'. Various motives have been suggested for this. Perhaps Kang Sheng was making a bid for control over the Party School (Fogel 1987: p. 33). True or not, it was certainly the case that the movement was used to settle old scores and the relative unity amongst scholars was shattered.

There has been much discussion concerning the role of Mao in the Anti-rightist movement of 1957. Suffice it to note here that he was able successfully to shift its focus away from literary concerns to economic matters (Solomon 1971). As we have seen, when ground was laid for that massive production drive known as the Great Leap Forward, large numbers of economists were criticised as 'conservative' and those who wished to give greater weight to market relations were silenced. Of particular note here was the demographer President of Beijing University Ma Yinchu who was accused of Malthusianism when, for a short time, Mao declared that a big population was a good thing (Hsia 1961).

During the Great Leap Forward, scholars were urged to become propagandists and Chen Boda became most active in promoting its ideals. Historians were no exception. Many were told to go down to the factories and the countryside to write the history of the masses. Those and the historians who remained in their studies were told to 'make the past serve the present' (*gu wei jin yong*) and that 'history should be led by theory'. Whilst most Marxist historians did in fact see the need to have history informed by theory, their position depended on the nature of the theory. The theory in question, of course, centred on class struggle which, when taken to an extreme, meant that historical figures were portrayed in stereotypical form (depending on class origin) and the forces which propelled history were seen as anonymous. Dissatisfaction began to grow.

There were also striking changes on the literary front. The old sterile socialist realism was now to be supplemented by 'revolutionary romanticism', for in Guo Moruo's words it did not matter if a piece of work was realist or romantic as long as it was revolutionary. Above all, works of art had to be positive, and critical literature, which pointed to the dark side of society, came under attack. The Party preferred happy peasants singing folk songs and sought to propagate the idea of everyone engaging in literary creation ('the million poems campaign'). Though a lot may be said for the de-mystification of élite literature and the popularisation of artistic creation (when exhausted workers had time for it), it was inevitable that the literary élite would respond. Consider the case of Tian Han, head of the Dramatists Association.

Tian had led the Anti-rightist movement in that association and
extolled the Great Leap. He was unwilling, however, to revert to the
old idea of portraying class enemies in crude terms. His reticence
here was later taken by Cultural Revolution activists to be a sign
that he had been put in charge of the Anti-rightist movement in the
association by Zhou Yang in order to negate it. One doubts the
charge but it is certainly true that Tian Han was worried about
political excesses. He responded not in critical reformist but in
militant mode. His play *Guan Hanqing*, produced on the 700th
anniversary of that Yuan dynasty playwright, attacked the corrupt
influence of a faction at the court of Kublai Khan, which could be
taken as a critique of those such as Chen Boda who had become
influential in the Great Leap Forward. Significantly Kublai Khan
rectified the situation, and so, one might suppose, could Mao. Here
Wagner (1987: pp. 205–10) points out, Guo Moruo, who was close
to Mao, responded with a play about the legendary Cao Cao who
maintained the importance of a collective agriculture. Critical
reform literature had given way to the old genre of militant stories
about historical heroes – 'making the past serve the present'.

After the Great Leap

As we have noted, the economic dislocation facing China in the
aftermath of the Great Leap saw the régime's first serious crisis of
legitimacy. It resulted in attempts being made to repair the science
and technology network and to restore the morale of scientists. To
that end authoritative press comments declared that science was
outside the parameters of class struggle. Economists were also
accorded greater respect and a number of them, on the periphery
of the state system, were bought to centre stage in the industrial
arena. Though some economists were reluctant to assume that role
many were quick to respond since they had complained during the
previous Hundred Flowers Campaign that they had not been made
full use of and had been denied statistical material. They were aided
here by the decision taken in July 1958, during the Leap, to bring
the Institute of Economics jointly under the Academy of Sciences
and the State Planning Commission and by the establishment of
links with the State Economic Commission concerned with im

nediate planning. By the early 1960s many economists felt that they vere actual participants in the restructuring process (Halpern 1987:). 48).

Under the guidance of Li Fuchun, head of the State Planning Commission, economists conducted investigations and participated n drawing up the 'seventy points on industry' discussed earlier. They also helped compile a textbook on industrial management under the guidance of a deputy director of the State Economic Commission, Ma Hong. Prominent in this whole process was Sun Yefang (with strong ties to Li Fuchun) who drafted a number of very critical and controversial reports during the period calling for greater enterprise autonomy, stressing the importance of profits and of setting the investment rate in accordance with the state of consumers' livelihood (Halpern 1987: pp. 57–61). As Sun saw it, the primary role of the state concerned 'expanded reproduction' (net new investment), leaving a major role for the enterprise in simple reproduction'. Sun was later denounced for this 'market socialism', though markets did not play a major role in his advocacy of planning according to the 'law of value'; indeed Barry Naughton describes him as advocating 'market socialism without markets' (Naughton 1986: p. 143).

In agriculture, however, where, as we have seen, a sixty-point charter was drawn up, the influence of professional economists was not marked. As Nina Halpern remarks, this was because Mao took direct interest in that sector and preferred to rely on strictly Party bodies and indeed supervised the drafting of the sixty articles himself. As already noted, Mao was extremely worried about what e felt to be the negation of innovations in agriculture and did not rust people outside the Party apparatus. In any case specifically Party bodies had always been considered more important in rural matters than in industrial ones. Because of agriculture's decentralised nature and because of regional variations, moreover, it was logical that the centre should rely on powerful provincial leaders (who were Party secretaries). A third reason why professional economists were less active in agriculture was that agriculture was not the central concern of the State Planning Commission under Li Fuchun (Halpern 1987: pp. 54–7). The influence of professional economists in the early 1960s, therefore, was limited to industry and not very effective even there, but a precedent had been set for the late 1970s.

The economic relaxation which followed the demise of the Great Leap, therefore, led to an attempt once again to recruit the services of intellectuals who had been alienated by the Leap's extreme policies. Both Zhou Enlai and Chen Yi criticised the excessive amount of time which intellectuals had been forced to devote to political study and, freed from excessive political strictures, they engaged in great debates on all fronts, particularly in the period 1961–2. Now once again economists studied Keynes, Smith and Marshall and philosophers turned to Hegel, Kant and many others Some economic historians entered into heated argument on why the 'sprouts of capitalism' did not mature in China several centuries ago. Other historians and philosophers attempted to reverse the verdict on a number of historical figures, culminating in a conference supervised by Zhou Yang in November 1962. Reference was made to the famous philosopher Feng Youlan who employed Marx's *German Ideology* to portray Confucius as progressive because of the universal nature of some of his teachings and because he was the forerunner of the feudal system which was seen crudely as more advanced than the slave society which it was supposed to have replaced. Others praised Confucius' stress on practice rather than contemplation and went on to argue that the Confucian concept of *ren* (benevolence) transcended feudal society from which it had arisen (Goldman 1981: pp. 53–5; Levenson 1962) Predictably, discussions of transcendence inflamed the tension in Marxism between universals and historical circumstances and between class struggle and national struggle.

One tenet of official history which came under attack was Mao's notion that peasant struggles were the motive force of history Notable here was Jian Bozan, the head of the history department and later vice president of Beijing University. Jian, who during the height of the Leap affirmed the notion of the 'two line struggle on the historical front' (reflecting class struggle), soon changed tack noting that Chinese history was characterised by dynasty after dynasty making concessions to peasants and buying them off; class reconciliation rather than class struggle had improved the peasants livelihood (Goldman 1981: pp. 56–7). Moving away from class struggle, Jian came to declare his commitment to the broader notion of historicism (*lishi zhuyi*) (Edmunds 1987). By historicism he meant the commitment of a historian to seeing events in their context and their full complexity. Thus he held that whilst allowing history to be led by theory was not erroneous, when taken to extremes such a view could lead to dogmatism. On the other hand, focusing only on the peculiarities of a particular nation could lead to what in the idiom of the time was called 'revisionism'. Though, indeed, history should 'serve the present' it was much more than looking for historical antecedents of present policies; it was not just propaganda. Finally, in a provocative speech to the Nanjing Historical Society in June 1962, Jian argued that the dominant tendency during the Leap had not been to lead history with theory but to *replace* history with theory. This was a violation of the Marxian stress on concrete reality.

Amongst writers and artists there was also much criticism of the Great Leap Forward. Some rightists capped in 1957 and rehabilitated in 1962 (such as Wang Ruowang) carried on where they had left off and added to their criticism denunciation of the Great Leap (Rubin 1987: p. 240). The focal point was a conference convened by Zhou Yang at Dalian in August 1962 to consider the plight of peasants. Here, incensed by the portrayal of 'one dimensional characters with red faces', Shao Quanlin, a confidant of Zhou Yang and a prominent leader of the Chinese Writers Union (echoing Hu Feng whom he had once criticised), praised 'people in the middle', extolling the virtues of the writer Zhao Shuli who was sensitive to the un-heroic complexity of peasant life (Goldman 1981: pp. 47–50).

In Cultural Revolution retrospect, the most notorious satirical pieces of writing emanated from the Beijing municipal establishment. In November 1961, Beijing's mayor, Peng Zhen, instructed his deputies to examine responsibility for the recent hunger. Deng Tuo, a former editor of *Renmin ribao* and now head of the Beijing Party Secretariat, was entrusted with the task of examining directives issued during the leap (Cheek 1986) and, together with the Vice Mayor, Wu Han, and Liao Mosha, director of the Beijing Party's United Front Work Department, he wrote a number of biting essays (*zawen*) criticising the policies of that time. These were collected together as *Notes from a Three Family Village* (appearing in the Beijing magazine *Qianxian* [Front Line] between 1961 and 1964) and *Evening Talks at Yanshan* (appearing in Beijing newspapers from 1961 to 62), as well as a series which appeared in the pages of *Renmin ribao*. Deng Tuo's targets were many and varied. By historical analogy, he implied that Mao had been misled by flattery, that he was stubborn, cut off from reality, went back on his word, suffered from amnesia and even followed 'the tyrant's way'. Deng Tuo denounced 'grandiose schemes which could not be realised', failure to follow the time-honoured policy of storing grain, and 'throwing out one's teacher' (the Soviet Union), and even may have proposed reconciliation with the United States. By analogy he also defended Peng Dehuai who, we remember, had opposed the 'petty bourgeois fanaticism' of the early Great Leap. The scope of Deng Tuo's sarcastic forays was broad indeed. For his part, Wu Han joined Deng Tuo in some of his endeavours but perhaps his most notorious play was entitled *Hai Rui Dismissed from Office* which was also a satire on the dismissal of Peng Dehuai and an attack on the Great Leap Forward. The play derived from an earlier essay in *Renmin ribao* of 1959, which had enjoyed the encouragement of Deng Xiaoping's associate Hu Qiaomu, and on an opera script which had been widely acclaimed. There were others who followed the lead of the Beijing authorities, some going much further to suggest the formation of different political parties, but such voices gradually fell silent after the Tenth Plenum of the Party Central Committee in the autumn of 1962 (Pusey 1969; Fisher 1986; Goldman 1981: pp. 25–38) at which Mao, returning to the 'front line', issued a call never to forget the class struggle.

In the early 1960s there was disquiet also in the central propaganda apparatus of the Party. Writers associated with that apparatus such as Xia Yan, Tian Han and Yang Hansheng joined in the criticism of the class struggle motif indirectly or by historical analogy. Some writers took pains to depict 'middle characters' (neither heroes nor villains) and others extolled 'ghost plays' or fairy tales suggesting the revenge of the masses for unjust rule (Goldman 1981: pp. 33–4). Perhaps the most interesting of the central propaganda figures, however, was Zhou Yang – later called a cultural 'tsar', who pronounced authoritatively the 'correct line' on every single contentious issue. As seen above, Zhou had taken an active part in the previous purges with considerable zeal. Yet Zhou had come to question Mao's infallibility and to regret the Great Leap. Like many of his colleagues, Zhou, thinking of the Leap, spoke about forced labour in Chinese history and castigated mass campaigns (Goldman 1981: pp. 39–41). He sought to allow the scope of literature to expand from the confines of socialist realism and revolutionary romanticism. As a literary bureaucrat, however, he was eventually forced to return to Mao's line. Thus in 1963, in a famous speech against 'revisionism', Zhou (1964) affirmed the struggle theme and denounced those who borrowed Marx's discussion of 'alienation' to talk about non-capitalist societies. In retrospect it seems that Zhou made the speech because he was sympathetic to Wang Ruoshui, a protegé of Deng Tuo, who had moved from an affirmation of the Great Leap to a more moderate position which foreshadowed his later conclusion that alienation, which had existed before the advent of capitalism, could continue into socialist society (Brugger and Kelly 1990: p. 148).

Whereas the Beijing Party establishment and the central propaganda apparatus were centres of resistance to a reaffirmation of the ideology of class struggle, the Shanghai Party committee and the Institute of Philosophy and Social Sciences of the Chinese Academy of Sciences housed a number of thinkers who affirmed the class struggle theme. Prominent in Shanghai was Zhang Chunqiao who had attracted Mao's attention for his radical support of some of the more extreme ideas of the Great Leap, and Yao Wenyuan, known by the nickname 'the stick' because of his alacrity in attacking 'rightists' and others. Yao was eager to join battle in the early 1960s, criticising, for example, Zhou Gucheng for denigrating class struggle in his depiction of 'spirit of the age', but this time in mild tones which allowed for Zhou to mount a defence. The Shanghai group was quite weak at that stage when faced with the power of the central propaganda apparatus, but its power was to grow. Through the intermediary of Ke Qingshi, First Secretary of the Shanghai Party Committee and Politburo member, Zhang and Yao formed an association with Chen Boda and Mao's wife Jiang Qing who had provided Mao with material on films and other works and was developing an interest in revolutionising Beijing opera with modern themes.

Amongst the Academy of Sciences group were Guan Feng, Qi Benyu, Lin Youshi and Lin Jie. Guan Feng and Lin Youshi took issue with Feng Youlan, employing the term 'historicism' to claim that Feng had not located Confucius in his historical context. But that did not stop many scholars coming to Feng's defence nor did it stop the publication of the second volume of his *History of Chinese Philosophy* which argued precisely the point Guan Feng was attacking. Qi Benyu, the historian, criticised Jian Bozan for denigrating class struggle and sought to refute Yang Hansheng's positive verdict on the Taiping leader Li Xiucheng who, Qi maintained, sold out to the Imperial court; this latter charge resulted in a major historical conference as Zhou Yang tried to keep the criticism within bounds. Guan, Qi and Lin Jie also wrote criticisms of Wu Han at that time but, they subsequently alleged, some were prevented from being published (Goldman 1981: pp. 65–72).

Wu Han was perhaps too close to Peng Zhen to be attacked openly at that stage. Peng was Mayor of Beijing and close to the central propaganda apparatus. Significantly in 1964, Peng Zhen was entrusted with the task of supervising literary reform. Peng, it appears, was hardly enthusiastic about Jiang Qing's attempts to revolutionise Beijing Opera, a task she performed under the aegis of the People's Liberation Army; this was not because he opposed reform, merely that he was determined it should be under proper guidance, not that of Jiang Qing whom he resented for taking unilateral action without the permission of the cultural authorities. Conspicuously, when a Festival of Beijing Opera on Contemporary Themes took place in Beijing in 1964, it was the cultural establishment which made all the speeches not Jiang Qing. In such a situation, it was later alleged, Jiang Qing and Kang Sheng supplied Mao with 'false information' which led him to take a very jaundiced view of the progress of literary and artistic reform. This was reflected in his *in camera* statements and in his poems. It was clear that Mao was becoming increasingly dissatisfied. Perhaps, observing that dissatisfaction, leaders of opportunistic bent, such as the Central South Region's Tao Zhu, presented themselves as arch-enthusiasts for the new opera (Goldman 1981: pp. 74–88).

The rectification of 1964–5, carried out under Peng Zhen's aegis, was mild indeed. Significantly, its first major targets for denunciation were hardly members of the quasi-humanist élite. Sun Yefang was attacked as early as 1963 for following the profit-oriented ideas of the Soviet economist Liberman, a charge he firmly denied. Mao, at Kang Sheng's instigation, gave the green light for Sun to be 'struggled against' in 1964 but Sun defended himself against his accusers (Naughton 1986 pp. 146–7). Another target was the ultra-materialist Yang Xianzhen, off and on head of the Central Party School, who, as we have noted, had been labelled a rightist for a time for implying that Mao Zedong Thought was too idealist. Now he was attacked for the work of two of his students who had put forward the notion that whereas one divides into two, 'two could unite into one'. This was taken to be a plea for class reconciliation rather than struggle. Significantly, in one of his last ideological forays, Ai Siqi denounced Yang as a Deborinite (Goldman 1981: p. 98), a conclusion at odds with Yang's orthodox materialist view that one should be mindful of the objective limits to the human spirit, which, one will remember, he had voiced as early as 1955.

Another feature of the rectification movement of 1964–5 was a criticism of people such as Shao Quanlin who stressed the role of 'middle characters' and dramatists such as Xia Yan and Tian Han who depicted them. In their place was offered selfless ordinary people such as the soldier Lei Feng (the rustless screw, referred to earlier) who lived an ordinary life in the service of Mao and died most unceremoniously, and Ouyang Hai who gave his life pushing a cart of ammunition away from the path of an oncoming train. Accordingly the philosopher Feng Ding came under attack for denigrating selfless sacrifice and stressing the improvement of people's livelihood. Those, like him, who gave greater attention to biology than class, were sometimes labelled 'social Darwinists'. There was criticism too of romantic love which should never be allowed to divert attention from the goals of the revolution (Goldman 1981: pp. 101–10).

But, we have noted, despite all the noise, the rectification movement of 1964–5 was mild. A few people were criticised for 'bourgeois thought' and 'revisionism' and some of Zhou Yang's close associates such as Shao Quanlin, Tian Han and Xia Yan lost their official posts, yet they were not labelled 'enemies' as in the past. Minister of Culture, Mao Dun was removed but replaced by Lu Dingyi, another close associate of Zhou Yang. Significantly, even some of the critics such as Yao Wenyuan were themselves criticised for going too far (in his attack on Zhou Gucheng). That is perhaps why some of the more vehement attacks were made by anonymous writing groups such as that based in Shanghai called *Luosiding* (screw) which argued that intellectuals belonged to the bourgeoisie. Clearly, when Zhou Yang brought the mild rectification movement to a close in April 1965, Mao was even more dissatisfied and was beginning to develop the kind of thinking which was to result in the Cultural Revolution (Goldman 1981: pp. 110–16).

The Cultural Revolution

Mao's dissatisfaction with the rectification of 1964–5 resulted in a largely academic struggle becoming a bloody political one. Under Mao's guidance and with the help of Jiang Qing and Zhang Chunqiao, Yao Wenyuan wrote a denunciation of Wu Han for satirising the Great Leap which was blocked by the propaganda and cultural authorities but eventually published. Peng Zhen and the establishment tried to confine the debate to academic matters and to deflect criticism on to Western and Soviet writers. But denunciations escalated. Zhou Yang, Xia Yan, Tian Han, Yang Hansheng, Jian Bozan and others came under severe attack and were persecuted. Sun Yefang was vilified and his reports of the early 1960s were used against him by Chen Boda. Sadly, while the spirit of Lu Xun was extolled for its spirit of rebellion against authorities, many of Lu Xun's associates were pilloried and the ideals he stood for trampled under foot.

Before long denunciation escalated to engulf Wu Han, Deng Tuo, Lu Dingyi, Peng Zhen and the whole of the central cultural establishment as leadership of the movement passed to a Central Cultural Revolution group headed by Chen Boda, Jiang Qing, Zhang Chunqiao, Lin Jie and Wang Li. Thousands of senior professors and scholars were subjected to struggle meetings and humiliated, with particular venom directed against university authorities such as Beijing University's Lu Ping, the successor of Ma Yinchu. Lu was the subject of a bitter wall poster written by a philosophy tutor Nie Yuanzi which, at the instigation of Mao through Kang Sheng, was broadcast over the mass media. Soon red guards and red rebel groups had formed all over the country and were denouncing intellectuals as 'the stinking ninth category'.[1] The Eleventh Plenum of the Eighth Central Committee in August gave them instructions on proper targets which excluded scientists, though those instructions were disregarded and many scientists were denounced as 'science for the masses' was extolled. Indeed, mass creativity in general became the watchword and authors who

---

[1] They were ranked after the counter-revolutionary 'five black classes' of earlier days (landlords, rich peasants, counter-revolutionaries, bad elements and rightists) and the newly added categories of renegades, enemy agents and unrepentant persons taking the capitalist road.

wrote about the masses but had not been part of them were given short shrift.

By the autumn of 1966 the attack had reached state chairman Liu Shaoqi and Party General Secretary Deng Xiaoping; and even Tao Zhu, who had adopted a stance in favour of class struggle, was felt to be too bureaucratic and swept aside. The movement escalated even further in January 1967, as we have seen, when attempts were made to model the administration of Shanghai along what were believed to be the lines of the Paris Commune of 1871. In this Zhang Chunqiao took the lead but soon changed tack as Mao came to feel the Cultural Revolution was becoming too 'anarchistic'. Zhang, who had mobilised mass activism, was now seen to be suppressing it. Then when Mao and the Central Cultural Revolution group felt the reaction to chaos had been too extreme, the military and others were criticised for applying too heavy a hand. This led to another outburst of denunciation, with Qi Benyu conducting a savage attack on Liu Shaoqi. By mid-year, faced with the opposition of the military commander of Wuhan who arrested for a time two members of the Central Cultural Revolution group, Lin Biao acted to suppress mutiny, which led to renewed and more savage denunciation of the army, a rebel takeover of the foreign ministry, the burning of the British mission and utter chaos.

In such a situation, Mao turned against some Beijing-based Cultural Revolution activists, including some members of the Central Cultural Revolution group. A 'May 16th Group' was identified as 'ultra-leftist', leading in September 1967 to the removal of Guan Feng, Lin Jie, Wang Li and Lin Youshi. This was followed in December 1967 by the ouster of Qi Benyu. The Beijing activists were silenced but the Shanghai Group backed away and, together with Kang Sheng, joined in the denunciation of 'ultra-leftism'. From the autumn of 1967 through until the Ninth Party Congress in April 1969, constant attempts were made to restore order, punctuated by outbreaks of ultra-left activity as red guards felt they had been betrayed. As we saw in Chapter 1, increasingly the military played a major role in charting the new order.

By 1969 some of the famous intellectuals were dead. For example Deng Tuo had committed suicide in 1966 (leaving perhaps his last testimony in the hands of Peng Zhen), Jian Bozan had committed suicide in 1968 and Wu Han and Tian Han had perished after persecution in 1968–9. Many thousands of others had been imprisoned, lost their posts or sent to the countryside. Culture was in tatters. It had become unwise for established writers to write anything and cultural fare was reduced to local operas, group compositions and a few prescribed Beijing operas with modern themes which were constantly revised to ensure 'correctness' according to changing views on class struggle. Universities had not taken in any new students for three years and were demoralised. As intellectuals saw it, the régime faced a new crisis of legitimacy. Yet some research and writing clearly went on, considering the speed with which some works appeared following the easing of publication restrictions in the early 1970s. For all that, large numbers of embittered intellectuals and Party leaders waited for the opportunity to return and turn the tables on those who had humiliated them. Their thirst for revenge, however, was not satiated for a decade.

By 1969, the Cultural Revolution had come to an end, though nowadays official Chinese comments speak of the 'ten years cultural revolution' which apparently lasted from 1966 to 1976. As noted earlier, they do this because the years 1969–76 were characterised by a struggle between those who sought to restore order and régime legitimacy, led by Zhou Enlai and following his rehabilitation in 1973 Deng Xiaoping, and those who sought to preserve what they called 'the socialist new things' of the Cultural Revolution, led by the Shanghai group whose intellectual leaders were Jiang Qing, Zhang Chunqiao and Yao Wenyuan. The period was characterised by intermittent campaigns of considerable complexity (Goldman 1981: pp. 156–231; Goldman 1975; Starr 1976; Price 1977).

The first drive to restore order resulted in the arrest of Chen Boda and considerable pressure being put on military personnel surrounding Lin Biao, who allegedly responded with his abortive coup. By that time (1971), there had occurred a *rapprochement* with the United States and a series of decisions had been taken to import and utilise Western and Japanese technology. Gradually, as universities reopened, efforts were made to restore part of the pre-Cultural Revolution system. Prominent in this task was Zhou Peiyuan, the Vice President of Beijing University, who extolled the value of basic as opposed to the excessively applied research of more radical times. He was to be strongly criticised by defenders of the Cultural Revolution who began to organise into anonymous writing groups (including *Luosiding* [screw]). Those groups endeavoured to 'go against the tide'.

The backlash took the form of four major ideological movements between 1973 and 1976 which, in the manner described earlier, used reinterpretations of history to score political victories. During those movements Mao adopted an ambivalent position, seeking on the one hand to preserve the spirit of class struggle and on the other to restore the authority of the Party. The first of these campaigns, 'The Movement to Criticise Lin Biao and Confucius', started out as an attack on the conspiracy of Lin Biao and then developed into an attack on and a defence of Zhou Enlai as a 'Confucian' who was said to hark back to a golden age – that of the Confucian model, the Duke of Zhou. One of the progenitors of the movement, the Guangzhou Professor Yang Rongguo, moved from a position moderately supporting Confucius (and the bureaucracy) to an outright denunciation of Confucianism in the spirit of the reaction to the reassessment of Confucius in the early 1960s. The venerable Feng Youlan, who had once championed the 'progressive' nature of Confucius, now joined the denunciation of Confucius. Most of the polemics, however, were carried on by anonymous writing groups which used ancient texts to make contemporary political points.

The most convoluted of those debates concerned Qinshihuang (the first emperor of Qin who unified the country over two millenia ago). Qinshihuang was a code name for Mao which had been used by the supporters of Lin Biao when plotting their coup. Now the history of the Qin dynasty was reinterpreted by a host of writing groups variously to attack or praise Zhou Enlai, Zhang Chunqiao and others. There were debates too on the Han, Tang and Song dynasties and much else, with praise and criticism accorded to famous empresses (analogues no doubt of Jiang Qing). The code was difficult to crack.

But not all the debates were in code. Some scholars joined in because no one had heeded their scholarship for years and some activists were concerned to address questions which had not been part of the agenda of the Cultural Revolution (such as the 'Confucian' subordination of women). There was much confusion and, one suspects, much of it deliberate as the debates became abstruse to the point of producing mass incomprehension. Not all the polemics, however, were obscure. Jiang Qing's criticism of pessimistic portrayals of China in foreign films and the importation of romantic music from the West were easy to understand, as indeed was her discouragement of local operas which challenged her prescribed Beijing forms. Nevertheless, by 1974, the campaign had run out of steam. Perhaps its last gasp took the form of the Li Yizhe 'big character poster', discussed earlier, which denounced Confucian rites in the name of Cultural Revolutionary activism and ended up by affirming the 'rule of law'.

The Li Yizhe poster of 1974 was prepared for the attention of the National People's Congress which met in January 1975 for the first time since the Cultural Revolution. As we saw in Chapter 1, that congress reiterated the slogan 'observe the four modernisations' and ironed out what seemed to be a compromise leadership. Within three weeks, the compromise was shattered by the launching of a campaign to 'study the theory of the dictatorship of the proletariat'. Now for the first time in years, Zhang Chunqiao and Yao Wenyuan wrote under their own names, advocating the restriction of 'bourgeois right'. Their followers extolled 'open door education' (mass education and 'taking society as school') and opposed the reconstruction of an intellectual élite. There was, of course, once again a backlash, with Minister of Education, Zhou Rongxin, denouncing the idea of 'taking society as school' as the 'bourgeois educational ideas of Dewey'. Even the central Party press argued that one should be on guard against 'dogmatism' as much as against 'revisionism'.

The third campaign in late 1975 was directed at the time-honoured vernacular novel *The Water Margin* which told the tale of a group of outlaws in the Song dynasty which took up arms against a corrupt court. Now the novel was interpreted in terms of the capitulation of the second leader of the group, Song Jiang (Zhou Enlai), and his fostering a second in command Lu Junyi (Deng Xiaoping) to help him destroy the group's mission once the first bandit leader (Mao) had died. *The Water Margin* campaign dragged on into 1976 and, after the death of Zhou Enlai in January, was used by some to attack his successor às Premier, Hua Guofeng.

During the Campaign to Study the Theory of the Dictatorship of the Proletariat, Mao put forward three directives. In addition to studying the theory of the dictatorship of the proletariat, people were enjoined to promote unity and further the national economy. To this end three documents were prepared by Hu Yaobang, Hu Qiaomu and others under Deng Xiaoping's aegis to impart vitality to the industrial economy by opening it up, restoring material incentives and developing systems of responsibility, to de-politicise the Chinese Academy of Sciences and to reign in class struggle. Steps were also taken to revive academic journals and restore normal academic life. Deng once again put forward the view, aired in the early 1960s, that science, technology and education in general constituted part of the 'productive forces' and were not the site of class struggle. Chapter 1 has already noted that these documents and proposals were vehemently attacked as 'poisonous weeds' by those who stressed 'class struggle' as the 'key link' in all programmes.

As 1975 drew to a close, a savage poster campaign at Qinghua University exploded into national concern, with *Renmin ribao* celebrating the new year by affirming the importance of class struggle. As we saw in Chapter 1, the death of Zhou Enlai removed the main supporter of normalisation, and when a demonstration held in Tiananmen Square in his memory on the occasion of the *Qingming* festival in April resulted in violent repression, Deng Xiaoping was blamed. Throughout 1976 there unfolded a movement to criticise Deng and to restore the spirit of the Cultural Revolution which had started ten years before. During the movement there was much noise but, unlike ten years previously, little mass response. Amidst a faltering economy beset by natural disasters (such as the Tangshan earthquake), there was no enthusiasm for continued revolution. Within one month of the death of Mao in September, the Shanghai group now called the 'Gang of Four' was arrested and China's leaders began once again to take stock.

The Post-1978 Situation

The two years following the death of Mao, which occasioned much confusion in the Party, also saw much confusion among intellectuals. The victory of Deng Xiaoping at the Third Plenum resulted in a determination to recruit the services of intellectuals. It was followed, therefore, by a conference on theory convened by the Propaganda Department of the Party and the newly established Chinese Academy of Social Sciences under the aegis of Hu

Yaobang. That conference, which lasted from January to April 1979, echoed many of the concerns of the democratic activists, although most of its participants remained aloof from the mass movement. The journal *China Youth*, which Hu Yaobang had done much to revive, had argued back in 1978 that democracy was a prerequisite for the 'four modernisations'. That theme was taken up by the activist Wei Jingsheng (discussed earlier) who talked about the 'fifth modernisation' and found echoes in the theory conference itself which talked about instituting limited terms of office for officials, the importance of the ballot box and the need to shake off the 'feudal' patriarchal heritage (Goldman 1991). Despite that, many activists probably suspected that the 'democracy' espoused by intellectuals was seen merely as a 'benevolent gift'. Unlike the assembled intellectuals, many of them had lost confidence in the capacity of a Marxist-Leninist régime to act in any way other than the patriarchal. They reflected a deepening crisis of legitimacy. Predictably, their exercise in what had been known in the Cultural Revolution as 'extensive democracy' was curtailed. In April, Wei Jingsheng was arrested, tried (according to dubious legal procedures, discussed in Chapter 5) and sentenced to fifteen years' imprisonment. By 1981, many of his associates had also been arrested, though this time without trial.

Though the first half of the theory conference abounded with reform proposals, its second half was dominated by Hu Qiaomu, who had blazed the trail for the 'practice faction' by his famous speech of 1978 declaring that the Party had to adhere to 'objective economic laws' (1978). It was Hu who drafted the speech for Deng Xiaoping with which to close the conference elaborating his 'four cardinal principles', which we have discussed many times before. From then on, as we noted in Chapter 2, Hu, as head of the newly established Chinese Academy of Social Sciences, achieved prominence as the authoritative spokesperson on matters intellectual. For the next half decade he was to utter the 'correct' verdict on a host of intellectual matters, eclipsing even Zhou Yang who had also been rehabilitated. But many intellectuals wished to go beyond Hu Qiaomu and received some backing from Hu Yaobang, who had instigated reform in the Chinese Academy of Sciences, the rebirth of *China Youth* and the theory conference of 1979. Hu Yaobang together with Zhao Ziyang were responsible for promoting or encouraging a large number of intellectual reformers.

We have already described the various political cycles of the 1980s. The first of these, which outlasted the theory conference of 1979, was one of considerable optimism. This was particularly the case amongst economists. Following the rehabilitation of the veteran economist Sun Yefang, there was much talk of utilising the 'law of value' in planning which resulted in a conference on the subject in April 1979. At that conference, Liu Guoguang, insisting on a much more positive role for the market, and He Jianzhang, advocating guidance rather than mandatory planning, went far beyond Sun. Increasingly Sun, who had been lionised after his rehabilitation was seen as somewhat 'conservative'. Throughout 1979 and into 1980, the debates continued, with even more innovative proposals emerging, such as Jiang Yiwei's 'theory of an enterprise-based economy' according to which economic enterprises would become independent units totally responsible for their profits and losses (Sung and Chan 1987). Such proposals raised further questions, bearing in mind that such an economy could not operate so long as prices were planned. Indeed, the bounds of orthodoxy were considerably stretched.

Economists, in pragmatic mode, debated energetically the impediments to efficiency, rejecting much of Mao's teleology. Yet some philosophers, notably Wang Ruoshui, were not content with the simple slogan 'practice is the sole criterion for evaluating truth'. Practice, he argued, had to be related to teleological concerns (see Brugger and Kelly 1990: pp. 127–32). Reformers had to be mindful of a socialist purpose whilst examining the impediments to rational modernity – one of which was said to be the 'peasant mentality'. In the spirit of 'emancipating the mind', Wang Ruoshui explained the cult of Mao in terms of that mentality as outlined in Marx's *Eighteenth Brumaire of Louis Bonaparte* (an old Trotskyist theme and highly subversive). Considerations of the peasantry, moreover, spilled over once again into questioning the former orthodoxy that peasant wars had been the motive force of Chinese history, into discussions of 'agrarian socialism' and into considerations of Marx's 'Asiatic Mode of Production' (recalling the thaw period after the death of Stalin). As Wu Dakun saw it, that Marxian concept was valid for China and by extension could be used to explain misrule in recent years (Brugger and Kelly 1990: pp. 20–8).

There was also the beginnings of a discussion on academic freedom, a major issue in the 1979 theory conference. One began to hear statements that there were no 'forbidden zones' in academic work and academic mistakes should not be equated with political mistakes. Accordingly, Wu Han, Zhou Yang, Jian Bozan and Deng Tuo were rehabilitated (the later two, posthumously) in 1978–9, their earlier works were republished and the debates they had pioneered reopened. Though they were presented correctly as 'victims of the uncontrolled criticism of the ruling élite' rather than martyrs to the cause of civil liberties (Israel 1986), their very rehabilitation did offer hope for greater freedom. Hope also accompanied the positive reassessment of Jian Bozan's historicism (Edmunds 1987: pp. 92–106). Yet old habits die hard. In the manner of the Great Leap, the Cultural Revolution and the attempts to revive it in the early 1970s, the past was once again used to satirise the present but this time to criticise Mao. Discussions concerning peasant rebellions were also clearly bent to oppose the emphasis on class struggle. On the other hand the reform movement of 1898 was also mentioned as an analogue of the succession struggle in contemporary China, serving a warning that reforms might be going too fast (Edmunds 1987: pp. 102–3). Indeed, there was a virtual explosion of historical plays which referred obliquely to recent events (Fisher 1986: p. 177).

On the literary front the early period of 'emancipating the mind' saw the outpouring of what became known as the 'literature of the wounded generation', narrating horrors endured in the Cultural Revolution. It was all right to denounce the past but soon denunciation of the past spilled over into critique of the present. When writers of 1957 vintage such as Wang Meng and Liu Binyan reappeared, they engaged in much the same kind of critical reform writing as they had in the mid-1950s and that always engendered a reaction from elements in the Party. Hostility was exacerbated as they and many younger disillusioned Cultural Revolution activists voiced a new distrust of authority. The new critical reformers were eager to unmask what seemed to some to have developed into a new 'social bourgeoisie'. Party leadership was still affirmed but the mood was decidedly more democratic and some writers sailed very close to the wind. Wang Ruowang, for example, not content to attack officially sanctioned targets of the Cultural Revolution, looked to the conditions which had allowed the 'Gang of Four' to rise – conditions which had existed for decades. He castigated those who had declared that writers lacked (the proper) virtue and praised leadership by inaction (*wuwei er zhi*) symbolised by Zhou Enlai and the ex foreign minister Chen Yi. Perhaps most galling of all, he compared his life in a *Guomindang* prison with that in a prison in the People's Republic for counter-revolutionary activities (six years). The latter, he felt, was worse, since he did not receive food from the outside, could read only Mao's works and did not quite know who the enemy was (Rubin 1987: pp. 240–50).

Rather than literature serving politics, Wang Ruowang declared, politics was 'the younger brother of literature' and the quality of writers had deteriorated after the imposition of the political criterion. Recalling Wang Shiwei's 'Wild Lily', Wang was most contemptuous of the practice of labelling literary works 'poisonous weeds'. Here he recalled Lu Xun's comment that politicians could not tolerate people who stood out (Rubin 1987: p. 244). The theme of literature's function was later taken up by Wang Ruoshui on the fortieth anniversary of the Yan'an Talks: both politics and literature should serve the people. In the meantime, however, the first major reaction set in.

In 1981, we have noted, fears concerning disorder led the Party to urge that intellectuals bide their time and submit to the new leadership until reform had sufficiently strengthened their position. Gradually, it seemed, political reform was to be postponed until economic reform was much more advanced. Such thinking, of course, strengthened the hand of more orthodox Party leaders, especially it seems in the military who moved to criticise the writer Bai Hua for the film *Kulian* (Unrequited Love) which painted far too pessimistic a picture about the new régime. The ban was soon lifted but at least the Bai Hua event demonstrated early on the fragility of the new critical literature (Wagner 1987: pp. 219–20; Fisher 1986). It showed that the medium of film, because of its wide appeal and the fact that not-very-literate leaders were more familiar with it, was the most sensitive to Party censure, and indeed a dozen films had been halted in progress in 1980 following a speech by Hu Yaobang on script writing, warning about the 'social effects' of literature and art (Kraus 1986: pp. 201–2).

We noted also fears about the state of central finances in 1981 and the salience of Chen Yun's theory of 'comprehensive balance'. Economists such as Liu Guoguang who felt that reform and readjustment were complementary, protested but in vain. Indeed, in the two years prior to his death Sun Yefang probably felt

vindicated (Sung and Chan 1987). In that period of hesitation
Deng Liqun, one of the more orthodox bureaucrats who had
declined to act as chairman of the 1979 theory conference, took
over the propaganda network. He abetted the renewed criticism of
writers, the reintroduction of taboos in scholarship by Hu Qiaomu
and continued the rethinking on restricting the scope of economic
reform. Legal reforms also seemed faced with considerable ob
stacles. We saw earlier that there was much discussion on the need
to replace the 'rule of persons' with the 'rule of law' but few figure
stand out as path-breaking in that endeavour. The new legal
profession still had to contend with a situation where matters were
regularly solved by Party bodies which applied administrativ
sanctions. When the Criminal Code was restricted because it was
felt to limit necessary state action, one can think of no prominent
legal scholars who protested (Feinerman 1987). Literary figures had
to do it for them and Wang Ruowang was not slow to bemoan the
relative absence of the rule of law in the popular journal *Minzhu y*
fazhi (Democracy and the Legal System) (Rubin 1987: p. 241). A
criticism of the legal system was mounted from outside, it appeared
that the new legal profession had a long way to go before it became
a major intellectual force.

The Twelfth Party Congress in September 1982 paved the way for
renewed reform which became clear at a National Conference on
Ideology and Political Work in January 1983. Those who wanted
industrial reform were excited by agricultural decollectivisation, the
speed of which seems to have taken everyone by surprise. It was an
opportune moment to cast aside hesitation. In the new climate Zhao
Ziyang sought out the 'jack of all trades' reformer Yu Guangyuan
and economist Xue Muqiao to explore new reforms and facilitate
the appointment of Ma Hong as Head of the Chinese Academy of
Social Sciences. Proposals for economic reform came thick and fast
Once it was decided to replace the delivery of enterprise profits by ta
and that enterprises could borrow capital from the banks, the
parameters of the old debate about restrictions on the law of valu
were broken and the arguments of 1979–82 seemed archaic, at leas
until the profit contract system of the late 1980s.

At the same time Hu Yaobang, seeking to advance cultural
reforms, launched a campaign to create a new 'spiritual civilisation
That movement was not just a profession of virtue but constitute
in part a reaction against much of the scientism which had gripped

ocial thinkers after the 'four modernisations' policy was restated. In the words of Ru Xin, the one-time critic of humanism now urned humanist, science needed the 'guiding light of philosophy' (*Renmin ribao*, 20 July 1983: p. 5). The official slogan was to create modernisation with Chinese characteristics'. This meant much more than just importing scientific know-how from the West and Japan. It meant no less than establishing philosophical guidance over the whole modernisation process. It meant asking what the aim of socialist production was.

In the new spirit of 'developing' Marxism (rather than the old slogan of 'upholding' it), Western philosophy of science was studied and attempts were made to modernise Engels' *Dialectics of Nature*. This was a sore point with the astro-physicist Fang Lizhi who had criticised the pseudo-science of the 'Gang of Four', which had defended Engels against the 'big bang theory' and had persecuted Fang (Williams 1990: pp. 462–9). Fang Lizhi still had to contend with Zha Ruqiang of the Natural Dialectics Research Office. Others, however, sought a reconciliation by using the insights gained from Ilya Prigogine's 'theory of dissipative structures'. That theory criticised equilibrium thinking and dangerously talked about the natural occurrence of 'great leaps'.

The new spirit also involved using Marxist categories to analyse contemporary Chinese society, asking whether alienation existed in that society and how one might overcome it. It led to a flowering of critical Marxism. Here Wang Ruoshui (1985) enlarged upon his earlier writings about alienation, arguing specifically that three sorts of alienation continued to exist in socialist society. The first form, Wang felt, was ideological alienation. This manifested itself as superstition, dogmatism and the cult of Mao. The second form was political alienation, manifested in the 'servants of the people' becoming the 'masters of the people'. Third came economic alienation, the separation of producers from one another, their product and their 'species being'. This was caused by people not fully understanding 'objective economic laws', bureaucratism and elements in the social structure. Though Wang objected most strongly, officials detected a Cultural Revolution flavour in his analysis. Referring to political alienation, Wang recalled Marx's discussion of the Paris Commune, a theme used by advocates of the Cultural Revolution. His argument about economic alienation was, of course, quite different. Advocates of the Cultural Revolution saw bureaucratism and structural factors in terms of the 'restoration of capitalism', and Wang (1980: p. 99) insisted that one could not restore capitalism since capitalism was never dominant anyway. If there was going to be any restoration it would be the restoration of feudalism. Nevertheless, despite Wang's distancing himself from the radicals of those times, some officials saw how his humanist Marxism could be bent in the same radical direction as the Marxism of the activists of the mid-1960s. Those who harboured paranoia about another Cultural Revolution were alarmed. For example Yang Xianzhen, ever the materialist, smarting at his denunciation by Wang Ruoshui nearly twenty years previously, once again denounced Wang's idealist views on 'the identity of thought and existence' as an ideological cause of the Great Leap Forward (Brugger and Kelly 1990: pp. 91–3). He presumably saw Wang in the same vein as his old enemy Kang Sheng and the theorist of class struggle Guan Feng.

The discussion of alienation in socialism, pioneered by Wang Ruoshui, resulted in hundreds of articles in one of the most lively debates in China for many years. Even Zhou Yang, on the hundredth anniversary of the death of Marx, joined in, using much the same words as Wang Ruoshui (*Renmin ribao*, 16 March 1983: p. 5) and engendering considerable opposition as senior Party leaders tried to prevent the publication of Zhou's speech in *Renmin ribao*. It could only be a matter of time before the lively debate was brought to an abrupt if temporary halt. In a speech to a Party plenum in October 1983, Deng Xiaoping (1984) urged those in charge of matters intellectual and particularly Deng Liqun to tighten discipline. So began the Campaign against Spiritual Pollution in which a broad range of targets were selected, ranging from those who spoke about alienation, who were accused of inciting people to seize back power in Cultural Revolution mode (*Guangming ribao*, 3 Dec. 1983: p. 3), to those who advocated 'modernist' (subjectivist) literature instead of (socialist) realism (Pollard 1985) and those who imported pornography. Zhou Yang made a careful confession, admitting that his words might incite people with 'ulterior motives' (*Guangming ribao*, 6 Nov. 1983: p. 1). The editor of *Renmin ribao*, Hu Jiwei, together with his outspoken deputy Wang Ruoshui, lost their posts and Hu Qiaomu made a long statement giving the 'correct' reading of Marx and rejecting the idea that alienation might be found in socialist society (*Renmin ribao*, 27 Jan. 1984: pp. 1–5). Throughout the campaign, however, most of the leading humanist scholars, with the notable exception of Ru Xin, remained obdurate. Wang Ruowang refused to participate and Wang Ruoshui (1984) wrote a polite but firm letter of reply to Hu Qiaomu. Within six weeks the main campaign petered out though literary figures continued to be criticised well into 1984. The campaign, while short-lived, cost Party leaders a degree of legitimacy amongst intellectuals; they could not afford to lose much more if the modernisation drive faltered. By October 1984, Deng had switched the focus of criticism back to 'leftists' and even extended rectification into the People's Liberation Army (Hamrin 1987: p. 297). Though Deng Liqun retained his post, *de facto* control over the propaganda network passed to Hu Qili who was more in tune with the humanist critics and who demanded 'academic freedom under the guidance of Marxism'.

The new 'hundred flowers' movement which exploded in 1984 saw an avalanche of new writing submitted for publication. Wang Ruoshui resumed polemics, extending the scope of his defence of humanism, and Wang Ruowang continued his interventions. All this was a backdrop to the economic reforms in the industrial sphere discussed earlier. In all this Zhao Ziyang stressed the importance of the new technological and information revolution and cybernetics and 'informatics' were widely discussed. The new discipline of futurology (*weilaixue*) flowered as Chinese scholars pored over the work of Daniel Bell, John Naisbitt and Alvin Toffler. Toffler, in particular, was warmly endorsed by Hu Yaobang and Premier Zhao Ziyang; and attempts to reconcile Toffler's work with Marxism appeared in profusion. Toffler argued, following his book *The Third Wave*, that China might leap from 'first wave' agrarian society to a 'third wave' society based on the information revolution without enduring the traumas of 'second wave' industrialism as experienced by the West and Japan. Indeed, Toffler rekindled 'great leap' thinking and added to the growing interest in futurology as a huge project was launched to chart possible futures for China by the year 2000. To that end a new journal *Towards the Future (zou xiang weilai)* was launched and scholars such as Jin Guantao did their best to combine new Western thinking with Marxism (Brugger and Kelly 1990: p. 70–9).

The 'hundred flowers' movement of 1984–6 was breathtaking. There was renewed criticism of China's feudal heritage and advocacy of new political reforms to accompany economic reforms, the birth of a Chinese political science pioneered amongst others by the physicist-turned social scientist Yan Jiaqi, calls for human rights, and demands for more freedom in the science and technology fields. There was exultation in the explosion of freer literature and art, pressure for more academic autonomy, suggestion of areas where Marx's political economy might need revising and, most remarkable of all, observations that the vanguard role of the proletariat had been replaced by that of the intellectuals. We have noted the backlash.

The backlash of the mid-1980s has to be seen in the context of a chaotic economic situation resulting from the accelerated reform of late 1984. Mounting inflation strengthened the hands of the cautious who began to move against unorthodox economists. Faced with economic disequilibrium, newspapers stressed that Prigogine's discussion of 'far from equilibrium states' did not contradict the need for economic equilibrium (*Guangming ribao*, 6 Nov. 1985: p. 3). Up until 1985, economics (as a 'science') had enjoyed more freedom than most fields of scholarship. Now Hu Qiaomu mounted an attack on Song Longxiang (Ma Ding) who had criticised those who sought answers to every question in Marx's *Capital* (Brugger and Kelly 1990: p. 117). Hu Qiaomu also became involved in denouncing Fang Lizhi's latest research interest – quantum cosmology – as 'bourgeois idealism' and *Beijing ribao* returned to the old theme of the 'idealist and metaphysical doctrine' of a finite universe (Williams 1990: p. 474). Hu Jiwei, now in charge of drafting a new publications law, came under pressure from those who stressed the duties of journalists; they now included the once vocal social critic Wang Meng who was to become Minister of Culture in 1986. A Party conference in September stressed the importance of Marxism which was increasingly interpreted in an orthodox manner, after which Hu Qili's pleas for freedom of creation were joined by pleas for social responsibility. Yet throughout early 1986, the 'hundred flowers' spirit still raged and pressure for democratic reform continued (Schell 1988), ranging from the cautious advocacy of Su Shaozhi to the vehement protests of Fang Lizhi. Fang Lizhi was quite blunt: socialism in China had been a failure, Sweden was more socialist, China needed to develop Western democracy and human rights and Deng's 'four principles' upheld superstition and dictatorship (Williams 1990: pp. 476–9, 484).

Reaction after the Sixth Plenum resulted in the removal of Hu Yaobang. Fang Lizhi, whose university in Hefei had witnessed some of the most vehement demonstrations, was dismissed from the Party. The same fate awaited Liu Binyan and Wang Ruowang and other intellectuals were transferred from their posts. Ironically Su Shaozhi was also removed from his post only two months before the Thirteenth Party Congress officially adopted his theory of stages, talking about 'the primary stage of socialism' (Zhao 1987). The accusations, summed up as promoting 'bourgeois liberalisation', included neglecting the role of the Party and suggesting that capitalist democracy might be superior to socialism. To counter this, Deng's 'four principles' were stressed and many articles were published condemning 'total westernisation' (sometimes tracing the trend back half a century to Hu Shi), assuring people that socialism was superior to capitalism, and revealing strenuous efforts to stamp out non-registered publications.

The backlash softened and petered out after the Thirteenth Party Congress. But, by turning on intellectuals who could have given it a new image, the Party had lost even more legitimacy. Wang Ruowang went on to claim that he was 'the father of bourgeois liberalisation', and Fang Lizhi, defiant throughout 1987–8, became something of a democratic hero, using science as a 'civil discourse'. Many of his writings were circulated by the central authorities for criticism, only to enjoy the acclaim of many students. This was no mean feat since many intellectuals were complaining that students were either apathetic or had sunk into blatant careerism; indeed there was a rush of students to join the Party in 1988. But, many felt, the Party had let them down. The question, however, was not just one of career prospects. There were also good intellectual grounds for disaffection. People such as Yan Jiaqi and Su Shaozhi directed much of their criticism at the persistence of 'feudal' ways of thought which required democratic correction. Others, however, as noted in Chapter 2, proposed '*xin quanwei zhuyi*' (neo-authoritarianism). They sometimes claimed that they were inspired by the American political scientist Samuel Huntington whose writings were translated (see Liu Jun and Li Lin 1989; Sautman 1992). They looked to certain newly-industrialising economies in Asia which experienced non-democratic rule in the crucial stages of economic development prior to proceeding to democracy. Such thinking, as we have seen, appealed apparently to Zhao Ziyang, who was more likely by such means to weather the inflationary consequences of market reform. Yet there was an obvious objection; one might finish up not with some new authority but with what Zhao Ziyang would have detested, the despotism of the old kind.

As described earlier, according to Deng the events of 1989 were largely the result of backstage manipulation by officials and intellectuals. Certainly some institutions such as the Beijing Social, Economic and Technological Research Institute, China's first private think-tank (headed by Chen Ziming), and other bodies such as the Stone (computer) company offered students financial and other support. Certainly a few intellectuals such as Liu Xiaobo and Zhou Duo did join the students' hunger strike. In general, though, intellectual support occurred behind the scenes. Many prominent reform intellectuals urged caution and others sought to act as go-betweens. Many of them felt that the heroics, the adventurism and the inflammatory speeches of student leaders such as Wuer Kaixi and Chai Ling were extremely imprudent. Nevertheless, the perception of back-stage manipulation led to the arrest of some of the reform intellectuals discussed earlier (for example, Chen Ziming, Li Honglin and Wang Ruowang), and the exile of others (such as Su Shaozhi and Yan Jiaqi). Fang Lizhi eventually departed for America after a period in the United States Embassy, for which he was branded a 'traitor'.

The persecution of the leaders of dissident groups continued into 1992 with 600 arrested in June (Leung 1993: p. 21.4). Later in the year, however, the régime attempted to present itself in a new light. We have discussed the new stress on modernisation in 1992, affirmed by the Party Congress of that year. At that Congress General Secretary Jiang Zemin (1992: p. 22) spoke of the enormous value of intellectuals, the need to respect them and the official policy of welcoming Chinese intellectuals back from abroad whatever their past political views. There is no doubt that a new thaw is occurring and intellectual inputs will be required. But will they be democratic?

Conclusion

At the beginning of this chapter we characterised intellectuals as people concerned to discuss universal values in a publicly accessible form. We saw that science was the pre-eminent universal discourse. For that reason, many of the debates discussed in this chapter turned on the question of science versus non-science or pseudo-science. In a scientistic climate, emerging 'civil discourse' will inevitably be couched in the language of science, as is evident from the writings of Yan Jiaqi and Fang Lizhi. When we object to the latter's silly statement that philosophy is merely an instrumental arm of physics, we must be mindful of that process. Of course, Ru Xin, like most philosophers, is quite correct in stating that science needs to be guided by philosophy and much of today's scientism in China needs an antidote. We are considering, however, a society in which many intellectuals claim that philosophical guidance has often been wrong and has produced adverse effects. Attempts to rehabilitate the philosophical elements of civil discourse have as yet borne little fruit with sad consequences for the legitimacy of the régime.

Civil discourse, of course, must develop outside official channels and must involve wide community participation. We have noted, however, that severe inhibitions have been placed on debates which extend beyond narrow academic confines. Many of the struggles narrated above concern not so much what was said but where it was said or published and at what time. Academic dissension meant simply dissension behind relatively closed doors; public dissension invited 'struggle'. That is why literature, film and television, which could not be confined, was always seen as the most subversive. China is, of course, not unique here, though the coercive measures which may be applied are unusually extreme. Nor is China alone in having a very strong anti-intellectual element in its ruling party; this is reflected in its older leaders, especially among those with a voracious appetite for learning who are largely self-taught. We are familiar with such politicians in the West, eager to tap mass aversion to what appears to be a self-serving élite. As Alexis de Tocqueville argues and as we noted in Chapter 4, the perception of privilege without power incites more animosity than the simple exercise of power and, as Wang Ruowang reminded us in the mid-1950s, was used to keep many intellectuals out of power. As the Cultural Revolution demonstrated, privilege is easy to detect and easy to tear down; power is much more opaque.

This chapter has concentrated on public intellectual struggles. It has touched on ordinary academic debate only when it involved

Party leaders or provided the basis for subsequent struggles. The picture presented is far from pretty. Most senior intellectuals swayed with the political wind and we cannot always be sure whether their 'confessions' constituted a genuine change of heart or concessions to authority in traditional Confucian mode. Integrity suffered and may have damaged reputations, yet a few scholars who held fast to their views emerged later, fighting the battles of previous decades, and often appeared slightly ridiculous. Scholarship on China in the West echoes that process. We recall our Introduction. We now witness a vulnerable generation which came to a favourable view of China in the 1960s and early 1970s confronted by old cold warriors of an earlier vintage. The latter often accuse the former of lacking integrity and the former frequently see the latter as ridiculous throw-backs. Both offer caricatures and mirror the insensitivity of recent Chinese debates.

Meanwhile, the observer of China sees a continuation of a Chinese intellectual theme, which dates from at least the May Fourth Movement of 1919. There is oscillation between, on the one hand, contempt for the West, affirmations of patriotism and the old belief that Western scholars are incapable of understanding China, and, on the other, an undifferentiated enthusiasm both for Western virtues and Western shallowness. This kind of oscillation is, of course, not particularly Chinese. It may be found in any country facing a crisis of legitimacy.

7

Family and Gender Relations

Pre-twentieth-century Chinese society was patriarchal, patrilineal and virilocal. Most of contemporary Chinese society still is. Of course, much has changed and is still changing but scholars are divided as to the significance of those changes. In the study of gender and the family 'socialist transition' is rarely seen nowadays as a simple unilinear process. The debate has been influenced by considerations of the 'unhappy marriage' between feminism and Marxism and a rejection of economic determinism which sees gender simply as a dependent variable. Feminist scholarship has eloquently revised Engels' proposition that participation in production is the most significant step towards women's liberation and the argument that women's liberation depends on the successful outcome of class struggle. Nor is 'modernisation' seen as a simple unilinear process. Scholars have been forced to consider arguments that modernisation does not automatically erode the power of the family and even that kinship networks (especially Confucian ones) might strengthen and be strengthened by that process. Discussions on China, moreover, have had to take into account arguments about revolutionary motivation. Whereas gender equality might be a motivating factor amongst intellectual revolutionaries, peasants might be concerned simply to restore the security of traditional family life, as we noted in Chapter 3. Our Introduction hinted that an extreme form of such analysis can go on to argue that the association between socialism and gender equality is a short-term 'marriage of convenience', resulting in 'patriarchal socialism' perhaps by way of the intermediate Chinese stage 'new democratic patriarchy' (Stacey 1983: pp. 108–94) – in Pateman's (1988) terms a new 'fraternal social contract'. Once scholars begin to argue like that, they tend to believe that revolutionary leaders never really intended to achieve gender equality. Others, however, react by saying that revolutionary leaders have been forced to make tactical compromises, and although the enforcement of patriarchy was not the intention it was the effect of those compromises (Wolf 1985: pp. 25–6). After all, the early Bolsheviks alienated much support by pursuing the cause of combating patriarchy and were forced to change tack. The Chinese Communist Party was not to repeat that mistake. Even the modest moves taken towards liberation in China had to be modified in the face of practical obstacles which could have endangered the whole revolutionary movement.

We are left with three basic positions. The first echoes official Chinese arguments that much progress has been made when one considers the past. Though few feminists would be satisfied with the degree of progress, such is clearly the case. The second position argues that the intention was never to end patriarchy but to redistribute its beneficiaries which, whilst true of many local leaders, is extremely difficult to sustain as a general proposition. The third stresses the effect of compromise and arguments centre on the necessity for particular compromises. A short chapter of this kind cannot explore relative degrees of necessity. It can, however, describe points of compromise and prepare the reader for more detailed consideration. (For a balanced appraisal of developments in 'socialist' states, see Molyneux 1981).

Pre-Twentieth-Century China

Official texts in pre-twentieth century China depict it ideally as one family writ large. The basic subdivisions of that country were extended families, each headed by a male and made up of a number of households held together by ties of loyalty and filial piety. Five basic relations governed society – between sovereign and subject (characterised ideally by justice), between father and son (characterised by love), between husband and wife (characterised by separate spheres of responsibility), between elder and younger brothers (informed by due precedence) and between friends (characterised by good faith). Each of these tended to be interpreted hierarchically with women's virtues (propriety in behaviour, speech, demeanour and employment) always seen as subordinate.

The values, both explicit and implicit, in that Confucian ideal ('the great tradition') were those of the gentry, the reality of peasant family relations being hardly worthy of the attentions of the authors of the texts, the *literati* of the bureaucratic élite.

Peasant life, or the 'little tradition', on the other hand, was basically that of a simple peasant commodity economy in which the family with its land (either directly owned or leased) was the basic unit. Despite being so described in recent texts, society was not 'feudal' in the sense of being static and land was alienable. Though extended families existed, even amongst the not-so-rich in areas where particular crops required a large labour force (Stacey 1983: p. 25), they were by no means the norm in the twentieth century. Surveys carried out in the 1930s and 1940s showed that the average size of a Chinese family was between four and six persons, only slightly higher than today. The eldest son usually remained in the family, whilst the other sons left it, thus forming what sociologists term a 'stem family' or *famille souche* (Buck 1964: p. 368; Levy 1949). There was clearly a strong moral component to the economic behaviour of those small peasant households but, given that a sizeable amount of crop production was marketed, one is hesitant to speak of the Chinese peasant economy as a 'moral economy' characteristic of subsistence farming (Stacey 1983: pp. 26–8). Yet one must be aware of the ideological basis of society – a patriarchy founded on the exchange of women among lineages (and villages) – and avoid an excessively economistic explanation. Such, Kay Ann Johnson (1983: pp. 22–6) reminds us, has led to the facile and erroneous view, noted above, that a transformation of economic relations leads automatically to a transformation of gender relations.

Clearly both ideological and economic considerations resulted in the male peasant child standing a much better chance of survival than the female. Though male infanticide was not unknown, female infanticide was much more common. Ideologically, males were more valuable because they preserved the eternal family line. Economically, rearing a male child was a much better investment than rearing a female child since sons would be expected to help the father in the fields as soon they were old enough and care for their parents in old age. The only return to be expected on a female child was her service during youth and the price she would fetch when sold into marriage (offset by the dowry she would take with her).

That is not to say, however, that the greater value attached to th
male resulted in discrimination against female children in the perio
of early infancy, though there was clearly a readiness to marry th
girl off as soon as possible (Lang 1946).

Both male and female children were treated with a great degree o
permissiveness during the early years (the male more so), thoug
later the boy was supposed to come under the supervision of th
father whilst the girl stayed with the mother (Levy 1949). From
about the age of four, families were ideally to separate the sexe
though that was virtually impossible in poor peasant families an
ties of affection between mother and son often remained ver
strong. These were seen as a useful emotional investment since late
the mother might formally be subject to the son's rule. Constantly
moreover, mothers manipulated traditional values subtly to pre
serve the loyalty of sons, creating what Margery Wolf (1985: p. 9
calls a 'uterine family'; that uterine family might be used to subver
the power of the formal family. Such must be borne in mind whe
we consider the passivity and 'conservatism' attributed to tradi
tional Chinese women. Indeed, as Johnson argues, the manipulatio
of 'conservative' patriarchal norms by women might be seen as
subtle way of achieving very non-patriarchal ends. For all tha
women's struggle for subjectivity made them complicit in the large
social system which subordinated them (Johnson 1983: pp. 22–4).

The father, on the other hand, would inculcate in the boy th
virtue of filial piety until he came to accept what Johnson (1983: p
1) calls an 'essentially androgynous vision of the universe' – mor
specifically, to see the world of both today and yesterday as a vas
hierarchy of families, each headed by a male whom it was his dut
to serve in return for which he would get material reward. The first
born son and to a lesser extent other sons knew that some day the
would be in the same position as their father – head of a family. Th
son's attitude towards his father was characterised more by fear an
avoidance than love and respect or even rivalry and contempt. Th
strictness of the boy's upbringing, reinforced by school if he had th
chance to go, resulted in him becoming by the early teens eithe
submissive or a rebel for life (Mao's own career is illustrative of th
latter possibility).

Whether one takes the family as an economic or an ideologic
unit, marriage was essentially a contract between two families i
two lineages (or villages). Arranged by matchmakers, it wa

frequently concluded without any regard for existing emotional ties. Indeed, the ideal marriage was one where emotional ties between husband and wife were minimised for fear of alienating the husband's mother (Wolf 1985: p. 7). Amongst the very poor this might be achieved by child marriages which were almost guaranteed not to generate sexual love. Marriage and sex, therefore, were often separated. The scion of the gentry class could satisfy his desire for sex or romantic love (which, contrary to some relativists, was not simply a Western invention) by taking a concubine or by frequenting brothels which, although never completely respectable, were accorded a status which they seldom acquired in the West. Peasant youths, however, rarely had the means to engage in such activities. They sought sexual outlets and romantic love in extra-marital relations, which often would be tolerated so long as they did not contribute to the breakup of the family. Extra-marital relations were usually seen as contributing to the disruption of the family only when they involved the waste of hard-earned resources. Illicit sexual relations were commonly entered into between a married man and a widow, since custom scorned a widow who remarried unless (and this was very rare) her new husband agreed to take the name of her former husband and thus preserve the integrity of the eternal family of the deceased. The Qing Legal Code, however, offered an inducement to violate custom by requiring the surrender of a widow's dowry (the property of the conjugal as opposed to the patrilineal unit) to her former husband's family in the event of remarriage; amongst better-off families, where dowries were larger, there was thus an incentive to secure her remarriage (Stacey 1983: p. 54).

Legally the wife was to obey her husband in all things and, on his death, her eldest son. She could rarely divorce her husband though he could divorce her on a number of grounds, one of which was 'talkativeness', the catch-all word. Though she was safeguarded by a number of clauses offering protection if she had no home to go back to or if she had fulfilled the appropriate mourning period for her husband's parents, these could generally be overruled since marital cases seldom reached the courts and purely practical issues determined her fate. One very important practical issue was, of course, the degree to which the family unit demanded the woman's manual labour. Clearly it was not always possible to separate farming tasks between those suitable for males and those suitable for females. Where males and females shared the same tasks, there might be a greater degree of gender equality and sexual freedom, as Mao Zedong noted on his inspection of the peasant movement in Hunan province in 1927 (Schram 1969: p. 258). But Hunan, where women had always engaged in farm work, was by no means typical. In China as a whole in the 1930s only some 13 per cent of farm work was undertaken by women and in North China very much less than that (though the figure may be underestimated since recent studies stress that important contributions by women to agriculture have been overlooked) (Judd 1990: p. 25). One might also question Mao's Engelsian proposition that participation in a single labour force is the most significant step towards emancipation. It was certainly the case, however, that among poorer peasants women were less isolated and could form informal support groups to resist mistreatment (Wolf 1985: pp. 8–9).

Whatever sexual equality existed amongst the peasants was surely complicated by generational considerations. The gentry ideal saw Chinese society as a gerontocracy with the patriarch accorded considerable power and respect. It may be demonstrated, however, that as one descends the social hierarchy, power becomes more and more dependent upon responsibility. A well-to-do patriarch might be able to exercise power without much responsibility, but a senile peasant grandfather rarely did. When the peasant grandfather became incapable of exercising responsibility, he lost power in decision-making and might even be pushed to a colder part of the communal *kang* on which the family in North China sleep. The demotion of the grandfather did not, of course, mean that much real power passed to women, yet some women had much more power than others. Often, in practical terms, the wife's mother-in-law was portrayed as the real tyrant of the home, appearing as a stern defender of patriarchal values in order to maintain her uterine family against her daughter-in-law who had the advantage of sharing her bed with the older woman's son. Interesting to note is the fact that suicide rates among women were very high for newly-weds, tapered off at age 30, then rose again at age 50, reflecting those mothers-in-law who could no longer compete with their son's wife for his affections (Wolf 1985: p. 11). The desire to preserve or create a uterine family by family division, moreover, explains the rivalry of sisters-in-law who manipulated fraternal conflict (Stacey 1983: p. 55).

Though a case may be made that there was less overt male oppression among the poorer peasants, at middle levels women were most cruelly exploited. It was to these families of landlords, rich peasants and minor gentry that servant girls were sold and where wives might be discarded in favour of concubines. At the highest levels, however, where males were often engrossed in extra-familial matters, some women had greater power in domestic affairs, though there women could more easily be isolated since they had no support network. Though overt gender relations varied according to families' position in the social hierarchy, at all levels extra-familial matters were the prerogative of the male head of the family. Whilst matchmaking was carried on by females, the male head was particularly concerned about the marriage of his daughter, since that involved her leaving to join another family (and in rural areas another village) in return for a bride-price. That bride price was very important among the relatively poor though among the more affluent a dowry was considered more significant since it bought appropriate favour. The wife, on the other hand, concerned herself with the marriage of her son. Formally this was an internal matter since he remained within the family, but practically it was crucial in maintaining her uterine family. Occasionally, a family without sons might conclude a uxorilocal marriage though this was rare, considered a second class arrangement and invited contempt for a male participating in such an arrangement (Johnson 1983: p. 12).

Transitional Society

The late nineteenth and early twentieth centuries saw dislocation in rural areas and the growth of a rural proletariat which depended on seasonal work to make a living. The precariousness of that existence led to banditry and to a drift to the cities. There were many causes of social dislocation. Judith Stacey (1983: p. 89) makes the case that the traditional family system generated contradictions which led to its undoing. The demand for male heirs and partible inheritance caused fragmentation of families and the proliferation of patriarchal units competing for land. Competition was intensified since patrilineal prestige caused the head of each family to strive to pass on to his heirs an amount of land at least equal to that which his father had inherited. There was also conflict between lineages and government. Chronic rural debt, moreover, was exacerbated by the high cost of marriage ceremonies. Whilst it would be ludicrous to claim that the rural family crisis (the undermining of the Confucian family's material and ideological foundations) caused the revolution, it was a factor which should be taken into account. The result was a shrinkage in the size of families, more rapid family division and an increase in the numbers of unmarried people. Women suffered more from the crisis than men; the 1953 census showed a ratio of 107.5 men for every 100 women after decades of war had witnessed large numbers of male deaths.

The crisis resulted in protest movements by women before the end of the Qing dynasty though scholars disagree as to the extent (Holmgren 1981: pp. 149–52). Some of those scholars argue that women's activity in secret societies increased and that the early days of the Taiping Revolution of mid-century, which promised gender equality, were marked by quite spectacular mobilisation. Some minor reforms were enacted by the old régime in its dying days though not to the satisfaction of large numbers of women who took part in the 1911 Revolution. Not long after that revolution there developed a Chinese suffragette movement. Significant numbers of women became politically active long before political parties mobilised people behind the banner of class struggle, influenced in many cases by the West but responding largely to the family crisis (Croll 1978: pp. 37–79; Stacey 1983: pp. 61–5). Whilst women's activism increased (especially in urban areas), there was also much female resistance to change in rural areas. Some women saw the forced unbinding of feet as tantamount to rape since by that act they often lost their respectability. Others resisted contraception in a situation where they needed constantly to bear children in the hope that one might survive to sustain parents in their old age (Wolf 1985: p. 14).

Whilst the family crisis may be explained first in terms of internal tensions in the patriarchal system, it must be seen in the context of war, which devastated agriculture in some areas and caused the disappearance of large numbers of males into the armed forces, and industrialisation which caused the collapse of some local handicraft industries (largely employing women) and migration to the cities. Early industrialisation followed a pattern familiar in what later became known as the third world. Many male peasants who migrated to the towns left their families behind, giving women in rural areas greater scope for exercising public roles. Where husband and wife were in factory employment, the line between breadwinner and domestic manager became blurred though men rarely participated in household chores. The urban wife who was not employed rarely saw her husband because long shifts were the norm. She was solely responsible for the training of young children until they were old enough for school or, more frequently, were old enough to be employed in the factories.

As for those women who were employed, most (over 80 per cent in the 1930s) were under 25 years of age (Davin 1976: p. 180); the unmarried ones commonly handed their wages over to their families and the married ones to their in-laws, even if the latter remained behind in the countryside. The women and children who migrated to the cities flocked into textiles and other light industries where they were often subject to the cruellest predations of the gang-boss system. Significantly the Green Gang, a notorious secret society, controlled the labour contracting network in textiles and prostitution in a number of cities since those occupations were the principal employers of women. Few women migrants to the towns were significantly liberated.

The Communist Party and Changing Gender Relations

The May Fourth Movement of 1919 which attacked tradition was, of course, concerned with gender discrimination, and a few intellectuals argued, against Marxist orthodoxy but in accordance with the moral calculus in which Chinese Marxism was embedded, that only by transforming the family could more general social change be brought about (Stacey 1983: pp. 72–6). Some of those intellectuals were soon to become Marxists; indeed Mao Zedong, in his pre-Marxist days, wrote protesting about women being driven to suicide (Witke 1967). Western-inspired women's magazines, which had begun to appear a decade before, were now published in profusion but such writings could usually only be read by men. A lot of the protest literature, moreover, was directed at intellectuals. Indeed the popularity of Ibsen can have had little relevance for peasants, assuming they could get someone to read to them the

translated excerpts. Yet, literate or not, many women joined th
urban movement. By the mid-1920s, attention was drawn to th
'sisterhoods' of South China which had developed throughout th
nineteenth century as a secular haven for women (Buddhis
sisterhoods being, of course, much older); those sisterhoods ofte
reimbursed the families of their members for the traditional 'bride
price'. In more modern vein, strikes by women occurred, with th
active encouragement of the Communist Party's women's depart
ment and left *Guomindang* organisations. In those organisations
number of women leaders emerged such as Deng Yingchao (wh
married Zhou Enlai) and Cai Chang (who married Li Fuchun). Th
first soviet of Hailufeng formed the first women's peasant associa
tion, women activists were prominent during the Northern Expedi
tion and radical women's unions remained active in the towns unt
they were savagely suppressed in Jiang Jieshi's coup of 1927 (Crol
1978: pp. 80–152).

Yet all the time there was a subterranean tension. May Fourt
radicals and those inspired by the early Bolsheviks openl
proclaimed Western ideas of women's rights, whilst peasan
activists were suspicious of 'bourgeois feminists' (many influence
by Christian missions) who might detract attention from clas
struggle. There was also much misleading conservative propagand
concerning the power of 'immoral women' and the radica
'communisation of wives'. Worried that such propaganda woul
be deleterious to the war effort during the Northern Expedition o
1926–27, leaders urged caution (Croll 1978: pp. 148–9; Johnso
1983: pp. 39–50). Here we return to the question posed at th
beginning of this chapter: was this tension purely the result o
tactical considerations or did it reflect something deeper? Johnso
and Stacey are in no doubt; the deeper cause lay in differen
motivations for revolution on the part of intellectuals and peasants
Intellectuals and urban leaders were inspired by the Enlightenmen
elements in Marxism, whereas peasants were proceeding, i
Friedman's (1974: pp. 118–20) terms, 'backward to revolution'
They were rebelling against the consequences of a family crisi
which had destroyed all the old patriarchal decencies (Johnso
1983: pp. 27–35: Stacey 1983: pp. 105–6). They demanded 'all me
be brothers' (Pateman's 'fraternal sexual contract') – to replace old
style patriarchy by a new one. There was a need, therefore, t
appease both peasants and local leaders.

The same tension surfaced in the Jiangxi Soviet. The Marriage Regulations of 1931, perhaps more under the influence of the leadership which had moved from Shanghai than of local leaders, proclaimed the thorough emancipation of women, allowed divorce if any party wished it and gave women the prerogative in deciding on the custody of children. Some women, moreover, served in the Workers' and Peasants' Red Army, the most famous being Kang Keqing who married the commander Zhu De, though, unlike Kang, most did not serve regularly in combat posts. Yet, once again, a preoccupation with maintaining production and not alienating male peasants during land reform resulted in an implementation of the Marriage Regulations less thorough than many activists desired. Most of the provisions of 1931 were not acted on and, although many divorces occurred, cadres often refused to permit divorce. Indeed, many cadres tended to see the reform of marriage in terms of land reform, in effect distributing women to the poor, and large numbers of poor men were at last able to get married. Significantly the regulations were amended in the formal Marriage Law of 1934 which, whilst remaining radical, stipulated that the wife of a soldier could only obtain a divorce with her husband's consent and weakened the woman's prerogative in deciding on child support. Furthermore, Party propaganda insisted that people must not confuse 'freedom of marriage' with 'absolute freedom' and warned against moral degeneracy, which often meant simply an injunction not to offend peasant sensibilities (Johnson 1983: pp. 51–62; Stacey 1983: pp. 159–66; Croll 1978: pp. 188–98; Davin 1976: pp. 21–33). Nevertheless, although class status (*jieji chengfen*) was assigned to families (ignoring the particularities of women's status) and 'land to the tillers' often just meant 'land to the families of tillers', the spirit remained radical and the issue of peasant women had been placed firmly on the agenda. The *Guomindang* Civil Code of 1930, on the other hand, which granted gender equality in property rights and promised rights of inheritance and divorce to women, was a dead-letter in rural areas and Jiang Jieshi's 'New Life Movement' offered no more than, in Betty Friedan's term, a 'feminine mystique' which was only modified a little during the war against Japan (Croll 1978: pp. 153–84).

Having moved its centre to Yan'an in the late 1930s, the Party faced a much worse situation. There foot-binding was common, and only some 5 per cent of women worked in the fields – indeed, it was considered a disgrace to be seen doing so. The primary task, therefore, was to get women into the workforce and to support the war effort in the women's militia, a task preferred by the pre-Long March local leadership who were said to have looked askance at marriage reform. Now there was even more caution than before, with leaders showing concern to protect existing property rights under the United Front formula and ordering postponement of marriage reform until the masses had been fully mobilised. Yet when mobilisation took place, it was to serve the Production Movement of 1943 which had little time for anything but production, even to the point of forbidding women to attend mass meetings. The formation of mutual aid teams, co-operatives and even guerilla units reinforced kinship ties, demanding that women merely extend the scope of their traditional work; and in its care for the families of military dependents the Party reinforced existing patriarchal dependency.

In such a situation some intellectuals felt the movement for female emancipation to be insufferably slow. The writer Ding Ling, in a famous article commemorating International Women's Day on 8 March 1942, protested that women were caught in a familiar bind: they were expected to engage in production and still shoulder the bulk of household chores. She was severely criticised for 'outdated views' and for impeding the process of mass mobilisation, which she subsequently admitted to be 'errors'. Thereafter there was little talk of implementing the 1934 Marriage Law (Johnson 1983: pp. 63–75; Croll 1978: pp. 199–214).

The Civil War, which renewed land reform, revived somewhat the radical spirit, yet cadre behaviour was faulty. Whilst what was to become the People's Liberation Army generally behaved impeccably towards women, the Party's civilian cadres and activists were to prove much less blameless, regarding women as prizes or class or village assets (Hinton 1966: pp. 362, 398). Reports also state that although women joined peasant associations they rarely had the courage to speak out, and although in the land reform process they were allowed to obtain a portion of land in their own right they were often denied the opportunity to take it up. Clearly the dominant ideology which held the male to be the physical intellectual and moral superior of the woman remained strong and attempts to challenge that position were subsumed by questions of class struggle. For example, the power of women's associations was impaired once it was claimed that they consisted largely of middle and rich peasant women (which is not surprising since those had experience in production). The associations were attacked by poor peasant bands whose women were then denounced as 'loose'. This may be because they had often been coerced into unapproved sexual relationships, though the term 'loose' could be applied to anyone who departed from traditional norms. Women activists were caught in a double bind. If they were active in seeking gender equality they were 'loose', and if they were not active they were 'feudal'.

It was clear by 1948 that the Party was prepared to move against radical action in gender matters particularly when the struggle against landlords had turned into struggle against husbands. The contrast with land reform was marked. According to Mao, land reform required what some thought to be 'excesses' in order for cowed peasants to become psychologically equipped to take part. But no one was willing to create conditions for women to engage in struggle sessions against patriarchy of the land reform type (Johnson 1983: pp. 75–83).

The 1950s

A major institution in post-1949 China which ideally was to pursue the emancipation of women was the Women's Federation. This co-ordinated a huge number of women's organisations which were set up all over the country following the victory of the Communist Party (Davin 1976: pp. 53–69). The Federation, however, was designated, in United Front mode, as a 'transmission belt' of a Party which was more concerned with the pressing problems of land reform and reviving the urban administration and economy. During land reform, which, as we saw in Chapter 3, was now extended to the newly liberated three-quarters of the country, women were once again encouraged to participate in peasant associations, and in some areas 10–15 per cent of their leaders were said to be female, though the target of one-quarter to one-third of female membership was rarely reached. The Land Reform Law once again gave legal title to women, but legal reform did not address complicated matters such as the capacity of women to use the land, the implications of land title for traditional exogamous marriages, and bride-price. Nor could legal provisions prevent *de facto* title being given to male family heads. Though formal ownership of land by women might strengthen a woman's uterine family, her threat to withdraw land on divorce was usually an empty one (Johnson 1983: pp. 102–14; Diamond 1975: p. 26). In the towns, the virtual and relatively painless abolition of prostitution and the dramatic increase in urban employment were of great benefit to women. Yet women were still slotted into the lower-paid street industries and into the textile and service trades. The small street industries which proliferated usually did not offer special services for women; they remunerated workers on a daily basis and did not provide pensions (in marked contrast to the generous allowances made in state enterprises).

Yet, at least, provisions for legal reform appeared quite radical. The Marriage Law of April 1950 abolished child marriages, often practised by the poor who felt that adopting child brides was cheaper than paying the bride-price for an adult,[1] and stipulated a minimum age for marriage of 18 for women and 20 for men. It gave equal rights to women and insisted that an existing marriage which had been concluded by parents and which was unsatisfactory to the parties concerned, could be dissolved. Small *ad hoc* Marriage Law Committees were set up in town and country and, in the euphoria of the time, it is said that those committees sometimes went around actively encouraging divorce and causing much disruption. Though clearly there was a dramatic rise in the number of divorces (over three-quarters sought by women), one is not sure how general that disruption was since many women interviewed later could not remember much about the campaign (Wolf 1985: p. 134). The reports may have been published (in 1953) in order to lend weight to those Party leaders who were worried about the effect of the Marriage Law on rural reform. At that time it was claimed that implementing the law had resulted in tens of thousands of suicides and murders (Wolf 1985: pp. 19–21). Patriarchal ideology, it was said, resulted in the real beneficiaries of the Marriage Law often being males who wished to shuffle off unsatisfactory relationships. Peasants, on the other hand, were heard to complain that they had

---

[1] A number of additional factors account for these 'minor' marriages, such as the desire for amenable daughters, shortage of women and contribution to the labour force (see Davin, 1976: pp. 73–4).

supported the Party only to have their wives divorce them, and cadres once again were concerned to see that the poor peasants, the beneficiaries of land reform, did not lose their wives. Those cadres, moreover, were probably as shocked as before by the fact that many of the women most active in reform were considered 'loose'. They were alarmed also by resistance to reform coming not only from men but also from mothers-in-law, threatened by loss of their uterine family through divorce or being forced to exchange the traditional security of *de facto* divorce within the family structure for real divorce and consequent poverty. Indeed, mothers-in-law were often the object of bitter attack.

Many local cadres, therefore, tried to blunt the edge of what was a quite radical campaign or at least failed to respond to it. Thus in 1953, as land reform drew to a close, extensive preparations for a new campaign were made to overcome local resistance. Early accounts depicted the new campaign as extremely bold and there is little doubt that the central leadership was committed to an onslaught on the old family system; but Johnson goes to great pains to point out that those accounts were exaggerated. Care was taken not to alienate cadres, who could only be criticised by Party authorities, and the intent of the campaign was portrayed in less-than-radical terms as restoring the old harmonious family. Propaganda soon stressed that in rural areas the integrity of the family unit was vital to provide the only social security there was and to maintain sideline production. Fears were expressed about excessive 'leftism' which a few years later was said to be 'bourgeois'. In some areas the campaign was considered successful though it was very soon wound up. By 1955, the government had relaxed its proscription on matchmaking, though the matchmaker could no longer charge extravagant sums for her services. Divorce, moreover, became extremely difficult and mediation was geared to 'reconciliation'. Significantly it was noted that the main obstacles to divorce were husbands, mothers-in-law and (most important) cadres (Davin 1976: p. 99; Johnson 1983: pp. 115–53).

Was this an instance of the conflict between Enlightenment ideals and peasant populism referred to earlier? Was the Party abandoning the family revolution in the face of opposition? Or was it the case that the Party, which had never expressed any wish to destroy the conjugal family and had disbanded 'sisterhoods', was remaining true to form? We have already hinted at two sorts of answer. The first, that of Stacey (1983), is that a genuine revolution did occur and was essentially completed by 1953. The Party set out to destroy old-style patriarchy and had succeeded. It had basically achieved its objective of saving peasant families from destruction by creating a 'new democratic patriarchy'. That patriarchy was 'democratic' in the sense that it was more generally available to the masses. It was egalitarian in that it enforced monogamy, and it was 'new' in that it curtailed foot-binding, concubinage, taking child brides, infanticide and much of the old family order. In addition it had created the conditions to give women much more access to the public sphere. Restored virilocal marriage, however, restricted the opportunities for women to exercise leadership. Patrilineal organisation still gave excessive value to sons and patriarchal ideology reinforced the subordination of women. What had been created was, like 'new democracy' itself, neither bourgeois nor socialist. There had appeared not the atomised family ideal of bourgeois capitalism nor the collective ideal of socialism – simply the ideal of the small peasant patriarch (Stacey 1983: pp. 182–94).

Another sort of answer focuses simply on the fact that the thorough implementation of the spirit of the Marriage Law was too disruptive and was shelved because the government was embarking upon its First Five Year Plan (1953–7). The concern, once again, was with the priority of production and Engels' simple views on the liberating consequences of participating in production. The plan, however, which gave priority to heavy industry, discriminated in urban areas against women's employment. It required levels of education which many women did not have. Even when women were qualified, factories were unwilling to incur the extra costs of services by employing them. By 1953, once the urban service sector had been revived, there was a dramatic fall-off in urban employment opportunities for women and female unemployment increased sharply. The government, therefore, moved (not all that successfully, as we have seen) to halt migration into the cities, disadvantaging rural women who sought marriages in the towns with the added prize of urban registration. The result of all that was that female participation in the non-rural labour force increased only slightly during the period of the plan (from 11.7 per cent to 13.4 per cent) (Andors 1983: pp. 35–6). In such a situation, official publications went to great pains to insist that women should observe the 'four goods'. They should be good at uniting with neighbourhood families for mutual aid, doing housework, educating children, encouraging family production, study and work and engaging in study themselves (Andors 1975: p. 34). The media insisted that 'housewives can serve socialism', encouraged women to give up employment if it conflicted too much with household duties, stressed women's biologically ordained work, promoted fashion, and even defined women's role in terms of the 'double burden' about which Ding Ling had complained in 1942 (Andors 1983: pp. 35–6, 103; Davin 1976: pp. 108–10).

Official publications, however, still called upon women to participate in public life and criticised family resistance to activist wives and the 'low level of political awareness' of women in traditional families. More women became state officials despite the very callous job-assignment system which often employed husbands and wives in different cities. More women were elected as deputies to people's congresses and, as we have seen, women came to play the dominant role in mediation committees which settled disputes outside the formal courts and in residents' committees which handled basic level administrative matters. The latter form of activity was a mixed blessing. On the one hand it could enhance confidence in public participation. On the other hand, since residents' committees were charged with reporting on insanitary conditions and public security violations, they reinforced the male stereotype of the female 'busybody'.

In the rural areas, propaganda stressed the importance of female participation in the collectivisation drive which accelerated in 1955, and the National Programme for Agricultural Development of 1956 put forward a target of 120 work-days for women (compared with 250 for men). In addition the Women's Federation insisted that in every co-operative and brigade there should be a female director or deputy (Andors 1975: p. 35). The media heralded the formation of women's production teams and the establishment of projects with 'March 8th' (International Women's Day) in their name. At first sight it seemed that collectivisation was geared to the abolition of the family as an economic unit and one could envisage considerable scope for improving the lot of women. In particular, the introduction of a work-points system of remuneration could be seen as promising large numbers of women an independent earning capacity. Yet work-point allocation tended to be made to families rather than to individuals and heavy manual jobs undertaken by men earned more points. Was this simply the result of attitudes lagging behind a policy which was concerned that too great an opposition to gender discrimination might impede collectivisation? Such seems to be the case when one reads media articles pandering to peasant superstitions about the deleterious effects of women's public work (Stacey 1983: p. 208). Yet Stacey (1983: pp. 203–11) offers a broader framework of explanation. What was occurring, she says, was the first step in a transition from 'new democratic patriarchy' to 'patriarchal socialism'. Though Party leaders might have been dimly aware of it, collectivisation merely extended the basic principles of patriarchy, with collectives forming around traditional (often lineage) lines and the subsistence part of farming (private plots) remaining under family control.

The Great Leap Forward and After

The Great Leap Forward, of course, extended the process of collectivisation, abolished private plots and offered much greater employment opportunities for women. As massive attempts were made to substitute labour for capital, men were employed increasingly on construction projects and in rural industry and more and more women were required to enter the agricultural labour force. To achieve this, propaganda extolled 'bumper crop maidens', 'women innovators' and heroic all-women teams. An attack was launched against male obstruction, the hostility of mothers-in-law whose status had traditionally freed them from labour, and superstitious ideas such as that women working in the fields prevented rain. Initial resistance was overcome and some 80–90 per cent of women were soon engaged in collective labour; indeed, in some areas the majority of the agricultural labour force consisted of women. To assist this rapid transition, the Party established child-care facilities (covering 50–70 per cent of children in some units) and communal canteens. That surely was not a step towards 'patriarchal socialism'. Yet the very fact that it was not, Stacey argues, provided the major source of opposition.

That opposition resulted in women's 'double burden' being only slightly dented. Management of communal canteens and child-care facilities was classified as 'women's work' and continued to attract fewer work-points. Though the average number of work-points earned by women increased from 5–6 to 7–8, they were still fewer than the male norm of ten. Fewer points, moreover, were awarded to women doing the same job as men, and in handicrafts, where women proved to be much more productive than men, there was pressure to lower point allocation to agricultural levels. Although mass meetings might achieve an amelioration of inequity, equal pay was rarely achieved. The same applied to status. Though more and more women achieved leading positions in the communes, brigades and teams, especially in suburban areas where experienced women were transferred from urban posts, the majority of top leadership positions were held by men. Similar inequalities were found in the cities. Though women played a major role in the movement to establish urban communes, they were usually employed in service stations and subsidiary industries (especially collectives which produced items traditionally made in the home).

Women, of course, suffered from the frenetic pace of production during the Great Leap Forward. Pregnant women were sometimes given inappropriate work. More than men, they endured inadequate health-care facilities and bore the brunt of the official abandonment of birth control (though this was only temporary). Furthermore, as the shortcomings of the Leap became apparent they shouldered some of the blame. They were accused of running public canteens that were often very inefficient, dull and unhygienic; that inefficiency, however, was magnified by those who resented the Leap's attempt to break down the old division of labour. Many women were resented simply for their success. There is no doubt, however, that during the Great Leap more women achieved a rudimentary education than before and that there were more women university students. Inroads were made into traditionally male jobs; there were more women taxi-drivers and technicians, and more women had the hope of becoming doctors and engineers (Andors 1983: pp. 47–73; Croll 1978: pp. 260–88). Yet, as in Yan'an, the stress was on the contribution of women to production rather than women's all-round liberation (though unlike the situation in Yan'an there was little fear at first of causing disruption). Questions to do with marriage were rarely raised, the Marriage Law being probably considered as too individualistic. Perhaps to be consistent, Mao who stressed at the time the importance of 'walking on two legs' (combining the traditional and the modern and much else) should have extended his advocacy to include integration of men's and women's particular tasks rather than seeking to make women more like men (Johnson 1983: pp. 161–8).

As we saw earlier, one of the first measures taken to remedy problems in the Leap was to restore family plots and to decentralise the unit of account in the communes. Moving that unit of account nearer to the family probably deprived women of some of the clout they might have enjoyed in demanding equal pay at commune or brigade levels.[2] Later moves to contract production to households reinforced the norms of the new patriarchy. At the same time, there was a reduction in collective services (including the hated canteens), closing of wasteful industries and retrenchment of workers, with women the first to go. As the issue of women's emancipation receded from the media, the number of women in agriculture declined to between 50 and 60 per cent, with work-point earnings diminishing even faster. Indeed, in the early 1960s many rural women only earned about half as many points as men and were often classified as 'half labour units'.

As Stacey (1983) sees it, the Great Leap had tested the limits of 'patriarchal socialism' and attempts were made in the early 1960s to consolidate it. The land revolution had eliminated élite patriarchy and the socialist revolution had eliminated partible inheritance. What was left after the chaos of the Great Leap subsided were atomised male dominated rural units which women had to leave on marriage. The Party governed with the camaraderie it had learned from the army and transmitted to the militia. Party members tended to marry other Party members or at least people with impeccable puritan standards and presided over a patriarchy which had socialised some functions hitherto performed by the family but which were kept under male control. That local Party leadership, the defenders of 'public patriarchy', depended on the support of poor peasants and the young, who had become active in the Great Leap often at the expense of older women (Stacey 1983: pp. 211–47; Croll 1981: pp. 80–107).

If Stacey is correct, the 'socialist patriarchy' consolidated after the Great Leap resisted both greater demands for gender equality and

---

[2] But there was a case noted later where the earnings of specialist women's teams (in tea-picking) were undervalued by brigade accounting (see Diamond 1975: p. 30).

the restoration of traditional family life. The Socialist Education Movement, which commenced in 1962, was designed to combat tradition. In that campaign the Communist Youth League played a role, along with the Women's Federation. There were widespread complaints about the revival of 'feudal practices', together, as we have noted, with campaigns to emulate the experiences of the Daqing oil-field and the Dazhai Production Brigade. Both continued Great Leap themes. The former sought to employ the dependents of workers in the oil-field in subsidiary factories and in agriculture. The latter advocated the participation of women in hazardous farming conditions; though older women did participate, there was exceptional praise for the younger ones of the 'Iron Girls Brigade'. Collective determination of education was also emphasised as a counterweight to the idea that it was not worthwhile educating a girl who would be married off to another family (though school-fees militated against this). The emphasis, moreover, on part-work part-study schemes greatly improved the prospects of women but again in a stratified labour market. As we have seen, much was also made of the technical transformation of agriculture, and women technicians (of which there were very few) were held up as models. At the same time the development of sideline production was promoted both for simple economic reasons and because it could provide the cash to purchase items which were formerly produced in the home. In addition there was a new emphasis on birth control and late marriages but again with a view to economic goals rather than women's freedom of choice (Croll 1981: pp. 60–79). That emphasis bore fruit in urban areas where there was a housing shortage and where unit cadres were required to give permission for marriage but not in rural areas where housing was more plentiful and where the cadres required to give permission could be one's kin.

By the mid-1960s there were some teams in which some 30 to 40 per cent of the labour force were women, yet there were not that many women who were qualified to become technicians and birth control measures were woefully inadequate. Such considerations led to a spate of articles arguing, in orthodox Marxist vein, that women's lack of freedom was determined technologically by the backwardness of the 'system'. Other articles, however, stressed the importance of residual 'feudal consciousness' and the great gains which would be achieved by overcoming it, reflecting the wider ideological cleavage of the time.

In the cities women's situation was better. The preference for virilocal marriages and for sons declined and urban women were much more likely to inherit paternal property than their rural counterparts. Whilst the continued practice of passing on the jobs of retired workers to members of the family favoured sons, employment opportunities for women improved. After the initial retrenchments of the early 1960s, street industries were revived and female employment in the regular industrial sector grew rapidly. Factories provided services specially for women though the problem of the 'double burden' was too difficult to address. Gradually also women made significant inroads into heavy industry (especially in plants set up during or after the Great Leap Forward) though the bulk of them remained in light industry and service trades. Women were increasingly accepted in the professions in which men still dominated and more women were elected to the National People's Congress in 1964 (18 per cent of deputies) than to the previous congress (12 per cent). There was also much debate about why women ought to participate in production. Should they do so to serve the revolution or gain material reward? At that time large numbers of female temporary workers were taken on. 'Correct motivation' and the 'iniquities' of temporary employment were seen as two burning issues in the Cultural Revolution but at that time there seemed to be little concern with women (Andors 1983: pp. 74–100).

The Cultural Revolution and After

Women's emancipation was not one of the major issues of the Cultural Revolution and the legacy of that revolution was ambiguous. Early on the Women's Federation was attacked, along with all united front bodies, as 'revisionist'. That federation had rarely been at the forefront of social change but it did provide a forum for advocating women's issues as opposed to reducing everything to class. Now, once again, it was assumed that gender inequality would automatically be the outcome of successful class struggle. Indeed, to raise questions of particular gender inequalities might be seen as 'selfish' and 'bourgeois'. Thus separate women's organisations and women's solidarity groups were suspended (Croll 1985: pp. 69–74). Dong Bian, the editor of *Zhongguo funu* (Women in China), was accused of having a 'bourgeois' disregard of class and the magazine ceased publication (Croll 1978: pp. 307–10). Despite the fact that the revolution started off by attacking the 'four olds', it was criticised later for seeking only 'bourgeois' targets and thus reinforcing 'feudal' practices particularly by its populist puritanism. Many of those 'bourgeois' targets (such as the novelist Ba Jin) were, of course, activists of the May Fourth generation who had campaigned for an end to the 'feudal' patriarchal system (Johnson 1983: pp. 178–93).

Such an attitude was deleterious to women but it is fair to say that the concern for inequalities in the Cultural Revolution could have positive implications. The mobility of youth broke stifling parental ties. The massive participatory thrust saw women activists demanding a say in decision-making in industry, educational institutions and local government. Each of these could empower women or cause very unfortunate consequences. We have already considered the contradictory outcomes of participation in residents' committees. Now such participation could be used to settle personal scores and serve the interests of those who wished to bring to an end the rustication programme which had split families up. Indeed, residents' committees might be attacked once they attempted to send back to the countryside youth who had taken advantage of the confusion to come home. Strife also might be caused by the assignment of invidious labels to certain families. Street-level participation had mixed results.

The cause of women might also be advanced by criticism of the contract labour system. Yet it was clear that the economy could not accommodate its immediate abolition, and bodies which formed to denounce it were soon considered excessively 'anarchistic' and banned. Such action did not enhance popular faith in the value of participation. Similarly the attack on piece-rates could be very divisive. Many women workers saw these as resulting in sweated labour similar to that of former times but others felt they had benefited from them. Few women, however, one might suppose, had any qualms about the repudiation of excessive factory regulations which encouraged general passivity (particularly that of women) or the integration of urban and suburban economic activities promoted at that time. Nor, one would imagine, was there much opposition amongst ordinary peasants to the provision of mobile health teams and the rapid employment of 'barefoot doctors', half of whom were women. Yet the gradual spread of radical ideas to the rural areas (if not revolutionary activity itself) engendered the same sorts of opposition encountered in previous movements. The numerous groups set up to study Mao Zedong Thought were seen as too time-consuming and, more alarmingly, as wasteful in the sense that 'women could not study' (Andors 1983: pp. 101–23).

Bitter memories of violence, and the fact that the revolution devalued things that for many women relieved the sheer monotony of rural life (Wolf 1985: p. 80) have impeded a sober assessment of the immediate effects of the Cultural Revolution on gender relations and relations between parents and children. People remember with bitterness children informing on parents and denouncing them yet people do not remember the many red guards who forsook power and excitement because of kin obligations. Suffice it to repeat that the youthful activists did not enjoy power for long; few women leaders emerged during the revolution's most active days and the revolutionary committees which developed out of it were still dominated by men. It was only as the revolution began to die down that gender relations were explicitly addressed. Of note here was the movement to criticise Lin Biao and Confucius, discussed earlier, which went beyond narrow questions of 'revisionism' to look at the ideological system which generated gender oppression (Croll 1978: pp. 323–31). At that time, much was made of Mao's slogan that 'women hold up half the sky' and Jiang Qing publicised a model village (Xiaojinzhuang, near Tianjin) to show how gender equality might be achieved. Going beyond mere criticism of traditional practices such as betrothal gifts, the media praised activism outside the family and stressed that denial to women of access to skills was a root cause of their subordination. Revolutionary committees set up women's committees to ensure the acquisition of those skills and flexible schedules were introduced in educational institutions to encourage the attendance of women. New importance was attached to training women technicians in industry and in the drive to mechanise agriculture. To free women for education, moreover, attention was given once again to male participation in household chores. To enhance their confidence, women's histories began to be written and various regions demanded the recruitment of women Party members in rural brigades and teams. At the same time a campaign was launched to promote marriage at an age even later than that stipulated in the early 1960s. In the countryside the recommended minimum age tended to be 25 for women and 28 for men and in the rural areas 23 for women and 25 for men, though the recommendations varied across the country. Couples were also urged to allow more space between having children; in rural areas it was recommended that couples should wait three years before having a second child and in urban areas at least four. Finally, uxorilocal marriage was promoted. As Johnson points out, this was particularly significant in that it struck at the heart of the traditional patriarchal system founded on the exchange of women by lineages (or villages) where women were seen as temporary members of the family of their birth (Johnson 1983: pp. 197–200).

The results of the campaigns of the early 1970s were again mixed. This time the campaign for late marriages had some impact on women in the rural sector (Wolf 1985: pp. 146–51; Croll 1981: pp. 68–70). A drive to increase the proportion of women in the Party, however, resulted in women comprising only 27 per cent of those admitted from 1966 to 1973. Women constituted only some ten per cent of the Party Central Committee (with 17 per cent of alternates) and 20 per cent of the Standing Committee of the National People's Congress (1978). A major source of upward mobility, the People's Liberation Army, was still over 97 per cent male by the end of the decade. Nevertheless, though women were grossly under-represented in leadership positions, the situation in China compared well with capitalist countries and was about the same as other socialist states (Whyte and Parish 1984: p. 211). By the late 1970s, there were more women factory managers, more women employed in heavy industry and gradually the gender division of labour in the textile industry (men as technicians, women as workers) began to change. In street industries there was increased interchange between basic level units and regular state enterprises which encouraged the upward mobility of women. Yet, observing the situation in 1980, Wolf (1985: pp. 63–4) noted that street industries were not effective stepping-stones to regular employment. Indeed, progress was painfully slow. Throughout the period there were constant complaints about lower pay for the same job and discriminatory allocation of work-points for women (Thorborg 1978: pp. 550–4). There were complaints also about the unwillingness of rusticated males to marry local women, an act which would jeopardise their chances of returning home and risk the curtailment of parents' remittances, considered necessary because they were not well looked after. Those who did marry received extravagant praise (Croll 1981: pp. 103–5). But administrative decentralisation made implementation uneven. In parts of Hebei the campaign of 1974 was apparently quite successful whilst in Guangdong it appeared superficial. Scholars, of course, are divided as to whether any such movement can achieve very much. Most sociologists consider that structural factors are crucial in effecting change. Such an approach returns us to the economic determinism criticised by writers such as Johnson. It is fair to say, however, that such movements may provide legitimacy for existing protest and support for the already aggrieved. The point, in Johnson's (1983: pp. 204–7) opinion, was that the movement involved insufficient mobilisation and was accorded insufficient commitment by the leadership.

By the end of the decade, more detailed research on gender inequality became possible and more official statistics became available. At that time, Wolf's (1985: p. 184) sample shows, the number of stem families was increasing after a sharp decline in urban areas in the 1950s and 1960s, reaching 54 per cent of those married in urban areas in the 1970s and 74 per cent of those married in rural areas. Simple conjugal families in urban areas had declined from 46 per cent of those married in urban areas in the 1960s to 33 per cent of those married in the 1970s whereas in rural areas they remained very few. The above would suggest that there was no clear trend towards what are commonly called 'nuclear families', though some scholars have referred to samples indicating the contrary (Lau Chong-chor 1993: pp. 20.4–7).

As for education, official statistics (1981) revealed that females constituted 44 per cent of students in primary schools, 39 per cent of those at regular secondary schools, 33 per cent of those at specialised secondary schools and 24 per cent of those in tertiary education (Wolf 1985: p. 128). These were much better than those of previous decades but still inadequate. The figures, however, mask serious problems in rural areas. There people commonly believed that women were less intelligent than men and that their intelligence declined sharply after puberty (which rationalised a high female drop-out rate as chores mounted). There was a reluctance to impart skills to women and the women who did obtain education were rarely considered suitable marriage partners by less-well-educated men. Some 31 per cent of rural women under 40 were illiterate compared with 4 per cent of urban women of the same age. In marked contrast to urban areas, there were few nursery schools (Wolf 1985: pp. 121–39).

In urban employment, Wolf's (1985) sample of 1980 (officially selected and certainly not typical) showed urban women's earnings to be some 70 per cent that of men. Whyte and Parish's (1984: pp. 200–10) sample shows 77 per cent, which compares well with developed countries (median 60 per cent), East European socialist states (median 66 per cent) and one third-world country, Egypt (61 per cent in 1970). There was a positive correlation between educational levels and women's wages but not men's (where seniority was more important in promotion than educational level). Women and men often started out with fairly equal wages for the same job, but women were slotted into jobs where seniority was less important, though segregation by gender was more moderate than most other countries. But as in most other countries, women remained at each promotion level longer than men. Women, moreover, retired earlier than men, often surrendering their jobs to their children, receiving lower pensions and losing the opportunity to undertake leading roles at the very age when men achieved such positions (Croll 1983: p. 13); unlike men, they could rarely stay at their place of work in an advisory capacity. The major cause for slowness in promotion was surely that men's freedom from domestic chores, similar in relative though not absolute terms to other countries (Whyte and Parish 1984: pp. 216–21), allowed them to earn extra merit by engaging in technical innovation and being more willing to accept overtime. Women's slowness to achieve promotion, however, was rationalised in physiological and psychological terms and such explanations were often accepted by women themselves. Wolf (1985: pp. 64–78) noted that women were less committed to their job, felt they made poorer leaders and regarded men as incompetent home managers and rearers of children.

In the rural areas by the end of the 1970s, the growth of light industry had resulted in a widespread feminisation of agricultural labour. In places where rural industrialisation was most marked, such as parts of Jiangsu, only 11 per cent of men remained in the less-rewarding agriculture. Frequently men did the ploughing but left other farming tasks to women. The rationale behind this was once again that women were not suited to heavy work, though Wolf observes that it is strange that women pulled heavy carts whilst men engaged in the supposedly 'heavier' work of driving tractors. Furthermore, some two-thirds of women worked part-time and were regularly laid off in slack seasons (Thorborg 1978: p. 596). Once again they would earn an average of 6–7 work-points per day compared with men's 10 and might even earn fewer points for attending the same meetings. Whilst women might in theory earn more than men in sideline operations, their earnings tended to disappear into collective coffers and to generate dissatisfaction with collective endeavour. Though there were still protests about unequal work-point allocation, many cadres felt that to equalise it would devalue work-points and decrease male motivation (Thorborg 1978: p. 551). Men also controlled the distribution of cash. Commune industries paid wages in cash and the cash distributed annually tended to be at the disposal of male family heads. Women often had control only over daily rations and annual surplus grain distribution and did not have direct access to cash.

The rural picture painted by Wolf (1985: pp. 56–111) and others of the final period of collective agriculture, therefore, shows that many of the hopes of the Great Leap Forward had been dashed Old superstitions about women polluting the land remained (though were not admitted to). The term *neiren* (inside person) for wife was used approvingly. There was still concern about widows remarrying and courtship was bedevilled by continued gender separation. Many women, moreover, desired to withdraw from collective labour as soon as they had a replacement. In some cases there were new restrictions on women. Marriage outside the village (brigade), for example, had to be negotiated through brigade and commune cadres. That kind of marriage continued to be the norm, though it was probably the case that women who remained in the village stood a much better chance of assuming leading roles (Diamond 1975: p. 28) and many parents sought increasingly to marry their daughters to someone nearby so that the woman could help both her natural parents and her in-laws.

Despite the stipulations of the Marriage Law, interference in marriage still occurred and matchmaking was referred to a 'introductions'. Though completely traditional forms of marriage were declining, most marriages were somewhat less than complete free choice (Croll 1981: pp. 24–40). Betrothal gifts and bride-price were frequently still paid, dowries given as a sign of status (with customary items in different areas) and extravagant wedding feasts held (Croll 1981: pp. 121–6). Despite the urging of Cultural Revolution years, weddings frequently cost the equivalent of two years' income and resulted in considerable debt. It was also still the case in rural areas that many couples were unknown to each other before they became engaged (though rarely before marriage) and divorces were difficult to obtain (Wolf 1985: pp. 151–81). Family divisions still caused traumas and might be instigated at the whim of the male head. Yet change was occurring. Perhaps most significant was the fact that increasingly marriage no longer required women to break ties with their natal families (Honig and Hershatter 1988: p. 167). Family divisions might occur because women found the family too large to manage. A man who neglected his parents might lose control of his parents' rations which the team would turn over directly to them. Mothers-in-law, once castigated as family tyrants, increasingly found themselves doing most of the household chores whilst the younger womenfolk worked in the fields. Some must have regretted the passing of the old society which promised a degree of leisure and power in old age. Now many became simply overworked which caused the Party to insist repeatedly that one should 'be kind to one's mother-in-law' (Wolf 1985: pp. 221–37; Honig and Hershatter 1988: pp. 168–73).

Changes in the towns were much more evident. There the role of the father had been restricted. He was no longer the sole link between the family and the outside world and was required less than before to provide opportunities for his sons (though spectacular cases of 'back-door' treatment were remarked on). Though he might still be very reluctant to engage in household tasks, he tended to spend more time with his children. Increasingly women managed the family budget (Whyte and Parish 1984: p. 217). While daughters might still hand over their wages to their families (now increasingly their mothers) before marriage, the wages of a young woman after marriage was often split after negotiation between her own uterine family and the larger economic family unit in which she lived. She might even make remittances to her mother as well as (or instead of) her mother-in-law (Wolf 1985: pp. 193–4). Indeed, as there was a greater promise of security in old age, urban mothers-in-law were less likely to regard their daughters jealously. On the other hand, young women, who could now maintain continued close relations with their own mothers, were less likely to put up with being humiliated by mothers-in-law and quarrels between the two became more common (Wolf 1985: pp. 212–13). Job mobility also obliged some women to leave their children with their grandparents. There was, therefore, much more freedom for women in the cities, though, some feminists argue, less than appeared at first sight. Whereas in the countryside family heads were still all-important, in the cities cadres played a major role in controlling marriage in what Stacey calls 'public patriarchy'.

The 1980s

In 1978 the formal reconstruction of the Women's Federation at a national level saw the return to power of a number of veteran women leaders such as Kang Keqing, Deng Yingchao and Song Qingling (widow of Sun Zhongshan) who tended to look back on the 1950s as expressing the correct policy towards women (Andors 1983: pp. 150–4). At that time the gender issue was seen as secondary, and so it was after 1978. In addition, hostility towards the Cultural Revolution obscured the serious attempt to combat women's oppression in 1973–4. The plight of women, like much else, was blamed on the 'ten years of turmoil' and Jiang Qing was subject to extremely sexist attacks. In this climate, the 'iron maidens' of earlier years were ridiculed as simply an example of the Cultural Revolution's ill-conceived plan to change human nature. In their place, women role-models were portrayed as tireless workers for economic reform, famous personages (in the acting profession, for example), daring heroines and loyal wives (Honig and Hershatter 1988: pp. 23–31).

Once again media comments seemed to accept the auxiliary role of women and women's 'double burden', reinforced by what Chodorow calls the 'reproduction of mothering' across the whole of society (Robinson 1985). Though the publications of the Women's Federation and the advice columns in the many women's magazines which appeared stressed that the idea of women's inferiority was a sign of 'feudal thought' and urged women to take part in production, the implicit message was that the proper employment for women was still seen in public extensions of old household duties, the caring professions, teaching and the service trades. This was justified by old arguments about women's weakness, biological aptitude and inferior rational intellect, though this time dressed up in pseudo-scientific language, with controversial 'scientific' evidence published simply as fact (Honig and Hershatter 1988: pp. 13–23). Whilst it is not altogether surprising that advice columns should perform in that way, the role of the Women's Federation bears further analysis. In promoting extensions of women's domestic role, was the Federation merely echoing the Party line as it had done in the past or was it just concerned with seeking any employment for women (Jacka 1990: pp. 16–8)? As Marilyn Young (1989: pp. 258–60) points out, China after the 'ten years of turmoil' was not unlike the post-war West where women were under pressure to withdraw from an active life and to fulfil the role of bearers of harmony. In such a situation the Women's Federation was eager to preserve what gains it could.

One may push the analogy further. In Roxann Prazniak's (1989: p. 275) words, the 'ten years' was often remembered as 'bitter' yet 'self-strengthening'. Hardly any women responded positively to Western scholars' suggestion that the Cultural Revolution could have had any merits, yet clearly its legacy in urban areas acted against any return to the old values of women's submissiveness. Instead the Women's Federation fostered the development of household management skills (Honig and Hershatter 1988: pp. 173–81). At the same time, there was much promotion in urban areas of fashion and romance, punctuated by denunciation of the commercialisation of sexuality and such manifestations of 'spiritual pollution' as outlandish clothing which occasioned lewd behaviour, pornography (extremely broadly defined) which was said to lead to psychological disorders and crime, and masturbation which was said to cause damage to the nervous system (Honig and Hershatter 1988: pp. 41–80). The result was occasional good sense (the critique of advertising) but usually a mixture of self-righteous (and often misleading) sex education and a 'feminine mystique', last described with reference to China by Croll in her discussion of the *Guomindang*.

By the 1980s the government considered the economy too backward to provide the social services of more radical days. Whereas more direct state investment in child-care facilities took place in the cities and a range of services were provided (usually for only the better-off) by retired people and youth no longer rusticated, rural services were grossly inadequate. Thus the revised Marriage Law of 1980 required children to care for their parents in their old age and the inheritance law of 1985 rewarded those who did, thus favouring males (Davin 1988: pp. 169–97). Indeed, parents had a right to demand care and up to five years' imprisonment might be imposed for abandoning elderly parents. Such a provision contradicted somewhat the provisions of the 'five guarantees' which applied to rural collectives. Every member of a collective was guaranteed in their old age adequate food, clothing, housing and medical expenses. If such were to be provided at collective expense, one wonders about the need for the above provision of the Marriage Law. Perhaps the answer lies in Wolf's (1985: pp. 196–9) finding that, whilst the childless had no course but to rely on the five guarantees, many rural people would feel a sense of shame if they had to receive such benefits. In any case there was some doubt about whether the guarantees could be honoured once the collectives began to fall to pieces and rural welfare funds decreased. More generally a rapidly aging population severely stretched the capacity of authorities to meet the cost of the five guarantees. There was little problem in the cities where informants felt that the state would take care of the aged or, failing that, their daughters would. But in the countryside, where pension plans were still rare and experimental, parents still relied more on their sons than on the state or their daughters. Having a son was still not only the most important source of status a woman could have but the surest guarantee for old age. However good the relationship between mother and daughter might be, being forced to live with a daughter in old age often involved considerable loss of face.

The incentive to have sons increased with the adoption of policies aimed at dramatically reducing population growth (Wolf 1985: pp. 238–59). The 1980 Marriage Law raised the minimum legal age of marriage from 18 for women and 20 for men (according to the 1950 Law) to 20 for women and 22 for men, (much less than the recommended age) but many more direct policies were deemed necessary. According to the 'one child family' policy adopted in 1979, planned quotas were adopted from national right down to unit level, though with considerable variation. In factories the progress of the movement was recorded with as much zeal and detail as the fulfilment of production targets, with open displays of information about women's menstrual cycles and the like. All the traditional mobilisation techniques were brought into play – shame, guilt, material incentives and sharp penalties. Employees in state enterprises were required to sign a pledge to have only one child, which, so long as it was adhered to, might result in a bonus of up to 8 per cent of average monthly salary until the child reached the age of 14 or later, though it was not clear whether the man's or woman's wage was to be augmented.[3] They were also granted priority in housing, extra maternity leave, free education and medical services for the child, preference in job placement for the child when she or he left school and increments to retirement pensions. Many of the incentives, however, could not be extended to small collective enterprises which were developing faster than state enterprises; job placement, for example, had no meaning in that context. Priority, moreover, was difficult to define in a situation where the overwhelming majority of couples were to be its beneficiaries. Rural incentives varied considerably in different areas. Collectives, so long as they existed, might award up to 20 or 30 extra work-points per month, pay a flat cash amount or make gifts of household appliances. In both urban and rural areas, of course, exceptions had to be made if, for example, the first-born had an accident, if one partner brought an existing child into the relationship or had adopted a child because of temporary infertility.

The penalties for breaking the pledge were severe. Cash subsidies had to be returned, medical services had to be paid for, the child's grain had to be bought on the higher-priced open market and there might be a wage reduction of up to 10 per cent until the child reached the age of 14. More seriously there might be forced sterilisations or abortions, sometimes as late as the fifth month. Press articles went to great pains to criticise some of these excesses but one must remember that the issue of coercion is very difficult to determine in any mass mobilisation campaign. 'Agreement' to abortion under considerable pressure was quite common especially among those who had a third child, for which the state formally was prepared to allow no exceptions.

---

[3] Dalsimer and Nisonhoff had great difficulty soliciting an answer to this question. Respondents finally agreed that the 'family' should be rewarded. They surmise that this answer was given because if the man received the increment the woman's subordinate position would be underlined, and if the woman received it, it would be lower (Dalsimer and Nisonhoff 1984: p. 19).

The consequences of the campaign were alarming both from humanistic and from feminist perspectives. It caused the disappearance of the system whereby impoverished families with many dependents, now considered profligate, could borrow grain from collectives to be repaid when those children were old enough to earn; such 'deviant' families were often headed by women (Davin 1988: p. 144). It led to alienation of peasants who resented the ridicule poured on their ancestral rites. It gave rise to discussions of eugenics and preventing the birth of retarded children. It caused more women to be beaten for bearing female children and to a revival of female infanticide. Infanticide was, of course, officially condemned and punished, though cases are on record of it being carried out at the behest of the authorities (Bianco and Hua 1988; p. 158; Chang 1988: p. 260). More generally, it was difficult to detect, as is clear from examination of birth statistics. In some areas the ratio of male to female live births increased significantly, prompting one to question where the missing females were. According to one estimate, a quarter of a million girl babies might have been killed in 1981 (Honig and Hershatter 1988: pp. 274–6). It was usually women who received punishment when detected. Indeed, women bore the brunt of the considerable risk-taking during the campaign as statistics were falsified and opposition to the programme (especially in Guangdong) mounted. One should consider also that in rural areas, responsibility for contraception was considered to be largely that of women. Condoms were disliked and vasectomies rare (due to the old belief that they weaken men).

The 'one child family' policy enjoyed moderate success in limiting births in the cities where state control was much tighter and where excessive births were not much of a problem anyway. There, where technology might be married to patriarchy, amniocentesis plus abortion is surely better than traditional sex-prediction charts plus infanticide, though to be fair the preference for sons in the cities has declined significantly. The relative success of the campaign in the cities can be expected to reduce municipal welfare costs, though not significantly the amount of time mothers spend on child care. Currently mothers spend about half an hour a day extra for a second child; but as the one child is seen as increasingly precious, or indeed spoilt, the result might be more housework rather than less (Robinson 1985: pp. 54–5).

In the countryside, however, the success of the campaign is problematic. According to a 1988 survey, '93 per cent of rural women who had one child gave birth to a second, 47 per cent of those with two children gave birth to a third; and 28 per cent of those with three children had a fourth'. Thus 'slightly over half of the total births in 1990 were not first-born children' (Yeh 1992: p. 508). National figures show that the birth rate rose from under 18 per thousand in 1979 to almost 21 in 1981, fell markedly until the mid-1980s, then rose reaching almost 21 again by 1990. The rate of natural increase rose from under 12 per thousand in 1979 to 14.6 in 1981, fell until the mid-1980s and then rose again to reach almost 14.7 in 1990. According to the 1990 census ten provincial-level units had a rate of natural increase of over 17 per thousand and only five had a rate below 10. These figures do not necessarily mean failure since one has to take into account the demographic bulge of the early 1960s, the women of which are now producing children. It was anticipated that the peak year would be 1992 and indeed 1993 figures indicate a significant decline. A sober analysis, however, must conclude that the initial hopes vested in the movement were optimistic and the original population target of 1.2 billion by the year 2000 will be exceeded (Yan Hao 1988). As noted, the population in 1991 was 1.158 billion and will probably reach 1.3 billion by the year 2000.

Those who claim 'success' for the campaign argue that it slowed down a rise in the birth-rate which was bound to occur. Yet few would deny that other government policies undermined its effectiveness at least in the short run. One of these is the de-collectivisation of agriculture. Those who stress the 'demographic transition curve' might argue that in the long run the improvement in standards of living brought about by that de-collectivisation will create the conditions for a lower birth rate. Initially, however, the result was the opposite.

Contracting farming to individual households has greatly strengthened the family as an economic unit. Male family heads now calculate the economic benefit of having more children as against the costs of violating the 'one-child family' policy. Local authorities have countered this by pairing a land contract with a contract to reduce births, often with some degree of success (Davin 1985: pp. 63–4); though, in general, birth contracts are difficult to enforce. Fearing disruption and eager to maintain a buoyant rural economy, local birth control campaigns have oscillated in their mix of coercive, remunerative and normative measures, with penalties often becoming less and less strict and incentives more and more difficult to provide (Greenhalgh 1990; Bianco and Hua 1988: pp. 159–64). Nevertheless, a combination of the birth control campaign and household contracting has resulted in a renewed incentive to have sons, scarcely offset by the consideration that the domestic labour of girls becomes valuable at a younger age than that of males. Significantly one of the earlier relaxations of the one-child policy in local areas consisted in permitting a second child if the first were female. Often peasants simply violate the law. Since family heads require the labour of children (and especially sons) as soon as and as cheaply as possible, they often disregard the law concerning marriage age and have reintroduced disguised child engagement, *de facto* child daughters-in-law and the 'exchange of relatives' (marrying the daughter and son of one family to the son and daughter of another). According to one calculation, such practices might make the reproduction of a rural generation some ten years shorter than one in urban areas.

The initial allocation of land, moreover, when calculated according to labour force units, has discriminated against households with a larger proportion of women (half units) (Judd 1992: pp. 340, 346). Economic calculations have also resulted in marriages once again concluded in settlement of debt, and in other cases with the highest bidder (Honig and Hershatter 1988: pp. 94–97). More generally, the value of betrothal gifts has risen which leads families to marry daughters earlier than sons in order to accumulate funds for the subsequent acquisition of a daughter-in-law (Croll 1985: p. 124). Furthermore, the enhanced role of the male family head has deprived women of opportunities to seek remission of labour from community leaders. Women have also been considerably disadvantaged by the collapse of many rural services and schools following the demise of the collectives (despite new calls for the socialisation of domestic labour), and women, more than men, have experienced the effect of medical expenses being to a much greater extent met out of the family budget. The strengthening of the family farm, moreover, has enhanced the concern for family prestige, resulting in more lavish exchange of wedding gifts and expensive wedding ceremonies, which might take place years after formal registration precisely because it could require the equivalent of several years' income. This has occurred despite much propaganda and the promotion of collective weddings which may involve up to 700 couples (Honig and Hershatter: 1988: pp. 137–66).

Women, it seems, have suffered from the new discovery of a huge rural labour surplus. As men move into construction work, contract work for urban factories and into commerce, the low-paid agricultural labour force, engaged in producing staples, consists more and more of married women. Rural industry, however, which consists of a rough gender balance in employment and pays much better, absorbs many more single women. But leadership positions in such industries usually go to men, and skilled workers, often recruited from outside the village, are invariably male. Indeed, women in responsible positions are usually the relatives of men in such positions. It may be argued also that a third alternative for female employment – work in 'sideline' activities, now designated as mainstream – remains under the direct control of male family heads. But here one is not so sure. The development of what were once sideline activities has resulted in the formation of 'specialised households' which do offer women greater independence. Encouraging women to engage in specialised production for the market, therefore, has been a preferred strategy of the Women's Federation and has been endorsed by at least one Western observer (Judd 1990). But one wonders whether the consequent gain in autonomy is sufficient to offset Delia Davin's (1988) conclusion that, in general, family farming has made women live a more subordinate and more isolated life.

The relationship between autonomy and isolation is notoriously unclear and in this specific case requires much more research. So also does the contribution of rural changes to violence against women. Infanticide and beating wives for producing daughters and the violent consequences of forced marriages are obvious examples. Perhaps less obvious are the consequences of a shortage of women to marry. In 1982 men outnumbered women by a ratio of 106:100.[4] More modest reports in 1991 speak of there being 20 million more men than women – a figure which would probably reach 50 million

---

[4] Some take this to be the 'natural' ratio. A more meaningful figure based on birth ratios of the 1960s is said to be 104:100. Some demographers place the late 1980s birth ratio at 109 or 111:100 due to the loss of baby girls. One may speculate on the future consequences (Chang 1988: p. 261).

by the year 2000. This imbalance has contributed to the revival of practices such as selling girl children and the abduction of Southern girls to provide future wives in the North (Honig and Hershatter 1988: pp. 273–98). The problem will worsen if infanticide continues. One understands, though with much disgust at its callous sexism, the argument against infanticide on the grounds that it might produce a situation where, in future, men would not be able to find wives (Wolf 1985: p. 271). There is also the possibility that the imbalance could result in an increase in cases of rape.

Most scholars have concluded that economic reform in rural areas has served the cause of patriarchy well. That is not to deny, however, that there are many women who feel better off than ever before. Clearly, women who sell produce on the open markets have more access to cash for their personal use and the simple acquisition of money earned in local enterprises instead of discriminatory work-points has produced much satisfaction, even though abolishing work-points took away from many individuals public recognition of the value of outside work (Davin 1988: pp. 141–2). Many of the new specialised households, moreover, as we have noted, are headed by women. In Shandong in 1987, it is said these constituted some 42 per cent of specialised households, accounting for over 40 per cent of the value produced by such households (Judd 1990: p. 35). There are also well-off areas in Guangdong with large numbers of Overseas Chinese relatives and a shortage of resident men (who have gone off to the towns) where the vast majority of women feel a new sense of power and over half of family heads are women. They know they live in a patriarchal society where sons are valued more, marriages are arranged at a considerable price and men are favoured in employment but, often earning more than their male kin, they do not care (Woon 1991). The question arises: what will happen if the feminisation of agriculture continues, men depart for the towns and are simply not available to exercise practical day-to-day dominance? Research in other third world countries indicates that matriculture does not advantage women in general and women farmers with husbands in the towns still depend upon them. Those Guangdong areas, however, are atypical in being rich and favoured by Overseas Chinese connections (and by government policy towards Overseas Chinese). One can see the development of new types of gender relations in various parts of South China which will still be patriarchal but in a new sense. This must be remembered as we conduct research into what must surely be seen as the development of new forms of production in the vibrant South.

The Guangdong example cited above and the growth of specialised households, headed by women in other areas, only slightly dents the case that patriarchy has been well served by recent reforms in rural areas. The case also holds for the towns, though less so. The first major reform of the early 1980s was to switch the focus in economic policy to light industry dominated by collectives which, as we have seen, employ more women than men and which offer few services. Commenting on the two greatest achievements for women in the first five years of the reforms (1978–83), Kang Keqing highlighted the growth of 3.3 per cent in female employment but failed to note that it had occurred largely in that deprived sector (the other achievement was success in athletics) (Wolf 1985: p. 261). Economic reform, moreover, has also boosted the small-scale private sector and the putting-out system which usually offer no services at all. In the state sector, the adoption of a 'floating wage' to replace fixed wages in textiles has been calculated according to women's original wages which were always lower than men's (Dalsimer and Nisonhoff 1984: pp. 23–8).

Furthermore, the stress on enterprise profitability has resulted in management being reluctant to take on women because of the extra cost of services, their relative inflexibility in undertaking overtime and fears about their absences to take care of children. That men are considered a better investment is reflected in the fact that women usually have lower priority in housing allocation, that two-thirds of young people 'waiting for employment' in the early 1980s were female, that labour bureaux reported that government departments were unwilling to offer jobs to women tertiary graduates (which were only 25 per cent of the total) and that women sitting entrance exams for employment in enterprises had to achieve higher marks than men. Local ordinances, moreover, concerned with 'women's health', discontinued the employment of women in tasks defined as 'heavy' and enterprises granted 'prolonged maternity leave' (at lower wages and minus the chance to earn bonuses).

All this was a response to a developing urban employment crisis in the mid-1980s brought on by an emphasis on the productivity of labour, the effect of the baby boom of the 1960s and the end of the policy of sending youth down to the countryside. One might note in this context that, whilst increasing numbers of women were being laid off, female employment was actually growing. Some economists, under pressure to provide a solution to the crisis, advocated laying off more women against the protests of the Women's Federation. More commonly women were forced into the more acceptable less-taxing (lower-paid) and part-time work. That women were unhappy with the situation is testified to by the fact that many on short-time or laid off undertook temporary jobs such as house-cleaning. Women have been ill-served by employment policies which have resulted in gender segregation (Jacka 1990; Honig and Hershatter 1988: pp. 243–55) though a number of ameliorating measures have proposed. Suggestions have been made to make the costs of having children a charge on both husband's and wife's work unit and experimental enterprise funds to which all employees contribute have been set for the purpose (Jacka 1990: pp. 20–2). But solutions to the problem demand much more than considerations of funding.

Gender discrimination is still rife in the cities, yet there is clearly more freedom of choice in marriage partners. Revived united front policies have weakened discrimination against families with 'bad' backgrounds, though women's disdain for marriage partners with 'dirty' jobs and preference for intellectuals has probably increased now that the class rubric has formally changed. In general, economic criteria have become much more important. There is also more sexual freedom, as is evident in the advice columns of magazines, but this is combined with appalling sexual ignorance. The mystique of women's chastity remains (though often criticised) and although abortions are readily available, they still carry a stigma and the 'backyard' variety still occurs out of considerations of secrecy. A concern with 'spiritual pollution', moreover, has led to condemnation of Western-style promiscuity, semi official sanctions imposed for adultery and sometimes the requirement that marriage certificates be presented by those sharing a room in a hotel (Honig and Hershatter 1988: pp. 90–104; 181–6; 219–24).

In the cities, divorce has become much easier. This has been due in part to the 1980 Marriage Law which maintains that 'alienation of affection' should be the prime ground for divorce. If affection (*ganqing*) has been destroyed and if mediation fails, divorce should be granted. The implication here is that political and economic concerns should not override considerations of affection. In addition, the scope for manipulation and paternalism has been restricted by the demand that a divorce 'should be granted' if only one party applies and mediation fails rather than 'may be granted' as the 1950 law put it (Croll 1981: p. 83). As a consequence divorce rates in the cities have risen. They are, however, still quite low and we cannot predict any long-term trends. This is because of a rush to dissolve 'Cultural Revolution' marriages and those of former rusticated youth entered into on political grounds which no longer apply. Rapid change in the urban status hierarchy has resulted in types of divorces which may soon no longer be prevalent (Honig and Hershatter 1988: pp. 206–19).

A particular problem in the cities is referred to in sexist language as the 'problem of old maids'. This seems to be a demographic problem arising from the baby boom of the late 1940s and early 1950s. Since men usually marry women several years younger than themselves, men born in the period 1944–53 have more women born between 1946 and 1955 to choose from. Some women, therefore, cannot find marriage partners, and these include women who postponed thoughts of marriage in the radical days of the late 1960s and early 1970s and are now considered too old. The argument that the demographic situation might be reversed in the 1990s is no consolation to those people (Honig and Hershatter 1988: pp. 104–10). But perhaps demography is assisting a re-evaluation of the importance of marriage.

Despite greater sexual freedom, another major problem in the cities is still the problem of meeting a mate. Matchmaking is still deemed necessary. For many years the Communist Youth league and other organisations had acted as unofficial matchmakers. That practice was officially sanctioned in 1984 when Chen Yun and Hu Yaobang paved the way for the establishment of matrimonial agencies (run by the Youth League and the Women's Federation). Before long prizes were instituted for 'outstanding match-makers' though the success rate of those official bodies has not been high. Their activities have been supplemented by personal adver-tisements in national magazines but some consider that the process in general treats people as commodities.

We have argued that changes in both rural and urban areas have furthered patriarchy, reinforced by official ideology which stresses the role of wife and mother and the educative role of women in creating a 'new socialist spiritual civilisation'. Once again media comment stresses the value of housework, on which more time is spent than in almost any other country in the world. Surveys in several cities show that women spend from three to five hours per day on household tasks compared with two to four for men, for which the prescribed solution is more part-time work. The socialisation ideals of the Great Leap Forward are now discredited and one hears arguments that the employment of live-in maids (*baomu*) is a step towards socialisation (Honig and Hershatter 1988: pp. 255–63). Almost as crude as the old message that participation in labour would solve the problem of gender inequality, the new tidings, in the spirit of the 'four modernisations', are that problems caused by housework will be solved by technology. Mao once said to André Malraux that washing machines did not liberate women. Indeed research in other countries has shown that, whereas a domestic appliance might be liberating in that it shortens the time to do a particular household task, it might generate other tasks which can result in more time being spent on domestic labour than before. It will be some time before we have sufficient data on the effects of technology on Chinese domestic life. In the meantime, while there has been a dramatic increase in the sale of domestic appliances, which may now be purchased on credit, peasants who have recently become better off prefer to spend their money on inputs to the family farm, or on such things as bicycles, simple plumbing, and means of family entertainment (television etc) rather than on items which are believed to reduce housework, which is still almost universally defined as the task of women (Robinson 1985: pp. 42–50; Dalsimer and Nisonhoff 1984: pp. 31–3).

Conclusion

Most Chinese sources and most Western analysts agree that whereas much has been done to emancipate Chinese women in the past half century, much remains to be done. They disagree, however, on the sources of the problems. A typical Chinese list of sources would be the residues of 'feudalism', the consequences of the 'ten years of turmoil' and the impact of the West. Problems caused by the modernisation policies themselves and the central structure of power are only sometimes noted. Official publications seem to regret the fact that women only constitute 7.5 per cent of the Party Central Committee elected in 1992 (less than previously) but it will perhaps be some time before there develops in China the kind of critical analysis which has animated feminists in the West. There are, however, signs of change. Women's studies have appeared in university curricula and conferences have been held on developing such studies (Wan Shanping 1988). A critical literature which might broadly be described as feminist has also appeared (even though its authors might reject the term) (Prazniak 1989: Honig and Hershatter 1988: pp. 308–33). Yet one suspects that the Party is as sensitive now as it was in its early days about the 'bourgeois' nature of such developments.

It would be arrogant in the extreme to attempt to impose Western models on China where the reality of class is so different. But some general propositions might be made. This chapter, like most of the Western literature, has pointed to the need to examine the problematic relationship between participation in public production and emancipation. It has been sceptical of the view that socialist transition or the development of the productive forces automatically solves the problem of gender discrimination. It has demanded an examination of the relationship between patriarchy and state-led or market-led modernisation. It has affirmed the need for more attention to ideology, though not of the excessively class-reductionist kind nor the 'feminine mystique' of 'socialist spirituality'. Throughout there has been an implied criticism of the capacity of centrally led bodies, controlled by a Party with a broader set of priorities, to pursue gender equality. The Women's Federation, for instance, has frequently been found wanting. In the Cultural Revolution it was attacked for 'bourgeois individualist' concerns, and in the 1980s it has often been considered insensitive to many of the sources of gender inequality. In recent years, popular pressure has made that Federation take a stand against discrimination in employment and the driving of women back to the home, and to recognise the existence of local spontaneously generated women's organisations and private research centres (previously considered 'bourgeois') (Honig and Hershatter 1988: pp. 317–25; Croll 1983: pp. 23–4; Dalsimer and Nisonhoff 1984). The Federation, however, in promoting women's activism and women's studies, might come to co-opt such bodies and bend them to an attenuated agenda set by the Party. Such has occurred before. Yet this is not just a problem of one-Party states.

A case may be made that in liberal régimes, the concern for substantive gender justice has been co-opted by a 'femocracy' which, in striving for gender justice, is locked into a procedural logic which perpetuates substantive gender injustice. That procedural logic is enshrined in the 'rule of law', to which many Chinese reformers aspire, but, as we have argued, have not attained. That rule of law, some maintain, legitimates liberal capitalist patriarchy just as surely as Mao's new democracy legitimated 'new democratic patriarchy' and socialist transition legitimated 'patriarchal socialism'. The only safeguard lies in the development of independent organisations with their own priorities and a willingness to engage in a battle of priorities in the terrain of substantive politics.

8

Minority Nationalities

Both liberalism and Marxism, as universalist belief systems, tend to handle the question of national and sub-national identity rather badly. Early liberalism, in proclaiming the 'rights of man', often ended up merely proclaiming the 'rights of Frenchmen' or other dominant nationalities. The result was a severe 'romantic' reaction. Marxism, moreover, in proclaiming the universality of 'class struggle', incurred the wrath of those whose struggles were not based on class and the incredulity of others as the working class rallied to the national banner during the First World War. In both cases, however, there has been a communitarian correction. From its inception, liberalism has been forced to incorporate a subversive communitarian critique and Marxism was soon influenced by its Austrian variety which was developed initially to deal with the multi-national Hapsburg Empire. Nowadays many communitarians believe that in both cases the correction has been inadequate. They are wary of liberals who talk about voluntary 'integration' rather than 'assimilation' on the grounds that the conditions necessary to make a voluntary commitment themselves demand a change in identity which destroys community. The same goes for their Marxist counterparts who might, in Chinese parlance, prefer voluntary 'melding' (*ronghe*) to 'assimilation' (*tonghua*). One is never sure, however, what communitarians' own solution might be. In the meantime, the fate of indigenous peoples in one country after another has proved to be one of the greatest tragedies of the twentieth century. This chapter will examine the experience of the Chinese Communist Party which started off as well-intentioned as any recent Australian government and finished up scarcely any better.

305

Policies in Imperial and Republican China

It is very difficult to define a 'minority nationality' in any society
Universalistic empires such as the Chinese usually did not bother
The official imperial view held that the capital was the centre of a
culture which became diluted the further away one went. In tha
process one encountered various 'barbarians' who occasionally
might rise up and invade the heartland but who inevitably
succumbed to the majority Han culture and adopted the Confucian
bureaucratic ideology. Such was the eventual fate of the Liao, Jin
Yuan and Qing dynasties which resulted from such invasions
Policy, therefore, tended to be assimilationist. That assimilation
was sometimes brutal (when rebellion occurred), but often it was
not, since the dominant humanist Confucian ideology, whilst
disdaining those it considered 'inferior', was held to be an inclusive
doctrine which could usually tolerate (though never respect) local
religions and other affirmations of particularistic identity.

With such a world view, Confucian officials felt no need to
consider how one would specify an ethnic group nor to ask how
many ethnic groups existed in China. Ethnicity was a subjective
phenomenon capable of transformation by appropriate instruction
Such was a very convenient view. It prevented examination of
historical claims to ethnic independence and offered solace to Han
officials who resented alien rule. But it was obviously false. The
nineteenth century was marked by major Muslim risings and many
minor ones amongst peoples who clearly could not be assimilated
and the cataclysmic Taiping revolution capitalised on hostility to
ethnic inequalities. The final years of the Qing dynasty, moreover
were marked by considerable tension between Han officials and
their Manchu and Mongol counterparts, the objects of positive
discrimination who were never intended to be assimilated. In the
final years of the empire, institutions were set up to train Tibetan
and Mongolian officials signifying the open abandonment of
assimilation in those areas through Confucian generalist education
The revolution of 1911 saw risings by Mongolians to reverse the
tide of Han immigration and by Tibetans resentful of a recent
central government invasion. The republic of 1912, therefore, had
to accord official recognition to four non-Han ethnic groups -
Manchus, Mongols, Hui (Muslims or those claiming Muslim
ancestry) and Tibetans. Nevertheless, until just before his death

when he forged an understanding with the Soviet Union, the 'father of the republic' Sun Zhongshan denied the significance of minority ethnicity and, in the years which followed, some local warlords were more sympathetic to minority nationalities than the *Guomindang*. A sinicised Yi, Long Yun came to rule Yunnan. The Hui Ma clan ruled Qinghai and Ningxia; it promoted Islam and Hui officials while engendering hostility to its authoritarian rule. In Xinjiang a succession of warlords culminated in Sheng Shicai, a leader with Soviet support (until 1941) who promoted Uygurs and Kazaks to high posts. Despite the rise of local régimes sympathetic to greater ethnic minority power, the Jiang Jieshi régime denied the identity of different nationalities. It saw local nationalism as a factor which prevented China's effective unification.

The situation was compounded by the fact that the Japanese made much of the national question in defence of its creation, Manchukuo, in establishing autonomous regions for Mongolians and in wooing the Hui away from the central government. Japan capitalised on detestation of Han migration into Inner Mongolia and Jiang Jieshi's refusal to limit the opening up of arable regions at the expense of pasture land. In the deeply sinicised Manchukuo, Japan encouraged the use of the Manchu language (a forlorn hope) and promoted Manchu officials. In many areas, the Manchukuo authorities developed minority education and it is significant that what later became the Yanbian Korean autonomous *zhou* developed the highest level of education of any minority nationality area in China, and of the two Mongolian banners with the highest literacy rate in the 1950s, one had been under Japanese control in Manchukuo (Lee Chae-jin 1986: p. 143). Manchukuo is now seen internationally as a *bête noire* and little good is found within it; such an attitude has prevented a sober assessment of the Japanese appeal.

In 1945, upon the Japanese defeat, the country was once again plunged into civil war and *Guomindang* fears of national disintegration escalated. Of particular concern were divisions amongst the Mongols exacerbated by border clashes with the Mongolian People's Republic, significant Korean involvement on the side of the Chinese Communist Party (Lee Chae-jin 1986: pp. 51–8) and the creation of an independent (pro-Soviet) East Turkestan Republic in the predominantly Kazak region of Ili in Xinjiang (Moseley 1966b: pp. 12–23) which the government handled less than honestly. Perhaps the eventual compromise with leaders in the area prevented the loss of Xinjiang to the Soviet Union but by 1949 there is no doubt that the *Guomindang*'s demonstrated commitment to assimilation had made it many enemies among minority nationalities and had exacerbated anti-Han sentiment (Barnett 1963: pp. 157–295; Dreyer 1976: pp. 15–41).

Early Policy of the Chinese Communist Party

The Chinese Communist Party, however, was constrained tactically and ideologically to take a non-assimilationist view. Soon after its formation, the Party adopted a federal solution for China, allowing for ethnic secession, and this was written into the Constitution of the Jiangxi Soviet in 1931 (Moseley 1966a: pp. 163–7). But relations between the Party and ethnic groups were mixed. During the days of the United Front with the *Guomindang*, Communists were active in the Mongolian People's Revolutionary Party and, indeed, a separate Communist Party with its own military organisation operated in Inner Mongolia. Following the break with the *Guomindang* in the late 1920s, two of the Party's first soviets established in Guangxi derived their vigour from the Zhuang (the largest nationality). At that time the Party proved itself not very sensitive to the ethnic issue (Lary 1972). During the Long March, relations were established with the warlike Yi people, said by some to be good and by others to be characterised by bribery. Relations with the peoples of Eastern Tibet, however, were uniformly hostile; indeed according to Edgar Snow, this was the first time the Party had 'faced a populace united in its hostility to them' (Snow 1961: pp, 213–14).

By the 1930s the Party had become much more mindful of the need for minority nationality support, since Japan had made much of the theme of 'national independence' in its intention to wrest territory away from China. Thus it appealed to the Hui, Mongol and other peoples to join it in resisting Japan. Reaction was again mixed. Many Koreans joined the North East Anti-Japanese United Army whilst others inclined towards Japan or supported the anti-communist nationalists. The Hui of Gansu were not particularly moved but the Yan'an administration did manage to create distinct Hui military units and in the civil war forged links with various groups seeking autonomy in Inner Mongolia. This explains why the Inner Mongolian autonomous region was established as early as 1947, though there was still active Mongolian opposition to the Party right up until 1949. In Xinjiang relations were established with the East Turkestan Republic though there were considerable fears throughout the civil war that the *Guomindang* offer of concessions to the Soviet Union might impair the success of the Communist Party and endanger the frontiers (Moseley 1966b: pp. 13–14). In 1945 an alliance had been concluded between the *Guomindang* government and the Soviet Union, and relations between Mao and Stalin, who, as we saw in Chapter 1, thought Mao another Tito, were much worse than they later appeared. In the South there were some Communist successes. Of note was the Li rising in Hainan, under Feng Baiju which started in 1943 and continued until the arrival of Lin Biao's forces at the end of the civil war. What was crucial in the South, however, was not so much Communist successes but *Guomindang* failures. Significantly the *Guomindang* failed to establish a base in Xikang, a province established in 1939 in part of what was known colloquially as 'Eastern Tibet', and was forced to retreat to Taiwan (Dreyer 1976: pp. 61–92).

The Stalinist Classification of Nationalities

Although relations with the Soviet Union were far from perfect, the Party was, of course, influenced by the official Soviet views on the nationalities issue. Back in 1914, Stalin had made a name for himself for his work *Marxism and the National Question* which established four criteria for national identity: a common language, common territory, common economic life and 'a typical cast of mind manifested in a common culture'. That orthodoxy was accepted by the Chinese Party though senior Party spokespersons noted that it could not be 'dogmatically applied' (Moseley 1966a: p. 36). It was clear to anyone who had thought about the national question in China that some peoples who saw themselves as distinct ethnic groups would be disqualified according to Stalin's criteria, either because they spoke several languages (for example the Jingpo), or because they spoke the Han language or the language of another specified nationality. The latter included the Hui, who were identified only by their Muslim faith or Muslim ancestry, and who could hardly be said to have a common territory, being spread over most of the country (Gladney 1991). Common economic life, moreover, applied to various regions in which a number of peoples claiming distinct ethnic identity might live.

Common culture distinct from other cultures, moreover, when taken to an extreme, could result in pure subjectivity, since any group which thought of itself as a nationality might be considered as one (Dreyer 1976: p. 145). Thus a group on Hainan Island, which ethnographers consider to be Yao, is classified as Miao because that is what they say they are (Heberer 1989: p. 33). Such subjectivity is worrying for Marxist-Leninists who stress the objective determinations of social phenomena. A subjective interpretation also creates major administrative problems. If minority nationalities are to be the object of separate laws and policies which at times benefit them, what is to stop a proliferation of nationalities each claiming a degree of autonomy? In the early 1950s, when the government called for the registration of minority nationalities, some four hundred groups responded. The government then undertook lengthy examination of the applications, recognising 54 nationalities by 1957, adding one (the Jinuo) in 1979. These are listed in Table 8.1.

Such groups are many and varied. They inhabit between 50 and 60 per cent of Chinese territory and in 1990 constituted some 8 per cent of the population (91 million). Several of them extend beyond China's borders.[1] Traditional lifestyles vary considerably, ranging from that of herds-people in the steppes to that of settled farmers in the South. Until recently the variation was even starker; consider that the Yi (Norsu) maintained a slave-society (Winnington 1959: pp. 13–122), the Va were head-hunters and the Jingpo were slash-and burn cultivators (Winnington 1959: pp. 125–72, 75–205; Dessaint 1990). Minority nationalities have been influenced by a variety of religions – Islam, Buddhism and various kinds of Christianity and also practice forms of animism and shamanism (see Schwarz 1984).

---

[1] Miao, Hani, Dai, Jing, Jingpo, Lahu, Lisu, Va, Yao, Yi and Zhuang exist in Vietnam, Laos, Thailand and Burma. Mongols, Kazaks, Kirgiz, Tajik, Tartar, Uygur, Daur, Ewenki, Oroqen, Hezhen and others may be found in the various newly independent republics of Central Asia. Koreans and Mongolians are, of course, the majority in their own states (Heberer 1989: p. 16).

Table 8.1 *Minority Nationalities (1990 Census)*

		Language group
Zhuang	15,489,630	Sino-Thai
Manchu	9,821,180	Tungusic
Hui	8,602,978	Han
Miao	7,398,035	Miao-Yao
Uygur	7,214,431	Turkish
Yi	6,572,173	Tibeto-Burmese
Tujia	5,704,223	Tibeto-Burmese
Mongolian	4,806,849	Mongolian
Tibetan	4,593,330	Tibeto-Burmese
Bouyei	2,545,059	Sino-Thai
Dong	2,514,014	Sino-Thai
Yao	2,134,013	Miao-Yao
Korean	1,920,597	Korean
Bai	1,594,827	Tibeto-Burmese
Hani	1,253,952	Tibeto-Burmese
Kazak	1,111,718	Turkish
Li	1,110,900	Sino-Thai
Dai	1,025,128	Sino-Thai
She	630,378	Han
Lisu	574,856	Tibeto-Burmese
Gelo	437,997	Sino-Thai
Lahu	411,476	Tibeto-Burmese
Dongxiang	373,872	Mongolian
Va	351,974	Austro-Asiatic
Shui	345,993	Sino-Thai
Naxi	278,009	Tibeto-Burmese
Qiang	198,252	Tibeto-Burmese
Tu	191,624	Mongolian
Xibe	172,847	Tungusic
Mulam	159,328	Sino-Thai
Kirgiz	141,549	Turkish
Daur	121,357	Mongolian
Jingpo	119,209	Tibeto-Burmese
Salar	87,697	Turkish
Bulang	82,280	Austro-Asiatic
Maonan	71,968	Sino-Thai
Tajik	33,538	Iranian
Pumi	29,657	Tibeto-Burmese
Achang	27,708	Tibeto-Burmese
Nu	27,123	Tibeto-Burmese
Ewenki	26,315	Tungusic
Jing	18,915	Sino-Thai

Table 8.1 continues overleaf

Table 8.1 continued

Jinuo	18,021	Tibeto-Burmese
Deang	15,462	Austro-Asiatic
Uzbek	14,502	Turkish
Russian	13,504	Slavic
Yugur	12,297	Turkish/Mongolian
Bonan	12,212	Mongolian
Moinba	7,475	Tibeto-Burmese
Oroqen	6,965	Tungusic
Drung	5,816	Tibeto-Burmese
Tatar	4,873	Turkish
Hezhen	4,245	Tungusic
Gaoshan	2,909	Austronesian
Lhoba	2,312	Tibeto-Burmese
Other	749,341	

Source: Beijing Review, 52, Dec. 1990: p. 30.

Securing the Frontiers

The chaotic situation inherited by the Communist Party in Xin
jiang, Inner Mongolia and other areas dictated its first task afte
assuming power – to secure the frontiers. The outbreak of th
Korean War, of course, made the Korean frontier vulnerable, bu
general support for North Korea in the Yanbian and other region
assisted the establishment of Chinese control during the campaig
to 'resist America and aid Korea'. An autonomous region (*qu*) wa
set up in 1952 which, after standardisation in 1955, was designate
as an autonomous prefecture (*zhou*) (Lee Chae-jin 1986: pp. 51–66)
In Xinjiang the military forces of the East Turkestan Republic wer
incorporated into the People's Liberation Army and a Productio
and Construction Corps was formed initially out of Han garrison
which had defected to the Communist side in the civil war an
members of the People's Liberation Army. When it seemed that th
Soviet Union had no immediate predatory designs on the area
China and the Soviet Union conducted joint surveys of resource
though the presence of Soviet influence everywhere was deepl
resented. By 1955, the region was felt sufficiently stable to set u
an autonomous region, ranking at provincial level. In Yunnan an
Guangxi, attempts were made to secure the borders, thoug
Guomindang troops which had fled to Burma continued to moun

raids and in 1951 launched a large-scale invasion of Yunnan. Considerable importance, therefore, was given to disarming 'bandits' and establishing autonomous or coalition governments along the frontier, under the supervision of the People's Liberation Army. Very soon members of minority nationalities were recruited into the self-defence forces (Moseley 1973: pp. 33–47).

In Tibet, memories of British and Russian designs caused some concerns about security which were also exacerbated by the outbreak of the Korean War. Evidence as to whether the United States and other foreign powers were involved in destabilising Tibet at that time is confused but one can understand the fears of the Chinese government (Grunfeld 1987). Unsure of the degree of foreign support, the traditional aristocratic governing body in Tibet – the *Kashag* – decided both to prepare for negotiations and to shore up its troops in the Qabdo (Chamdo) region in what was then Xikang province. Those troops were defeated in October 1950 but the People's Liberation Army did not enter Tibet proper until after a formal agreement was signed in May 1951. It was later claimed that the agreement was signed under duress though that was unlikely since nothing was said about duress at the time (Grunfeld 1987: pp. 108–10). According to the agreement, the Tibetan government recognised the region's inclusion in the People's Republic and accepted 'regional national autonomy'. The *Kashag* remained in existence and agreed to institute a reform of what the Chinese government considered to be a system of monastic serfdom. For its part, the Beijing government agreed not to abolish the powers of the Dalai Lama and not to carry out reform through compulsion.

Moderation and Cautious Reform

The policy of the Chinese Communist Party towards minority nationalities in the early 1950s was cautious and gradualist, providing an interesting contrast with the Soviet Union. In that country policy towards nationalities had at times been quite brutal even though the Constitution contained the formal right of separation from the union. In China, policy was lenient though the original commitment to a federal state and the right of separation was rescinded. Probably the main reason for this was a combination of security concerns and traditional ideas about the integrity of the Chinese nation (*Zhonghua minzu* – the latter being the same word as used for nationalities). But, of course, that was not the way leading spokespersons defended the change. Zhang Zhiyi argued that although the Party had supported federalism from 1921 to 1940 the war had forced nationalities together so that by 1949 there was no need for a federal state. In any case, minority nationalities comprised less than 10 per cent of the population, whereas in Russia in 1917 more than half of the population were non-Great Russians, some of them more 'advanced' than the Great Russians themselves. The 1954 Constitution, therefore, accepted the principle of self-government but not separation. Such a policy, Zhang admitted, was different from that of Lenin (Moseley 1966a: pp. 5–56, 67–79).

Whilst separation was not permitted, attempts were made to define the special minority nationality regions. To this end the General Programme for the Implementation of Regional Autonomy was issued in 1952 and formalised by 1956. Gradually temporary administrations were abolished and some very small autonomous areas were incorporated into larger units. The largest units, ranked at provincial level, were known as 'autonomous regions' (*zizhiqu*) and have already been mentioned in the case of Inner Mongolia and Xinjiang. They were joined by Ningxia (Hui) and Guangxi (Zhuang) in 1958 and later by Tibet (formally established 1965). At levels intermediate between province and *xian*, there were 'autonomous districts' (*zizhizhou*) and below that autonomous administrations existed at *xian* and *xiang* levels. As in other areas, however, legal guarantees of autonomy were always subject to changes in Party policy and these began to occur in the mid-1950s. The status of minority areas were by no means fixed and some were abolished in more radical times only to be restored later.

In the first half of the 1950s, however, the mood was far from radical. Summing up policy in 1956, Zhang Zhiyi noted that an assimilationist policy was ruled out, since such a policy could lead to national movements led by non-proletarian elements. Thus all references to assimilation (*tonghua*) were expunged from policy statements in favour of the word 'melding' (*ronghe*). Under the guidance of the Party's United Front Work Department and the State Council's Nationalities Affairs Commission, Han names of minority regions were replaced and the derogatory 'dog' radical in characters pertaining to minorities was replaced by the 'person' radical. But dissatisfaction in the use of names remained; as we have noted when nationalities were asked what they called themselves prior to the elections of 1954, several hundred names were reported and only some could be adopted (Dreyer 1976: p. 143).

Official policy also stressed the toleration of religion. According to Zhang Zhiyi, any attempt to suppress religion only produced martyrs, and a Marxist position held that it was pointless to attempt to destroy religion unless, at the same time, one destroyed its class basis (Moseley 1966a: pp. 113–14). A lot here, however, depends on what one defines as religion. It is easy to show respect for formal mainstream religions but some of the traditional animist practices, mating festivals (classified by Zhang Zhiyi as not injurious) and 'witch-vengeance' (which involved murder and was classified as harmful) (Moseley 1966a: p. 118) must have struck local cadres not as religion but as simple superstition often brutal or lewd. There is no doubt that cadres did intervene to stop some of those practices. In Tibet, moreover, even measures restricting the power of local officials to levy taxes, allowing cadres to hunt and fish, building schools which taught sacrilegious things and setting up bodies to conduct propaganda were seen as interference in religion, as indeed was the Chinese installation of the Bainqen Erdini Quoiqyi Gyancain (Panchen Lama) in Tashilhunpo Monastery in 1952, which rekindled rivalry dating some hundreds of years.

Policy demanded that Han cadres 'make friends' with local people including the traditional upper-strata which continued to enjoy privileges from which their Han counterparts had long been deprived (Moseley 1966a: p. 132). Where reform was carried out it was often extremely moderate compared with that in Han areas. Consider, for example, the description by the journalist Alan Winnington (1959: pp. 13–122) of reforms among the slave-owning Yi. Though one must be mindful that Winnington was predisposed to be sympathetic, there is no reason to doubt his account. In the reforms of 1956 Winnington noted that only those who owned more than ten slaves were singled out as targets for reform. Even after the slave-owners had lost their slaves, however, they still enjoyed political rights and still remained influential in local government. Sometimes they were even paid compensation. In the Yi region, opium cultivation (the main agricultural activity) was still permitted for fear of damaging the local economy.

For all that, reports spoke of fear and hostility on the part of some minority nationalities and over-zealous action by Han cadres. While, in the words of A. Tom Grunfeld (1987: pp. 104–26), the mood in Tibet in the early 1950s might be described as one of 'honeymoon', there were palpable tensions. For example, when the Chinese government took measures to deal with local inflation and initially failed, it incurred much blame. There was opposition also to the building of roads and a coal mine. That, together with religious hostility and resentment of the superior airs of Han cadres, resulted in the formation of anti-Chinese associations. When the Chinese general Zhang Jingwu demanded that two of the leaders of such an association be dismissed from government office, he was accused of unwarranted intervention.

In Inner Mongolia the Party's major spokesperson Ulanhu had to calm fears about Han immigration (which continued throughout the 1950s) and in 1951 stressed the need to educate the Han in combating 'great Han chauvinism' (Hyer and Heaton 1968). He had also to handle the delicate question of pan-Mongolian sentiment. Significantly, in 1954, the body of Genghis Khan was re-buried in that region. Ulanhu also had to deal with problems of land reform. Unlike Tibet, Inner Mongolia and places inhabited by Koreans carried out land reform in arable areas at the same time as most Han regions but care was taken not to antagonise pastoralists. As a result, some Mongols found themselves subject to regulations concerning land reform while others of the same nationality (pastoralists) were not. Zhuang areas soon followed in implementing land reform but were more fortunate in not having to deal with the problem of pastoralists. In parts of Xinjiang a number of local religious and temporal leaders were removed from office and some land was redistributed in the very early years but after 1952 the operative slogan was 'no struggle, no liquidation and no distinction of classes' (Moseley 1966b: p. 28). Again special care was taken to calm the fears of pastoralists and model farms were established and then handed over to local people. In some other areas in the South, however, minority regions were temporarily exempted from land reform. Invidious comparisons began to be made.

According to investigations in 1952, there were numerous examples of 'overdue haste' in implementing change. In Guizhou there were cases of anti-Buddhist actions, felling 'holy trees' and forcing minority nationalities to wear Han dress. In Guangxi, minority nationality people were forced to sell silver bracelets to meet the local bank's savings target. In certain areas minority nationalities could not become urban cadres because they were excluded from towns. In others land reform gave land to minority nationalities poorer than that designated for the Han. Such criticism reached a high point just prior to the promulgation of the Constitution of 1954. After that, a more pressing problem was how to deal with the limited powers given to autonomous units to adapt laws to local minority conditions. Which minorities should remain exempt from land reform? How was one to modify the marriage law and in which areas? Implementation of exceptions was extremely difficult. In a few areas the provision of special treatment proved to be impossible. How, for example, should one treat the hedonist Jingpo who, when given pigs, slaughtered them for huge feasts and who objected to work points and accounting in general as signifying the policies of ungenerous people who 'lacked a heart'? What did one do with runaway Yi slaves when there was nowhere they could be employed and who might be killed on discovery? The problems were immense and complaints continued (Dreyer 1976: pp. 93–137). For example, another major investigation in 1956 revealed the old problems of insufficient cadre training, infringement on minority rights, usurpation of minority cadres' functions and restrictions on the use of local languages. To these was added lack of financial autonomy in the newly established autonomous regions (Dreyer 1976: pp. 141–8).

Despite all the above and despite sporadic risings among Muslims and Tibetans (Gladney 1991: p. 136; Grunfeld 1987: pp. 127–9), it is fair to say that most nationalities questions were handled with sensitivity in the early 1950s. Work teams were sent out to engage in medical and propaganda activities and measures were taken to foster trading relations between Han and minorities, to improve educational facilities, to publish material in minority languages, to set up local people's councils and to form mutual aid teams. A Central Nationalities Institute with provincial offshoots was also established to train cadres though the demand for cadres far exceeded supply.

Whilst the central government was concerned to promote development, it appreciated that levels of development varied widely in minority nationality areas. In that spirit, leading anthropologists Fei Xiaotong, Lin Yuehua and others embarked on a huge seven-year project to slot minorities into the orthodox progression from primitive communism through slavery and three types of feudalism to the present, presumably with an eye to adopting the appropriate policies for peoples at each particular stage.

But the speed-up in collectivisation which occurred after Mao's famous call of mid-1955 (though usually some six months later in most minority regions) was bound to affect minority nationality areas and raise questions about appropriate policies. By March 1956, 72.7 per cent of herding families in Inner Mongolia had been co-operativised. In the Ili Kazak autonomous *zhou* (the old capital of the East Turkestan Republic) in Xinjiang, nomads were enjoined to settle down and to form co-operatives based initially on traditional clans; shares were issued to herd owners which were later bought by the authorities. In the Zhuang area of Guangxi, the Yanbian Korean autonomous district and agricultural parts of Qinghai, 70–90 per cent of households had been co-operativised by 1956 and, in the Hui autonomous *xian* in Hebei, over 90 per cent had been so organised (Moseley 1966: pp. 104–5). Progress in the South West was much slower. As elsewhere, there was some resistance and, as one might expect, the slaughter of animals prior to collectivisation amongst Mongolian pastoralists was quite marked (Hyer and Heaton 1968: p. 116).

Hostility to accelerated co-operativisation was one of the major issues to surface in the movement of 1957 'to let a hundred flowers bloom'. In addition, members of minority nationality peoples complained that the 'unified purchase and sale of grain' discriminated against them, that education policies had served a strategy of 'divide and rule' and once again that lack of financial autonomy made 'autonomous regions' purely formal. Some Hui people, moreover, objected to serving in the People's Liberation Army, declaring that their religion forbade them to bear arms except in the case of a *jihad* (holy war) (Dreyer 1976: pp. 149–50). Among the Kazaks, there were demands for the re-establishment of the East Turkestan Republic and insistence by pro-Soviet elements that whilst they were not opposed to socialism they wanted to build it themselves (Moseley 1966b: pp. 60, 72). Perhaps the largest source of friction, however, was not the result of any government policy to transform the life of minority nationalities. It was the consequence simply of migration into minority nationality areas. This age-old process continued through the early 1950s but accelerated after the middle of the decade due to considerations of security, doubts about the loyalty of peoples who straddled border areas and the simple desire to tap the resources of 'virgin lands' (Schwarz 1963). Of particular note here was the connection established between Shanghai and Xinjiang with the latter taking in large numbers of rusticated Shanghai youth (White 1979). The Han population of Xinjiang increased from 6.2 per cent in 1953 to 40 per cent in 1973 (Heberer 1989: p. 93). In Inner Mongolia, the ratio of Han to Mongolian jumped from 4:1 in 1947 to 6:1 in 1958. The result was a decline in per capita grain production and the area of pastoral farming. This and other grievances was also a factor in separatist movements among the Uygurs and Kazaks.

The Problem of 'Eastern Tibet'

Of course, some Han cadres were cavalier in implementing change. An equally important problem was the literal manner in which many cadres carried out their formal instructions. Consider for a moment the fact that policies governing Tibet applied to Tibet proper (outer Tibet), whereas in the early 1950s two-thirds of Tibetans lived outside what became known (in preparatory form) as the Tibetan autonomous region where inhabitants were subject to different regulations. In such areas, census registration was carried out, which was taken by the paranoid as a move preparatory to arrest. Moves were made to prevent nomadism and to confiscate weapons, which were felt by nomads to be prized possessions, and reforms were set in motion which would not have been dreamt of in outer Tibet (Grunfeld 1987: pp. 120–2). Critics claimed once again that these reforms involved interference in religion, and since there was no separation between religious and temporal authority, changes in property relations in Xikang, Qinghai and Sichuan in 1952–3 must have been seen in that light. As noted earlier, sporadic risings of Tibetans in parts of Qinghai and Eastern Tibet occurred at that time. They flared up again in 1954, and during the 'little leap' of 1955–6 there was another rising among the Khampas of Sichuan. This continued for several years and was to some extent aided by foreign countries (Grunfeld 1987: pp. 127–9, 147–60). That rising influenced Tibetans in outer Tibet. Whereas scrupulous cadres felt they acted legitimately in carrying out reforms amongst Tibetans outside Tibet proper, Tibetans were not concerned with such administrative niceties; they were not interested in the abolition of Xikang province, which was divided between Tibet and Sichuan in 1955 and must have caused Han officials great administrative problems. As Tibetans saw their situation, there was only one Tibetan people, regardless of boundaries. Although the Khampas were often hostile to the authorities in Lhasa, they expressed allegiance to the Dalai Lama, who at that time was embarrassed by their fervour (Norbu 1979). Increasingly Tibetans began to doubt Mao's assurance in his speech 'On the Correct Handling of Contradictions among the People' (*Selected Works*, 5: p. 406) that no changes should take place in Tibet during the Second Five Year Plan (up to 1962) and it was an open question as to whether they should take place in the Third (up to 1967). Despite the fact that Tibet proper remained relatively untouched, an explosion was brewing.

The Anti-rightist Movement

The existence of separatist tendencies was a major element in the Anti-rightist movement of mid-1957 which ended the policy of 'blooming and contending'. Less than a year after Zhang Zhiyi's book had declared that 'only where big Han nationalism has been energetically resisted and fundamentally overcome can the tendency toward local nationalism be satisfactorily overcome' (Moseley 1966a: p. 153), the emphasis in Party policy was reversed. In Xinjiang there was a purge of Soviet-oriented Kazak intellectuals including Jahoda, the governor of the Ili Kazak autonomous *zhou* who was accused of attempting to exclude the Han, giving shelter to rightists and insisting that language reform (the abandonment of Cyrillic script for a Latin one) was no business of the Han. There was also denunciation of Uygur demands for an independent Uygurstan or East Turkestan with some leaders of both nationalities sentenced to labour reform (Moseley 1986b: pp. 57–76; Lo 1961: pp. 103–4). Action was also taken against some Hui leaders in Gansu, Henan and Shandong who were said (not implausibly) to have been egged on by the Jiang Jieshi régime on Taiwan (Dreyer 1976: pp. 150–2). There was similar reaction, it was said, in the

Yanbian Korean region, against declarations of Korean 'super-iority' and expressed desire to join Korea (Lee Chae-jin 1986: pp. 79–81). The issue of 'localism', however, was much wider than that of minority nationalities. Significantly, the ex-warlord Long Yun of Yunnan was removed from office for allegedly demanding 'Yunnan for the Yunnanese', and Feng Baiju, who had organised Communist guerillas in Hainan during the civil war and had protested about excessive mainland control to the Eighth Party Congress, was accused of fomenting armed resistance (described as 'a minor Hungarian incident') in 1956 and demoted (Vogel 1969: pp. 211–16). We are not sure how much the nationality question was involved in either case. We may surmise, however, that the creation of an autonomous region in Guangxi at the time had less to do with issue of nationalities than Beijing's desire to exercise control over the local administration, since opposition to its establishment was considered no less 'rightist' than 'local nationalism' (Moseley 1973: pp. 81–6). The same may be true of Ningxia.

Yet for all that, whilst separatist tendencies were dealt with summarily and despite the fact that some Dai fled to Burma, Laos and Thailand, the Anti-rightist movement was in general not severe in minority nationality areas. Although some leaders were purged and although one increasingly heard repetition of the class struggle theme, many of the traditional élite remained in office. Although eradicating 'local nationalism' took priority, 'Han chauvinism' was still criticised and policy insisted that members of minority nationalities and not Han cadres were in general to launch the criticism. Moves were made, moreover, to redress the grievances about taxation, allowing regions to retain some taxes or a portion of them. The Anti-rightist movement did not strain gradualist policies unduly: it was, in June Dreyer's (1976: p. 158) words, 'a gentle push'.

The Great Leap Forward

During the Great Leap Forward, push came to shove, leading some minority nationalities later to speak of 'twenty lost years' (1958–78) in contrast to the 'ten lost years' of the Cultural Revolution (1966–76) (Gladney 1991: p. 135). Echoing one of the dominant themes of the Leap, cadres strove to bring about a situation where minority nationalities 'caught up' with Han areas in three to five years. This was reflected in 1961 by the journal *Minzu yanjiu* (Nationalities Research) being taken over by the significantly titled *Minzu tuanjie* (Nationalities Unite). The scope whereby special characteristics were to apply was progressively narrowed. New enthusiasm for learning the Han language was discovered and cadres were told only to speak the Han language at meetings. Two years after the Party had defended local customs, minority nationalities were found to be discarding them, though one wonders how willingly Muslims in Xinjiang discarded polygamy and traditional divorce practices once exceptions to the Marriage Law were rescinded (Lo 1961: p. 101). As greater stress was put on the class struggle motif, the ambitious seven-year programme in minority anthropology and history was reduced to a one-year project and its leaders criticised for 'bourgeois scientific objectivism'. Apparently, in the voluntarist vein noted in earlier chapters, the 'poor and blank' (in Mao's words) could transcend the various prescribed evolutionary stages. Considerations of class struggle, furthermore, led the Party to stress the cruelty of Genghis Khan who had been re-buried with much pomp only a few years before. Yet, despite that stress, some upper-class minority leaders were still invited to visit nationalities institutes and study minority nationality policy (Moseley 1973: pp. 131–2).

In most (but certainly not all) minority areas, communes were formed and everything was geared to serve production. There was renewed pressure to turn pastures into arable land, to force nomads to 'settle down' within the new organisations and to subvert traditional patterns of production organised along kinship lines. Minority peasants were enjoined to spend their money on 'useful' things such as wheelbarrows rather than national dress which impeded work. Exemptions to the funeral laws granted to minorities were rescinded as cemeteries were moved from usable land. Dai women, who had never worked in the fields, were made to do so, and Hui peasants, whose dietary régime was strictly Muslim, were required to eat in communal canteens like everyone else. As communes increased in size, moreover, mixed nationality communes were formed, which may have contributed to ethnic tension. Indeed there was much scope for conflict, as Han cadres gave vent to feelings for which they had been criticised in the early 1950s. In some areas they even went so far as to prevent traditional songs and dances and to curtail the training of local cadres (Dreyer 1976: pp. 159–7).

Once again, however, the major bone of contention was migration. There was an accelerated influx of Han into Xinjiang, facilitated by the opening of a new railway to Lanzhou (Moseley 1986b: pp. 88–115). This led to a rising in 1958 and the subsequent movement of thousands of Kazaks and Uygurs across the border into the Soviet Union, often with their herds. Migration was both illegal and legal as Soviet authorities became willing to issue passports. By 1963 it was estimated that some 70,000 refugees had crossed into Soviet Kazakstan. Disaffection among the Kazaks as a result of the Great Leap was said to have been a factor contributing to the rising of Kazaks in the Ili region in 1962. There were disturbances too among the Hui and the Yi and once again amongst peoples in Inner Mongolia. There, accelerated migration resulted in the Han-Mongol ratio changing from 6:1 in 1958 to 9:1 in 1960, reaching 12:1 a decade later (Heberer 1989: p. 93; Hyer and Heaton 1968: p. 117). The virgin lands policy in that region proved eventually to be as harmful as Khrushchev's in the Soviet Union. Hostility to migration and to the interventionist policies of the Great Leap resulted in the slogan *minzu tuanjie* (nationalities unite), designed with obvious assimilationist intent, being reinterpreted to mean exactly the opposite – the solidarity of particular nationalities in the face of outside interference (Gladney 1991: p. 313).

Though there was no Great Leap Forward in Tibet proper in 1958–9, a revolt was sparked off in March 1959 by the Khampa rising in Sichuan which had been going on for three years, It was influenced also by China's changed international position as a result of the Leap and renewed foreign interest in Tibet. We shall not go into the details here. Suffice it to say that the People's Liberation Army quelled most opposition and the Dalai Lama fled to India. He was nevertheless recognised in Beijing as Tibet's titular head and member of the Standing Committee of China's National People's Congress until December 1964. Upon the Dalai Lama's departure, the State Council moved, on 28 March, to abolish the traditional government (the *Kashag*) and transfer power to the Preparatory Committee for the Tibet autonomous region (URI 1968b: pp. 37–58). Though the titular head of the committee remained the Dalai Lama, its effective head was now to be the Bainqen Erdini.

After the rising, social change was pursued rapidly. Peasant associations were formed and a series of measures for 'democratic reform' were instituted. The operative slogan was *'sanfan shuangjian'* ('three abolitions and two reductions'). The 'abolitions' here referred to rebellion, forced labour and personal servitude and the 'reductions' to land rent and interest. The land of supporters of the rising was confiscated and nobles implicated in the rebellion were made to stand with heads bowed and hear the former serfs 'speak their bitterness'. Various monasteries were punished for their involvement and many were closed, the number of religious institutions declining from 2,716 with over 100,000 monks in 1959 to 553 with under 7,000 monks by the time of the Cultural Revolution (*Beijing Review*, 43, 26 Oct. – 1 Nov. 1987, p. 23). Some new monks, however, continued to be trained. This interference with religion was prominent in what the government referred to as 'left excesses' in the late 1970s and early 1980s.

After the Great Leap

The Tibetan rising took place at a time when the Communist Party had already decided that the Great Leap had caused too much disruption in other areas and attempts were being made to soften its impact on minority nationality areas. Though there was a change in policy for a few months after the Lushan plenum of 1959 (which had a marked effect on the Ili Kazak autonomous *zhou*) (Moseley 1966b: pp. 83–5), the general trend in minority areas was towards de-radicalisation. This reflected developments in other parts of the country but was given added impetus by rapidly worsening relations with India and the Soviet Union. The class struggle theme received less emphasis and local-level cadres were once again castigated for 'Han chauvinism'. Rusticated youth were warned not to put on airs and many took advantage of the disruption to return whence they had come. Decentralisation of the unit of account in communes, moreover, reduced the tension in communes organised with more than one nationality and in 1961 a few communes in Dai, Lisu and some Tibetan areas were abolished. A more liberal policy concerning canteens was also adopted. The return of private plots, contracting land to households, permitting 'sideline production' and reopening rural fairs revived traditional trading relations and contributed to the lessening of friction. Minority nationality peoples were consulted about some of the changes made in agricultural techniques during the Leap and not a few were changed. Of particular concern here (particularly of Ulanhu) was the situation in herding areas. The Party admitted that the loss of animals had occurred and that excessive amounts of pasture land had been turned over to arable farming. New plans were made to safeguard livestock, compensation was paid to families who had surrendered animals and they were allowed once again to own some, officially not exceeding 10 per cent of the total. By 1961 nomadic pastoralism was once again acknowledged as a valid form of production and in general the living standards of pastoralists improved. The former policy, stressing self-sufficiency in grain, was seen as harmful, though in certain areas, such as Yunnan, forest clearing continued with considerable ecological consequences (Heberer 1989: pp. 60–1).

By the early 1960s, official statements stressed once again the importance of special characteristics, local religions (but not superstition), the value of regional autonomy and respect for traditional upper strata. Former 'rightists' such as Long Yun and various Hui leaders were rehabilitated, the value of the old social history project, truncated during the Great Leap, was reaffirmed and considerable attention was given to local languages. Of all languages, Mongolian was given most emphasis and the sinicised Ulanhu started to learn it. Symbolising the new mood, the 800th anniversary of the birth of Genghis Khan was duly celebrated (Dreyer 1976: pp. 173–91). In Yanbian also, separate Korean schools were re-established and various senior leaders, mindful of the delicate position of North Korea in the Sino-Soviet split, visited the region (Lee Chae-jin 1986: pp. 86–8).

The general mood of de-radicalisation was also felt in Tibet proper, which had only commenced reforms after the rising of 1959, and, as in other areas, tardiness in carrying out reform was one of the charges levelled at Liu Shaoqi in the Cultural Revolution. Liu, as we know, was concerned about disruption and must have worried about continued foreign subversion throughout the 1960s. In Tibet, rural reorganisation was indeed slower than one might have expected just after the rising. Mutual aid teams were established though communes did not form until the eve of the Cultural Revolution and did not cover the bulk of land until the mid-1970s. Of course, the closing of monasteries displaced many monks but new opportunities were opening. These included the employment of large numbers of lower-level Tibetan cadres as the region was incorporated into the regular administration of the People's Republic, though the top levels of administration were dominated by Han. There were also new opportunities in education, communications, agriculture and to some extent industry (though again Liu Shaoqi was blamed for the slow growth in that area). That is not to say, however, that the situation was rosy. In the late 1970s, the government admitted that economic policies had been mistaken. There had been excessive capital construction, and the forced planting of wheat to replace the traditional barley was not only unsuitable to the soil but caused disquiet among those used to a traditional diet. There was hostility also to the movement of large numbers of Han into the area though it is misleading to refer to that process as 'genocide' (International Commission of Jurists 1960: pp. 11–63). The general picture of Tibet in the early 1960s, therefore, was mixed (Grunfeld 1987: pp. 161–7). Though there were some positive aspects of the reforms, they were *imposed* reforms, and the subsequent admission by the government that regional autonomy was merely a formality must be taken seriously as must the admission of general 'leftist excesses'. Even the Bainqen Erdini protested about the latter in 1962 which must have been a factor in his dismissal during the radical climate of 1964.

As we have seen, in China as a whole, the new radical climate was ushered in at the Tenth Plenum of the Eighth Central Committee in 1962 and took the form of a Socialist Education Movement. In minority nationality regions, that movement was much more limited than elsewhere though the propaganda message was similar. There was general condemnation of slandering the 'three red banners' of the Great Leap Forward, denunciation of Soviet 'revisionism' and the selection of a number of minority nationality heroes to accompany Lei Feng. Gradually the class struggle theme became more strident. It reappeared in research reports and was employed by the various culture teams which toured minority nationality areas in 1965. By that time the Party examined the class origin of minority nationality cadres and united front work came under suspicion. Li Weihan, the director of the Party's United Front Work Department, was removed for 'capitulationism' and the vice governor of Qinghai, the 'living buddha' Shirob Jaltso, was replaced by a former Tibetan carpenter. In general though, there were few concrete changes during the Socialist Education Movement (Dreyer 1976: pp. 191–204) – a fact which convinced many activists in the Cultural Revolution that minority nationality work had been dominated by a 'revisionist' line after the Great Leap.

The Cultural Revolution

Despite the efforts of various leaders to prevent the movement of red guards into some minority nationality areas (for example Zhou Enlai with regard to Tibet) and formally to suspend the movement in Inner Mongolia and Xinjiang, the Cultural Revolution followed the same course in those areas as it did in other places in China (Heberer 1989: pp. 23–9; Dreyer 1976: pp. 205–35). Yet there were added dimensions. The first stage of the revolution, it will be remembered, saw a campaign against the 'four olds' (ideology, customs, culture and habits). The movement of red guards across the country to implement it had a particularly severe impact on minority nationalities. Second, emphasis on collapsing the national question into one of class, as we have seen, resulted in a condemnation of united front policies (referred to as 'capitulationism') and attacks on differential treatment for national groups. Indeed, Liu Shaoqi was accused of stating that national questions were merely linked to class (rather than being reducible to it) and was condemned for including clauses on regional autonomy in the 1954 Constitution which were said to negate the 'dictatorship of the proletariat'. Similar charges were levelled at Deng Xiaoping, who was additionally accused of allowing a former prime minister of the Tibetan *Kashag* to emigrate to India after he had opposed Party policies; that man turned out later to be a leader of the 1959 insurrection. The stress on class, moreover, allowed disgruntled Han residents in minority areas to attack local leaders who were felt to have obtained their position because of discrimination in favour of 'feudal elements'. The same went for students in the Central Nationalities Institute in Beijing who sought to achieve upward mobility by removing traditional leaders. A third element which appears regularly in China to subvert rational thought was the ugly theme of 'patriotism' which was counterposed to 'nationalism'.

The consequences of all the above was severe discrimination against minority nationalities. Even now we are not sure of the extent. Because the Cultural Revolution was largely an urban phenomenon and most of the accounts we have deal with towns in which the overwhelming majority of participants were Han, we are uncertain about the degree of disruption in the countryside, and accounts vary (compare Dreyer 1976 and the bleaker Heberer 1989). Revulsion against the Cultural Revolution in the pas decade has generated many lurid stories, and many of the charge are no doubt exaggerated yet deserve listing since all contain more than a little truth.

A rigid uniformity was said to have been imposed. Even more than in the Great Leap Forward, minorities were enjoined to live in normal houses, wear unpretentious Han clothes and were forbidden to celebrate national holidays and religious festivals, engage in superstitious practices, dubious health cures and traditional singing and dancing. They were discouraged from speaking their native languages and books in those languages were removed from the shelves (though Mongolian, Tibetan, Uygur, Kazak and Korean were too widespread to suppress). Once again the Han language became the only language prescribed for meetings or hearing legal cases (such as there were). Minority languages ceased to be taught in schools, admission quotas for minority nationalities were denounced as discriminatory and special minority schools were often closed down. Nationalities institutes, moreover, were said to be 'hotbeds of the bourgeoisie'. There was a reduction in the number of minority cadres. Several autonomous areas were abolished and the Inner Mongolian region was reduced in size by a half (though here defence against the Soviet Union was said to be a major factor).

Real or imaginary political associations were suppressed. Of note was the Revolutionary People's Party of Inner Mongolia, set up, it is said, under the aegis of Ulanhu who had not been forgiven for taking measures to end the policy of fusion, for halting the encroachment on pastures and for convening a conference to heal the breach between pastoralists and agriculturalists (Hyer and Heaton 1968). He was accused of pan-Mongolian sentiments or at least trying to establish a separate 'independent kingdom'. We are not sure how far he was defended by specifically Mongol supporters but it does seem to have been the case that Ulanhu put up fierce resistance to the Cultural Revolution, that groups mobilised in his defence (perhaps including the so-called Genghis

Khan Combat Squads) and that military force had to be used in the region. In the Yanbian Korean autonomous *zhou* a 'local Khrushchev', similarly accused, was removed from office, and red guards antagonised both Koreans in China and the régime of Kim Il-sung (labelled a 'fat revisionist'). Many Chinese Koreans fled to that country (Lee Chae-jin 1986: pp. 88–95). There was fighting too in Xinjiang and some of the old leaders were removed. There the local leader Wang Enmao was accused of fostering nationalism though he survived relatively unscathed. In Yunnan, the local First Secretary of the Party committed suicide after being accused of being more concerned with minority living standards than with class struggle, though we do not know to what extent class struggle policies affected some of the remote minorities. Similar charges were made against Li Jingquan, the First Secretary of Sichuan who had been responsible for dissolving some communes in the early 1960s. In Guangxi, particularly bloody clashes occurred in 1968 resulting in many tens of thousands of deaths and corpses floating down the Xijiang to the port of Hong Kong. There again it is impossible to know how many local nationalities were affected since most urban Zhuang who had participated in the fighting had long been assimilated. Suffice it to say that the local leader, Wei Guoqing, survived, rose to high office and, though a Zhuang, did not appear to have been accused of 'local nationalism'. Throughout that turbulent period, factional fighting occurred in many areas, such as the Li Miao autonomous *zhou* on Hainan and the Tibet autonomous region from which there was a new flight of refugees.

Economic policies were also affected. For the first time, as we have noted, communes were introduced into Tibet, though these had populations scarcely larger than production brigades elsewhere. Under pressure to 'grow grain everywhere' forests were cut down with renewed intensity and Xinjiang and Inner Mongolia saw once again a reduction of pasture land. As one might expect from the above there was a general disrespect for religion and the religious were often humiliated. Indeed it is said that Muslims were sometimes made to keep pigs; those criticised were forced to eat pork or masquerade as pigs; pork eating rituals became a prerequisite for Party or army membership and sometimes wells were polluted by pig carcases (Heberer 1989: p. 109; Gladney 1991: p. 138). One recalls that Zhang Zhiyi had observed and denounced some of those practices as early as 1956 (Moseley 1966a: pp. 144–5). There was also much destruction of religious monuments and buildings. Churches, mosques and monasteries were demolished or ransacked. These included many Christian institutions and the famous Jokhang monastery in Lhasa. Clearly much of the damage was done by Han red guards from parts of China other than minority nationality areas. Yet it too easy to assign all the blame to them. One should note that the formation of red guard units in places such as Tibet and Xinjiang proceeded in much the same way as in other parts of the country with the same sorts of ideological cleavage and factionalism. As elsewhere, the military was used to end internecine strife and its action resulted in much greater Han control over the top levels of administration and heightened detestation of the Han. Significantly, the Tibet and Xinjiang autonomous regions were among the last to establish revolutionary committees, revealing the extent of the disruption. In both of those areas there was considerable worries about security. In the latter there was concern both about defence installations, including the nuclear facilities at Lop Nor, and sympathy for pan-Turkik movements which were felt to expose the North Western frontiers to a very hostile Soviet Union. Indeed, at that time, Radio Tashkent was broadcasting propaganda to Uygur, Kirgiz and Tajiks in China, claiming how much better life was the other side of the frontier and denouncing Chinese nationality policy.

As the Cultural Revolution wound down after 1969, there was a gradual easing of restrictions on minorities. That process was accelerated after Lin Biao's alleged abortive coup of 1971 and by the removal of several of Lin's associates who had been appointed to high office in minority regions. Official comment maintained that Lin had sabotaged the Party's policy towards minority nationalities and had held them in low esteem. By that time a number of figures prominent in nationalities affairs since the establishment of the régime such as Ngapoi Ngawang Jigme (former head of the Tibet autonomous region) and Saifudin (a one time leader of the East Turkestan Republic and later governor of Xinjiang) were seen to have retained significant posts and were joined by some new minority leaders who had risen during the Cultural Revolution.

Gradually broadcasting and publishing in minority languages recommenced and Han cadres were instructed to learn them. Much was made once again of the provision of new Latin-based scripts for minorities in Xinjiang as well as the importance of the traditional script in Inner Mongolia. This was obviously dictated by the security threat along the Soviet borders, which clearly demanded not just insulating minorities from Soviet propaganda but also improving relations in case hostilities should break out. Minorities in that region were treated with a barrage of propaganda about the Russification of Soviet nationalities and archeological exhibitions went to great pains to show that Xinjiang had been under Chinese influence since antiquity. Doubtless also it was security concerns which resulted in more rusticated youth being sent to Xinjiang and other vulnerable frontier regions. It was claimed in 1974 that some 200,000 of such youth had settled in the region in the past six years. To prevent those youth causing inter-ethnic tension, the majority were kept in state farms or organised separately under the aegis of the Production and Construction Corps. A similar provision was made by the Production and Construction Corps in Inner Mongolia and Tibet, and rusticated youth in other areas, such as Guangxi, were usually kept separate from the indigenous population.

Unlike Xinjiang and Inner Mongolia, the security situation in Tibet improved considerably. The Nixon visit to China in 1971 saw the end of covert United States actions. Gradually, as in other regions, there was a cautious revival of religion. A campaign to 'eradicate those who used religion to restore serfdom' came to an abrupt end in 1971 and a few monasteries were repaired. By 1974 the government had proclaimed 'four basic freedoms' – to practise religion, engage in trade, lend money with interest and to keep servants. There was even talk in the early 1970s of the return of the Dalai Lama though hopes on that score were dashed in 1973 and criticism of the Dalai Lama resumed. Together with this, there was a renewed stress on communisation and parts of Tibet were held out as Dazhai-style models of how backward areas could easily be developed.

By 1972 the Central Nationalities Institute reopened and training of new cadres made considerable headway. Much was made of nationality cadres holding responsible jobs and efforts were undertaken to recruit minorities into the Party. The process, of course, was uneven and was no doubt influenced by the various movements to revive the spirit of the Cultural Revolution after 1973 during which Jiang Qing is reported to have asked why one needed minority nationalities. Some persecution continued. In 1973, for example, a Miao Christian clergyman was executed in Yunnan and his family members were forced to renounce their faith after his sentence was read (Heberer 1989: p. 109). More significantly a rising occurred amongst Hui in Yunnan in 1975 in which a whole village was razed and some 1,600 Hui massacred (Gladney 1991: pp. 137–40). Yet increasingly there was talk once again of 'special characteristics', and factories producing national dress and artifacts were given prominence in the media. Trade fairs recommenced, restoring a vitality to depressed minority areas, and a renewed concern for preventative health measures resulted in the training of large number of minority 'barefoot doctors'.

Despite the measures taken to revive the Cultural Revolution, it was evident in most minority nationality areas throughout the early 1970s that its influence was gradually being eroded. Significantly Ulanhu was rehabilitated at the Tenth National Congress of the Party in 1973 along with Li Jingquan, the First Secretary of the Sichuan Party who a few years before was accused of pandering to minority sentiment in dissolving communes. The new Constitution, approved by the National Peoples Congress in 1975, moreover, seemed to offer hope of stability (Dreyer 1976: pp. 237–59). But the winding-down of the Cultural Revolution was soon felt to have been inadequate. As we have seen, the death of Mao ushered in two years of soul-searching culminating in the Third Plenum of 1978, after which the whole question of policy towards nationalities was reassessed.

The Post-1978 Situation

As in so many areas, after the Third Plenum in 1978, the Chinese government admitted errors made in its past handling of minority nationalities, particularly its treating minority nationality questions solely in terms of class. Once again the government listened to demands by some nationalities to discard derogatory names (Heberer 1989: pp. 37–9). When it became clear that minority nationalities were to enjoy a degree of positive discrimination, there was a rush of groups to obtain minority nationality status and applications from individuals for their nationality to be reclassified (some of which were said to be fraudulent). As a result the minority nationality population registered in some areas doubled. Consider, for example, that the 2.4 million Manchus registered in 1953 had grown merely to 2.6 million in 1978. By 1982 there were 4.3 million, rising to 9.8 million in 1990.

But the criteria for minority nationality status were no more clear then than they had been in the 1950s. Are the 2,000 'Jews' who applied for registration really Jews? Why are some groups which manifest a distinct lifestyle classified as Han, or certain groups which speak an Iranian language classified as Uygur (whose language is Turkik) (Heberer 1989: p. 30)? Do the Yugur not have a better claim to ties with the ancient Uygur empire than the nationality bearing that name, even though some of them speak Mongolian (Gladney 1991: p. 301)? Perhaps even more important, does the exercise in classification not call into question the very concept of Han nationality which comprises groups of varied origin and language (Gladney 1991: pp. 306–12)? The result has been much argument, and by 1990 some 750,000 persons remained unclassified.

The point is that so much of the historical analysis as to ethnic origins and independent status in the past evokes what Benedict Anderson (1983) calls 'imagination' rather than objective historical analysis. Ethnic identity in China, as elsewhere, draws upon affective ties rationalised by a half-remembered history as well as considerations of simple instrumentalism on the part of both the state and the minority nationalities. The state registers minority nationalities to enhance its control, and minority nationalities, so registered, use their official status to further local ends. While obviously the nation state did not create minority nationalities, it played a large part in setting their official boundaries and perhaps drawing the lines of future cleavage (see Gladney 1991). From the perspective of the 1990s we can say that the Soviet Union has fallen apart along fault lines of its own making. The Chinese government in the early 1980s, of course, could not foresee the break-up of the Soviet Union and was unaware of the dangers of an official 'objective' ethnography which turns out to be more imaginative than historically objective. It did, however, take considerable care in its official pronouncements concerning the historical determinants of national identity.

Ethnic identification remains problematic. So indeed does freedom of religion, proclaimed once again in the 1980s and written into the 1982 Constitution. This time, however, the clause 'freedom not to believe' which had occurred in the 1954 Constitution was omitted as it implied covert discrimination. At the same time efforts were made to restore the damage done to religious institutions, though only a little could be achieved. In Tibet, out of the 533 religious institutions of 1966 only ten were said to have been left intact. By 1984, 45 monasteries were functioning. Some monks, moreover, were recruited as teachers in government schools (Postiglione 1992: p. 36). Moves were also made to repair relations with religious leaders. Overtures were made to the Dalai Lama who sent delegations to Tibet. When one of those delegations, however, was greeted by demonstrations for independence in 1980, the prospect for reconciliation receded.

There are many problems associated with 'freedom of religion'. Freedom of conscience is relatively easy, but what does one do when traditional leaders attempt to use the new policy to impose observance of old religions on those who had chosen apostasy? How should the Party react when more people listen to the local *ulama* than to local Party committees, or violate the Marriage Law? And how does one define religion? As in the early 1960s, a distinction was made between mainstream religions and 'superstition'. Practices such as geomancy and exorcism remained banned but were more and more openly practised. The new policies, furthermore, were imperfectly implemented and cases of religious persecution occurred during the political movements of the 1980s such as the campaigns to combat 'spiritual pollution' and to impede 'bourgeois liberalisation'. In both of those campaigns , there was a concern with what was described as 'obscenity' which was sometimes applied to local 'superstitious practices'. Such imperfect implementation of policies fuelled religious resentment and contributed to the risings of Muslims in Kashgar in 1981 and 1989–90 and the troubles in Tibet from 1987 to the present.

But 'obscenity' is double-edged. While some 'religious' practices are seen officially as obscene, protests against 'obscenity' may serve the cause of those of a more puritan bent in the central leadership. The belief in the pure and true (*qingzhen*), espoused by the Hui, is not exclusively Koranic. Here we recall what has been termed China's Salman Rushdie affair. While students were engaged in demonstrations which were to culminate in the massacre of 4 June 1989, demonstrations were occurring in Beijing and elsewhere, with official support, against the publication of the book *Sexual Customs*, which compared minarets with phalli, the Meccan pilgrimage with orgies and made reference to sodomy with camels. That silly book was banned, copies were destroyed and burned, the editors dismissed from office and the authors, after temporary arrest, driven into hiding, Salman Rushdie-style. We can perhaps all do without such 'obscenity'. But consider, along with Dru Gladney (1991: pp. 1–4) the comparison with the contemporary obscenity of 4 June 1989.

Consider also the problem of the legal status of minority nationalities worked out in the early 1980s. The Law of Regional Autonomy of the Nationalities of the People's Republic of China (1984) specified the nature of self-determination and the relationship among 'autonomous' and other units. But there is no doubt that Party leadership constricted the implementation of the law (Heberer 1989: pp. 42–3). In the early 1980s, minority nationality representatives complained about the cavalier way 'autonomous' units were abolished in the Great Leap Forward and Cultural Revolution and subsequently restored. Yet despite the new law, the Li and Miao autonomous *zhou* in Hainan (abolished in 1959, restored in 1962, abolished in 1966 and restored after the Cultural Revolution) was abolished again in 1988, when that region was re-designated as a province (Heberer 1989: pp. 41–2). By 1989, there were five autonomous regions at provincial level, 31 autonomous *zhou* (called *meng* [leagues] in Inner Mongolia), 105 autonomous xian (called *qi* [banners] in Inner Mongolia) and some 3,000 autonomous *xiang*. In the light of the above and the fact that one-sixth of all minority nationalities are in mixed regions (with more than one nationality) one might expect those numbers to change.

Even before the Law on Regional Autonomy which specified that leading cadres in minority regions should come from the relevant nationalities, attempts were made to recruit local nationality cadres. But again there are problems. In the late 1970s the Party proposed to ensure that two-thirds of all cadres in Tibet were Tibetans (the figure in 1982 had reached 60 per cent). There were, however, insufficient numbers of trained people and, in the meantime (1988), Han cadres in Tibet were ordered to learn Tibetan. To accelerate training of local cadres, nationality schools were re-established, universities set up special courses introducing quotas for minority nationality students (6.1 per cent in 1987) and by the 1990s twelve nationalities institutes (*minzu xueyuan*) were operating (Heberer

1989: p. 50; Postiglione 1992: p. 38). Here new attention was paid to minority languages. In 1949, eleven written minority languages were in regular use, with seven others used sporadically. Since then, twenty-five written languages have been codified. Implementation of this policy varies, of course, from area to area. In some places the overwhelming majority speaks the local language, but in others (such as Guizhou) it has been reported that 35 per cent of the population of local nationalities did not know the language of the group to which they had been classified (Heberer 1989: pp. 16–17, 51). There is an additional problem, common in other countries, in that whereas local languages may aid upward mobility at lower levels, a formidable barrier has to be surmounted once one reaches institutions where instruction has to be in the dominant language. That problem is not adequately addressed by policies of positive discrimination which grant minority nationality students entry to universities with lower marks in the unified examination system (Lee Chae-jin 1986: pp. 104–5). Difficulties might also arise from the proliferation of single-language ethnic schools and not long after their establishment moves have been made in some areas to promote de-segregation (Postiglione 1992: p. 37).

Then there is, of course, the problem of sheer poverty in minority nationality areas. A further set of policies have been put forward to alleviate the hardship in many minority nationality areas. In 1988 it was said that 29 per cent of the minority nationality population did not have adequate food and clothing, one-quarter of all people deemed to be earning less than the living wage belonged to ethnic minorities, and the rate of illiteracy or semi-literacy of people aged 12–50 (43 per cent) was much higher than for China as a whole (32 per cent), with considerable variations among different ethnic groups (Pien 1990; Heberer 1989: pp. 46, 50; Postiglione 1992: pp. 29–30). Minority regions have received huge influxes of cash. Particularly favoured here has been Tibet which also enjoys generous tax holidays. But as we shall see, discrimination in favour of poor regions is no guarantee against disaffection.

Considerations of the plight of minority nationalities caused the government initially to exempt minority nationality areas from its 'one child policy' for reducing population growth, discussed in earlier chapters. Such a policy, it was felt, would cause undue hardship since infant death rates in those areas, which were higher than in those of the Han, caused families to aim for a larger number of children to care for their members in old age. The policy would also exacerbate fears about assimilation. Yet it was abundantly clear that overall growth rates amongst most minority nationalities were higher than among the Han, and exercises of simple arithmetic led some Han cadres to the facile conclusion that eventually minorities would become majorities. It was also clear that although there has been considerable development of educational institutions in minority areas, increased birth rates there meant that the percentage of children unable to attend school was higher than in Han areas (Postiglione 1992: p. 31). Policies aimed at population restriction were soon extended to some minority areas. Even in the early 1980s, one heard of forced sterilisation and abortion in Gansu and Tibet. Soon official policy began to change. By 1982, minority nationality areas were urged to work out their own family planning policies, and in 1984 the 'one child' policy was laid down for minorities of over ten million people (there was only one, the Zhuang). The tightening of official policy led to the adoption of different regulations in different areas. In many regions the stipulations for Han and minorities varied and in some there appeared different regulations for different minorities. Sometimes regulations were strict (in parts of Qinghai), and sometimes very loose, particularly those regulations involving nomads who would migrate the moment they felt them to be unbearable. The general result of all this was to add to resentment between Han and minorities and among minorities. Families of the latter sometimes hid their children whenever an official approached.

One can expect that population of minority nationalities, in general, will continue to grow faster than that of the Han. This, however, will not be the case amongst the very small hunting minorities in the North (for example the Ewenki), where disease and alcoholism,[2] consequent upon the destruction of traditional hunting lifestyles, has produced despair and the prospect of imminent extinction. Amongst such peoples, the government's prohibition of marriage amongst relatives has not only caused hostility but has resulted in marriages with the Han. The

---

[2] The problem of excessive alcohol consumption has been noted officially in other areas, for example among the Jinuo of Yunnan (*Beijing Review*, 36, 5-11 Sept. 1988: pp. 28–9).

government's assurance that this will lead to an increase in the population of such peoples because children of mixed marriages can claim minority status, is hardly consoling since such children will surely soon be totally assimilated (Heberer 1989: pp. 74–101).

Population policies, therefore, have caused resentment. Many nationalities continue to oppose their regions being opened up for the exploitation of raw materials with resulting ecological damage. They have protested also about an economic strategy which favours the Eastern coastal areas where few minority nationalities live (Postiglione 1992: pp. 27, 45). Though it has been stated officially that the proportion of Han living in Tibet declined after 1982 (*Beijing Review*, 33, 17 Aug. 1987: p. 20), resentment remains and there have been continued demonstrations in Xinjiang and Inner Mongolia against Han migration (Heberer 1989: p. 43). In Tibet there is still dislike of Han cadres who receive substantial allowances for being in what is considered to be a 'hardship post'. There is annoyance at government attempts to prevent the growth of smuggling which has increased as the Tibetan borders have become more open and, above all, unabated resentment of the Han dating from the Cultural Revolution (Grunfeld 1987: pp. 207–17). The demonstrations in Tibet from 1987 to 1989 have to be seen in that light.

According to Beijing government sources, the recent disturbances in Tibet were the result of 'external factors'. It would be more true to say that some of them were designed to capitalise on external occurrences. During the mid-1980s the government went to great pains to portray Tibet as a show-case of Beijing's generosity and of rapid development in a very poor region. Journalists flocked to Tibet and tourism burgeoned, culminating in 1987 in the visits of ex-President Jimmy Carter and Chancellor Helmut Kohl to the region. Those who sought independence felt a need to counter the favourable propaganda. The first disturbance in 1987 occurred as the Dalai Lama was addressing the United States House of Representatives Human Rights Committee. As a result tourism declined sharply and few journalists were allowed to remain. After the second disturbance in March 1988, the Beijing government sought to enter into dialogue with the Dalai Lama, inviting him to return but rejecting his demands for a plebiscite and what seemed like an extension of the 'one country two systems' formula, whereby a government in Lhasa would be responsible for Tibet's internal affairs (Chang Ya-chun 1989).

The third disturbance in December 1988 was timed to coincide with the fortieth anniversary of the Universal Declaration of Human Rights, and the fifth, in March 1989, with the fortieth anniversary of the rising in which the Dalai Lama fled. This rising saw the imposition of martial law in Tibet for the first time since 1959. If the aim of the demonstrators was to capture world attention, they certainly succeeded, though, one might argue, their extremism makes it difficult to believe the demonstrations were carried out at the Dalai Lama's behest and that he saw them contributing to a negotiated settlement. At the time of writing (1993) new demonstrations are occurring in Tibet, attempting to put pressure on the Chinese government. It is clear that the legitimacy of the Chinese government depends on continued success in economic development and the continued goodwill of foreign countries. Such pressure may be expected to continue.

Conclusion

The introduction to this chapter stated that the Communist Party's policies towards indigenous peoples started off well-intentioned and finished up scarcely better than those of any recent Australian government. The economic and cultural reasons for this are much the same. But there are crucial differences in outcome. The Chinese Party has been able to inflict much more harm by its greater centralised control over the country but, by the same token, has greater power to enforce remedial measures. China, moreover, has seen a great part of the minority nationality question in strategic terms. But strategic factors change, as we have seen in the late 1980s. There is no longer any Soviet threat and that very fact has removed one basis of what solidarity there was among Han and minority nationalities. The example of what is happening in what was once the Soviet Union, moreover, has caused considerable unrest along the borders with Kazakstan. And considerable apprehension has been expressed by Chinese leaders about developments in Outer Mongolia. This chapter has also noted the continual recrudescence of separatist tendencies. We may expect these to become more acute. From 1989 to 1992, we have seen risings in many places in Xinjiang led, among other groups, by the Free East Turkestan Movement and backed by Mujahedeen groups in

Afghanistan. Such disturbances were clearly on the agenda of foreign minister Qian Qichen on his visit to Turkey where some separatist movements were said to be based (Postiglione 1992: pp. 25–7). Clearly, Islamic sentiment in China, more than previously, takes international developments as a reference point with many of its fundamentalist implications. We think again about China's equivalent to the Salman Rushdie affair.

We have remarked in this chapter that opposition to the central government might occur both in both times of hardship and times of improvement. If Tocqueville is right, the latter could be more dangerous. In recent years the greatest disturbances in the Chinese People's Republic have occurred in Tibet where economic conditions have improved markedly and where the régime has been trying to establish a show-case. The point, as we noted earlier, is that expectations rise faster than economic performance. We may expect disturbances in Tibet to continue. We may also expect continued unrest in Xinjiang. The end of the post-war order promises to herald an era of nationalism. Let us hope this time that both liberals and Marxists understand with more clarity how to reconcile the universal and the particular. China is not yet falling apart along fault lines of its own making. It is unlikely to do so since the fault lines are remote. Remote regions, however, provide a festering sore which have the capacity to haemorrhage a far from healthy core.

Bibliography

Anagnost, A. (1992) 'Socialist Ethics and the Legal System', in J. N. Wasserstrom, and E. J. Perry, *Popular Protest and Political Culture in Modern China: Learning from 1989* (Boulder, Westview Press) pp. 177–205.

Anderson, B. (1983) *Imagined Communities; Reflections on the Origin and Spread of Nationalism* (London, Verso).

Andors, P. (1975) 'Social Revolution and Woman's Emancipation: China During the Great Leap Forward', *Bulletin of Concerned Asian Scholars*, vol. 7, no. 1 (January–March) pp. 33–42.

Andors, P. (1983) *The Unfinished Liberation of Chinese Women: 1949–1980* (Bloomington, Indiana University Press).

Andors, S. (1974) 'Factory Management and Political Ambiguity: 1961–63', *China Quarterly*, 59 (July–September) pp. 435–76.

Ash, R. (1991) 'The Peasant and the State', *China Quarterly*, 127 (September) pp. 493–526.

Aubert, C. (1988) 'China's Food Take-off', in Feuchtwang, Hussain and Pairault, pp. 101–36.

Bachman, D. (1985) *Chen Yun and the Chinese Political System* (Berkeley, University of California, Center for Chinese Studies), *China Research Monograph*, no. 29.

Barnett, A. D. (1963) *China on the Eve of Communist Takeover* (New York, Praeger).

Bastid, M. (1973) 'Levels of Economic Decision Making', in Schram, pp. 159–97.

Baum, R. (1969) 'Revolution and Reaction in the Chinese Countryside: The Socialist Education Movement in Cultural Revolutionary Perspective', *China Quarterly*, 38 (April–June) pp. 92–119.

Baum, R. (1971) 'The Cultural Revolution in the Countryside: Anatomy of a Limited Rebellion', in T. Robinson (ed.), *The Cultural Revolution in China* (Berkeley, University of California Press) pp. 367–476.

Baum, R. (1975) *Prelude to Revolution: Mao, the Party and the Peasant Question*, 1962–66 (New York, Columbia University Press).

Baum, R. (1986) 'Modernization and Legal Reform in Post-Mao China: The Rebirth of Socialist Legality', *Studies in Comparative Communism*, vol. 19, no. 2 (Summer) pp. 69–103.

Baum, R. and Teiwes, F. (1968) *Ssu-Ch'ing: The Socialist Education Movement of 1962–1966* (Berkeley, University of California, Center for Chinese Studies), *China Research Monographs*, no. 2.

Bennett, G. and Montaperto, R. (1971) *Red Guard: The Political Biography of Dai Hsiao-ai* (New York, Doubleday).

Berman, H. J., Cohen, S. and Russell, M. (1982) 'A Comparison of the Chinese and Soviet Codes of Criminal Law and Procedure', *Journal of Criminal Law and Criminology*, vol. 73, no. 1 (Spring) pp. 238–58.

Bernstein, T. (1967) 'Leadership and Mass Mobilisation in the Soviet and Chinese Collectivisation Campaigns of 1929–30 and 1955–56: A Comparison', *China Quarterly*, 31 (July-September) pp. 1–47.

Bernstein, T. (1968) 'Problems of Village Leadership after Land Reform', *China Quarterly*, 36 (October-December) pp. 1–22.

Bernstein, T. (1977) 'Urban Youth in the Countryside: Problems of Adaptation and Remedies', *China Quarterly*, 69 (March) pp. 75–108.

Bianco, L. and Hua Chang-ming (1988) 'Implementation and Resistance: The Single-Child Family Policy', in Feuchtwang, Hussain and Pairault, pp. 147–68.

Blaustein, A. P. (ed.) (1962) *Fundamental Legal Documents of Communist China* (South Hackensack, N.J., Fred B. Rothman).

Blecher, M. (1991) 'Sounds of Silence and Distant Thunder; The Crisis of Economic and Political Administration', in Goodman and Segal, pp. 35–63.

Bodde, D. and Morris, C. (1967) *Law in Imperial China* (Cambridge, Mass., Harvard University Press).

Bonner, J. (1976) 'Yu P'ing-po and the Literary Dimension of the Controversy over Hung lou meng', *China Quarterly*, 67 (September) pp. 546–81.

Bradsher, H. (1973) 'China: The Radical Offensive', *Asian Survey*, vol. XIII, no. 11 (November) pp. 989–1009.

Brady, J. P. (1982) *Justice and Politics in People's China: Legal Order or Continuing Revolution?* (London and New York, Academic Press).

Brugger, W. (1971) 'The Male (and Female) in Chinese Society', *Impact of Science on Society*, vol. 21, no. 1 (January-March) pp. 5–19.

Brugger, W. (1976) *Democracy and Organisation in the Chinese Industrial Enterprise (1948–1953)* (Cambridge University Press).

Brugger, B. (1981a) *China: Liberation and Transformation, 1942–1962* (London, Croom Helm).

Brugger, B. (1981b) *China: Radicalism to Revisionism, 1962–1979* (London, Croom Helm).

Brugger, B. (1981c) 'Soviet and Chinese Views on Revolution and Socialism: Some Thoughts on the Problems of Diachrony and Synchrony', *Journal of Contemporary Asia*, vol. IX, no. 3, pp. 311–32.

Brugger, B. (1985) 'Democracy and Organisation in Chinese Industry: New Directions', in G. Young (ed.), *China: Dilemmas of Modernisation* (London, Croom Helm) pp. 61–99.

Brugger, B. (1989) 'Ideology, Legitimacy and Marxist Theory in Contemporary China', in Cheng, 1989, pp. 1–33.

Brugger, B. and Kelly, D. (1990) *Chinese Marxism in the Post-Mao Era* (Stanford University Press).

Buck, J. L. (1964) *Land Utilization in China* (New York, Paragon Book Reprint Corporation).

Buckley, C. (1991) 'Science as Politics and Politics as Science: Fang Lizhi and Chinese Intellectuals' Uncertain Road to Dissent', *Australian Journal of Chinese Affairs*, 25 (January) pp. 1–36.

Bucknall, K. (1989) *China and the Open Door Policy* (Sydney, Allen & Unwin).

Burns, J. P. (1989a) 'China's Governance: Political Reforms in a Turbulent Environment', *China Quarterly*, 119 (September) pp. 481–518.

Burns, J. (1989b) 'Chinese Civil Service Reform: The 13th Party Congress Proposals', *China Quarterly*, 120 (December) pp. 739–70.

Burns, J. (1989c) 'Civil Service Reform in Post-Mao China', in Cheng, 1989, pp. 95–129.

Chan, A. (1991) 'The Social Origins and Consequences of the Tiananmen Crisis' in Goodman and Segal, pp. 105–30.

Chan, A. (1993) 'Revolution or Corporatism? Workers and Trade Unions in Post-Mao China', *Australian Journal of Chinese Affairs*, 29 (January) pp. 31–61.

Chan, A., Rosen, S. and Unger, J. (1985) *On Socialist Democracy and the Chinese Legal System: The Li Yizhe Debates* (Armonk, M. E. Sharpe).

Chan, S. (1980) 'The Blooming of a "Hundred Flowers" and the Literature of the Wounded Generation' in B. Brugger, *China Since the 'Gang of Four'* (London, Croom Helm) pp. 174–201.

Chang, M. H. (1988) 'Women', in Wu Yuan-li *et al.*, pp. 250–67.

Chang, P. (1970) 'Research Notes on the Changing Loci of Decision in the Chinese Communist Party', *China Quarterly*, 44 (October–December) pp. 169–94.

Chang, P. (1975) *Power and Policy in China* (University Park, Pennsylvania State University Press).

Chang Ya-chun (1989) 'Communist China's Difficulties in Ruling Tibet', *Issues and Studies*, vol. 25, no. 1 (January) pp. 110–27.

Chao Kuo-chün (ed.) (1963) *Economic Planning and Organization in Mainland China: A Documentary Study (1949–1957)* (Cambridge, Mass., Harvard University, East Asian Research Center), *Harvard East Asian Monographs*, no. 7, 2 vols.

Cheek, T. (1986) 'Deng Tuo: A Chinese Leninist Approach to Journalism', in Hamrin and Cheek, pp. 92–123.

Chen, C. and Ridley, N. (1969) *Rural People's Communes in Lien-chiang: Documents Concerning Communes in Lien-chiang County, Fukien Province, 1962–1963* (Stanford, Hoover Institution Press).

Chen Nai-ruenn (1967) *Chinese Economic Statistics: A Handbook for Mainland China* (Edinburgh University Press).

Cheng, J. (ed.) (1989) *China: Modernisation in the 1980s* (Hong Kong, The Chinese University Press).

Cheng, J. and Brosseau, M. (eds.) (1993) *China Review 1993* (Hong Kong, the Chinese University Press).

Cheng, J. and Ting Wang (1993) 'Administrative Reforms in China in 1992: Streamlining, Decentralization and Changing Government Functions', in Cheng and Brosseau, pp. 4.1–20.

Cheng Renqian (1983) 'Some Questions on the Reassessment of Rosa Luxemburg' in Su Shaozhi *et al.*, *Marxism in China* (Nottingham Spokesman Books) pp. 96–113.

Chevrier, Y. (1990) 'Micropolitics and the Factory Director Responsibility System', in Davis and Vogel, pp. 109–33.

Chi Wen-shun (1970) 'Liang Shu-ming and Chinese Communism', *China Quarterly*, 41 (January–March) pp. 64–82.

CCP (Chinese Communist Party) (1956) *Eighth National Congress of the Communist Party of China, Documents* (Peking Foreign Languages Press) 3 vols.

CCP (1981) 6th Plenum of 11th Central Committee, 'Resolution on Certain Questions in the History of our Party Since the Founding of the People's Republic of China', 27 June 1981, *Beijing Review*, 27 (6 July) pp. 10–39.

Cohen, J. A. (1968) *The Criminal Process in the People's Republic of China, 1949–63* (Cambridge, Mass., Harvard University Press).

Cohen, J. A. (ed.) (1970) *Contemporary Chinese Law: Research Problems and Perspectives* (Harvard University Press).

Cohen, J. A. (1971) 'Drafting People's Mediation Rules', in Lewis, pp. 29–50.

Copper, J. F. (1988) 'Human Rights and the Chinese Political System', in Wu Yuan-li *et al.*, pp. 56–76.

Copper, J. F., Michael, F. and Wu Yuan-li (1985) *Human Rights in Post-Mao China* (Boulder and London, Westview Press).

Croll, E. (1978) *Feminism and Socialism in China* (London, Routledge and Kegan Paul).

Croll, E. (1981) *The Politics of Marriage in Contemporary China* (Cambridge University Press).

Croll, E. (1983) *Chinese Women Since Mao* (London, Zed Press).

Croll, E. (1985) *Women and Rural Development in China* (Geneva, International Labour Organisation), *Women, Work and Development*, 11.

Croll, E. (1988) 'The New Peasant Economy in China', in Feuchtwang, Hussain and Pairault, pp. 77–100.

Dalsimer, M. and Nisonhoff, L. (1984) 'The New Economic Readjustment Policies: Implications for Chinese Urban Working Women', *Review of Radical Political Economics*, vol. 16, no. 1 (Spring) pp. 17–43.

Davin, D. (1976) *Woman-Work, Women and the Party in Revolutionary China* (Oxford, Clarendon Press).

Davin, D. (1985) 'The Single-child Family Policy in the Countryside', in E. Croll, D. Davin and P. Kane (eds.), *China's One-Child Family Policy* (London, Macmillan) pp. 37–82.

Davin, D. (1988) 'The Implications of Contract Agriculture for the Employment and Status of Chinese Peasant Women', in Feuchtwang, Hussain and Pairault, pp. 137–46.

Davis, D. (1989) 'Chinese Social Welfare: Policies and Outcomes', *China Quarterly*, 119 (September) pp. 577–97.

Davis, D. (1990) 'Urban Job Mobility', in Davis and Vogel, pp. 85–108.

Davis, D. and Vogel, E. (eds.) (1990) *Chinese Society on the Eve of Tiananmen* (Harvard University, Council on East Asian Studies).

Davis, S. B. (1987) 'The Death Penalty and Legal Reform in the PRC', *Journal of Chinese Law*, vol. 1, no. 2 (Fall) pp. 303–34.

Deng Xiaoping (1984) 'Speech at the Second Plenary Session of the Twelfth Central Committee of the Chinese Communist Party', 12 October 1983, *Issues and Studies*, 4 (April) pp. 99–111.

Dessaint, A. (1980) *Minorities of South West China; An Introduction to the Yi (Lolo) and Related Peoples and an Annotated Bibliography* (New Haven, Human Relations Area Files Press).

Diamond, N. (1975) 'Collectivization, Kinship and the Status of Women in Rural China', *Bulletin of Concerned Asian Scholars*, vol. 7, no. 1 (January–March) pp. 25–32.

Dicks, A. (1989) 'The Chinese Legal System: Reforms in the Balance', *China Quarterly*, 119 (September) pp. 540–76.

Dirlik, A. (1989) *The Origins of Chinese Communism* (Oxford University Press).

Dirlik, A. and Meisner, M. (eds.) (1989) *Marxism and the Chinese Experience* (Armonk, M. E. Sharpe).

Domes, J. (1973) (trans. Rüdiger Machetzki), *The Internal Politics of China, 1949–1972* (London, Hurst and Co.).

Dreyer, J. (1968) 'China's Minority Nationalities in the Cultural Revolution', *China Quarterly*, 35 (July–September) pp. 96–109.

Dreyer, J. (1976) *China's Forty Millions* (Cambridge, Mass., Harvard University Press).

Dreyer, J. (1980) 'Limits of the Permissible in China', *Problems of Communism*, vol. 29, no. 6 (November–December) pp. 48–65.

Dutton, M. (1992) *Policing and Punishment in China: From Patriarchy to 'the People'* (Cambridge University Press).

Edmunds, C. (1987) 'The Politics of Historiography in Jian Bozan's Historicism', Goldman, Cheek and Hamrin, pp. 65–106.

Edwards, R. R. (1986) 'Civil and Social Rights: Theory and Practice in Chinese Law Today', in R. R. Edwards, L. Henkin and A. J. Nathan, *Human Rights in Contemporary China* (New York, Columbia University Press) pp. 41–75.

Esmein, J. (1973) *The Chinese Cultural Revolution* (New York, Anchor Books).

Feinerman, J. V. (1987) 'Law and Legal Professionalism in the People's Republic of China', in Goldman, Cheek and Hamrin, pp. 107–27.

Feuchtwang, S., Hussain, A. and Pairault, T. (eds.) (1988) *Transforming China's Economy in the Eighties, vol 1: The Rural Sector, Welfare and Employment* (Boulder, Westview Press).

Fisher, T. (1986) 'Wu Han: The "Upright Official" as a Model in the Humanities', in Hamrin and Cheek, pp. 155–84.

Fogel, J. (1987) 'Ai Siqi: Professional Philosopher and Establishment Intellectual', in Goldman, Cheek and Hamrin, pp. 23–41.

Foucault, M. (1979) *Discipline and Punish: The Birth of the Prison* (Harmondsworth, Peregrine Books).

Friedman, E. (1974) *Backward Toward Revolution: The Chinese Revolutionary Party* (Berkeley, University of California Press).

Fukuyama, F. (1992) *The End of History and the Last Man* (New York, the Free Press).

Gardner, J. (1969) 'The Wu-fan Campaign in Shanghai: A Study in the Consolidation of Urban Control', in A. D. Barnett (ed.), *Chinese Communist Politics in Action* (Seattle, University of Washington Press) pp. 477–539.

Gelatt, T. A. (1982) 'The People's Republic of China and the Presumption of Innocence', *Journal of Criminal Law and Criminology*, vol. 73, no. 1 (Spring) pp. 259–316.

Gelatt, T. A. (1982) 'Law Reform in the PRC After June 4', *Journal of Chinese Law*, vol. 3, no. 2 (Fall) pp. 317–25.

Gellhorn, W. (1987) 'China's Quest for Legal Modernity', *Journal of Chinese Law*, vol. 1, no. 1 (Spring) pp. 1–22.

Gladney, D. C. (1991) *Muslim Chinese: Ethnic Nationalism in the People's Republic* (Cambridge, Mass., Harvard University, Council on East Asian Studies).

Gold, T. (1990a) 'Autonomy versus Authoritarianism', in Hicks, pp. 196–211.

Gold, T. (1990b) 'Urban Private Business and Social Change', in Davis and Vogel, pp. 157–78.

Goldman, M. (1962) 'Hu Feng's Conflict with the Communist Literary Authorities', *China Quarterly*, 12 (October–December) pp. 102–37.

Goldman, M. (1964) 'Writers' Criticism of the Party in 1942', *China Quarterly*, 17 (January–March) pp. 205–28.

Goldman, M. (1975) 'China's Anti-Confucius Campaign 1973–74', *China Quarterly*, 63 (September) pp. 435–62.

Goldman, M. (1981) *China's Intellectuals: Advise and Dissent* (Harvard University Press).

Goldman, M. (1991) 'Hu Yaobang's Intellectual Network and the Theory Conference of 1979', *China Quarterly*, 126 (June) pp. 219–42.

Goldman, M., Cheek, T. and Hamrin, C. L. (eds.) (1987) China's Intellectuals and the State (Harvard University, Council on East Asian Studies).

Goodman D. and Segal, G. (1991) *China in the Nineties: Crisis Management and Beyond* (Oxford, Clarendon Press).

Gray, J. (1973) 'The Two Roads: Alternative Strategies of Social Change and Economic Growth in China', in Schram, pp. 109–57.

Greenhalgh, S. (1990) 'The Evolution of the One-Child Policy in Shaanxi, 1979–88', *China Quarterly*, 122 (June) pp. 191–229.

Grunfeld, A. T. (1987) *The Making of Modern Tibet* (London, Zed Books).

Guojia tongjiju (1988) *Zhongguo tongji nianjian*, 1988 (Zhongguo tongji chubanshe).

Halpern, N. (1987) 'Economists and Economic Policy-Making in the Early 1960s', in Goldman, Cheek and Hamrin, pp. 45–63.

Hamrin, C. L. (1986) 'Yang Xianzhen: Upholding Orthodox Leninist Theory', in Hamrin and Cheek, pp. 51–91.

Hamrin, C. L. (1987) 'Conclusion: New Trends Under Deng Xiaoping and His Successors', in Goldman, Cheek and Hamrin, pp. 275–304.

Hamrin, C. L. and Cheek, T. (eds.) (1986) *China's Establishment Intellectuals* (Armonk, M. E. Sharpe).

He Baogang (1992) 'The Party('s) Human Rights White Paper: A Basis for its Self-legitimation and for Political Dialogue?', unpublished paper given to the June Fourth Memorial Seminar, the Australian National University, Canberra.

Heberer, T. (1989) *China and Its National Minorities: Autonomy or Assimilation* (Armonk, M. E. Sharpe).

Henderson, G. (1990) 'Increased Inequality in Health Care', in Davis and Vogel, pp. 263–82.

Hicks, G. (ed.) (1990) *The Broken Mirror: China after Tiananmen* (London, Longman).

Hinton, W. (1966) *Fanshen: A Documentary of Revolution in a Chinese Village* (New York, Vintage Books).

Ho Ming (1978) 'On the Way to the Rule of Law', *Qishi niandai*, 4, April 1978, *Chinese Law and Government*, vol. 11, nos. 2–3 (Summer-Fall) pp. 115–27.

Holmgren, J. (1981) 'Myth, Fantasy or Scholarship: Images of the Status of Women in Traditional China', *Australian Journal of Chinese Affairs*, 6, pp. 147–70.

Honig, E. and Hershatter, G. (1988) *Personal Voices: Chinese Women in the 1980's* (Stanford University Press).

Hsia, R. (1961) 'The Intellectual and Public Life of Ma Yin-ch'u', *China Quarterly*, 6 (April–June) pp. 53–63.

Hsiao, G. T. (1965) 'Legal Institutions', *Problems of Communism*, vol. 14, no. 2 (March–April) pp. 112–21.

Hu Qiaomu (1978) 'Observe Economic Laws, Speed up the Four Modernizations', Speech to State Council, 7 July 1978, *Beijing Review*, 45 (10 November 1978) pp. 7–12; 46 (17 November 1978) pp. 15–23; 47 (24 November 1978) pp. 13–21.

Hussain, A. and Feuchtwang, S. (1988) 'The People's Livelihood and the Incidence of Poverty', in Feuchtwang Hussain and Pairault pp. 36–76.

Hyer, P. and Heaton, W. (1968) 'The Cultural Revolution in Inner Mongolia', *China Quarterly*, 36 (October–December) pp. 114–28.

Ikels, C. (1990) 'New Options for the Urban Elderly', in Davis and Vogel, pp. 215–242.

International Commission of Jurists (1960) *Tibet and the Chinese People's Republic: A Report to the International Commission of Jurists by its Legal Inquiry Committee on Tibet* (Geneva, International Commission of Jurists).

Ishikawa, S. (1984) 'China's Economic System Reform: Underlying Factors and Prospects', in N. Maxwell and B. McFarlane (eds), *China's Changed Road to Development* (Oxford, Pergamon Press) pp. 9–20.

Israel, J. (1986) 'Foreword', in Hamrin and Cheek, pp. ix–xix.

Jacka, T. (1990) 'Back to the Wok: Women and Employment in Chinese Industry in the 1980s', *Australian Journal of Chinese Affairs*, 24 (July) pp. 1–23.

Jencks, H. W. (1991) 'China's Army, China's Future', in Goodman and Segal, pp. 131–59.

Jiang Zemin (1992) 'Accelerating Reform and Opening Up', report to the 14th National Congress of the Chinese Communist Party, 12 October 1992, *Beijing Review*, 43 (26 October–1 November 1992) pp. 9–32.

Joffe, E. (1975) *Between Two Plenums: China's Intraleadership Conflict, 1959–1962* (Ann Arbor, University of Michigan, Center for Chinese Studies), *Michigan Papers in Chinese Studies*, no. 22, 1975.

Johnson, K. A. (1983) *Women, the Family and Peasant Revolution in China* (University of Chicago Press).

Joint Publications Research Service (ed.) (1974) *Miscellany of Mao Tse-tung Thought (1949–1968)* (Arlington, Virginia).

Jones, W. C. (ed.) (1974) *Basic Principles of Civil Law in China* (Armonk, M. E. Sharpe).

Judd, E. (1990) 'Alternative Development Strategies for Women in Rural China', *Development and Change*, vol. 21, no. 1 (January) pp. 23–42.

Judd, E. (1992) 'Land Divided, Land United, *China Quarterly*, 130 (June) pp. 338–56.

Kamenka, E. (1965) 'The Soviet View of Law', *Problems of Communism*, vol. 14., no. 2 (March–April) pp. 8–16.

Kamenka, E. and Tay, A. (1971) 'Beyond the French Revolution: Communist Socialism and the Concept of Law', *University of Toronto Law Journal*, vol. 5, no. 21, pp. 109–40.

Kamm, J. (1989) 'Reforming Foreign Trade', in E. Vogel, *One Step Ahead in China: Guangdong Under Reform* (Harvard University Press) pp. 344–45.

Keith, R. C. (1991) 'Chinese Politics and the New Theory of the "Rule of Law"', *China Quarterly*, 125 (March) pp. 109–18.

Kelly, D. (1990) 'Chinese Intellectuals and the 1989 Democracy Movement', in Hicks, pp. 24–51.

Knight, N. (ed.) (1992) *The Philosophical Thought of Mao Zedong: Studies from China, 1981–89, Chinese Studies in Philosophy: A Journal of Translations*, vol 23, nos. 3–4 (Spring-Summer).

Kojima, R. (1988) 'Agricultural Organization: New Forms, New Contradictions', *China Quarterly*, 116 (December) pp. 706–35.

Kolenda, H. (1990) 'One Party, Two Systems: Corruption in the People's Republic of China and Attempts to Control It', *Journal of Chinese Law*, vol 4., no. 2 (Fall) pp. 189–232.

Konrád, G. and Szelényi, I. (1979) *The Intellectuals on the Road to Class Power: A Sociological Study of the Role of the Intelligentsia in Socialism* (New York, Harcourt Brace Jovanovich).

Kraus, R. (1986) 'Bai Hua: The Political Authority of a Writer', in Hamrin and Cheek, pp. 185–211.

Kueh, Y. Y. (1989) 'The Maoist Legacy and China's New Industrializing Strategy', *China Quarterly*, 119 (September) pp. 420–47.

Kuo, L. (1972) *The Technical Transformation of Agriculture in Communist China* (New York, Praeger).

Lang, O. (1946) *Chinese Family and Society* (New Haven, Yale University Press).

Lardy, N. (1983) *Agriculture in Modern China's Economic Development* (Cambridge University Press).

Lardy, N. (1992) 'China's Foreign Trade', *China Quarterly*, 131 (September) pp. 691–720.

Lary, D. (1972) 'Communism and Ethnic Revolt: Some Notes on the Chuang Peasant Movement in Kwangsi, 1921–31', *China Quarterly*, 49 (January–March) pp. 126–35.

Lau Chong-chor (1993) 'The Chinese Family and Gender Roles in Transition', in Cheng and Brosseau 1993, pp. 20.1–18.

Lau Kwok-yu (1993) 'Urban Housing Reform in China amidst Property Boom Year', in Cheng and Brosseau 1993, pp. 24.1–35.

Lee Chae-jin (1986) *China's Korean Minority: The Politics of Ethnic Education* (Boulder, Westview Press).

Lee, P. N. S. (1987) *Industrial Management and Economic Reform in China, 1949–1984* (Oxford University Press).

Lee Ta-ling (1988) 'Intellectuals and "Democratic Elements": A Distrusted Underclass', in Wu Yuan-li *et al.*, pp. 154–92.

Lee Yok-shiu F. (1988) 'The Urban Housing Problem in China', *China Quarterly*, 115 (September) pp. 387–407.

Lee Yok-shiu F. (1989) 'Small Towns and China's Urbanization Level', *China Quarterly*, 120 (December) pp. 771–86.

Leng Shao-chuan (1967) *Justice in Communist China: A Survey of the Judicial System of the Chinese People's Republic* (Dobbs Ferry, Oceana Publications).

Leng Shao-chuan (1982) 'Criminal Justice in Post-Mao China: Some Preliminary Observations', *Journal of Criminal Law and Criminology*, vol 73, no. 1 (Spring) pp. 204–37.

Leng Shao-chuan and Chiu Hungdah (1985) *Criminal Justice in Post-Mao China: Analysis and Documents* (Albany, State University of New York).

Leung, K. K. (1993) 'Pro-Democracy Movement in the People's Republic of China and Overseas', in Cheng and Brosseau, pp. 21.1–14.

Levenson, J. R. (1962) 'The Place of Confucius in Communist China', *China Quarterly*, 12 (October–December) pp. 1–18.

Levy, M. (1949) *The Family Revolution in Modern China* (Cambridge Mass., Harvard University Press).

Levy, R. (1975) 'New Light on Mao: His Views on the Soviet Union's "Political Economy"', *China Quarterly* 61, March pp. 95–117.

Lewis, J. (ed.) (1971) *The City in Communist China* (Stanford University Press).

Li, V. (1971) 'The Evolution and Development of the Chinese Legal System', in J. M. H. Lindbeck *China: Management of a Revolutionary Society* (Seattle, University of Washington Press) pp. 221–55.

Li, V. (1978) *Law Without Lawyers: A Comparative View of Law in China and the United States* (Boulder, Westview Press).

Li Zhengtian (1985) 'Lawless Laws and Crimeless Crime' (1979), in Chan, Rosen and Unger, pp. 163–75.

Liang Huixing (1985) 'On the Principle of Planning and the Principle of Contract Freedom in Our Country's Contract Law', *Faxue yanjiu*, 4 July 1982, pp. 44–48, *Chinese Law and Government*, vol. 18, no. 1 (Spring), pp. 73–89.

Liao Gailong (1981) 'Historical Experiences and our Road of Development', Report on the History of the Communist Party to National Party

School Forum, 25 October 1980, *Issues and Studies*, 10 (1981) pp. 65–94; 11 (1981) pp. 81–110; 12 (1981) pp. 79–104.

Lin, P. (1990) 'Between Theory and Practice: The Possibility of a Right to Free Speech in the People's Republic of China', *Journal of Chinese Law*, vol. 4, pp. 257–76.

Lippit, V. (1975) 'The Great Leap Forward Reconsidered', *Modern China*, vol. 1, no. 1 (January) pp. 92–115.

Liu Jun and Li Lin (eds.) (1989) *Xin quanwei zhuyi* (Beijing jingji xueyuan chubanshe).

Liu Shaoqi (1968–9) *Collected Works*, vols. 2–3 (Hong Kong, Union Research Institute).

Lo, C. W-H. (1989) 'The Theory of Socialist Law and the Legal System in Post-Mao China: A Legal Awakening, 1979–1987', unpublished Ph. D. thesis, Adelaide, The Flinders University of South Australia.

Lo, J. P. (1961) 'Five Years of the Sinkiang-Uighur Autonomous Region', *China Quarterly*, 8 (October–December) pp. 92–105.

Lo, L Nai-kwai (1993) 'The Changing Educational System: Dilemma of Disparity', in Cheng and Brosseau, pp. 22.1–42.

Lubman, S. (1970) 'Methodological Problems in Studying Chinese Communist "Civil Law" ', in Cohen 1970, pp. 230–60.

Ma Guonan and Garnaut, R. (1992) *How Rich is China: Evidence from the Food Economy* (The Australian National University, Research School of Pacific Studies, Department of Economics and Research Centre for Developmental Studies), *Working Papers in Trade and Development*, no. 92/4 (July).

Macartney, J. (1990) 'The Students: Heroes, Pawns or Power-Brokers', in Hicks pp. 3–23.

MacFarquhar, R. (1973) 'Problems of Liberalization and the Succession at the Eighth Party Congress', *China Quarterly*, 56 (October–December) pp. 617–46.

MacFarquhar, R. (1974) *The Origins of the Cultural Revolution, vol. I, Contradictions Among the People: 1956–1957* (New York, Columbia University Press).

Manion, M. (1992) 'Politics and Policy in Post-Mao Cadre Retirement', *China Quarterly*, 129 (March) pp. 1–25.

Mao Zedong (1965/1977) *Selected Works*, vols. 3–5 (Beijing Foreign Languages Press, 1965, 1977).

Maxwell, N. and McFarlane, B. (eds.) (1984) *China's Changed Road to Development* (Oxford, Pergamon Press).

Meisner, M. (1986) *Mao's China: A History of the People's Republic* (New York, The Free Press, 1977); revised as *Mao's China and After: A History of the People's Republic* (New York, The Free Press 1986).

Molyneux, M. (1981) 'Women's Emancipation Under Socialism: A Model for the Third World?' (Brighton, University of Sussex, Institute of Development Studies) *Discussion Papers*, 157.

Moseley, G. (ed.) (1966a) *The Party and the National Question in China* (Cambridge, Mass., M.I.T. Press).

Moseley, G. (1966b) *A Sino-Soviet Cultural Frontier: The Ili Kazakh Autonomous Zhou, Harvard East Asian Monographs*, 22 (Cambridge, Mass., Harvard University Press).

Moseley, G. (1973) *The Consolidation of the South China Frontier* (Berkeley, University of California Press).

Murdoch University, Asia Research Centre (1992) *Southern China in Transition: The New Regionalism and Australia* (Canberra, Department of Foreign Affairs and Trade).

Nathan, A.J. (1986a) 'Political Rights in Chinese Constitutions', in Edwards, Henkin and Nathan pp. 77–124.

Nathan, A.J. (1986b) 'Sources of Chinese Rights Thinking', in Edwards, Henkin and Nathan, pp. 125–64.

NPC (National People's Congress) (1982) 'Constitution of the People's Republic of China' adopted on 4 December 1982, *Beijing Review*, 52 (27 December) pp. 10–29.

NPC (1986) 'General Principles of the Civil Code of the People's Republic of China', adopted by the fourth session of the Sixth National People's Congress, 12 April 1986, Chapter 5, BBC, *Summary of World Broadcasts: Far East*/8240/C1–20, 23 April 1986.

NPC (1988) 'Administrative Litigation Law of the People's Republic of China (draft)', November 1988, BBC, *Summary of World Broadcasts: Far East*/0315/B1–4, 23 November 1988.

NPC (1991) 'Revised Code of Civil Procedure (1991)' BBC, *Summary of World Broadcasts: Far East*/1066/C1/1–21, 8 May 1991.

Naughton, B.J. (1986) 'Sun Yefang: Toward a Reconstruction of Socialist Economics', in Hamrin and Cheek, pp. 124–54.

Naughton, B.J. (1988) 'The Third Front: Defence Industrialization in the Chinese Interior', *China Quarterly*, 115 (September) pp. 351–86.

Nolan, P. (1976) 'Collectivisation in China: Some Comparisons with the USSR', *Journal of Peasant Studies*, vol. 3, no. 2 (January) pp. 192–220.

Norbu, D. (1979) 'The 1959 Tibetan Rebellion: An Interpretation', *China Quarterly*, 77 (March) pp. 74–93.

Odgaard, O. (1992) 'Entrepreneurs and Elite Formation in Rural China', *Australian Journal of Chinese Affairs*, 28 (July) pp. 89–108.

Oi, J. (1986) 'Peasant Grain Marketing and State Procurement; China's Grain Contracting System', *China Quarterly*, 106 (June) pp. 272–90.

Oi, J. (1989) *State and Peasant in Contemporary China: The Political Economy of Village Government* (Berkeley, University of California Press).

Oksenberg, M. and Tong, J. (1991) 'The Evolution of Central-Provincial Fiscal Relations in China, 1971–1984', *China Quarterly*, 125 (March) pp. 1–32.

Oldham, J.R. (ed.) (1986) for the *Columbia Journal of Transnational Law, China's Legal Development* (Armonk, M.E. Sharpe).

Palmer, M. (1988a) 'China's New Inheritance Law: Some Preliminary Observations', in Feuchtwang, Hussain and Pairault, pp. 169–97.

Palmer, M. (1988b) 'The Revival of Mediation in the People's Republic of China: (1) Extra-Judicial Mediation', in W.E. Butler (ed.), *Yearbook on*

Socialist Legal Systems (Dobbs Ferry, New York, Transnational Publishers) pp. 219–77.

Pateman, C. (1988b) *The Sexual Contract* (Cambridge, Polity Press).

PFLP (Peking Foreign Languages Press) (1961) *Constitution of the People's Republic of China* (20 September 1954) (Beijing).

Pfeffer, R. M. (1970) 'Crime and Punishment: China and the United States', in Cohen 1970, pp. 261–81.

Pien Feng-kuei (1990) 'The Population of Chinese Minority Nationalities', *Issues and Studies*, vol. 26, no. 4 (April) pp. 43–62.

Pollard, D. E. (1985) 'The Controversy Over Modernism', *China Quarterly*, 104 (December) pp. 641–56.

Postiglione, G. A. (1992) 'China's National Minorities and Educational Change', *Journal of Contemporary Asia*, vol. 22, no. 1, pp. 20–44.

Potter, P. B. (1986) 'Peng Zhen: Evolving Views on Party Organization and Law', in Hamrin and Cheek, pp. 21–50.

Prazniak, R. (1989) 'Feminist Humanism: Socialism and Neofeminism in the Writings of Zhang Jie', in Dirlik and Meisner, pp. 269–93.

Price, R. (ed.) (1977) *The Anti-Confucius Campaign in China* (Melbourne, La Trobe University, Centre for Comparative and International Studies in Education), *Asia Studies Papers, China Series*, no. 1.

Pusey, J. (1969) *Wu Han: Attacking the Present through the Past* (Cambridge, Mass., Harvard University Press).

Rawls, J. (1985) 'Justice as Fairness: Political not Metaphysical', *Philosophy and Public Affairs*, vol. 14, no. 3, pp. 223–51.

Rice, E. (1972) *Mao's Way* (Berkeley, University of California Press).

Richman, B. (1969) *Industrial Society in Communist China* (New York, Random House).

Riskin, C. (1987) *China's Political Economy: The Search for Development Since 1949* (Oxford University Press).

Robinson, J. C. (1985) 'Of Women and Washing Machines; Employment, Housework and the Reproduction of Mothering in Socialist China', *China Quarterly*, 101 (March) pp. 32–57.

Rosenbaum, A. L. (ed.) (1992) *State and Society in China: The Consequences of Reform* (Boulder, Westview Press).

Rubin, K. (1987) 'Keeper of the Flame: Wang Ruowang as Moral Critic of the State', in Goldman, Cheek and Hamrin, pp. 233–50.

Rui Mu (1986) 'New Developments in China's Economic Legislation', in Oldham, pp. 61–76.

Saich, T. (1989) 'Modernization and Participation in the People's Republic of China', in Cheng 1989, pp. 35–62.

Salaff, J. (1967) 'The Urban Communes and Anti-City Experiment in Communist China', *China Quarterly*, 29 (January–March) pp. 82–109.

Salaff, J. (1971) 'Urban Residential Communities in the Wake of the Cultural Revolution', in Lewis, pp. 289–323.

Sautman, B. (1992) 'Sirens of the Strongman; Neo-Authoritarianism in Recent Chinese Political Theory', *China Quarterly*, 129 (March) pp. 72–102.

Schell, O. (1988) *Discos and Democracy: China in the Throes of Reform* (New York, Pantheon).

Schram, S. (1969) *The Political Thought of Mao Tse-tung* (Harmondsworth, Penguin).

Schram, S. (ed.) (1973) *Authority, Participation and Cultural Change in China* (Cambridge University Press).

Schram, S. (ed.) (1974) *Mao Tse-tung Unrehearsed* (Harmondsworth, Penguin).

Schurmann, H. F. (1966) *Ideology and Organization in Communist China* (Berkeley, University of California Press).

Schwartz, B. (1968) 'On Attitudes Towards Law in China', in M. Katz (ed.), *Government Under Law and the Individual* (Washington D. C., 1957) pp. 27–39, repr. in Cohen, 1968, pp. 62–70.

Schwarz, H. G. (1963) 'Chinese Migration to North West China and Inner Mongolia, 1949–59', *China Quarterly*, 16 (November–December) pp. 62–74.

Schwarz, H. G. (1984) *The Minorities of Northern China: A Survey* (Bellingham, Western Washington University, Center for East Asian Studies), *Studies on East Asia*, vol. 17.

Scobell, A. (1988) 'Strung Up or Shot Down?: The Death Penalty in Hong Kong and China and Implications for Post-1997', *Case Western Reserve Journal of International Law*, vol. 20., no. 1, pp. 147–67.

Scobell, A. (1990) 'The Death Penalty in Post-Mao China', *China Quarterly*, 123 (September) pp. 503–20.

Selden, M. (1971) *The Yenan Way in Revolutionary China* (Cambridge, Mass., Harvard University Press).

Selden, M. (ed.) (1979) *The People's Republic of China: A Documentary History of Revolutionary Change* (New York, Monthly Review Press).

Selznick, P. (1957) *Leadership in Administration: A Sociological Interpretation* (Evanston, Ill., Row, Peterson).

Shue, V. (1980) *Peasant China in Transition: The Dynamics of Development Towards Socialism, 1949–1956* (Berkeley, University of California Press).

Sicular, T. (1988) 'Agricultural Planning and Pricing in the Post-Mao Period', *China Quarterly*, 116 (December) pp. 671–705.

Sidel, M. (1987) 'Recent and Noteworthy Legal Works Published in China', *Journal of Chinese Law*, vol. 1, no. 2 (Fall) pp. 251–69.

Skinner G. (1964–5) 'Marketing and Social Structure in Rural China', *Journal of Asian Studies*, vol. 24, no. 1 (November 1964) pp. 3–43 (Pt l); no. 2 (February 1965) pp. 195–228 (Pt II); no. 3 (May 1965), pp. 363–99 (Pt III).

Snow, E. (1971) *Red Star over China* (New York, Grove Press).

Solinger, D. (1992) 'Urban Entrepreneurs and the State: The Merger of State and Society', in Rosenbaum, pp. 121–41.

Solomon, R. (1971) *Mao's Revolution and the Chinese Political Culture* (Berkeley, University of California Press).

Stacey, J. (1983) *Patriarchy and Socialist Revolution in China* (Berkeley, University of California Press).

Stalin. J. V. (1972) *Economic Problems of Socialism in the U.S.S.R.* (1952) (Beijing, Foreign Languages Press).

Starr, J. (1976) 'From the 10th Party Congress to the Premiership of Hua Kuo-feng: The Significance of the Colour of the Cat', *China Quarterly*, 67 (September) pp. 457–88.

State Council Information Office (1991) 'Human Rights in China', *Beijing Review*, vol. 34, no. 44 (4–10 November) pp. 8–45.

State Statistical Bureau (1990) *China: Statistical Yearbook, 1990* (China Statistical Information and Consultancy Service Centre and the University of Illinois at Chicago).

Stavis, B. (1978) *The Politics of Agricultural Mechanization in China* (Ithaca, Cornell University Press).

Su Shaozhi and Feng Lanrui (1979) 'Wuchanjieji qude zhengquan hou de shehui fazhan jieduan wenti', *Jingji yanjiu*, 5, pp. 14–19.

Sung Y-W. and Chan T. M-H. (1987) 'China's Economic Reforms 1: The Debates in China', *Asian-Pacific Economic Literature*, vol. 1, no. 1 (May) pp. 1–24.

Teiwes, F. (1979) *Policies and Purges in China: Rectification and the Decline of Party Norms: 1950–1965* (White Plains, N.Y., M. E. Sharpe).

Thorborg, M. (1978) 'Chinese Employment Policy in 1949–78 with Special Emphasis on Women in Rural Production', in US Congress, Joint Economic Committee, *Chinese Economy Post-Mao*, vol. 1, *Policy and Performance* (Washington D.C., US Government Printing Office) pp. 535–604.

Tilly, C. (1985) 'War Making and State Making as Organised Crime', in P. Evans, D. Rueschmeyer and T. Skocpol (eds.), *Bringing the State Back In* (Cambridge University Press) pp. 169–91.

Townsend, D. E. (1987) 'The Concept of Law in Post-Mao China: A Case Study of Economic Crime', *Stanford Journal of International Law*, vol 24, no. 1, pp. 227–58.

Unger, R. M. (1976) *Law in Modern Society: Towards a Criticism of Social Theory* (New York, The Free Press).

URI (Union Research Institute) (ed.) (1968a), *The Case of P'eng Teh-huai* (Hong Kong).

URI (ed.) (1968b) *Tibet 1950–1967* (Hong Kong).

URI (ed.) (1971) *Documents of Chinese Communist Party Central Committee* (Hong Kong).

Vogel, E. (1969) *Canton Under Communism, Programs and Politics in a Provincial Capital, 1949–1968* (New York, Harper and Row).

Vogel, E. (1989) *One Step Ahead in China: Guangdong Under Reform* (Harvard University Press).

Wagner, R. G. (1987) 'The Chinese Writer in his Own Mirror: Writer, State and Society – the Literary Evidence', in Goldman, Cheek and Hamrin, pp. 183–231.

Walder, A. G. (1989) 'Factory and Manager in an Era of Reform', *China Quarterly*, 118 (June) pp. 242–64.

Walder, A. G. (1990) 'Economic Reform and Income Distribution in Tianjin, 1976–1986', in Davis and Vogel, pp. 135–56.

Walder, A. G. (1991) 'Workers, Managers and the State: The Reform Era and the Political Crisis of 1989', *China Quarterly*, 127 (September) pp. 467–92.

Walder, A. G. (1992) 'Urban Industrial Workers: Some Observations on the 1980s', in Rosenbaum, pp. 103–20.

Walder, A. G. and Gong Xiaoxia (1993) 'Workers in the Tiananmen Protests: The Politics of the Beijing Workers' Autonomous Federation', *Australian Journal of Chinese Affairs*, 29 (January) pp. 1–29.

Walker, K. (1965) *Planning in Chinese Agriculture Socialisation and the Private Sector, 1956–1962* (London, Frank Cass).

Walker, K., 'Chinese Agriculture During the Period of Re-adjustment, 1978–83', *China Quarterly*, 100 (December) pp. 783–812.

Walker, K. (1988) 'Trends in Crop Production, 1978–86, *China Quarterly*, 116 (December) pp. 592–633.

Wan Shanping (1988) 'The Emergence of Women's Studies in China', *Women's Studies International Forum*, vol. 11, no. 5, pp. 455–64.

Wang, J. (1992) *Contemporary Chinese Politics: An Introduction*, 4th edn (Englewood Cliffs, Prentice Hall).

Wang Ruoshui (1980) 'The Greatest Lesson of the Cultural Revolution is that the Personality Cult Should be Opposed', speech at conference on theoretical work of the Chinese Communist Party Central Committee, 13 February 1979, *Mingbao* (Hong Kong), 2, pp. 2–15, in Joint Publications Research Service, 75291, 12 March 1980 pp. 78–99.

Wang Ruoshui (1984) 'My Views on Humanism', *Jingbao* (Hong Kong) 83 (1984); Foreign Broadcast Information Service, *Daily Report*, 10 August 1984, W 5–7.

Wang Ruoshui (1985) 'Discussing the Problem of Alienation', *Chinese Studies in Philosophy*, vol. 16, no. 3 (Spring) pp. 25–38.

Wang Xizhe (1985) 'Mao Zedong and the Cultural Revolution', in Chan, Rosen and Unger, pp. 177–260.

Watson, A. (1984) 'Agriculture Looks for Shoes that Fit', in Maxwell and McFarlane, pp. 83–108.

Watson, A. (1993) 'Market Reform and Agricultural Growth: The Dynamics of Change in the Chinese Countryside', in Cheng and Brosseau, pp. 14.1–20.

White, G. (1993a) 'Prospects for Civil Society in China: A Case Study of Xiaoshan City', *Australian Journal of Chinese Affairs*, 29 (January) pp. 63–87.

White, G. (1993b) *Riding the Tiger: The Politics of Economic Reform in Post-Mao China* (Basingstoke, Macmillan).

White, L. (1971) 'Shanghai's Polity in Cultural Revolution', in Lewis, pp. 325–70.

White, L. (1972) 'Leadership in Shanghai, 1955–69', in R. Scalapino (ed.), *Elites in the People's Republic of China* (Seattle, University of Washington Press) pp. 302–77.

White, L. (1979) 'The Road to Urumchi: Approved Institutions in Search of Attainable Goals During pre-1968 Rustication from Shanghai', *China Quarterly*, 79 (September) pp. 481–510.

Whyte, M. (1992) 'Urban China: A Civil Society in the Making', in Rosenbaum, pp. 77–101.

Whyte, M. K. and Parish, W. L. (1984) *Urban Life in Contemporary China* (University of Chicago Press) 1984.

Wich, R. (1974) 'The Tenth Party Congress: The Power Structure and the Succession Question', *China Quarterly*, 58 (April–May) pp. 234–9.

Williams, J. H. (1990) 'Fang Lizhi's Expanding Universe', *China Quarterly*, 123 (September) pp. 459–84.

Winnington, A. (1959) *The Slaves of the Cool Mountains* (London, Lawrence and Wishart).

Witke, R. (1967) 'Mao Tse-tung, Women and Suicide in the May Fourth Era', *China Quarterly*, 31 (July–September) pp. 128–47.

Wolf, M. (1985) *Revolution Postponed: Women in Contemporary China* (Stanford University Press).

Woo, M. (1989) 'The Right to a Criminal Appeal in the People's Republic of China', *Yale Journal of International Law*, vol. 14, no. 1, pp. 118–60.

Woodward, D. (1978) 'Two Line Struggle in Agriculture', in B. Brugger (ed.), *China: The Impact of the Cultural Revolution* (London, Croom Helm) pp. 153–70.

Woon, Yuen-fong (1991) 'From Mao to Deng: Life Satisfaction Among Rural Women in an Emigrant Community in South China', *Australian Journal of Chinese Affairs*, 25 (January) pp. 139–69.

Wu-Beyens, I-chuan (1990) 'The Years of Reform in China: Economic Growth Versus Modernization', *L'Asie et Le Pacifique, Civilisations*, vol. 40, no. 1, pp. 101–32.

Wu Jianfan (1986) 'Building New China's Legal System', in Oldham, pp. 1–40.

Wu Yuan-li, Michael, F., Copper, J. F., Lee Ta-ling, Chang, M. H. and Gregor, A. J. (1988) *Human Rights in the People's Republic of China* (Boulder and London, Westview Press).

Wylie, R. F. (1979) 'Mao Tse-tung, Ch'en Po-ta and the "Sinification of Marxism", 1936–38', *China Quarterly*, 79 (September) pp. 447–80.

Yan Hao (1988) 'China's 1.2 Billion Population Target for the Year 2000: "Within" or "Beyond"', *Australian Journal of Chinese Affairs*, 19/20 (January/July) pp. 165–83.

Yang, M. M-H. (1989) 'Between State and Society: The Construction of Corporateness in a Chinese Socialist Factory', *Australian Journal of Chinese Affairs*, 22 (July) pp. 31–60.

Yeh, K. C. (1992) 'Macroeconomic Issues in China in the 1990s', *China Quarterly*, 131 (September) pp. 501–44.

You Ji (1991) 'Zhao Ziyang and the Politics of Inflation', *Australian Journal of Chinese Affairs*, 25 (January) pp. 69–91.

Young, G. (1989) 'Party Reforms', in Cheng 1989, pp. 63–93.

Young, M. (1989) 'Chicken Little in China: Some Reflections on Women', in Dirlik and Meisner, pp. 253–68.

Young, S. (1989) 'Policy, Practice and the Private Sector in China', *Australian Journal of Chinese Affairs*, 21 (January) pp. 57–80.

Zhang Chunqiao (1975) 'On Exercising All-Round Dictatorship over the Bourgeoisie', *Peking Review*, no. 14 (4 April) pp. 5–11.

Zhao Ziyang (1987) 'Advance Along the Road of Socialism with Chinese Characteristics', report to 13th National Congress of the Chinese Communist Party, 25 October 1987, *Beijing Review*, 45 (November 9–15), i–xxvii (inclusion).

Zhongguo Shehui Kexueyuan (eds.) (1983) *Renxing, rendaozhuyi wenti taolunji* (Beijing, Renmin chubanshe).

Zhou Yang (1964) 'The Fighting Task Confronting Workers in Philosophy and the Social Sciences', 26 October 1963, *Peking Review*, 1, pp. 10–27.

Index

358